FOURTH EDITION

EXPERT RESUMES

&LinkedIn PROFILES FOR

MANAGERS AND EXECUTIVES

Capture Attention ... Capture Opportunities

Wendy S. Enelow and Louise M. Kursmark
Certified Master Resume Writers

EMERALD
CAREER PUBLISHING

Expert Resumes and LinkedIn Profiles for Managers and Executives
Capture Attention ... Capture Opportunities

© 2020 by Wendy S. Enelow and Louise M. Kursmark

ISBN 978-0-9966803-6-3

Publisher:

 EMERALD CAREER PUBLISHING

www.emeraldcareerpublishing.com

Layout: Deb Tremper, Six Penny Graphics
http://sixpennygraphics.com

Distributor: Cardinal Publishers Group
www.cardinalpub.com

Printed in the United States of America

TABLE OF CONTENTS

ABOUT THIS BOOK

Consider this important data from the U.S. Department of Labor's Bureau of Labor Statistics (www.bls.gov):

- Total employment is projected to grow by 11.5 million jobs between 2016–2026.

- Employment within management and executive occupations is favorably positioned, with projections at 8.5% during that same decade.

- The percentage of growth is higher for management opportunities in these growth industries and professions: medical/health services (20.5%), finance and financial services (18.7%), and technology (12%).

- As has been the trend for several decades, employment in service industries will show strongest growth (81%) as compared to goods-producing industries at only 11.9%.

- The median annual wage of chief executives was $189,600 as of May 2018 (latest data), up by more than 8% from the previous decade.

As management and executive opportunities continue to increase in the U.S. and around the world, your challenge is to become a savvy manager of your own career. Acknowledge that career management is a lifelong process in which you must be actively engaged and not just a task to be undertaken when a job search or career move is imminent.

Two vital components of your career management plan are your resume and LinkedIn profile, which must position you as a well-qualified and highly competitive candidate. The easiest way to accomplish that is by developing powerful, performance-based resumes and profiles.

Resumes and profiles must include essential details, but both documents are much more than just your job history and academic credentials. They must be written to communicate your brand … your unique value proposition … by prominently showcasing your career highlights, most notable achievements, and unique skills and qualifications.

In this book, we'll teach you how to create a resume that will get you noticed by both human readers and electronic scanners. Read everything thoroughly, carefully review the 100+ resume and LinkedIn samples, and then use those tools to write, format, and design your own winning resume.

With the 4th edition of *Expert Resumes and LinkedIn Profiles for Managers and Executives* as your guide, you will succeed in developing a powerful and effective resume that captures attention, gets interviews, and helps you land your next great leadership opportunity!

INTRODUCTION

Why a special resume book just for managers and executives? Aren't their resumes, job-search letters, and LinkedIn profiles similar to everyone else's? No, they are not!

To understand what makes them different and why it's so critical, we must first explore the underlying actions of job search and career management. Both have become increasingly more complex and competitive—especially in management and executive ranks. According to the U.S. Bureau of Labor Statistics (BLS), keen competition will continue to be the norm for top executive positions because their prestige and high pay attract many qualified applicants.

Consider that "managers and executives" is a very large occupational group, represented in virtually every industry worldwide. On the one hand, that's great because there are so many senior-level opportunities. The vast number of positions also means there is a lot of transition as executives (1) move from one position to another, (2) re-career from one profession or industry to another, (3) start their own businesses or consulting ventures, or (4) retire.

Conversely, the competition is fierce, from entry-level managers to C-suite executives and board directors. Therefore, your challenge is to position yourself as a visible and attractive candidate to give yourself an edge over the competition. Step 1 in that process is to write a powerful resume that is rich in content, achievements, and visual appeal.

That document—your resume—will be at the forefront of your job search and career management efforts, so it must be the very best it can be. It's not enough to be great at your job; you have to **sell the fact** that you are great at your job, explain why and show how, to position yourself as a talented, interesting, and possibly perfect new hire!

The What, How, Which, and Where of Resume Writing

Before you begin writing your resume, address these 4 critical questions:

- **What types of positions are you pursuing?** Your current career goals dictate the entire resume writing, formatting, and design process—what you write, how and why you write it, and where you position it. If you're looking for a role similar to what you do now as a Senior Director of Supply Chain Management, you'll write your resume with one specific strategy and format. But if you're now interested in a COO position, your resume will be focused in an entirely different direction and will showcase a broader range of skills, qualifications, projects, and achievements.

- **How are you going to "paint a picture" of your skills and qualifications to position yourself as an attractive candidate for your targeted jobs?** What information are you going to highlight about your past experiences that ties directly to your current objectives? What accomplishments, skills, and qualifications are you going to showcase? How are you going to brand yourself to align with current and projected market opportunities?

- **Which resume format are you going to use?** Is a chronological, functional, or hybrid resume going to work best for you? Which format will give you the greatest flexibility to highlight the qualifications and achievements you want to bring to the forefront of your resume to support your career goals?

- **Where are you going to look for a job?** Once you have decided what type of position you are interested in, how do you plan to identify and approach those companies and organizations? How will you network? What online tools and platforms will you use? What is your job-search plan?

When you can answer the what, how, which, and where, you'll be prepared to write your resume and launch your search campaign. Without a clearly defined objective, resume writing becomes much more difficult because there is no direction for your resume and no clear guidelines for decision making.

Here is how this book will help you.

Use **Chapters 1 and 2** to guide you in developing the content for your resume and selecting the appropriate format and design. Your resume should focus on your skills, achievements, and qualifications, demonstrating the value and benefit you bring to a prospective employer. The focus should be on the "new" you—the role you want to fill now—and not necessarily what you have done in the past.

Chapter 3 will help you understand the complexities of online search, e-resumes, and resume scanning technology and how they will impact the document you create. Often, the beautifully formatted resume that you email or hand to someone is not exactly the same document that you upload to a resume database. We'll walk you through the various formats and explain what you'll need, why and when you'll need it, and how to prepare it.

Review the sample resumes in **Chapters 4 through 12** to see what other people have done—managers and executives in situations like yours and who faced similar challenges. You'll find interesting formats, unique skills presentations, achievement-focused resumes, project-focused resumes, branded resumes, and much more. Most importantly, you'll see samples written by the top resume writers in the world. These are real resumes that got real interviews and generated real job offers. They're the "best of the best" from us to you.

Next, review **Chapters 13 and 14** for best-in-class strategies, formats, and samples for your LinkedIn profile. As you'll read, your LinkedIn presence has become a vital element in managing your job search and your career.

Finally, don't overlook the appendices. We've provided 2 highly useful resources for managing your career now and in the future. **Appendix A** is a resume worksheet that you can use to develop your resume now and capture career information in the years ahead to make updating faster and easier. In **Appendix B** you'll find every resume writer's "secret weapon"—a list of powerful, distinctive, and descriptive verbs that will add meaning, impact, and variety to all of your career communications.

Once you've written powerful and well-focused career marketing documents, you're ready to launch your job search.

PART I

Resume Writing Strategies and Formats

CHAPTER 1

Resume Writing Strategies for Managers and Executives

If you're reading this book, it's likely you've decided to make a career move. It might be because of one or a combination of the following reasons:

- You're ready to leave your current position and move up the ladder to a higher-paying and more responsible management or executive role.

- The industry in which you've been working is in decline, so you've decided to pursue opportunities in other industries where the prospects for growth and stability are much stronger.

- You've decided on a career change and will be looking at opportunities both within and outside your current industry.

- You're unhappy with your current employer or senior management team and have decided to pursue opportunities elsewhere.

- You've been laid off, downsized, or otherwise left your position and must find a new one.

- You've completed a contract assignment or interim position and are looking for a new contract, consulting, or permanent opportunity.

- You've decided to resign your current position to pursue an executive-level entrepreneurial opportunity.

- You're relocating to a new area and need to find a new management opportunity.

- You're returning to the workforce after several years of unemployment or retirement and are ready for new senior management opportunities.

- You've just earned your graduate degree and are ready to take a step upward in your career.

- You're simply ready for a change.

No matter the reason behind your move, a powerful resume is an essential component of your search campaign. In fact, it is virtually impossible to conduct a search without a resume. It is your calling card that briefly, yet powerfully, communicates the skills, qualifications, experience, and value you bring to a prospective employer. It is the document that will open doors and generate interviews. It is the first thing people will learn about you when you forward it in response to a job posting and the last thing they'll remember when they're reviewing your qualifications after an interview.

Your resume is a sales document and you are the product! You must identify the *features* (what you know and what you can do) and *benefits* (how well you do your job and how you can help your next employer) of that product and then communicate them in a concise and hard-hitting written presentation. Remind yourself over and over, as you work through the resume process, that you are writing a marketing document designed to sell a product—YOU—into a new management or executive-level position.

Your resume can have tremendous power and a phenomenal impact on your job search. Don't take it lightly. Rather, devote the time, energy, and resources that are essential to developing a resume that is well written, visually attractive, and effective in communicating *who* you are and *how* you want to be perceived.

Resume Strategies

Following are 8 core strategies for writing effective and successful management and executive resumes.

RESUME STRATEGY #1: Write to the Job You Want

Now that you've decided to look for a new position, the very first step is to identify your current career interests, goals, and objectives. This task is critical because it is the underlying foundation for *what* you include in your resume, *how* you write it, and *where* you position it. You cannot write an effective resume without knowing, at least to some degree, what type or types of opportunities you are targeting. This requires more than the simple response of "I'm looking for an executive role." You must be more specific to create a document that powerfully positions you for such opportunities.

There are 2 concepts to consider here:

- **Who you are:** This relates to what you have done professionally and/or academically. Are you a CEO, COO, CIO, CTO, or CFO? Are you a director of manufacturing, a director of purchasing, or a director of training and development? Are you a business manager, program manager, or technology manager? Have you just returned to school to complete your MBA or another advanced degree?

- **How you want to be perceived:** This relates to your current career objectives. If you're a CFO seeking a position as CEO, don't focus solely on your financial skills. Put an equal emphasis on your success in general management, strategic planning, organizational leadership, joint ventures, team building, and business development. If you're a production manager seeking a promotion to the next tier of management, highlight your accomplishments in reducing operating costs, improving productivity, streamlining operations, eliminating product defects, and contributing to the bottom line.

The strategy, then, is to connect these 2 concepts by using the *who you are* information that ties directly to the *how you want to be perceived* message to determine what information to include in your resume, how, and where. By following this strategy, you're painting a picture that allows a prospective employer to see you as you want to be seen—as an individual with the qualifications for the types of leadership positions you are pursuing.

WARNING: If you prepare a resume without first clearly identifying what your objectives are and how you want to be perceived, your resume will have no focus and no direction. Without the underlying knowledge of *"This is what I want to be,"* you will not know what to highlight in your resume. In turn, the document becomes a historical overview of your career and not the sales document it is designed to be.

RESUME STRATEGY #2: Sell It to Me...Don't Tell It to Me

We've already established that resume writing is sales. You are the product, and you must create a document that powerfully communicates the value of that product. One particularly effective strategy for accomplishing this is the "Sell It to Me...Don't Tell It to Me" strategy that impacts virtually every word you write on your resume.

If you "tell it," you are simply stating facts. If you "sell it," you promote it, advertise it, and draw attention to it. Look at the difference in impact between these examples:

Tell It Strategy: Supervised customer service operations for 2 large sales locations.

Sell It Strategy: Led strategic planning, operations, and P&L for 2,000-employee customer-service organization supporting $125M+ in annual sales for world's largest automotive brake manufacturer. Closed FY19 $250K under budget with 98% customer-satisfaction rating.

Tell It Strategy: Managed a large-scale reorganization of one of Telescope Corp's manufacturing facilities.

Sell It Strategy: Spearheaded plant-wide reorganization of Telescope's flagship manufacturing facility, impacting 1,000 employees and $450M in annual product throughput. Slashed operating costs 22%, introduced lean manufacturing techniques, and added $14M+ to bottom-line profits.

What's the difference between "telling it" and "selling it"? In a nutshell...

Telling It	Selling It
Describes features.	Describes benefits.
Tells what and how.	Sells why the "what" and "how" are important.
Details activities.	Includes results.
Focuses on what you did.	Details how what you did benefited your employer, department, team members, customers, and so on.

RESUME STRATEGY #3: Integrate Critical Keywords

No matter what you read or who you talk to about job search, the concept of keywords is sure to come up. Keywords are words and phrases specific to an industry or profession. For example, general management keywords include *strategic planning, organizational design, team building, revenue growth, profit improvement, cost reduction, productivity improvement, business planning, operating management,* and hundreds more.

When you use these words and phrases—in your resume, in your job-search letters, in your LinkedIn profile, or during an interview—you are communicating a very specific message. For example, when you use *marketing management* in your resume, your reader will most likely assume that you have experience in strategic market planning, market positioning, new product launch, new business development, competitive analysis, multimedia marketing, promotions, and more. As you see, people will make inferences about your skills based on the use of just 1 or 2 individual words.

Here are a few other examples:

- When you use the words **corporate financial management,** people will assume you have experience with budgeting, tax, treasury, cash management, banking, investor reporting, financial analysis, financial reporting, and more.

- By referencing **technology leadership,** you convey that you likely have experience in identifying technology needs, developing new technologies, training technical staff, managing technology projects, and related functions.

- When you include **human resources** as one of your areas of expertise, most people will assume you are experienced in recruitment, training and development, benefits, compensation, employee relations, performance evaluation, and more.

- When you mention **educational administration,** readers will infer that you have experience in curriculum development, instructional materials design, technology-based learning, teacher selection and training, and much more.

Keywords are also an integral component of the resume-scanning process, whereby employers and recruiters electronically search resumes for specific terms to identify candidates with the skills, qualifications, and credentials for their particular hiring needs. In online job search, keyword-based electronic scanning has replaced the more traditional method of initial resume reviews done by people. Therefore, to some degree, the *only* thing that matters is that you have included the right keywords to match the company's or the recruiter's needs. Without the right keywords, your resume (and you) will be passed over.

Once your resume passes the keyword scan, it will then be read by human eyes, so it's not enough just to throw together a list of keywords. In fact, it's not even necessary to include a separate keyword summary on your resume. A better strategy is to incorporate keywords naturally into the text within the appropriate sections of your resume—summary, job descriptions, education notes, and wherever else they fit into the text that you are writing.

Keep in mind, too, that keywords are arbitrary; there is no defined set of keywords for a CEO, sales director, telecom manager, hotel manager, or VP of engineering. Employers develop a list of terms and core competencies that reflect the specifics they desire in a qualified candidate. These might be a combination of professional skills, job titles, years of experience, college degrees, and other easily defined criteria along with soft skills such as leadership, decision-making, and communications.

How can you be sure that you are including all the keywords and the right keywords? Just by describing your work experience, achievements, educational credentials, technical qualifications, and the like, you will automatically include most of the terms that are important in your field. To cross-check what you've written, review online job postings for positions that are of interest to you. Look at the precise terms used in the postings and include them in your resume (as appropriate to your skills and qualifications).

RESUME STRATEGY #4: Use the "Big" and Save the "Little"

When deciding what you want to include in your resume, try to focus on the big things—revenue and profit growth, new initiatives and ventures, special projects, cost savings, productivity improvements, new products, technology implementations, sales successes, new market launches, and more. Give a good broad-based picture of what you were responsible for and how well you did it. Here's an example:

> Senior Finance and Operating Executive with full responsibility for corporate finance, daily operations, corporate administration, and HR/employee benefits. Concurrent responsibility for identifying and negotiating acquisitions to accelerate growth and expansion. Recruit, train, and lead a staff of 120 through 12 management reports.
>
> - Delivered strong and sustainable financial gains:
>   - 300% increase in revenues and 400% increase in profitability.
>   - $160,000 cost reduction in staffing and employee costs.
>   - $1 million collected in outstanding receivables.
>   - $95,000 savings in vendor and lease costs.

Then save the little stuff—the details—for the interview. With this strategy, you will accomplish 2 things: You'll keep your resume readable and at a reasonable length (while still selling your achievements), and you'll have new and interesting information to share during the interview. Using the preceding example, when discussing this experience you could elaborate on your specific achievements—namely, *how* you increased revenues and profits, *how* you were able to reduce personnel costs while still managing all operations, *what* you did to collect the $1 million in outstanding debt, and more.

RESUME STRATEGY #5: Make Your Resume "Interviewable"

One of your greatest challenges is to make your resume a useful interview tool. After it's been determined that you meet the primary qualifications (you've passed the electronic keyword scan or initial review) and you are contacted for an interview, your resume becomes all-important in leading and prompting your interviewer during your conversation.

Your job, then, is to make sure the resume leads the reader where you want to go and presents just the right information to stimulate a productive discussion. To improve the interviewability of your resume, consider these tactics:

- Make good use of Resume Strategy #4 (Use the "Big" and Save the "Little") to invite further discussion about your experiences, achievements, credentials, and other distinguishing information.

- Be sure your greatest selling points are featured prominently, not buried within the resume.

- Conversely, don't devote lots of space and attention to areas of your background that are irrelevant or less than positive; you'll only invite questions about things you don't want to discuss.

- Make sure your resume is visually pleasing and easy to read—this means plenty of white space, short paragraphs and bullet points, an adequate font size, and a logical flow from start to finish. Feel free to add some graphic elements—borders, shading, tables, charts, logos, unique lettering, a touch of color—but don't overdo it. Management and executive resumes should be conservatively distinctive in design.

RESUME STRATEGY #6: Eliminate Confusion with Structure and Context

Keep in mind that your resume will be read very quickly by hiring authorities. You might agonize over every word and spend hours working on content and design, but the average reader will skim quickly through your masterpiece and expect to pick up important facts in just a few seconds. Try to make it as easy as possible for readers.

- Prominently position your name and contact information at the top of your resume where everyone will look for it.

- Be consistent; for example, put job titles, company names, and dates in the same place for each position.

- Make information easy to find by clearly defining different sections of your resume with large, highly visible headings.

- Use bold, color, or other font enhancements to further differentiate the various sections of your resume and/or prominent career highlights.

- Define the context in which you worked (for example, what the company does, what your specific organization/department does, any notable challenges you overcame) before you start describing your activities and accomplishments. This strategy creates a logical flow that is easy for readers to understand.

RESUME STRATEGY #7: Use Function to Demonstrate Achievement

A resume that focuses only on your job functions can be dry and uninteresting and will say very little about your unique activities and contributions. Consider the following example:

> Responsible for all operations at the 235-room Marriott Hotel in downtown Washington, D.C.

Now consider using that same function to demonstrate achievement and see what happens to the tone and energy of the information. It comes alive and clearly communicates that you deliver results.

> Profitably manage 235-room luxury Marriott property that generates $150M+ in annual revenues. Revitalized property from loss position to double-digit profitability within 2 years through complete redesign of sales, catering, front desk, and security operations. Currently ranked #3 for customer service out of 560 Marriott properties nationwide.

Translate your functions into achievement statements and you'll create much more powerful, interesting, and engaging resume content.

RESUME STRATEGY #8: Remain in the Realm of Reality

We've already established that resume writing is sales. And, as any good salesperson does, you might feel inclined to stretch the truth, just a bit. However, you must stay within the realm of reality. Do not push your skills, qualifications, achievements, and success stories outside the bounds of what is truthful. You never want to be in a position where you have to defend something you've written on your resume. If that happens, you'll lose the opportunity before you ever get started.

Resume Writing Standards

One of the greatest challenges in resume writing is that there are no rules to the game. There are certain expectations about information that you will include: principally, your employment history and educational qualifications. Beyond that, what you include is entirely up to you. What's more, you have tremendous flexibility in determining how to feature the information you have selected. In Chapter 2, you'll find a complete listing of sections you might include in your resume, the type of information that should be contained in each, preferred formats for presentation, and sample text you can edit and use.

Although there are no rules, there are a few standards to adhere to as you write your resume. The following sections discuss these standards in detail.

CONTENT STANDARDS

Content is, of course, the text that goes into your resume. Content standards cover the writing style you should use, items you should be sure to include, items you should avoid mentioning, and the order and format in which you should list your qualifications.

Writing Style

Always write in the first person, dropping the word "I" from the front of each sentence. This style gives your resume a more assertive and more professional tone than the passive third-person voice. Here are some examples.

First Person:

(I) Manage 12-person team leading the global market launch of new OTC pharmaceuticals for Bayer's Consumer Division.

Third Person:

(He) Manages a 12-person team leading the global market launch of new OTC pharmaceuticals for Bayer's Consumer Division.

By using the first-person voice, you are assuming ownership of that statement. You did such-and-such. When you use the third-person voice, it reads as though someone else did it.

Stay Away From...

Try *not* to use phrases such as "responsible for" or "duties included." These words create a passive tone and style. Instead, use active verbs to describe what you did.

Compare these 2 ways of conveying the same information:

Duties included scheduling, job assignment, and management of more than 200 production workers, engineers, and maintenance support staff for a $52 million poultry-production facility.

OR

Directed daily operations, scheduling, and job assignment for more than 200 production workers, engineers, and maintenance support staff at a $52 million poultry-production facility.

The second example above has a stronger tone and impact, which is precisely what you want. Eliminate unnecessary, passive words to create the best impression.

Resume Style

The traditional **chronological** resume lists work experience in reverse-chronological order (starting with your current or most recent position and working backwards). The **functional** style de-emphasizes the where and when of your career and instead groups similar experiences, talents, and qualifications regardless of when or where they occurred.

Today, however, most resumes follow neither a strictly chronological nor strictly functional style; rather, they are an effective mixture of the 2 styles, usually known as a **combination** or **hybrid** style.

Like the chronological, the hybrid includes specifics about where you worked, when you worked there, and your job titles. Like a functional resume, a hybrid emphasizes your most relevant qualifications—in the headline and summary at the top of your resume, integrated into your job descriptions, highlighted in achievement statements in multiple sections throughout your resume, or in many other ways.

Most of the examples in this book are hybrids and demonstrate a wide range of organizational structures that you can use as inspiration when crafting your own resume.

Resume Formats

Resumes, principally career summaries and job descriptions, are most often written in a paragraph format, a bulleted format, or a combination of both. Following are 3 job descriptions, all very similar in content, yet presented in each of the 3 different writing formats. The advantages and disadvantages of each format are also addressed.

Paragraph Format

Division Manager   2014 to 2020

National Medical Research Center, Lewiston, ME

Created and led strategic planning, finance, accounting, administration, contracting, and partnerships for the start-up of a new entrepreneurial division launching new ventures in emerging healthcare markets. Developed business plans and directed operating budgets for 8 distinct profit centers worldwide.

Identified opportunity; then structured, negotiated, and closed joint venture with Central Health, the largest non-profit hospital system in the region. Created Limited Liability Corporation (LLC) to manage and market community-based health-care programs. Appointed to Board of Directors.

Created a portfolio of financial models, indices, and analyses to monitor/evaluate performance of all new ventures, new products, and new service-delivery programs. Collaborated with business partners to create a new respiratory-care company. Won 21 contracts with projections for an additional 12 by end of year 3 ($2+ million in revenue). Established program to facilitate new business opportunities in research, case management, and clinical services. Delivered $4 million in first-year revenue. Negotiated joint venture with medical technology company that included a valuable insider equity position prior to IPO.

Advantages

Requires the least amount of space on the page. Succinct and to the point.

Disadvantages

Achievements get lost in the text of the third paragraph. They are not visually distinctive, nor do they stand alone to draw attention to them. It is very easy to overlook key information in this format because no one wants to read long and text-heavy paragraphs.

Bulleted Format

Division Manager   2014 to 2020
National Medical Research Center, Lewiston, ME

- Created and led strategic planning, finance, accounting, administration, contracting, and partnerships for the start-up of a new entrepreneurial division launching new ventures in emerging healthcare markets. Developed business plans and directed operating budgets for 8 distinct profit centers worldwide.

- Identified opportunity; then structured, negotiated, and closed joint venture with Central Health, the largest non-profit hospital system in the region. Created Limited Liability Corporation (LLC) to manage and market community-based health-care programs. Appointed to Board of Directors.

- Created a portfolio of financial models, indices, and analyses to monitor/ evaluate performance of all new ventures, new products, and new service-delivery programs.

- Collaborated with business partners to create a new respiratory-care company. Won 21 contracts with projections for an additional 12 by end of year 3 ($2+ million in revenue).

- Established program to facilitate new business-development opportunities in research, case management, and clinical services. Delivered $4 million in first-year revenue.

- Negotiated joint venture with medical-technology company that included a valuable insider equity position prior to IPO.

Advantages

Quick and easy to peruse.

Disadvantages

Responsibilities and achievements are lumped together with everything of equal value. In turn, the achievements get lost farther down the list and are not immediately recognizable.

Combination Format

Division Manager   2014 to 2020

National Medical Research Center, Lewiston, ME

Created and led strategic planning, finance, accounting, administration, contracting, and partnerships for the start-up of a new entrepreneurial division launching new ventures in emerging healthcare markets. Developed business plans and directed operating budgets for 8 distinct profit centers worldwide.

- Identified opportunity; then structured, negotiated, and closed joint venture with Central Health, the largest non-profit hospital system in the region. Created Limited Liability Corporation (LLC) to manage and market community-based health-care programs. Appointed to Board of Directors.

- Created a portfolio of financial models, indices, and analyses to monitor/ evaluate performance of all new ventures, new products, and new service-delivery programs.

- Collaborated with business partners to create a new respiratory-care company. Won 21 contracts with projections for an additional 12 by end of year 3 ($2+ million in revenue).

- Established program to facilitate new business-development opportunities in research, case management, and clinical services. Delivered $4 million in first-year revenue.

- Negotiated joint venture with medical-technology company that included a valuable insider equity position prior to IPO.

Advantages

Our recommended format. Clearly presents overall responsibilities in the introductory paragraph and then accentuates each achievement as a separate bullet.

Disadvantages

If you don't have clearly identifiable accomplishments, project milestones, or other notable information to share, this format is not as effective. It also might draw unwanted attention to positions where your accomplishments were less notable; this can be less than favorable if those jobs were recent.

PRESENTATION STANDARDS

Presentation refers to the way your resume looks. It has to do with the fonts you use, the way it looks onscreen in both Word and PDF files, the paper you print it on, any graphics or visual enhancements you might include, and how many pages your resume should be.

Font

Use a typestyle that is clean, conservative, and easy to read. Stay away from anything that is too fancy, glitzy, curly, and the like. Here are a few recommended fonts:

Arial	Century Schoolbook
Arial Narrow	Garamond
Bookman	Georgia
Book Antiqua	Gill Sans MT
Calibri	Lucida Sans
Cambria	Tahoma
Century Gothic	Verdana

We recommend that you not use Times New Roman font. Because it was the default font on Microsoft Word for years, it became overused and now looks extremely dated.

Your choice of typestyle should be dictated by the content, format, and length of your resume. Some fonts look better than others at smaller or larger sizes; some have "bolder" boldface type; some require more white space to make them readable. After you write your resume, experiment with different fonts to see which one best enhances your document.

Type Size

Readability is everything! If the type size is too small, your resume will be difficult to read and difficult to skim for essential information. Interestingly, a too-large type size, particularly for senior-level professionals, can also give a negative impression by conveying a juvenile or unprofessional image.

As a general rule, select type from 9 to 12 points in size. However, there's no hard-and-fast rule, and a lot depends on the typestyle you choose. Take a look at the following examples:

Very readable in 9-point Verdana

Won the 2020 "Manager of the Year" award at Ford's Indianapolis plant. Honored for innovative contributions to cost reduction, product development, and profit growth.

Difficult to read in too-small 9-point Gill Sans

Won the 2020 "Manager of the Year" award at Ford's Indianapolis plant. Honored for innovative contributions to cost reduction, product development, and profit growth.

Concise and readable in 12-point Garamond

Senior Training & Development Manager specializing in the design, development, and presentation of multimedia leadership training programs for senior managers and executives nationwide.

A bit overwhelming and elementary-looking in 12-point Bookman

Senior Training & Development Manager specializing in the design, development, and presentation of multimedia leadership training programs for senior managers and executives nationwide.

Type Enhancements

Bold, *italics*, <u>underlining</u>, and CAPITALIZATION are ideal for highlighting certain words, phrases, achievements, projects, numbers, and other information you want to draw special attention to. However, do not overuse these enhancements. If everything is emphasized, nothing stands out.

Page Length

Our recommendation is 1 or 2 pages for a management or executive resume. Keep it short and succinct, giving just enough to entice your readers' interest.

However, in some instances a longer, 3-page resume might be appropriate. Let the amount of essential information you have to share be the determining factor. Do not feel as though it *must* remain on 1 or 2 pages, although that is the preference. What it *must* do is attract prospective employers to you.

Here are a few situations when a longer resume might be appropriate:

- You have an extensive list of relevant technical qualifications.
- You have extensive educational training and numerous credentials/certifications, all of which are important to include.
- You want to include many special projects, task forces, and committees that are relevant to your career objectives.
- You have an extensive list of professional honors, awards, and commendations. This list is tremendously valuable in validating your credibility and distinguishing you from the competition.
- You have an extensive list of media appearances and publications. Again, this list is extremely valuable in validating your credibility and distinguishing you from the competition. It must be included, even if just the highlights.

NOTE: In any of the above situations, often it's more beneficial to present these additonal items in an addendum—typically a 1-page optional addition to your resume. The resume remains sharply focused and concise, while the addendum shares additonal distinguishing information in a way that doesn't distract from the core message. You might also integrate the most notable of these items into your career summary.

If you create a resume that's longer than 2 pages, make it reader-friendly by carefully segmenting the information into separate sections. For instance, begin with your career summary and your work experience. This will most likely take 1 to 2 pages. Then follow with education, any professional or industry credentials, honors and awards, technology and equipment skills, publications, public speaking engagements, professional affiliations, civic affiliations, volunteer experience, foreign-language skills, and other relevant information you want to include.

Put each section into a separate category (under a separate heading) so that your resume is easy to skim and your reader can quickly grasp the highlights. You'll read more about each of these sections of your resume in Chapter 2.

Paper Color

In most cases, your resume will be sent electronically, so paper color is not a factor. However, for in-person networking meetings and job interviews, you will want to bring a printed version of your resume to share. Use good-quality paper in a conservative color. White, ivory, and light gray are ideal.

Graphics and Color

An attractive, relevant graphic can really add impact. When you look through the sample resumes in Chapters 4 through 12, you'll see many examples that use graphics effectively to enhance the visual presentation and strengthen the underlying message.

As you create your resume, consider adding a powerful chart or table to illustrate your management successes, revenue gains, stock price increases, growth in customers, and other metrics. Don't be afraid to add a touch of color to create a distinctive appearance. Just be sure not to get carried away; be tasteful and relatively conservative.

White Space

We'll say it again: Readability is everything! If people have to struggle to read your resume, they simply won't make the effort. Therefore, be sure to leave plenty of white space. It really does make a difference in how much time and effort individuals will put into actually reading your resume and learning about your career.

ACCURACY AND PERFECTION

The final step, and one of the most critical in resume writing, is the proofreading stage. It is essential that your resume be well written, visually pleasing, and free of any errors, typographical mistakes, misspellings, and inconsistencies. We recommend that you carefully proofread your resume a minimum of 3 times, and then have 2 or 3 other people also proofread it.

Always remember that your resume is an example of the quality of work you will produce on a company's behalf. Is your work product going to have errors and inconsistencies? If your resume does, it communicates to a prospective employer that you are careless, and that is likely to lead to a disappointing and frustrating search.

Take the time and put forth the effort to make certain that your resume is perfect in all the little details that make a big difference to those who read it.

CHAPTER 2

Writing Your Resume

For many managers and executives, resume writing is *not* at the top of the list of fun and exciting activities! How can it compare to negotiating a joint venture, solving a major production problem, reducing corporate debt, or launching a new product? In your perception, we're sure that it cannot.

However, resume writing can be an enjoyable and rewarding task. Once your resume is complete, you can look at it proudly, reminding yourself of all that you have achieved. It is a snapshot of your career and your success. When it's complete, we guarantee you'll look back with tremendous self-satisfaction as you launch and successfully manage your job search.

Resume writing is typically the first step in finding a new position or advancing your career and can be the most daunting of all job-search tasks. If writing is not one of your primary job functions, it might have been years since you actually wrote anything other than notes to yourself. Even if you write on a regular basis, resume writing is unique. It has its own style and a number of peculiarities, as any specialty document does.

To make the writing process easier, more fluid, and more efficient for you, we've consolidated it into 5 discrete sections:

- **Contact Information.** This identification—most often, your name, cell number, email, and link to your LinkedIn profile—provides recruiters, hiring managers, and network contacts with an easy way to respond and follow up.

- **Career Summary.** Think of your Career Summary as the corporate strategy of your resume. It is the big-picture view of everything that allows your organization to work—whether your organization is an entire company or just one individual department. It is the backbone of your leadership experience and the foundation of your resume.

- **Professional Experience.** The Professional Experience section is much like the operations that are the basis of your organization. These specifics support your achievement of the corporate strategy. Your professional experience demonstrates how you put all your capabilities to work.

- **Education and Certifications.** Think of this content as your organization's credentials, the third-party validation of your qualifications, knowledge, and expertise.

- **The "Extras"** (Publications, Public Speaking, Honors and Awards, Technology Qualifications, Training, Professional Affiliations, Civic Affiliations, Foreign Languages, Personal Information, and so on). This section of your resume includes your product and service features, the "extra stuff" that helps distinguish you from others with similar qualifications.

Step-by-Step: Writing the Perfect Resume

In the preceding section, we outlined the 5 core resume sections. Now we'll detail the particulars of each section—what to include, where to place it, and how to present it.

CONTACT INFORMATION

Let's briefly address the top section of your resume: your name and contact information.

Name

You'd think writing your name would be the easiest part of writing your resume! But there are several factors you should consider:

- Although most people choose to use their full, formal name at the top of a resume, it has become increasingly acceptable to use the name by which you prefer to be called.

- You want readers to feel comfortable calling you for an interview. Their comfort level might decrease if your name is gender-neutral, difficult to pronounce, or very unusual; they don't know whether they're calling a man or a woman or how to ask for you. Here are a few ways you can make it easier for them:

> Lynn T. Cowles (Mr.)
>
> (Ms.) Michael Murray
>
> Tzirina (Irene) Kahn
>
> Ndege "Nick" Vernon

Address

It is no longer a best practice to share your physical address (or mailing address) on your resume. You can omit location entirely or simply indicate your general area. Think about the following as you are making this decision.

If you are open to relocation, we recommend that you not include any information regarding your location. Why tell a prospective employer in Dallas that you currently live in Pittsburgh? All that does is give that employer a reason to exclude you from consideration.

The only time we recommend sharing your location is when your job search is restricted to the area in which you currently live and work. In that situation, include only your city, state, and zip code or your general area ("Chicago Metro")—the specific search terms someone will use if looking for candidates in their immediate vicinity.

Phone Number

Include just one phone number on your resume—the number where you can be reached most readily and where callers can leave a voice mail message for a speedy return call. For the vast majority of managers and executives, that number is your cell phone number; in rare instances it might be your home number. Never, of course, use your work number for your search.

Be sure to have a brief, professional-sounding voice mail greeting on your phone, and regularly monitor your messages.

Email Address

Always include a live link to your email address on your resume. Do not use your employer's email. Instead, use a personal email address through a provider such as Gmail, Outlook, Mail.com, Yahoo!, or iCloud.

LinkedIn URL

We recommend that you add a live link to your profile as part of your contact information. Employers and network contacts who want to know more will click through to review your profile, so be certain that it is interesting, insightful, and consistent with your resume and current career goals. (See Chapters 13 and 14 for guidelines and examples.)

Also, take the time to customize your LinkedIn URL so it does not include a string of random numbers after your name.

As you look through the resume samples in Chapters 4 through 12, you'll see how resume writers have arranged the many bits of contact information at the top of a resume. You can use these as models for presenting your own information. Bottom line, make it as easy as possible for employers to contact you.

Now, let's get into the nitty-gritty of the 4 core content sections of your resume.

CAREER SUMMARY

The Career Summary is the introductory section at the top of your resume that summarizes and highlights your knowledge, expertise, and, in many instances, some of your most notable achievements.

Although some resumes, even for managers and executives, still begin with Objective statements, we believe a Career Summary is a much more powerful introduction. The problem with Objectives is that they are either too specific (limiting you to an "engineering management position") or too vague (doesn't everyone want a challenging management opportunity with a progressive organization offering the opportunity for growth and advancement?). In addition, they can be read as self-serving because they describe *what you want* instead of suggesting *what you have to offer* an employer.

In contrast, an effective Career Summary allows you to position yourself as you want to be perceived and to immediately paint a picture of yourself that supports your current goals. It is critical that this section focus on the specific skills, qualifications, and achievements of your career that are related to your job targets. Your summary is *not* a historical overview of your career. Rather, it is a concise, well-written, and sharp presentation of information designed to *sell* you into your next position.

This section can have various titles, such as:

Career Summary	Leadership Profile
Career Achievements	Management Profile
Career Highlights	Professional Qualifications
Career Synopsis	Professional Summary
Executive Profile	Profile
Expertise	Summary
Highlights of Experience	Summary of Achievements
Industry Summary	Summary of Qualifications

Or, as you will see in the first format example below (headline format), your summary does not need a title at all. In fact, headlines have become increasingly popular because they immediately call attention to critical "who you are" information.

Here are 5 sample Career Summaries. Consider using one of these as the guide for developing your Career Summary, or use them as the foundation to create your own presentation. You will find some type of Career Summary in just about every resume included in this book because it is the preferred style of professional resume writers.

Headline Format

MANUFACTURING MANAGER / PRODUCTION MANAGER
Production Planning / Logistics / Multi-Site Operations
MBA – Executive Management
MS – Manufacturing Systems & Technology

Traditional Paragraph Format

CAREER SUMMARY
INSURANCE INDUSTRY MANAGER with an 18-year career highlighted by rapid advancement and consistent achievement in market, premium, and profit growth. Outstanding qualifications in building and managing relationships with sales producers and field management teams. Deep knowledge and expertise in underwriting and policy rating. Advanced technology skills.

Core Competencies Summary Format

SENIOR EXECUTIVE: Startup, Turnaround & High-Growth Companies

✓ **Twenty-year management career** with consistent and measurable achievements in:

- Revenue & Profit Growth
- Operating Cost Reductions
- Market & Customer Expansion
- Productivity & Efficiency Improvement

✓ **Success in overcoming market, technological, financial, and competitive challenges** to drive growth, profitability, and performance improvement. Expertise includes:

- Strategic Planning & Leadership
- Finance, Budgeting & Cost Management
- Marketing, Sales & New Business
- Contracts, Outsourcing & Partnerships
- Training, Development & Team Building
- Investor & Board Relations

✓ **Guest Speaker,** 2020 "Leadership Innovations" Conference

✓ **Winner,** 2018 McKenzie Award for Leadership Excellence

Achievement Format

CAREER SUMMARY

▶ **VP BUSINESS DEVELOPMENT, X-CO: Captured the #1 client in company history, now generating $40M annual revenue.** Defined and drove expansion strategy that produced opportunities in 7 new industries and 14 geographic markets.

▶ **MARKETING DIRECTOR, M&S Products: Launched iconic Spiff product line** with award-winning marketing and branding strategies that led to industry recognition as "Product of the Year."

▶ **ACCOUNT MANAGER, M&S Products: Delivered sales results in top 10% companywide** for 4 straight years.

▶ **SALES REPRESENTATIVE, First Financial: Achieved President's Club** in second year and built reputation for client-focused sales and support.

Category Format

PROFESSIONAL CAREER HIGHLIGHTS

EXPERIENCE:	12 years as a Director of Maintenance Operations for Dow Corning and its subsidiaries
EDUCATION:	Graduate Certificate in Facilities Maintenance & Engineering—University of Washington BS—Operations Management—University of Oregon
PUBLICATIONS:	"Improving Workforce Productivity Through Maintenance Systems Design & Optimization," *American Manufacturing Association*, 2019 "Redesigning Maintenance Processes to Enhance Productivity," *National Facilities Maintenance Association*, 2017
AWARDS:	Employee of the Year, Dow Corning, 2018 Employee of the Year, Bell Laboratories, 2009

PROFESSIONAL EXPERIENCE

Your Professional Experience is the heart of your resume—the "operations," as we discussed before. It's what gives your resume substance, meaning, and depth. It is also the section that will take you the longest to write. If you've had the same position for 10 years, how can you consolidate all you have done into one short section? If, on the opposite end of the spectrum, you have had your current position for only 11 months, how can you make it seem substantial and noteworthy? And, for all of you whose experience is in between, what do you include, how, where, and why?

These are not easy questions to answer. In fact, the most truthful response to each question is, "it depends." It depends on you, your experience, your achievements and successes, and your current career objectives.

Here are 7 samples of Professional Experience sections. Review how each individual's unique background is organized and emphasized. Consider your own background when using one of these as the foundation for developing your own Professional Experience section.

Achievement Format

Emphasizes each position, the overall scope of responsibility, and the resulting achievements.

PROFESSIONAL EXPERIENCE:

Human Resources Manager (2016 to Present)
ARNOLD & SMITH DISTRIBUTION CO., INC., Roanoke, VA

Recruited by principals and given complete responsibility for defining organizational culture, developing strategic HR plans, and positioning HR as a proactive partner to operations and business units nationwide. Scope of responsibility impacts 1,500 employees at 25 operating locations and 2 administrative office complexes. Supervise 3-person management team and 22 other HR employees.

Achievements

- Created best-in-class HR organizations, systems, processes and practices as Arnold & Smith has experienced dramatic growth and expansion over the past 4 years. Fully integrated 150 Prestige employees, 90 US General Life Insurance employees, and others as the company has accelerated growth through acquisition.

- Introduced a focused, yet flexible corporate culture to facilitate seamless integration of acquired business units, product lines, and personnel.

- Led recruitment and selection for key positions throughout the company, including the entire legal, finance, administrative, and accounting organizations.

- Designed and implemented HR infrastructure, benefit programs, and performance-based appraisal and incentive compensation system. Upgraded staffing models.

- Contributed $750K in salary cost reductions through redesign of staffing processes.

Challenge, Action, and Results (CAR) Format

Highlights the challenge of each position, the action you took, and the results you delivered.

Professional Experience

WIP Systems International, Bulverde, TX   2014 to Present

VICE PRESIDENT OF OPERATIONS (2016 to Present)
PLANT MANAGER (2014 to 2016)

Challenge: Plan and direct the turnaround and return to profitability of $42M technology systems manufacturer plagued with cost overrides, poor productivity, dissatisfied customers, and multimillion-dollar annual losses.

Action: Rebuilt the entire management team, introduced advanced technologies and systems to expedite production flow, retrained all operators and supervisors, and implemented team-based work culture.

Results:
- ■ Achieved/surpassed all turnaround objectives and returned the operation to profitability in first year. Delivered strong and sustainable gains:
  - **70%** improvement in operating efficiency.
  - **250%** reduction in cycle times.
  - **75%** improvement in product quality ratings.
  - **100%** on-time customer delivery.

- ■ Replaced obsolete equipment with state-of-the-art systems, redesigned and upgraded facility, introduced stringent standards to achieve OSHA compliance, and established in-house day-care facility (with dramatic reduction in absenteeism).

- ■ Restored credibility with key customer generating more than $30M a year in revenues to WIP. Resolved long-standing quality and delivery issues, implemented key account management strategy, and revitalized key business relationships.

- ■ Partnered with HP, IBM, and Dell to integrate their technologies into WIP's software applications. Received more than $200K in technology resources at no charge to the company.

- ■ Quoted in the National Manufacturing Association's annual publication as one of 2019's ***"Leaders in Manufacturing."***

Functional Format

Focuses on the functional areas of responsibility (tasks) within the job and associated achievements.

PROFESSIONAL EXPERIENCE:

Vice President — STAR FINANCIAL, INC., Dayton, Ohio   2017 to Present

Recruited by former advisor to help manage Star Financial, a large private equity investment firm operating as an incubator for emerging, undercapitalized, rapidly growing, and turnaround businesses requiring hands-on management and leadership. Challenged to identify strategic investment opportunities, develop innovative business models, conduct due diligence, structure transactions, and negotiate private placements.

- **New Venture Start-Up** – Founded and invested in X-TRA Distributors, Inc., a privately held business-to-consumer (B2C) direct marketing company. Created a portfolio of 8 consumer-based direct marketing products, orchestrated go-to-market strategy, developed best-in-class financial infrastructure and all financial systems, and launched new venture in 2018.

- **Organizational & Financial Infrastructure** – Created a unique business/finance model leveraging outsourcing to deliver operating expertise in product development, manufacturing, packaging, fulfillment, and customer service. Operated X-TRA with only 14 employees and a team of 12 core business partners/vendors. Controlled costs at less than 12% of revenue.

- **Financial Growth Through Strategic Marketing** – Rolled out national direct marketing campaign utilizing media to drive online and inbound telemarketing traffic. Generated $4.3M in sales within first 6 months and secured 70K+ web-based customers.

- **Corporate Roll-Up** – Structured and negotiated sale of X-TRA Distributors to a large international direct marketer to achieve economies of scale, improve operating efficiencies, and increase net profitability.

Career Track Format

Emphasizes career advancement, overall scope of responsibility, and notable achievements.

RYNCON AMERICA, INC. | Dallas, TX | 2010–Present

Vice President – Marketing Operations Worldwide (2017–Present)
Vice President – Sales (2015–2017)
Sales Director (2013–2015)
National Accounts Manager (2011–2013)
Sales Associate (2010–2011)

Fast-track promotion through a series of increasingly responsible positions to current role as Vice President of Marketing Operations Worldwide. Credited with building global marketing organization that led division to 6-fold growth in just 3 years. Recruited and developed talented staff of sales and marketing professionals who now serve as Ryncon's core marketing and sales management team.

- ☑ Built division from $20M in annual revenues to $120M+ in 2020.

- ☑ Achieved #1 market position in North America and maintained for 3 years.

- ☑ Surpassed all profit goals for 10 consecutive years, averaging 12%–15% annual profit growth.

- ☑ Conceived and implemented customer-focus strategy to drive long-term product development and service delivery. Currently maintain customer satisfaction rating of 97%+.

- ☑ Outpaced competition as first in the industry to enter the Northern Canadian, Puerto Rican, and Caribbean markets. Currently projecting more than $20M in new-market revenues by end of year 2.

Project Highlights Format

Details specific projects, their scope of responsibility, and associated achievements.

MOLTEN METAL TECHNOLOGY *($650M metal products design & manufacturing company)*

PROJECT MANAGER   2010 to Present

Travel to Molten facilities nationwide to orchestrate a portfolio of special projects and assignments. Delivered all projects on time and within budget for 10 consecutive years. Recent projects include:

- **Recycling Facility Development & Construction** ($12.8M). Co-led fast-track design and construction team bringing project from concept to completion in just 16 months. ***RESULT:*** *Built an environmentally safe and regulatorily compliant facility at 12% under projected cost.*

- **SAP Implementation Project** ($1.8M). Led 12-person technology and support team in a massive SAP implementation project impacting virtually the entire facility and workforce. ***RESULT:*** *Created a totally integrated technology environment linking inventory, production planning, quality, cost accounting, and other core manufacturing and support functions.*

- **OSHA Compliance Project** ($500K). Led year-long project to identify non-compliance issues and initiate appropriate remedial activity. ***RESULT:*** *Passed 2017 OSHA inspection with zero findings.*

- **Annual Shutdown & Maintenance Project** ($100K). Planned, scheduled, and directed annual plant shutdown and maintenance programs for 3 facilities involving as many as 100 craftsmen. ***RESULT:*** *Restored all facilities to full operation within stringent time constraints.*

Skills-Based Format

Puts initial focus on specific skills rather than when and where they were used. Helpful in bringing less-current skill sets to the forefront and avoiding emphasis on employment gaps.

FOUNDER AND GENERAL MANAGER — Law Offices of Earl W. Hadley — 2008 to Present

Founded specialized legal practice providing corporate advisory services to CEOs, COOs, and other senior executives across a broad range of industries and on a broad range of business issues. Built new venture from start-up to 3 locations and 12 employees. Achieved and maintained profitability for 12 consecutive years. Built and sustained an excellent reputation for ethical performance and integrity.

Serve in the capacity of a **Senior Operating Executive & General Counsel** to client companies, providing hands-on leadership in:

- Strategic Planning & Vision
- Policies & Procedures
- Growth & Expansion
- Market Analysis & Positioning
- Acquisitions & Valuations
- Letters of Credit & Intent

- Operations Management
- Cost Control & Avoidance
- Process Design & Analysis
- Banking & Corporate Finance
- Asset & Stock Purchase Agreements
- Licensing & Leasing Agreements

- Human Resources
- Technology
- Capital Assets
- Executive Compensation
- A/R & Collections
- Bankruptcy/Turnaround

Clients range from start-up ventures to $200M corporations engaged in software development, high-tech manufacturing, industrial manufacturing, consumer products, heavy equipment, transportation, automotive and marine dealerships, and professional services.

Firm responsibilities include: As **General Manager**, direct all daily and long-term business planning and management functions, staffing, technology, and business performance. As **Marketing & Business Development Executive**, lead client acquisition, networking, marketing, and relationship management. As **Principal Attorney**, manage all legal affairs and client representation.

Experience Format

Concisely describes specific highlights of each position. Best used in conjunction with a detailed Career Summary.

EXPERIENCE SUMMARY ————————————————————————————————

Office Manager, WEST-QUEST TECHNOLOGIES, Lewisburg, ID — 2018 to Present

- ❑ Implemented cost savings that slashed $150,000 from annual operations.
- ❑ Selected and directed implementation of new cloud-based network with advanced communication and multimedia capabilities.
- ❑ Recruited, trained, and supervised 12 administrative and office support personnel in 2 operating locations.

Office Manager, CENTURY TECHNOLOGIES, Ames, IA – 2015 to 2018

- ❑ Independently managed all office, administrative, and clerical functions for a small technology start-up venture in the "train-the-trainer" market.
- ❑ Designed all internal recordkeeping, reporting, accounting, project management, and client-management systems and processes.
- ❑ Selected office equipment and technology, negotiated leases, and coordinated installation.
- ❑ Represented owners at local business and Chamber of Commerce meetings/events.

Assistant Manager, GREENWALT ARCHITECTURAL SYSTEMS, Ames, IA – 2011 to 2015

- ❑ Worked with owners and architects to facilitate project completion by coordinating deadlines, deliverables, and client communications.
- ❑ Implemented PC-based project tracking and accounting systems.
- ❑ Coordinated all purchasing and inventory functions for office supplies and design materials.

EDUCATION AND CERTIFICATIONS

Your Education section should include college attendance and degrees, certifications, credentials, licenses, registrations, and continuing education. If any are particularly notable, be sure to highlight them prominently in your Education section and/or bring them to the top in your Career Summary (as demonstrated by the Headline format in the previous section on writing career summaries).

Here are 5 sample Education sections that illustrate a variety of ways to organize and format this information.

Executive Education Format

EDUCATION

➤ **Executive Development Program**	STANFORD UNIVERSITY
➤ **Executive Development Program**	UNIVERSITY OF CALIFORNIA AT LOS ANGELES
➤ **Master of Business Administration (MBA)**	UNIVERSITY OF CALIFORNIA AT LOS ANGELES
➤ **Bachelor of Science (BS)**	UNIVERSITY OF CALIFORNIA AT IRVINE

Academic Credentials Format

EDUCATION: **M.S., Management Science**, University of Colorado, 2006
B.S., Industrial Engineering, University of Nevada, 2000

Highlights of Continuing Professional Education:
- Organizational Management & Leadership, Colorado Leadership Association, 2018
- Industrial Engineering Technology in Today's Modern Manufacturing Organization, Purdue University, 2016
- SAP Implementation & Optimization, American Society for Quality Control, 2008
- Conflict Resolution & Violence Management in the Workplace, Institute for Workplace Safety, 2005

Certifications Format

Technical Certifications and Degrees

Nurse Executive-Board Certified (NE-BC), Helen Keller School of Nursing & Health Care Administration, 2006
Bachelor of Science in Nursing (BSN), Missouri State University at Columbia, 1998
Certificate in Advanced Cardiac Life Support (ACLS), State of Missouri, 1998
Certificate in Basic Cardiac Life Support (BCLS), State of Tennessee, 1996

Non-Degree Format

TRAINING & EDUCATION

UNIVERSITY OF TOLEDO, Toledo, Ohio
BS Candidate—Management & Administration (Senior class status)
UNIVERSITY OF MICHIGAN, Ann Arbor, Michigan
Dual Majors in Management & Human Resource Administration (2 years)
Graduate, 100+ hours of continuing professional education through the University of Illinois, University of Michigan, and University of Wisconsin.

No-College Format

PROFESSIONAL DEVELOPMENT

Management Training & Development	KELLOGG SCHOOL OF MANAGEMENT
Leadership Excellence	KELLOGG SCHOOL OF MANAGEMENT
Supervisory Training	CONNELLY COMMUNITY COLLEGE
Management Communications	PACE LEADERSHIP TRAINING

THE "EXTRAS"

The primary focus of your resume is on information (most likely, your professional experience and academic credentials) that is directly related to your career goals. However, you also should include things that will distinguish you from other candidates and clearly demonstrate your value to a prospective employer. And, not too surprisingly, it can be the "extras" that get the interviews.

Following is a list of the other categories you might or might not include in your resume, depending on your particular experience and your current career objectives. Review the information. If it's pertinent to you, use the samples for formatting your own data. Remember, however, that if something is truly impressive, you might want to draw attention to it in your Career Summary at the beginning of your resume. If you do that, it's not necessary to repeat the information at the end of your resume.

Honors and Awards

If you have won honors and awards, you can either include them in a separate section on your resume or integrate them into Education or Professional Experience, whichever is most appropriate. If you choose to include them in a separate section, consider this format:

❖ Winner, 2018 **"Sales Leadership Award,"** American Sales Association, for outstanding contributions to sales revenues, market penetration, and new business development.
❖ **"Corporate Sales Manager of the Year,"** ISP Systems, Inc., 2017
❖ **"Sales Manager of the Year,"** ISP Systems, 2015
❖ **"Sales Trainer of the Year,"** Delco Systems, 2012
❖ **Summa Cum Laude Graduate,** Yale University, 2002

Public Speaking

Experts are the ones who are invited to give public presentations at conferences, seminars, workshops, training programs, symposia, and other events. If you have public-speaking experience, be sure to include this impressive information in your resume. Here's one way to present it:

• Keynote Speaker, **"Advancing Technology Innovation In The Workplace,"** 2018 National Association on Technology Excellence Conference, New York

• Panel Presenter, **"Emerging Multimedia Technologies & Applications,"** 2017 National Association of Information Technology Executives, Dallas

• Keynote Speaker, **"Technology for the Entrepreneur,"** 2012 Entrepreneur's World Conference, Chicago

Publications

If you're published, you must be an expert (or at least most people will think so). Just as with your public-speaking engagements, include your publications in your resume. They validate your knowledge, qualifications, and credibility. Publications can include books, articles, online content, manuals, and other written documents. Here's an example:

- Author, *"Executive Compensation Systems,"* Society of Human Resource Management Annual Conference Proceedings, 2020
- Author, *"International Hiring, Employment & Retention,"* Society of Human Resource Management Journal, 2019
- Author, *"Expatriate Employment for U.S. Corporations,"* IBM Corporation Employee Bulletin, March 2017
- Co-Author, *"Hiring For Long-Term Retention,"* American Management Association Journal, April 2012

Technology Skills and Qualifications

If you are a manager or executive in a field unrelated to technology, you might include just a brief statement in your Career Summary that communicates your expertise For example:

Technology Qualifications: MS Office Suite, Salesforce CRM, Blackboard, Cognos, Tableau

However, if you're employed in a technology industry or have unique technology qualifications, you'll want to include a separate section with this information (if it's relevant to your current career objectives). You'll also have to consider placement of this section in your resume. If your target positions require strong technical skills, we recommend you insert this section immediately after your Career Summary. If, on the other hand, your technical skills are a plus rather than a specific requirement, the preferred placement is after your Education section.

Here is a sample for how you might present your technical qualifications:

Technical Competencies

C#.NET | R programming language | Python

Neo4j - graph database | SQL Server | Cypher Query Language

MicroStrategy | Java | Visual C++ | Visual Basic | Classic ASP/COM | Visual FoxPro

Visual Studio .NET | CA Agile Central | ASP.NET | JavaScript | JSON | RESTful Web Services

Teaching and Training Experience

Many managers and executives also teach or train at colleges, universities, technical schools, and other organizations in addition to training they might offer "on the job." If you have this type of experience (paid or unpaid), you will want to include it on your resume. Being asked to share your expertise communicates a strong message about your skills, qualifications, knowledge, and expertise. Here's a format you might use to present that information:

- **Faculty,** Department of Finance & Economics, Morgan State University, 2016 to Present. Teach graduate studies in Economics, Economic Theory, Advanced Statistics, and Management Communications.

- **Adjunct Faculty,** Department of Economics, Coppin State College, 2012 to Present. Teach Microeconomics and Macroeconomics to third-and fourth-year students.

- **Guest Lecturer,** Department of Business & Economics, Purdue University, 2009 to Present. Provide semiannual, daylong lecture series on the integration of economic theory into the corporate workplace.

- **Lecturer,** Maryland State University, 2006 to 2009. Taught "Principles of Management" for first-year college students.

Committees and Task Forces

Many managers and executives serve on committees, task forces, and other special project teams either as part of, or in addition to, their full-time responsibilities. Again, this type of information further strengthens your credibility, qualifications, and perceived value to a prospective employer. Consider a format such as this:

- **Chairperson**, 2017–18 Corporate Planning & Reorganization Task Force
- **Member**, 2016–17 Corporate Committee on Global Market Expansion & Positioning
- **Member**, 2012–14 Study Team on "Redesigning Corporate Training Systems To Maximize Employee Productivity"
- **Chairperson**, 2009–10 Committee on "Safety & Regulatory Compliance in the Workplace"

Professional Affiliations

If you are a member of any educational, professional, or leadership associations, be sure to include that information on your resume. It communicates a message of professionalism, a desire to stay current with the industry, and a strong professional network. Highlight any leadership positions you have held within these organizations. Here's an example:

AMERICAN MANAGEMENT ASSOCIATION
Professional Member (1998 to Present)
Professional Development Committee Member (2015 to 2017)
Recruitment Committee Member (2010 to 2012)

AMERICAN HEALTH CARE ASSOCIATION
Associate Member (2005 to Present)
Professional Member (2000 to 2005)
Technology Task Force Member (2000 to 2003)

INTERNATIONAL HEALTH CARE SOCIETY
Professional Member (2000 to Present)
Training Committee Member (2000 to 2010)

Civic Affiliations

Civic affiliations are fine to include if they are with a notable organization, demonstrate leadership experience, or might be of interest to a prospective employer.

However, affiliations such as treasurer of your local condo association and singer with your church choir are not generally of value in marketing your professional qualifications unless, of course, the skills you demonstrate in those organizations relate directly to the professional qualifications you are showcasing. Here's an example of what you might include:

- **Volunteer Chairperson,** United Way of America—Detroit Chapter, 2014 to Present
- **President,** Lambert Valley Conservation District, 2012 to Present
- **Treasurer,** Habitat for Humanity—Detroit Chapter, 2012 to 2015

Personal Information

Do not share personal information such as your birth date, marital status, number of children, and related data. However, in some instances it may be appropriate to add personal information. If it will give you a competitive advantage or answer unspoken questions about your background, then by all means include it. Here's an example:

- ☑ Born in Argentina. U.S. Permanent Resident since 1999.
- ☑ Fluent in English, Spanish, and Portuguese.
- ☑ Competitive Triathlete. Top-5 finish, 2018 Midwest Triathlon and 2014 Des Moines Triathlon.

Note in the preceding example that the job seeker is multilingual. Although this fact is listed under Personal Information in this example, such a critical selling point should also be mentioned in the Career Summary.

Consolidating the Extras

Sometimes you have so many extra categories at the end of your resume, each with only a handful of lines, that spacing becomes a problem. You certainly don't want to have to make your resume a page longer to accommodate 5 lines, nor do you want the extras to overwhelm the primary sections of your resume. Yet you believe the information is important and should be included. Or perhaps you have a few small bits of information that you think are important but don't merit an entire section.

In these situations, consider consolidating the information using the following format. You'll save space, avoid overemphasizing individual items, and present a professional, distinguished appearance.

PROFESSIONAL PROFILE

Education	BSEE, Florida State University
Affiliations	International Association of Electrical Inspectors American Electrical Association Florida Association of Electrical & Electronic Engineers
Public Speaking	Speaker, IEEE Conference, Dallas, 2020 Presenter, AEA National Conference, San Diego, 2018 Panelist, APICS National Conference, Miami, 2014
Languages	Fluent in English, Spanish, and German
Additional	Co-Chair, Education Committee, Tampa Technology Association Eagle Scout and Boy Scout Troop Leader Available for relocation worldwide

Writing Tips, Techniques, and Important Lessons

At this point, you've done a lot of reading, probably taken some notes, and highlighted samples that appeal to you. Now you're ready to plunge into writing your resume.

To make this task as easy as possible, we've compiled some "insider" techniques that we've used in our professional resume writing practices. We know they work, and they will make the writing process easier, faster, and more enjoyable for you.

GET IT DOWN—THEN POLISH AND PERFECT IT

Don't be too concerned with making your resume "perfect" the first time around. It's far better to move fairly swiftly through the initial process, getting the basic information organized into a Word file, instead of agonizing about the perfect phrase or ideal formatting. Once you've completed a draft, we think you'll be surprised at how close to "final" it is. Then, you'll be able to edit and tighten the text quickly while also improving the formatting and enhancing the design and visual presentation.

WRITE YOUR RESUME FROM THE BOTTOM UP

We guarantee that the process of writing your resume will be much easier if you follow this "bottom-up" strategy:

- **Start with the easy things**—Education, Technology, Professional Affiliations, Public Speaking, Publications, and any other extras you want to include. These items require little thought, once you've researched and collected all of the data, and can usually be completed in just a few minutes.

- **Write short job descriptions for your older positions, the ones you held years ago.** Be very brief and focus on highlights such as rapid promotions, achievements, metrics, innovations, honors and awards, or employment with well-respected, well-known companies.

Look at how much you've written in a short period of time! Now, you can move on to the next step:

- **Write the job descriptions for your most recent positions.** This will take a bit longer than the other sections you have written. Remember to focus on the overall scope of your responsibility, major projects and initiatives, and significant achievements. Tell your reader what you did and how well you did it. You can use any of the formats recommended earlier in this chapter or shown in Chapters 4 through 12, or you can create something that is unique to you and your career.

Now, see how far along you are? Your resume is 90% complete with only one small section left to do:

- **Write your Career Summary.** Before you start writing, remember your objective for this section. The summary should not simply rehash your previous experience. Rather, it should position you for your targeted next role by highlighting your skills, qualifications, and accomplishments that are most closely related to your current career objectives. The summary is intended to capture the reader's attention and *sell* your expertise.

That's it! You're done. Now, on to the next tip.

INCLUDE NOTABLE OR PROMINENT "EXTRA" STUFF IN YOUR CAREER SUMMARY

Remember the "extras" that are normally at the bottom of your resume? As we've mentioned, if this information is particularly significant or prominent—you won a notable award, spoke at an international conference, secured a patent for a new technology, or wrote an article for an industry publication—you might want to include it in your Career Summary to distinguish yourself from other qualified candidates. Refer to the sample Career Summaries earlier in this chapter for examples.

USE RESUME SAMPLES TO GET IDEAS FOR CONTENT, FORMAT, AND ORGANIZATION

This book is just one of many places where you can review the resumes of other managers and executives to help you in formulating your strategy, writing the text, and formatting your resume—these aids are published precisely for that reason. You don't have to struggle alone. Rather, use all the available resources at your disposal.

Be forewarned, however, that finding a resume that fits your life and career to a "T" is unlikely. It's more likely that you will use "some of this sample" and "some of that sample" to create a resume that is uniquely "you."

INCLUDE ALL DATES IF YOU ARE YOUNGER THAN 50

Unless you are over age 50, we recommend that you date all of your work experience and education to paint a complete picture of your professional life for your target audience of hiring managers and recruiters.

Most management and executive positions require years of experience, so there is no benefit to being vague about your age.

Early Work Experience Dates

If you are over age 50, dating your early positions must be an individual decision. Certainly you do not want to age yourself out of consideration by including dates from the 1970s, 1980s, and even the 1990s. On the other hand, those positions might be worth including for any number of reasons. Further, if you omit those early dates, you might feel as though you are misrepresenting yourself (or lying) to a prospective employer.

One strategy to overcome those concerns is to create a separate category titled "Previous Professional Experience" in which you summarize your earliest employment. Or, simply include the information at the very end of your Professional Experience section. You can tailor a brief statement to emphasize what is most important about that experience.

If you want to *focus on the reputation of your past employers,* include a statement such as this:

> • Previous experience includes mid- to senior-level management positions with **IBM, Dell,** and **Xerox.**

If you want to *communicate the rapid progression of your career,* consider this example:

> • Promoted rapidly through a series of **increasingly responsible operating management and leadership positions** with Zyler Form Molding, Inc.

If you want to *emphasize your early career achievements,* include a statement such as this:

> • Earned 6 promotions in 3 years with Procter & Gamble based on outstanding performance in revenue growth, market development, and customer retention. **Closed first year at 145% of revenue goal.**

By including any one of the preceding paragraphs, you are clearly communicating to your reader that your employment history dates further back than the dates you have indicated on your resume. In turn, you are being 100% honest and not misrepresenting yourself or your career. What's more, you're focusing on the success, achievement, and prominence of your earliest assignments.

Education Dates

If you are over age 50, we generally do not recommend that you date your education or college degrees. Simply include the degree and the university with no date. Why exclude yourself from consideration by listing a college graduation year of 1979, 1986, or 1989—possibly before the hiring manager was born? Remember, the goal of your resume is to share the highlights of your career and open doors for interviews. It is *not* to give your entire life story. As such, it is not mandatory to date your college degree.

NEVER INCLUDE SALARY HISTORY OR SALARY REQUIREMENTS ON YOUR RESUME

Your resume is *not* the correct forum for a salary discussion. First of all, you should never provide salary information unless a company has requested that information and you choose to comply. (Studies show that employers will look at your resume anyway, so you might choose not to respond to that request, thereby avoiding pricing yourself out of the job or locking yourself into a lower salary than the job is worth.)

When contacting **recruiters,** however, we recommend that you do provide salary information, but only in your letter. With recruiters you want to "put all of your cards on the table" and help them make an appropriate placement by providing information about your current salary and salary objectives. For example, you could write:

"Be advised that my current compensation is $170,000 annually and that I am interested in a position starting at a minimum of $200,000 per year."

Or, if you would prefer to be a little less specific, you might write:

"My annual compensation over the past 3 years has exceeded $150,000."

In some instances you will not have the option to omit salary information. A good example is an online application that requires you to submit your salary history and/or salary requirements along with your resume. In that case, be truthful and know that all candidates will be revealing similar information.

ALWAYS REMEMBER THAT YOU ARE SELLING

As we have discussed over and over throughout these first 2 chapters, ***resume writing is sales.*** Understand and appreciate the value you bring to a prospective employer, and then communicate that value by focusing on your achievements. Companies don't want to hire just anyone; they want to hire *the* someone who will make a positive impact and deliver results. Show them that you are that candidate.

CHAPTER 3

Formatting and Designing Your Resume

After you've worked so tirelessly to write a winning resume, your next challenge is design, layout, and presentation. It's not enough for your resume to simply read well and highlight your core skills, experiences, and accomplishments; your resume must also have just the *right* look for the *right* audience.

That audience might be a hiring manager or a recruiter, a close contact or a third-degree network referral. It might even be an automated resume scanner—a machine rather than a human being. So, while the content is supremely important, other considerations also come into play.

This chapter discusses those considerations and provides guidelines for preparing your resume so that any recipient can quickly read it and easily understand your value.

Throughout your job search you'll be transmitting your resume in different ways:

- Emailed to network contacts, to recruiters, and in response to job postings.

- Uploaded to company and recruiter websites, job search portals, and other sites that post positions and/or allow you to post your resume.

- In traditional printed/paper form when you meet for a networking event, a face-to-face encounter with a contact, or a job interview.

In each of these instances you'll want to be sure that your resume looks great and, just as importantly, is formatted to be read by human eyes or by electronic scanners.

Good news! In most cases, unless your resume is unusually formatted or very heavily designed, the same document will work for all of these purposes. Electronic scanning technology has evolved rapidly from its earliest days, when only plain-text documents were readable, to the point that scanners can now capture and interpret the vast majority of information in a Word or PDF document.

You will need to be aware of just a few formatting and design limitations as you prepare for today's web-based job search.

Guidelines for Scannable Resumes

Online job postings are easy to find and easy to respond to. That's great news for you—but also great news for hundreds if not thousands of other job seekers with similar qualifications and career interests. To generate a response and ultimately get an interview, your resume must be accurately read and highly scored to be among the handful of candidates who make the cut.

As you would imagine, the battle to the top is extremely competitive. You will give yourself the best odds of winning that battle by following these guidelines.

- **Match your resume to the job posting.** Because scanners look for keyword matches, the more closely your resume mimics the language used in the job posting, the higher your chances of being selected. Take the time to read the posting carefully and, if necessary, edit your resume a bit to better reflect the job requirements and integrate some of those critical keywords if they are not already there.

- **Use a chronological/hybrid format.** Functional resumes are not effective because resume-scanning Applicant Tracking Systems (ATS) cannot determine when and where you gained the experience and achievements listed in your resume and may discount the information entirely. If you're unsure about the functional versus chronological/hybrid format, refer back to Chapter 1 for details.

- **Do not use MS Word's "Insert Text Box" feature.** Scanning software no longer physically scans each page of text; rather, it reads the underlying code in your document. Because it views Text Boxes as graphics, it will not absorb any content within the box. Instead of Text Boxes, use Word's Tables feature to get the same effect.

- **Do not worry about lines, borders, shading, unusual fonts, font enhancements, and graphics.** Not so long ago all of these things were forbidden to ensure a clean scan. Today, ATS can read highly formatted text and will simply ignore any graphics. If you are using a graphic (a performance chart, for example), to be certain that information is read just make sure to mention the achievement in your text as well as showcasing it visually.

- **Do not put any essential information in a Header or Footer on page 1.** It's fine to use a header or footer on page 2 to repeat your name and contact information.

- **Upload a cover letter if given the opportunity to do so.** Just as with your resume, tailor your letter to the position and the company. Share specifics that will resonate with your target audience.

- **Carefully follow upload instructions every time you submit a resume.** Different sites may have file-format restrictions that are a factor of their ATS technology. Their instructions may differ from the guidelines we've provided, so take the time to read and adjust as necessary. Most importantly, follow instructions for type of file (most likely, Word.doc, Word.docx, or PDF) to be uploaded. If your resume file is rejected, you'll never even get the chance to rise to the top of the candidate pool.

Guidelines for Emailed Resumes

You will be emailing your resume frequently during your search, and you want to be sure it arrives exactly as you wrote, formatted, and designed it before sending. These guidelines will help.

- **Send a PDF unless instructed otherwise.** PDFs stand the best chance of retaining format integrity when opened by different operating systems.

- **Format properly.** The more carefully and correctly you format all of the items in your resume, the greater the likelihood your content will remain where you put it. We've all seen resumes where the dates don't fit nicely at the right margin, bullet points don't line up correctly, or a 2-page resume mysteriously spreads onto a third page. You can avoid many of these errors with careful formatting.

- **Write your cover letter as the email message.** Unless otherwise instructed, don't attach your cover letter as a separate file and don't combine it with your resume. Write a short, powerful email message that explains why you're writing and entices the reader to click on your resume.

Guidelines for Printed Resumes

Contrary to the norm in decades past, the printed resume is undoubtedly the least used in today's job search! However, on some occasions you will want to share your hard-copy resume:

- **When meeting in person with a network contact.** With a printed version, you can view the resume together and you and/or your contact can make notes directly on the page. Of course, you'll send a resume via email either before or after your meeting, but don't neglect to bring a printed copy with you.

- **When attending a networking event.** Again, because these are in-person events, the paper copy is the most useful. Bring a small stack laid flat in a portfolio or briefcase.

- **On every interview.** Yes, your interviewer has seen your resume and may even have a printed copy in hand when you meet. But why take that chance? Perhaps they've lost their copy. Or maybe you are invited unexpectedly to meet with another team member. Or a group interview includes a few more people than had been planned. Tuck a few printed resumes into your portfolio and offer to share at any time it seems appropriate.

Your printed resume will look exactly the same as your emailed resume. The difference is that it is printed, in sharp ink on high-quality paper, rather than sent electronically. Color can make your document really stand out, so experiment with different shades and intensities for colored lines, boxes, graphics, and other visuals to be certain you're making a memorable and favorable impression.

How Long Should Your Resume Be?

Like many aspects of resume writing, there is no hard-and-fast rule regarding resume length. Your resume needs to be long enough to tell your story and provide essential details of your qualifications and work history. For most managers and executives, a 2-page resume is the perfect length. A select few will need 3 pages to convey all the necessary information. And some executives are able to write sharply focused, concise 1-page resumes. You'll find excellent examples of all 3 options in this book.

When writing and formatting your resume, we recommend that you not go beyond 2 or at most 3 pages. Use the examples in this book to inspire you as you work to express your value in concise, hard-hitting terms. Remember, you want to entice hiring authorities and recruiters to call you to learn more and offer you the opportunity for an interview.

Are You Ready to Write and Format Your Resume?

To be sure that you're ready to write your resume, go through the following check-list. Each item is a critical step that you must take to ensure that you are writing and designing your very *best* resume—a resume that will open doors, generate interviews, and help you land a great new opportunity.

- ❑ Clearly define "who" you are and "how" you want to be perceived.
- ❑ Document your key skills, qualifications, and knowledge.
- ❑ Highlight your notable career achievements and successes.
- ❑ Identify one or more specific job targets or positions.
- ❑ Define one or more industries that you are targeting.
- ❑ Research and compile keywords for your profession, industry, and specific job targets.
- ❑ Determine which resume format best suits you and your career.
- ❑ Select an attractive and appropriate font.
- ❑ Look at resume samples for up-to-date ideas on resume styles, formats, organization, design, and language.
- ❑ Review the guidelines in this chapter for scannable, emailed, and print resumes so you are ready to create the versions you will need for your search.

PART II

Sample Resumes for Managers and Executives

CHAPTER 4

Presidents, CEOs, and Board Directors

- President and Chief Executive Officer—Global Insurance
- President and Chief Executive Officer—Medical
- Chief Executive Officer—International Technology and Industry
- International Executive—Global Consultancy
- C-Level Executive and Board Director—Talent Management
- Chief Executive Officer and President—Health Care and Durable Medical Equipment
- Global Chief Executive Officer—Sports and Lifestyle
- Senior Executive and Global Leader—Advanced Technology Ventures
- President and Chief Executive Officer—Aviation
- Chief Executive Officer and VC/PE Advisor—Technology
- C-Level Executive—Technology and Global Insurance

RESUME 1: *by Wendy Enelow, MRW, CCM, CPRW, JCTC • www.wendyenelow.com*

DANIEL L. LAKEWOOD

698.901.3471 ▪ dllakewood@gmail.com

View my profile on Linked in

PRESIDENT & CHIEF EXECUTIVE OFFICER
Driving transformational change to advance the business and build shareholder value

High-energy insurance executive with 20+ years of leadership experience with a Dow 50 insurer. Progressive background includes both field and home office roles, resulting in expert knowledge of nationwide independent agents, brokers, and alternative distribution channels to drive accelerated market growth.

Turnaround architect able to quickly assess a business, put out the fires, define a long-term vision and strategic plan, and then execute on the strategies to meet profit and performance goals. Background includes reimagining the business model, business platform, and organizational structure to create a highly scalable and efficient organization.

Expert in building and energizing teams and then leading from the front to deliver significant financial results. Create a culture built on a foundation of integrity, accountability, analytics, and execution success.

Signature Strengths

Strategic Visioning & Planning	P&L Management	New Business Development
Revenue & Profit Growth	Talent Recruitment & Development	Business Model Restructuring

EXECUTIVE PERFORMANCE

ALLSTATE OF THE AMERICAS

EVP, President of Cyber (2018–Present) **| EVP, Co-President, Business Insurance** (2016–2018)

> Stepped into Co-President role following the restructuring of the $12 billion Business Insurance division. Manage $4 billion P&L with general management responsibilities for Select Accounts, Specialized Distribution (National Programs, Seminole E&S, Seminole Trucking), and Agriculture.

- **Handpicked to lead the emerging Cyber business in 2018 and disrupt an industry projected to reach $8 billion in premiums in the next 3 years.** Currently working to put the distribution, marketing, lobbying, and product drivers in place to build out a robust product line that delivers top-line growth.

EVP, President and CEO, Select Accounts and Agriculture, Business Insurance (2006–2016)

> Returned to Allstate following the Erie/Allstate merger and promoted to drive profitable growth of the $2.8 billion small commercial division. Managed 1700 employees in the product and underwriting, sales and marketing, distribution, operations, IT, finance, product management, and actuarial functions.

- **Served as a key executive member of the post-merger transition team** and transferred the $650+ million small commercial book of business from Erie to Allstate.

  P&L: $2.8 billion
  Operating Income: $328 million
  Return on Equity: 13%

- **Pioneered end-to-end processing platform**, which was the foundation for the now-standard straight-through processing model in small commercial in the insurance industry. Received Chairman's Award (2010).
  - Transformed operating model and platform from 80% direct-touch underwriting to 80% straight-through processing, creating efficiency gain of 20% reduction in underwriting census.
  - Increased line of business quote activity 100%.

Strategy: Create a bold, distinctive appearance through dark-shaded headings as well as framed boxes that draw attention to the context/challenge of each position. Enhance readability through ample white space, a generous font size, bold type, and concisely written paragraphs and bullets.

DANIEL L. LAKEWOOD   Page 2 ▪ 698.901.3471 ▪ DLLAKEWOOD@GMAIL.COM

- **Elevated organizational capabilities by introducing new teams, structures, and competencies.**
  o Built a product management organization—unique to the commercial space—to drive profitable growth through a geographic-focused product and pricing management structure.
  o Stood up a Program Management Office to drive the effective execution of strategic business initiatives.
  o Restructured sales team to increase capacity to handle expanded distribution.
- **Expanded distribution opportunities 115%+ (to 10,500 agencies)** by redefining the market/distribution strategy.
- **Appointed to the Management Committee (2012) and Operating Committee (2010).**

ERIE INSURANCE COMPANIES

SVP, President and CEO, Small Commercial (2005–2006)

Recruited by CEO to turn around an unprofitable $700 million business with full responsibility for managing the P&L and strategic direction of the business. Oversaw all sales, underwriting, and operations with 600+ employees.

- **Strengthened the management team within 90 days** by replacing 60%+ of senior field leadership and 30%+ of home office leadership while establishing a dedicated sales organization.
- **Improved combined ratio from 97% to 92%** through rigorous re-underwriting of the core book.
- **Heightened profitability** by removing the least profitable programs and navigating the exit of medical malpractice.
- **Rebuilt the Small Commercial technology platform** to improve ease of doing business and replace void from newly exited medical malpractice. Growth rate in second year of new platform exceeded 7% and was a catalyst for the Erie/Allstate merger in 2004.

THE DONEGAL INSURANCE COMPANIES

Select Regional Vice President: Mid-Atlantic Region (2002–2005)

Managed small commercial P&L for a 6-state, $200 million region made up of Pennsylvania, Virginia, Delaware, Maryland, West Virginia, and Washington, DC. Defined and executed strategy for underwriting, sales, and operations.

- **Ranked among the Top 3 Regional VPs companywide** for profit and growth for 7 consecutive years and earned the #1 Select RVP ranking for 3 years.
- **Maintained a combined ratio at or below 94%.**

EDUCATION

Bachelor of Arts (BA) — Longwood University, Farmville, VA

Insurance Credentials:
Accredited Advisor in Insurance (AAI)
Chartered Property Casualty Underwriter (CPCU)

BOARD EXPERIENCE

Board Chairman, Midwest Chapter of the Susan G. Komen Breast Cancer Foundation, 2012–2014

RESUME 2: *by Alexis Binder, ACRW, MBA • www.greatresumesfast.com*

LUCA ACCOLA
Global Executive • Board Member

Naples, FL 34102 | lucaaccolatest@gmail.com | LinkedIn | 555.718.0494

Medical | Retail | Start-ups

Led HearingMatters USA to earn Star Tribune's "Top 100 Workplace" for 3 consecutive years. Repeatedly turned around businesses and drove 2X, 3X, and even 4X revenue growth.

Build lean and nimble organizations to cope with inevitable changes in the health care and retail market based on healthy company culture that fosters success and attracts the best talents. Achieve balance between long-term strategy and short-term measures to drive sustainable success. Lead through conviction, strategy, and fact-based approach.

Speak German • English • French.

EXECUTIVE CAREER

<u>HearingMatters Group</u> | 2001–Present

Promoted through progressive roles and challenged to overcome previously insurmountable obstacles to grow business.

ADVISOR ON REGULATORY AFFAIRS | June 2019–December 2019 .... **Naples, FL, US**

EXECUTIVE VICE PRESIDENT, AMERICAS | March 2017–June 2019 .... **Plymouth, MN, US**
Role was expanded from only North America to include Central and South America.

— Grew footprint in Canada and South America through store openings and acquisitions.

PRESIDENT/CEO, REGIONAL MARKET DIRECTOR | April 2009–March 2017
Full P&L and balance sheet responsibilities for organizations in US and Canada.

Defined and executed strategy to simplify go-to-market approach, **slashing back-office costs from $19M in 2008 to less than $11M in 2017** and reducing from 9 to 3 business units under the umbrella of HearingMatters USA. Delivered revenue and EBITDA growth in every business unit.

Miracle-Hearing, Inc.: *Franchise System with 1,500+ locations and ~200 individual owners. Best recognized hearing aid brand in US. Presence in Canada through corporate stores. Most profitable business unit (acquired in 1999).*

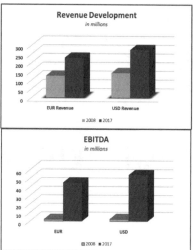

✓ **Doubled retail revenue and grew EBITDA >10X**, 2008 to 2017.

✓ Negotiated new contract with **Sears, Roebuck & Co.** in 2011, allowing us to initiate an exit strategy; exit from Sears completed in 2015 by moving **~600 stores** to freestanding locations.

✓ Introduced new POS system; all franchise locations now run on same platform, a first in franchise history.

Hearing Instrument Network: *Largest buying group and service provider for independent hearing health care professionals in the US with 1,600+ locations. Acquired by the HearingMatters Group in 2003.*

✓ **Tripled revenue** from 2008 to 2017.

✓ Implemented growth strategy through revamping Value Proposition with dramatically increased services for members as well as management change.

HearingMatters Health Care: *Organization in Managed Care/Health Benefit and Workers' Comp arenas, referring patients created through relationships to 2,500+ locations in US, using existing network of Miracle-Hearing/Hearing Instrument Network and independent providers. Acquired in 2003.*

✓ **Quadrupled revenue** from 2008 to 2017.

✓ Stipulated and successfully implemented strategy for key accounts in the insurance market, boosting growth (worked with most major US insurance companies: Aetna, Humana, Cigna, the Blues etc.).

Strategy: Highlight a few notable achievements at the very top of the resume and draw further attention with eye-catching graphs that instantly illustrate top performance.

Luca Accola | lucaaccolatest@gmail.com — Page | 2

HearingMatters Deutschland GmbH
GENERAL MANAGER | April 2005–April 2009 .... **Hamburg, Germany**
Conquered the German market, where HearingMatters had had no footprint prior to 2004. Established a headquarters in Hamburg and held full P&L and balance sheet responsibilities for the German Amplifon subsidiary.

— **Led acquisition of 25+ individual companies** in the hearing aid retail landscape, capturing 170+ locations in less than 3 years with a small acquisition team.

— Integrated acquisitions and set the base to work under one brand by harmonizing work contracts, unifying store signs and store concepts, and establishing common commission systems.

HearingMatters Hungary
GENERAL MANAGER | April 2003–April 2005 .... **Budapest, Hungary**
Entered the Hungarian market; established and expanded organization and footprint in Hungary. Full P&L and balance sheet responsibilities of the Hungarian HearingMatters subsidiary.

— **Doubled footprint** through openings and acquisition of Viton Hungary, the country's leading retailer of hearing aids.

— Established new management team.

Viennatone Hörgeräte GmbH (HearingMatters Group)
GENERAL MANAGER | January 2001–April 2003 .... **Vienna, Austria**
Managed full P&L and balance sheet responsibilities of the Austrian HearingMatters subsidiary.

— Successfully divested Viennatone Hörgeräte in 2003; sold to competitor owned by a hearing aid manufacturer.

HearingMatters AG
GENERAL MANAGER | January 2001–April 2003 .... **Baar, Switzerland**
Integrated acquisitions made prior to arrival and created uniform footprint of retail locations under the HearingMatters brand in Switzerland. Increased efficiency and productivity after integration.

— **Tripled sales** from CHf 13.5 million to CHf 40.0 million and increased EBITDA from losing CHf 3.5 million in 2001 to being profitable at CHf 8.0 million in 2007.

— **Became market leader in Switzerland with 20%+ market share.**

— Integrated two brands—microelectric and Surdité Dardy.

Sales & EBITDA
in millions CHf

EARLY CAREER

MEMBER OF THE GLOBAL MANAGEMENT TEAM | **Denmark** | **ReSound**
GENERAL MANAGER | **Austria** | **Viennatone Hearing GmbH**
GENERAL MANAGER | **Germany** | **Medizintechnik GmbH**

EDUCATION & BOARD EXPERIENCE

BACHELOR OF BUSINESS ADMINISTRATION, **University of Applied Science**, Zurich, Switzerland

PRESIDENT OF BOARD OF DIRECTORS, **HearingMatters Foundation** | 2010–2019

ERIC RODRIGUEZ

Boston, MA • 617-789-5432
eric.rodriguez@gmail.com • LinkedIn Profile

CEO

INTERNATIONAL TECHNOLOGY & INDUSTRIAL COMPANIES—EARLY STAGE TO EXPANDING GLOBAL ENTERPRISES

High-Growth Strategy & Operations • Turnarounds • Asian Startups, Distributorships & Supply Chains

> **Unlocking Value ... Identifying Opportunity ... Driving Strategic Growth**
> **Finding Winning Solutions for Businesses facing Growth Challenges**

- Extensive international operational, business development, and supply chain experience, notably in China and Japan.

- Deep functional expertise in Engineering, Operations, Product Management, Marketing, Sales, Business Development.

- Energetic, entrepreneurial, and principled leadership that inspires teams to reach for—and achieve—aggressive goals.

PROFESSIONAL EXPERIENCE

SunSystems, Inc. *(An innovator in solutions for solar and other renewable energy industries)*   Boston, MA • 2018–Present

COO, INDUSTRIAL SYSTEMS GROUP • CHAIRMAN OF THE BOARD, SUNSYSTEMS, INC.—2019–Present

> **Took on new challenge to turn around Industrial Systems Group.** Within months, transformed struggling business units to viable operations with strong growth prospects. Executed 2 divestments to return cash to parent company.

- Took specialty parts division from "unsaveable"—**$1M** losses, underperforming assets, ineffective management—to cash-positive in **6** months. Sold the retooled business for **$4M.**

- Invigorated efforts to commercialize advanced technology of SunSolar business unit. Within **7** months, validated new use in biotech engineering; signed a **$290M** agreement with an Asian sales channel; found a buyer; and negotiated sale of the business.

- As Board Chair, steered SunSystems toward higher growth sectors; currently on path to grow revenue **400%** by 2024.

PRESIDENT, SOLAR SYSTEMS GROUP, Ho Chi Minh City, Vietnam—2018–2019

> **Recruited by CEO to restructure/refocus the company toward growth segments.** Relocated to Vietnam to manage $300M business: P&L, Operations, Global Supply Chain, Sales and Service, Engineering, and Manufacturing.

- In **9** months, slashed operating expenses **25%** and implemented a highly flexible just-in-time supply chain strategy.

- In **12** months, improved return on sales from breakeven to **>25%** by focusing on most valuable market segments.

Diamond Manufacturing *(Leading manufacturer of rechargeable batteries)*   Phoenix, AZ • 2010–2018

CEO

> **Recruited to VC-backed company with challenge to drive profitable growth and global expansion.** Led the company through strategic pivot to an entirely new market segment and acceptance by Tier 1 automakers and OEMs.

- Grew the company from a 10-person R&D shop to high-volume production in Asia. Managed complex process to establish a JV in China. Shipped **1M+** batteries through major retail and industrial channels.

- Built an IP portfolio of **50+** patents. Negotiated a technology licensing agreement with Capital Energy.

- Created strategy to take advantage of fast-growing multibillion-dollar markets in auto and data-storage segments.

- In accelerated timeframe, passed rigorous multistage product and technology test programs to earn qualification by 3 global automakers—leading to selection for multiple passenger car platforms.

- Raised **$100M+** in new investment funding.

Strategy: Pare down career details to the essentials to create an easily readable resume that emphasizes challenges and results. Use bordered and shaded boxes to highlight context for each position.

ERIC RODRIGUEZ Page 2

PowerUp, Inc. *(Provider of power conversion products, energy systems, and engineering services)*   Phoenix, AZ • 2005–2010

PRESIDENT, POWER COMPONENTS

Created a top-3 global power supply business, combining 6 separate power supply companies with sales of $600M into a highly integrated business. Rapidly grew revenue **50%** to **$1.6B** while boosting profitability from **<5% to 15%.**

- Drove double-digit annual sales growth by refocusing market strategy, rationalizing product lines by more than **50%,** and shortening the new product introduction cycle by **6** months.
- Achieved similar EBIT gains by removing cost from the supply chain and doubling inventory turns to **12.**
- Steered a global enterprise, with direct, VAR, OEM, distributor, and manufacturer rep. sales worldwide and production facilities in the U.S., Mexico, Europe, and Asia.
- Restored profitability to X-TEC division—a world-leading but struggling $80M global power supply business.

Extol Systems *(Acquired by PowerUp, 2005)*   San Diego, CA • 2003–2005

VP, WORLDWIDE OEM PROGRAMS

Merged and led business to 48% sales growth and 63% EBIT growth, exceeding financial objectives every year. Managed **$150M** P&L and all Sales, Marketing, New Business Development, Product Development, Program Management, and Finance functions.

- Streamlined operations and integrated sales, marketing, and engineering organizations following merger of 2 OEM businesses that formed Extol.
- Launched sales and product development organizations in Europe and Japan to provide OEMs with custom products.

Early Career with EchoStar Corporation *(Leading provider of telecommunications technologies)*   Englewood, CO

Progressed rapidly through increasingly responsible roles in specialty engineering divisions.

- **Business Unit Manager, Machinery Diagnostics Systems:** Created and grew new business unit from startup to **$20M** in profitable sales, establishing EchoStar as the world leader.
- **Production Manager:** Directed 130-employee manufacturing facility. Reduced warranty costs from **>5%** to **<2%.**
- **Program Manager:** Held P&L responsibility for **$15M**/year sonar systems product line.
- **Product Specialist/Electrical Engineer:** Within 1 year, promoted to manage **$6M** line of analysis instruments.

EDUCATION

MBA, Stanford University
BSEE, University of Colorado

BOARD AFFILIATIONS

Board of Directors—SunSystems, Inc., 2018–Present; **Chairman of the Board,** 2019–Present
Advisory Board—University of Colorado Leadership Institute, 2010–Present

RESUME 4: *by Mary Schumacher, ACRW, CPRW, G3, CJSS, OPNS • www.careerframes.com*

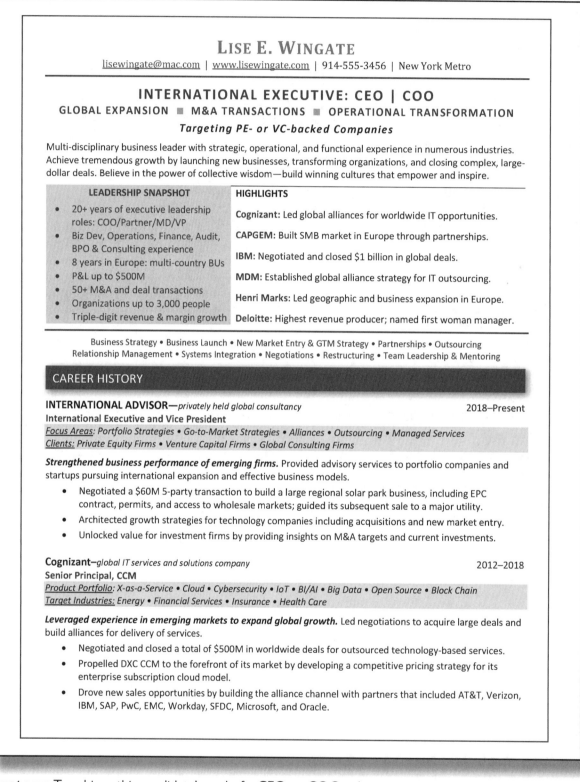

LISE E. WINGATE

lisewingate@mac.com | www.lisewingate.com | 914-555-3456 | New York Metro

INTERNATIONAL EXECUTIVE: CEO | COO
GLOBAL EXPANSION ▪ M&A TRANSACTIONS ▪ OPERATIONAL TRANSFORMATION
Targeting PE- or VC-backed Companies

Multi-disciplinary business leader with strategic, operational, and functional experience in numerous industries. Achieve tremendous growth by launching new businesses, transforming organizations, and closing complex, large-dollar deals. Believe in the power of collective wisdom—build winning cultures that empower and inspire.

LEADERSHIP SNAPSHOT

- 20+ years of executive leadership roles: COO/Partner/MD/VP
- Biz Dev, Operations, Finance, Audit, BPO & Consulting experience
- 8 years in Europe: multi-country BUs
- P&L up to $500M
- 50+ M&A and deal transactions
- Organizations up to 3,000 people
- Triple-digit revenue & margin growth

HIGHLIGHTS

Cognizant: Led global alliances for worldwide IT opportunities.

CAPGEM: Built SMB market in Europe through partnerships.

IBM: Negotiated and closed $1 billion in global deals.

MDM: Established global alliance strategy for IT outsourcing.

Henri Marks: Led geographic and business expansion in Europe.

Deloitte: Highest revenue producer; named first woman manager.

Business Strategy • Business Launch • New Market Entry & GTM Strategy • Partnerships • Outsourcing
Relationship Management • Systems Integration • Negotiations • Restructuring • Team Leadership & Mentoring

CAREER HISTORY

INTERNATIONAL ADVISOR—*privately held global consultancy*   2018–Present
International Executive and Vice President
Focus Areas: Portfolio Strategies • Go-to-Market Strategies • Alliances • Outsourcing • Managed Services
Clients: Private Equity Firms • Venture Capital Firms • Global Consulting Firms

Strengthened business performance of emerging firms. Provided advisory services to portfolio companies and startups pursuing international expansion and effective business models.

- Negotiated a $60M 5-party transaction to build a large regional solar park business, including EPC contract, permits, and access to wholesale markets; guided its subsequent sale to a major utility.
- Architected growth strategies for technology companies including acquisitions and new market entry.
- Unlocked value for investment firms by providing insights on M&A targets and current investments.

Cognizant—*global IT services and solutions company*   2012–2018
Senior Principal, CCM
Product Portfolio: X-as-a-Service • Cloud • Cybersecurity • IoT • BI/AI • Big Data • Open Source • Block Chain
Target Industries: Energy • Financial Services • Insurance • Health Care

Leveraged experience in emerging markets to expand global growth. Led negotiations to acquire large deals and build alliances for delivery of services.

- Negotiated and closed a total of $500M in worldwide deals for outsourced technology-based services.
- Propelled DXC CCM to the forefront of its market by developing a competitive pricing strategy for its enterprise subscription cloud model.
- Drove new sales opportunities by building the alliance channel with partners that included AT&T, Verizon, IBM, SAP, PwC, EMC, Workday, SFDC, Microsoft, and Oracle.

Strategy: To achieve this candidate's goal of a CEO or COO role at a startup, provide ample evidence of her measurable contributions across a diversity of growth markets.

Lise E. Wingate   Page 2 of 3

CAPGEM– *$11 billion global technology leader*   2010–2012
Vice President, Finance and Accounting Services
Product Portfolio: BPO • Asset Management • Decision Support • FP&A • Procurement • Transaction Processing
Scope: Deal Negotiation & Structure • Client Management • Product Portfolio Development • Acquisitions • Alliances

Catalyzed business unit performance through portfolio innovation and global growth strategies. Propelled revenue generation by identifying market and product opportunity gaps and driving solutions.

- Developed an integrated suite of F&A and source-to-pay outsourcing services, providing high-performance outcomes for clients through process innovation and transformational technology.
- Expanded capabilities by securing and integrating alliances and acquisitions, including a captive center acquisition in Poland. Built the SMB market in Europe through partnerships.
- Negotiated and closed deals totaling $250M.

IBM Global Services–*global professional services firm*   2007–2010
Senior Executive and Partner, Office of Risk Management
Product Portfolio: IT Outsourcing (ITO) • BPO • SI • AD/AO • R&D • Regulatory Compliance • Consulting
Target Industries: Pharmaceutical • Telecom • CPG • Manufacturing

Negotiated and closed $1 billion in global deals during tenure. Built client relationships and led projects combining strategy, technology, and services to improve clients' ability to address external volatility and internal complexity.

- Increased revenue and profitability by overhauling account management; protected delivery team progress by keeping financial and contract discussions solely within weekly executive review meetings.
- Formed a new Commercial Management function to standardize processes and provide internal guidance for deal negotiations, dispute resolution, governance, and resource management.

MDM Systems–*global information technology company*   2003–2007
Vice President, Global Strategy and Alliances
Product Portfolio: Information Technology Outsourcing (ITO) • Infrastructure Managed Services
Scope: Global Channels • Alliances • Solution Partners • Third Party Advisors

Spearheaded global strategy and partnership development for IT outsourcing and managed services business.
Managed P&L, opportunity pipeline, and partner relationships.

- Created a business vision, roadmap, and innovation culture; drove change and shaped a fast and flexible business. Developed a portfolio of offerings to leapfrog the competition with end-to-end services (collaboration, security, utility/cloud computing) to serve new clients and markets.
- Established a cost-effective Captive Shared Services Center in Budapest for IT support and application development. Launched additional smart sourcing locations in India and China.
- Launched a global Six Sigma Lean program and became a Certified Black Belt.

Henri Marks–*global leader in marketing communications*   1999–2003
Partner and COO Europe
Scope: International Expansion • Operational Performance • Automation • 14 countries • 900 FTEs/2,300 PTEs
Clients: Unilever • Coca-Cola • Pepsi • Whirlpool • Gillette • GSK • General Motors • Ford • Kraft • Colgate-Palmolive • L'Oreal • Nestle • IBM

Expanded international presence and tripled revenue. Provided executive leadership in an expatriate role. Named Europe Board Member, HM Partner Club, and member of Global Operations Committee.

- Transformed siloed European operations with a Pan-European operating model. Established a Captive Center in Croatia to centralize backroom operations, saving $800K annually. Managed 7 call centers with 400 total seats; automated manual processes, achieving 32% savings in direct costs.

Lise E. WIngate   Page 3 of 3

Henri Marks, continued

- Expanded footprint from 5 countries to 14 through 4 acquisitions, 3 greenfield businesses, and 6 licensees.
- Gained additional revenue through a Key Account Marketing Strategy and a centralized pricing process that achieved 20% increase in multi-country business from clients.
- Grew profitability from 8.8% to 13.4% during tenure.

Deloitte—*Big 4 audit, tax, and consulting firm*   1991–1999
Manager

Product Portfolio: Restructuring Services • M&A • IT System Conversions • Resource Management • SEC Reporting
Target Industries: Public Sector • Health Care • Financial Services • Manufacturing

Won acclaim as the firm's top revenue producer. Joined the Audit business and after 4 years advanced to the Consulting arm, becoming the firm's first woman manager. Conducted business development and closed agreements for consulting projects. Provided leadership for project teams and vendors.

- Captured $8M in sales for 7 consulting projects.
- Contributed to development and launch of a new Outsourcing line of business, now acquired by Xerox.

ADDITIONAL QUALIFICATIONS

EDUCATION
Executive MBA, The Wharton School, University of Pennsylvania—Philadelphia, PA   2005
B.S., Accounting and Economics, University of Pennsylvania—Philadelphia, PA   1991

CERTIFICATIONS
Six Sigma Champion, Sponsor, and Black Belt Certification, Juran Institute of Quality Management   2003
Certified Public Accountant—Pennsylvania and New York   1995

VOLUNTEER ACTIVITIES
Board Member, New York Theatre Arts
Volunteer Mentor, Restore Hope

RESUME 5: *by Wendy Enelow, MRW, CCM, CPRW, JCTC • www.wendyenelow.com*

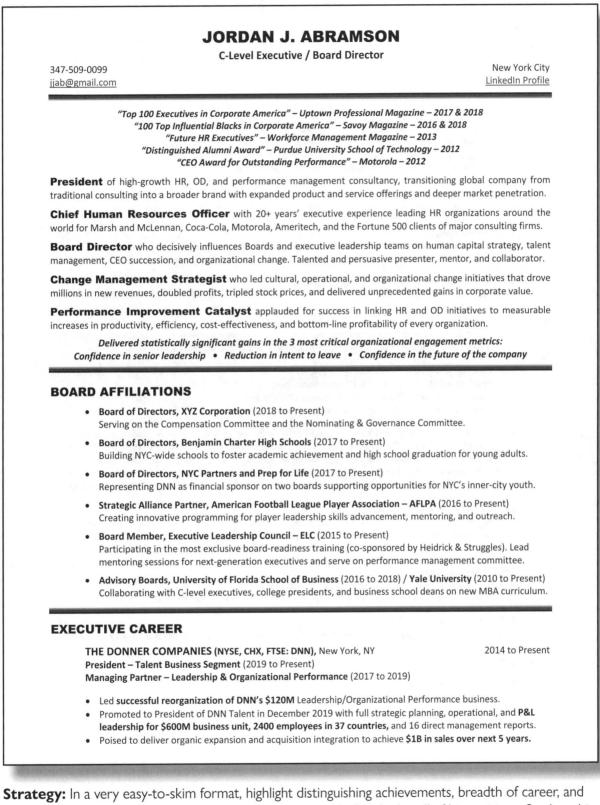

JORDAN J. ABRAMSON

C-Level Executive / Board Director

347-509-0099
jjab@gmail.com

New York City
LinkedIn Profile

"Top 100 Executives in Corporate America" – Uptown Professional Magazine – 2017 & 2018
"100 Top Influential Blacks in Corporate America" – Savoy Magazine – 2016 & 2018
"Future HR Executives" – Workforce Management Magazine – 2013
"Distinguished Alumni Award" – Purdue University School of Technology – 2012
"CEO Award for Outstanding Performance" – Motorola – 2012

President of high-growth HR, OD, and performance management consultancy, transitioning global company from traditional consulting into a broader brand with expanded product and service offerings and deeper market penetration.

Chief Human Resources Officer with 20+ years' executive experience leading HR organizations around the world for Marsh and McLennan, Coca-Cola, Motorola, Ameritech, and the Fortune 500 clients of major consulting firms.

Board Director who decisively influences Boards and executive leadership teams on human capital strategy, talent management, CEO succession, and organizational change. Talented and persuasive presenter, mentor, and collaborator.

Change Management Strategist who led cultural, operational, and organizational change initiatives that drove millions in new revenues, doubled profits, tripled stock prices, and delivered unprecedented gains in corporate value.

Performance Improvement Catalyst applauded for success in linking HR and OD initiatives to measurable increases in productivity, efficiency, cost-effectiveness, and bottom-line profitability of every organization.

Delivered statistically significant gains in the 3 most critical organizational engagement metrics:
Confidence in senior leadership • Reduction in intent to leave • Confidence in the future of the company

BOARD AFFILIATIONS

- **Board of Directors, XYZ Corporation** (2018 to Present)
  Serving on the Compensation Committee and the Nominating & Governance Committee.

- **Board of Directors, Benjamin Charter High Schools** (2017 to Present)
  Building NYC-wide schools to foster academic achievement and high school graduation for young adults.

- **Board of Directors, NYC Partners and Prep for Life** (2017 to Present)
  Representing DNN as financial sponsor on two boards supporting opportunities for NYC's inner-city youth.

- **Strategic Alliance Partner, American Football League Player Association – AFLPA** (2016 to Present)
  Creating innovative programming for player leadership skills advancement, mentoring, and outreach.

- **Board Member, Executive Leadership Council – ELC** (2015 to Present)
  Participating in the most exclusive board-readiness training (co-sponsored by Heidrick & Struggles). Lead mentoring sessions for next-generation executives and serve on performance management committee.

- **Advisory Boards, University of Florida School of Business** (2016 to 2018) / **Yale University** (2010 to Present)
  Collaborating with C-level executives, college presidents, and business school deans on new MBA curriculum.

EXECUTIVE CAREER

THE DONNER COMPANIES (NYSE, CHX, FTSE: DNN), New York, NY
President – Talent Business Segment (2019 to Present)
Managing Partner – Leadership & Organizational Performance (2017 to 2019)

2014 to Present

- Led **successful reorganization of DNN's $120M** Leadership/Organizational Performance business.
- Promoted to President of DNN Talent in December 2019 with full strategic planning, operational, and **P&L leadership for $600M business unit, 2400 employees in 37 countries,** and 16 direct management reports.
- Poised to deliver organic expansion and acquisition integration to achieve **$1B in sales over next 5 years.**

Strategy: In a very easy-to-skim format, highlight distinguishing achievements, breadth of career, and notable board affiliations before showcasing the great results he's had in all of his positions. Stack multiple positions with each company to save space and concentrate achievements and results.

JORDAN J. ABRAMSON
C-Level Executive / Board Director

347-509-0099
jjab@gmail.com

THE DONNER COMPANIES – *Continued*
Senior Vice President & Chief Human Resources / Communications Officer – Corporate HQ (2015 to 2017)
Senior Vice President & Chief Human Resources Officer – Corporate HQ (2014 to 2015)

- Member of 9-person, C-level executive team leading DNN through massive global rebranding and internal reorganization initiatives. Efforts drove **stock price from $19/share to $30/share in less than 3 years.**
- Reinvigorated operating management and leadership teams with new vision, energy, and direction, contributing to a **better than 7% gain in annual revenues worldwide.**
- As **#1 HR Executive for $10B+ company with 50K employees in 100+ countries,** held complete strategic, operating, and leadership responsibility for HR, OD, Comp & Benefits, Media Relations, and Communications.
- Led presentations on diversity, talent, HR strategy and success at Board and Governance meetings.

PEPSI (NYSE: PEP), Baltimore, MD   2011 to 2014
Group Director – Human Resources – Eurasia & Africa (2013 to 2014) – *Expatriate in Turkey*
Group Director – Corporate Center – Human Resources & Cultural Transformation (2011 to 2013)

- One of the top HR executives in the Pepsi organization, leading the company through a period of rapid growth and deeper global market entrenchment, **driving stock price from $41/share to $63/share.**
- Championed key organizational, strategic, cultural, and operational initiatives that contributed to strong and sustained **revenue growth averaging 15.25% annually** and **millions of dollars in annual cost savings.**
- Built and led the entire HR organization for newly created emerging markets business group with employees in 90 countries on 3 continents. **Achieved/surpassed all financial performance goals.**

HARRIS CORPORATION (NYSE: HRS), Boston, MA   2009 to 2011
Vice President – Global HR Strategy & Organizational Development (2011)
Vice President – Human Resources – North America (2010 to 2011)
Vice President & Director – Organizational Development (2009 to 2010)

- Second-in-command of global HR organization for 68K employees at 320 facilities in 73 countries. Delivered critical HR and OD innovations/solutions that helped **increase stock from $7/share to $26/share in 2 years.**
- Enabled leadership to streamline product development and fast-track new Razr phone. Efforts **won major media coverage, increased sales 53% in first year, and captured #1 market position in global cell market.**
- Streamlined worldwide HR organization, introduced self-service modules, and **reduced employee cost 33%.**

GRANT TUCKER CONSULTING, LLC, Boston, MA   2006 to 2009
Partner / Principal – Change Leadership Practice – Organizational Architecture, Leadership, Performance
Increased regional revenues year-over-year by exceeding expectations of Fortune 100 CEOs, COOs, Board Members, and other decision-makers. Promoted to Partner, the youngest in the firm by 15 years.

TECH-DRIVE, Chicago, IL   2003 to 2006
Director – Organizational Performance – 50-Person OD Team
Contributed to 50% increase in revenue per order and 26% gain in total annual revenues.

ANDERSEN CONSULTING, Chicago, IL   1999 to 2003
Senior Consultant – Change Management Group – Pharmaceutical, Insurance, Retail & Distribution Industries

EDUCATION

M.S., Industrial Technology (Human Resources Concentration), Yale University, 1999
B.S., Organizational Leadership, Yale University, 1997

Speaker: World Economic Forum | National Assoc. of Corporate Directors | Bentley University Ctr for Women
Published: Bloomberg BNA, HR Executive, NACD Bulletin | **Quoted:** SHRM Online, Conference Board Review

KRIS KING

555-700-1667 • McKinney, TX 75070

kriskingtest@gmail.com
http://www.linkedin.com/in/krisking

STRATEGIC EXECUTIVE LEADER
CHIEF EXECUTIVE OFFICER • PRESIDENT • CHIEF OPERATING OFFICER
Shape & Structure Operations | Cultivate Meaningful Partnerships | Build High-Performance Teams

◆ ◆ ◆

Develop new organizations, inspire best-in-class teams, and refine operations in competitive and highly regulated industries. Drive superior performance, achieving fast, sustainable growth through excellence in operations for mid-sized and start-up companies.

- ✓ Planned, raised capital, launched, and led an innovative healthcare company to achieve 35% EBITDA.
- ✓ Quadrupled angel-investor returns within 5 years.
- ✓ Established strategic relationship, initiating a joint venture and navigating a complex restructuring process.

—————————AREAS OF EXCELLENCE—————————

Contract Negotiation / Management	Strategic Planning	Capital Raising (Debt and Equity)
New Market Development & Execution	Board Reporting & Corporate Compliance	Team Building & Leadership
MSO/DSO Development & Implementation	Compliance & Tax	Financial Analysis & Reporting

EXECUTIVE HISTORY

SIMPLE SLEEP TODAY • Dallas, TX; Ft. Worth, TX; San Antonio, TX

CEO – 2017 to present | Board of Directors – 2011 to Present | President and COO – 2011 to 2016

Founded Texas-based MSO/DSO healthcare and durable medical equipment (DME) provider and built a first-of-its-kind provider, specializing in the diagnosis and treatment of obstructive sleep apnea.

Implemented and managed a marketing and advertising platform that became a model for other direct-to-patient, broadcast-driven businesses in the country, ultimately leading to a nationwide rollout of the concept via a joint venture with a public company *(see following Renew Your Sleep entry)*.

OPERATIONS DEVELOPMENT & DISTINCTION

- Created medical insurance-based model that maximized private payor reimbursement, yielding superior patient outcomes along with positive financial results. **Angel investors realized 5X return on capital within first 5 years.**
- Drove exponential revenue growth while navigating complex regulatory and legal requirements. Vetted and maintained all legal contracts pertaining to DSO and insurance carriers.
- **Reduced days in A/R 60%** by creating in-house revenue cycle department. Managed credentialing and carrier relationships with all major insurers in both in-network and out-of-network environments.
- Established inbound/outbound Call Center that processes **up to 2K unique prospective patient inquiries** per month.
- Built in-house direct-to-consumer marketing and advertising model by working directly with media companies.
  - o **Managed $2.5M annual marketing and advertising budget** and spearheaded diverse healthcare advertising using radio, TV, print, outdoor, and online activities.
  - o Ran all aspects of advertising, including campaign and creative development, advertising placement, management of online presence, brand management, and vendor relations.

STRATEGIC PARTNERSHIP

- **Fostered strong relationship among BoD** by creating and disseminating all reporting, documentation, and communication.
- Inspired culture of cooperation by building teams that prioritized patient care at every point in the organization.
  - o **Maintained <10% turnover rate YOY for 7 years.**
- Partnered with stakeholders to develop business plan and implementation strategy leading to successful raising of capital.
- **Achieved Joint Commission Accreditation,** establishing the only JCAHO-accredited facilities specializing in the treatment of sleep apnea using an FDA-cleared class II medical device.

Strategy: Combine a headline, brand attributes, a few strong and specific specific achievements, and diverse areas of excellence to create a powerful opening section that sets the stage for the executive history that follows.

KRIS KING

555-700-1667 | Page 2 of 2

RENEW YOUR SLEEP • Dallas, TX

Board of Directors / Consultant – 2016 to 2018

Partnered with an Australia-based, publicly traded medical device company to form joint venture to build a network of healthcare clinics across US specializing in the treatment of obstructive sleep apnea. Managed legal structuring and vetting of all contracts forming the venture.

- **Built a strong, experienced leadership team** by being a part of the recruiting, interviewing, and hiring process of key executives, including the CEO.
- **Positioned the company for success** by serving as an active consultant during the life of the business, including onboarding and training CEO and leadership team.
- **Navigated complex regulatory issues** by working with leadership team and counsel to ensure compliance with legal requirements by setting up state-specific DSOs and associated entities in 9 states.

BEST DENTAL SERVICES • Dallas, TX

President – 2010 to 2011

Launched and commercialized first compliance monitoring system for oral appliances used in treatment of obstructive sleep apnea.

- **Innovated the oral appliance market,** proving that compliance monitoring was both possible and practical on the same scale as other treatment modalities.
- **Managed FDA-clearance process,** providing a clear path for appliance manufacturers to incorporate the technology.
- **Negotiated and facilitated** the roll-up of the company into Simple Sleep Services in 2011.

───────PRIOR BUSINESS DEVELOPMENT EXPERIENCE───────

Business Development Leader – 2009 to 2011 | YELLOWSTONE BUILDINGS • Dallas, TX

- **Built infrastructure and carved out market share** in previously untapped industry.
- **Increased EBITDA 45% within 2 years** by selling, negotiating, and managing large-scale commercial projects.

Regional Services Manager – 2002 to 2009 | FOXWORTH LUXURY LUMBER COMPANY • Dallas, TX

Full P&L responsibility for construction services division of Texas, New Mexico, and Arizona region. Provided strategic leadership for operations, finance, sales, marketing, and regulatory functions.

- **Integrated multiple acquisitions** of large subcontractors into company's framework, including methodology of practices, accounting, reporting, management, and structure. Acquisitions included multiple large-scale operations throughout Texas, New Mexico, and Arizona.

EDUCATION

Bachelor of Applied Arts and Sciences (BAAS)
University of North Texas, Denton, TX

BOARD LEADERSHIP & AFFILIATIONS

Board of Directors, Simple Sleep Today, LLC
Board of Directors, Best Dental Services, LLC
Board of Directors, Renew Your Sleep, LLC

Association of Dental Support Organizations, Vistage Group #5887, Founding Member
American Academy of Dental Sleep Medicine

PAT DRISCOLL

773-555-5555 ▪ Chicago, IL
driscoll@gmail.com ▪ www.linkedin/in/driscoll

CHIEF EXECUTIVE OFFICER
ACTIVE LIFESTYLE ... PARTICIPATORY SPORTS ... INTERNATIONAL EVENTS

Entrepreneurial Business Executive with expertise in leveraging relationships with investors, board members, and like-minded individuals to create unique consumer experiences in the community, nation, and beyond. Articulate vision, rally teams, and drive results in iconic companies proud of their heritage. Rooted in corporate law.

► **Transformed early-stage nonprofit** into solidly structured, high-growth, global operation with new vision, branding strategy, and master growth plan. Grew revenues 250%, unrestricted assets 450%, and sponsorship 200%.

► **Launched new international business** with a unique concept in the global market. Partnered with investors to build the leadership team, governance, and technology platform. Negotiated major US/France sponsorship deal.

ORGANIZATIONAL LEADERSHIP ... BUSINESS DEVELOPMENT ... EMERGING & GROWTH VENTURES ... FAST-PACED ENVIRONMENTS
COMPETITIVE SPIRIT ... CREATIVE INNOVATION ... UNCONQUERABLE DESIRE TO WIN

PROFESSIONAL EXPERIENCE

WORLD SPORTS & LIFESTYLE   Chicago & Paris ▪ 2017–Present
Global CEO

Recruited to launch active lifestyle company focused on revolutionizing health and wellness with a unique brand of participatory fitness events. Created, developed, and introduced the "Festival of Sport" product on a global scale and initiated event pipeline planning throughout the US. Garnered positive media coverage for the new product, digital platform, and 3 highly regarded events in Paris.

► Built global leadership team (Business Development, Events & Operations, Strategy & Technology, Finance, Legal, Marketing) while establishing governance and startup operations in Paris and Los Angeles.

► Developed 5-year business plan with multimarket, multievent global footprint. Instituted risk management process and best practices, including event contingency plans, crisis communications, and event cancellation insurance.

► Negotiated and signed Nike as athletic footwear and apparel partner—an above-market deal for both US and French event markets and a breakthrough achievement for the new venture.

CHICAGO ROAD RUNNERS (CRR)   Chicago ▪ 2000–2017
President, CEO & Race Director, Chicago Marathon (10 years)
EVP & COO (5 years)
EVP, Administration (2 years)

Provided vision, direction, and strategic leadership to evolve organization into new era as preeminent leader in participatory running. Transformed business model from race organizer to lifestyle community brand. Rebuilt Board, executive team, and workforce as purpose-driven and inclusive. 160 F/T staff, 700 seasonal staff, 10K volunteers.

CEO / COO LEADERSHIP

► Ignited **250% revenue growth**—from $24.4M to $85.2M.

► Increased **net unrestricted assets 450%**—from $4.6M to $25.4M.

► Grew **sponsorship 200%,** including record-breaking, long-term deal with GEM Consultancy of Japan.

► Drove fundraising growth **from 0.5% to nearly 10%** of total annual revenue.

► Grew **Chicago Marathon to a world leader**—50K participants/100 countries; $340M economic impact to Chicago.

Strategy: Transform a text-dense, 4-page resume into a well-organized, easy-to-skim document that clearly communicates value and results. Notice how section headers highlight keywords while making long lists of bullet points easy to read and understand.

PAT DRISCOLL

773-555-5555 ▪ driscoll@gmail.com

CHICAGO ROAD RUNNERS, continued

MARKET GROWTH & BUSINESS PARTNERSHIPS

► **Following record-setting GEM deal,** laid the groundwork, developed the relationship, and negotiated key terms for industry-leading athletic footwear and apparel deal with Reebok.

► **Created and co-founded "Global Marathon League"** global alliance of marquee marathons (Chicago, Boston, NYC, LA, London, Berlin). Hosted major national championships, including USA Men's Olympic Trials.

EVENT DEVELOPMENT & COMMUNITY INVOLVEMENT

► **Worked with city agencies and CRR team** to create the Chicago Half Marathon and reinvigorate the Suburban Series, one of which grew to nation's largest—from 3.5K race finishers to 26K.

► **Championed growth of a youth running program**—from 5 children to over 200K annually in 6 years.

► **Created grass-roots neighborhood events** that reached new audiences of all ages—pre-K to elderly.

► **Led strategic promotional and investment initiatives** in the national market of middle and distance runners.

TECHNOLOGY, SOCIAL MEDIA & MULTIMEDIA

► **Transitioned CRR from laggard to leader** in leveraging data and technology to advance operations, programs, and marketing. Broadened fan base and engaged with runners through digital, social, and broadcast channels.

► **Advanced operations through technology**—real-time, data-driven safety and security systems, online customer support systems, spectator and athlete mobile apps, comprehensive website, and robust social media strategy.

► **Secured multiyear broadcast partnerships** with CBS, ESPN, and ABC national networks, enabling live coverage of the Chicago Marathon in more than 100 countries for the first time.

ANDERSON & LEWISTON, LLP   Cincinnati ▪ 1992–2000
Partner, Project Finance & Leasing Team (2 years)
Senior Associate, Project Finance & Leasing Team (3 years)
Associate, Corporate Team (7 years)

Joined firm directly out of law school to develop strong foundation of corporate law experience. Represented large US banks and insurance companies in complex, multijurisdictional, asset-based leasing and loan transactions.

► **Led deal teams and counter-party negotiations.** Coordinated client risk management and credit reviews.

► **Drafted finance documents** for aircraft, rail equipment, ships, and infrastructure assets in US, Africa, and Europe.

EDUCATION

Juris Doctor, University of Chicago Law School—Chicago, IL
Bachelor of Arts, Boston College—Boston, MA

AWARDS

CRR Leadership Award ▪ Inductee, IL Running Hall of Fame ▪ IL Business Leader of the Year
Boston College Outstanding Alumni ▪ Law Review Woman of the Year Award
USA Women's Olympic Marathon Trials Qualifier ▪ Chicago Women's Marathon Winner

RESUME 8: by Wendy Enelow, MRW, CCM, CPRW, JCTC • www.wendyenelow.com

MARIAH SUTER

SENIOR EXECUTIVE & GLOBAL LEADER – ADVANCED TECHNOLOGY VENTURES

Enterprise Technology | Blockchain | Cloud Computing | Information Technology | Telecommunications | SaaS

Highly entrepreneurial CEO with rich experience in emerging technologies. Built customer-centric businesses, captured market share, created successful business operations, and drove multichannel market streams. Exceptionally competitive in forging new markets and delivering compelling results in shifting business environments across multicultural landscapes.

Mergers | Acquisitions | IPOs | Corporate Fund Raising & Road Shows | JVs & Partnerships | Strategic Alliances

Greatest expertise and record of performance in strategic planning and development, emerging technology development and commercialization, new business start-up and leadership, multi-site operations, equity and venture funding, CRM, organizational design and operational efficiency, revenue growth and sustainability, M&As.

Board Member | Entrepreneur of the Year | Keynote & Featured Speaker | Major Media Spokesperson | Multilingual

PROFESSIONAL EXPERIENCE

NEX-COM-TEL   **The Netherlands** – 2018 to Present

BOARD DIRECTOR

Majority investor in revolutionary security solutions for blockchain technology and cryptocurrency transactions. Solutions eliminate risk of cryptocurrency theft and guarantee strong audit assurance for trading and transactions. Technology reduces business burden of wallet key management and cyber-threats that result from centralized key storage.

LUXTECH   **Belgium** – 2015 to Present

BOARD DIRECTOR

Board Director of pure-cloud infrastructure-as-a-service (IaaS) company offering highly available, flexible, enterprise-class hybrid cloud servers and cloud hosting solutions. Eleven operating locations, blue-chip customers in the US and Europe.

DREYER SYSTEMS & SOLUTIONS   **The Netherlands** – 2014 to 2018

CHIEF EXECUTIVE OFFICER & BOARD MEMBER

Leveraged recognition from MTM-A success to raise growth capital and acquire Dreyer, a larger, well-established US company struggling with financial and technological challenges. Orchestrated complex reverse acquisition and seamless integration of the 2 companies to expand footprint with new fully integrated software suite (desktop, mobile, cloud). Held full strategic planning, operating management, technology development, marketing, sales, and P&L responsibilities.

▸ Rebranded and relaunched Dreyer as multi-tenanted enterprise collaboration platform across desktop, mobile, and cloud technologies. Retooled business model into SaaS-enabled offerings, transitioned 98% of customers to new solution, and achieved 95% retention.

▸ Grew recurring annual revenue from $14M to $42M and delivered 5 highest revenue quarters in company's history.

▸ Reversed losses and restored company to profitability with new technologies, online sales, and $15M debt facility to support further investment and acquisitions.

▸ Orchestrated 3 successful acquisitions to expand solutions portfolio: M&A transaction management technology , mobile editing tool, and business social application.

Strategy: Create a dual-focus summary that emphasizes both executive and board contributions to position job seeker for new board opportunities. List current board positions first in the experience section before presenting more detailed CEO/executive experience.

MTM-A GLOBAL SOLUTIONS   **The Netherlands** – 2012 to 2014

CHIEF EXECUTIVE OFFICER & BOARD MEMBER

Majority investor of start-up company. Partnered with talent teams to develop technology concept, design product suite, and lead through rapid growth. Secured beachhead customers in legal, financial services, and government sectors.

▸ Successfully launched new technology within high-growth markets in the UK and Europe.

▸ Raised $30M capital to fund the acquisition of Dreyer, a larger company with highly visible market presence.

LORIMER SOFTWARE & SYSTEMS   **France** – 2005 to 2012

GROUP MANAGING DIRECTOR & BOARD MEMBER – Italy

Recruited by VC and investment banking group to help plan and orchestrate a financial, operational, and organizational turnaround at early-stage company. **Acting as President,** led a team of VPs and in-country Managing Directors. Guided a portfolio of 11 unique businesses in 11 European countries (each with its own P&L and operating requirements).

▸ Played a key role in driving operational performance and building revenue to more than $350M. Led corporate strategic growth, business development, and executive hiring.

▸ Turned around loss to profitability. Grew revenues annually with dominant positioning throughout key European markets. Delivered 22 consecutive quarters of growth, transitioning from negative to 35% positive EBITDA.

▸ Helped raise $450M in commercial and public debt over 10 years. Bought out 65% of initial investor group.

▸ Expanded into new markets (financial services, telecomm, media), generating 80% of sales from new segments.

▸ Forged partnerships with IBM, AT&T, and Accenture. Achieved and maintained 98% customer satisfaction rating.

3T# SOFTWARE   **US, Hong Kong, UK, Spain** – 2002 to 2005

VICE PRESIDENT INTERNATIONAL & GENERAL MANAGER

Member of executive team that structured, negotiated, and integrated 12 companies into 3T# over 2 years. Final acquisition was Delta Solutions (50% larger than 3T#). Reduced costs $18M. Full P&L responsibility.

▸ Drove international sales to $60M+ in 2 years (35% of total company revenues). Won major sales with Alpha Solutions, MasterCard, NEC, TelecomTech, Telia, and Xerox.

▸ Pioneered international expansion and launched offices in Europe and Asia. Created culture-specific operating and sales infrastructures. Led global marketing campaigns and built direct/indirect sales and support teams.

▸ Orchestrated South Korean JV, recruited/trained sales teams, and built profitable organization in first year.

▸ Guided new strategic alliances. Partnered with ATG, Baan, BroadVision, Cap Gemini, Clarify, KPMG, Vantive, and others to expand market presence. Developed reseller relationships in Asia (Compaq, Hitachi, NEC).

LAND-TECH SOLUTIONS (currently, a division of Dell)   **US** – 1999 to 2002

DIRECTOR, INTERNATIONAL SALES & BUSINESS DEVELOPMENT

Built division from start-up to $4.5M in first-year revenues and $10.5M in second-year revenues. Closed major sales with Diner's Club Europe, Dutch PTT, Sony, and others. Markets in Japan, UK, Australia. IPO in 1996; Dell acquisition in 1997.

PROJECT FIELD SYSTEMS, INC.   **US** – 1996 to 1999

INTERNATIONAL SALES & MARKETING MANAGER

Launched Asian and Latin American sales, expanded European markets, and increased international sales from 5% to 35% of total business. Built global distributor/agent network. Nurtured relationships with the UN and foreign governments.

EDUCATION | LANGUAGES

UNIVERSITY OF MASSACHUSETTS – Amherst, MA
MBA, Cum Laude • 1991 / **BA, Cum Laude** • 1990 *(9-month Graduate Internship with US Ambassador to South Korea)*

US & The Netherlands Citizen | Fluent English, French, Dutch | Conversational Spanish

Mariah Suter | +34 3822 906 377 | maiahsutertech@gmail.com | www.LinkedIn.com/in/mstech3824 | Page 2 of 2

RESUME 9: by Adrienne Tom, CERM, MCRS, CIS, CES, CCS • www.careerimpressions.ca

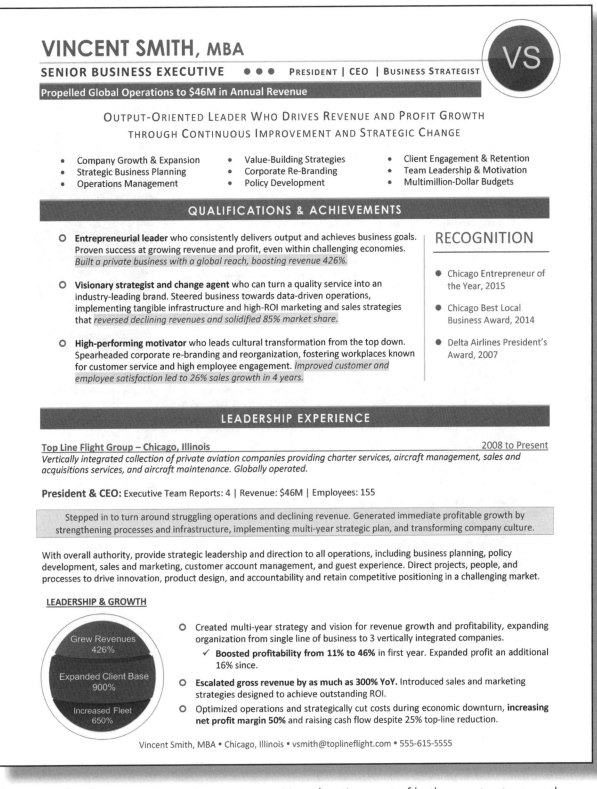

VINCENT SMITH, MBA

SENIOR BUSINESS EXECUTIVE ● ● ● PRESIDENT | CEO | BUSINESS STRATEGIST

Propelled Global Operations to $46M in Annual Revenue

OUTPUT-ORIENTED LEADER WHO DRIVES REVENUE AND PROFIT GROWTH
THROUGH CONTINUOUS IMPROVEMENT AND STRATEGIC CHANGE

- Company Growth & Expansion
- Strategic Business Planning
- Operations Management
- Value-Building Strategies
- Corporate Re-Branding
- Policy Development
- Client Engagement & Retention
- Team Leadership & Motivation
- Multimillion-Dollar Budgets

QUALIFICATIONS & ACHIEVEMENTS

○ **Entrepreneurial leader** who consistently delivers output and achieves business goals. Proven success at growing revenue and profit, even within challenging economies. *Built a private business with a global reach, boosting revenue 426%.*

○ **Visionary strategist and change agent** who can turn a quality service into an industry-leading brand. Steered business towards data-driven operations, implementing tangible infrastructure and high-ROI marketing and sales strategies that *reversed declining revenues and solidified 85% market share.*

○ **High-performing motivator** who leads cultural transformation from the top down. Spearheaded corporate re-branding and reorganization, fostering workplaces known for customer service and high employee engagement. *Improved customer and employee satisfaction led to 26% sales growth in 4 years.*

RECOGNITION

- Chicago Entrepreneur of the Year, 2015

- Chicago Best Local Business Award, 2014

- Delta Airlines President's Award, 2007

LEADERSHIP EXPERIENCE

Top Line Flight Group – Chicago, Illinois   2008 to Present
Vertically integrated collection of private aviation companies providing charter services, aircraft management, sales and acquisitions services, and aircraft maintenance. Globally operated.

President & CEO: Executive Team Reports: 4 | Revenue: $46M | Employees: 155

Stepped in to turn around struggling operations and declining revenue. Generated immediate profitable growth by strengthening processes and infrastructure, implementing multi-year strategic plan, and transforming company culture.

With overall authority, provide strategic leadership and direction to all operations, including business planning, policy development, sales and marketing, customer account management, and guest experience. Direct projects, people, and processes to drive innovation, product design, and accountability and retain competitive positioning in a challenging market.

LEADERSHIP & GROWTH

Grew Revenues 426%

Expanded Client Base 900%

Increased Fleet 650%

○ Created multi-year strategy and vision for revenue growth and profitability, expanding organization from single line of business to 3 vertically integrated companies.
   ✓ **Boosted profitability from 11% to 46%** in first year. Expanded profit an additional 16% since.

○ **Escalated gross revenue by as much as 300% YoY.** Introduced sales and marketing strategies designed to achieve outstanding ROI.

○ Optimized operations and strategically cut costs during economic downturn, **increasing net profit margin 50%** and raising cash flow despite 25% top-line reduction.

Vincent Smith, MBA • Chicago, Illinois • vsmith@toplineflight.com • 555-615-5555

Strategy: Emphasize most recent executive position, devoting most of both pages to strong and relevant achievements within specific areas of leadership. Add bold graphics to strengthen impact and accentuate large metrics.

INNOVATION & DEVELOPMENT

o **Differentiated company from competitors** with new industry-leading performance and financial reporting that helped secure 85% of market.
   - ✓ Sourced and deployed new modern enterprise software system within 90 days, **reducing reporting time from 8 hours to 2 hours** per aircraft.
o Implemented 5 major enterprise software applications across all major departments, automating work to **save over $125K annually.**
o **Expanded hangar space from 8,000 sq. ft. to 60,000 sq. ft.** Oversaw negotiation, design, and construction of new headquarters, delivering project on time and within budget.
o Re-energized corporate brand, making it synonymous with legendary customer service and more adaptable to economic realities. **Increased customer satisfaction 36%.**

CULTURE & SAFETY

o **Cultivated culture of "customer first" service excellence** by enhancing product and service offerings.
   - ✓ **Increased overall customer base 900%,** growing management customers from 2 to 25 and charter customers from 10 to 100.
o **Maintained perfect corporate safety record with 0 incidents or accidents.** Pursued and secured difficult industry accreditations to validate safety efforts:
   - ✓ Hold First-Rate status with US Department of Transportation.
   - ✓ IBS-BAO Certified, Contrail Aviation Safety Certified, and Argus Platinum Rating.

EMPLOYEES & COMMUNITY

o Instituted corporation-wide social responsibility plan, ensuring ethical, safe, and community-supportive services. Formed strategic partnerships with community players, together **donating over $500M to worthy causes.**
o **Raised employee engagement 62%,** launching numerous social and community initiatives designed to give employees a purpose alongside profits. Provided employees with 4 paid volunteer days each year.
o Inspired employees to generate workplace and system improvements. Recognized and rewarded employees for improvement submissions, **producing nearly 1 submission each day and 90% implementation rate.**

Peak Company Stats:

$46M Annual Revenue
•••

37,000+ Guests
•••

50,000 sq. ft. Hangar
•••

18,000+ Flight Hours
•••

36 Countries Flown To
•••

50,000+ Maintenance Hours
•••

1000+ Volunteer Hours
•••

100+ Charter Customers
•••

25 Management Clients
•••

Delta Airlines – Atlanta, Georgia   2003 to 2007
Manager, InFlight Standards & Training (2004 – 2007) | Customer Service Support (2003 – 2004)

Promoted during time of great corporate change, with low employee morale, to turn around service standards. Directed inflight customer service program, delivering operational and best practices training to 1600 flight attendants each year.

Increased Sales 26% in 4 Years

o Introduced new operational standards that streamlined processes and procedures, increasing operational efficiency 78%.
o **Recharged front-line services** by designing and delivering innovative customer service program focused on the idea that *"it's not what you do, it's how you do it."*
   - ✓ Raised employee satisfaction from 36% to 78%. Increased customer satisfaction 38%.

EDUCATION

Master of Business Administration (MBA): The University of Chicago, 2016
Bachelor of Science in Business Administration: Emory University, 1996
Professional Development Courses: Leadership Excellence • Customer Service • Change Management • Building Relationships

Vincent Smith, MBA • Chicago, Illinois • vsmith@toplineflight.com • 555-615-5555

RESUME 10: by Louise Kursmark, MRW, CPRW, CEIP, CCM, JCTC • www.louisekursmark.com

Serena Matthews

serena.matthews@mail.com ▪ 312-245-1234 ▪ <u>LinkedIn Profile</u>

CEO | VC & PRIVATE EQUITY ADVISOR | OUTSIDE DIRECTOR
Cloud, Colocation, Managed & Professional Services

Global Growth & Turnaround Strategist for cutting-edge IT operations—Fortune 500, mid-market, start-up. Career record of quickly achieving aggressive financial and operational goals, making smart decisions regarding organizational refocus and cultural change, and moving companies forward despite economic challenges and financial constraints.

"Top 10 Influencer," TechData Midwest (2020)
CEO of the Year, Chicago Business Journal (2019)
Industry Thought Leader and Conference Speaker (Business Trends, Technical Issues, M&A Activity)

PROFESSIONAL EXPERIENCE

ROBUST DATA CENTERS, LLC | Chicago, IL   2019–Present
Global provider of data infrastructure and services to 1100 enterprise-class customers; 300 employees; $385M revenue.

President and Chief Executive Officer | Company Director

Led rapid acquisition and relaunch of Data Corp's data center assets, teaming with Danforth Investment Partners to create new standalone company with $385M in revenue and 31 data centers in 11 countries and 25 markets.

- **In 6 months, executed complex transition.** Recruited executive leadership team, provided oversight on all legal discussions, and created and executed plan to build from scratch all business functions (Sales, Marketing, Finance, IT, HR, Legal, Operations, Engineering) and operating systems to stand up new entity within tight timeframe.

- **Established legal entities in 11 countries** and new U.S. headquarters. Recruited 50 new employees in 6 months.

- **Defined business strategy** as an enterprise-class retail colocation provider.

- **Raised $550M in debt** and achieved initial debt rating of B2 (Moody's) and B (S&P).

MATTHEWS GROUP | Chicago, IL   2016-2019
Management consultancy specializing in state-of-the-art data centers, cloud computing, and managed services.

Chief Executive Officer

Built consulting practice from start-up to $4.3M revenue and 40 employees, providing expertise to help PE, VC, start-up, SMB, and Fortune 1000 enterprise clients optimize IT investments, define business strategy, and jump-start growth.

- **Grew revenue 437% in 1 year** (2017–2018).

- **As CEO and primary rainmaker,** proposed, sold, and directed the delivery of 70+ unique projects for private equity, mid-market companies, and technology service providers.

- **Established partner agreements with ~20 companies** (Amazon Web Services, IBM, Microsoft) to complement internal capabilities.

- **Teamed with Danforth Investment Partners** to conduct commercial and technical due diligence and ultimately acquire the data center business from Data Corp—a transaction valued at $1.1B. Recruited to serve as CEO of the newly formed entity, Robust Data Centers.

GREAT PLAINS INTERNET SERVICES, INC. | Lincoln, NE   2013–2016
Mid-market PE-backed provider of enterprise-class data center, cloud, and connectivity service solutions.

Chief Executive Officer

Transformed regional colocation-only company to enterprise-class IT IaaS provider. Raised $89M senior secured debt in 2 rounds to restructure existing debt, lower capital cost, and provide funds for the business. Stabilized data center and built out 2 cloud platforms and a set of managed service offerings.

Strategy: Start with a headline, brief summary, and items of notable recognition to position this executive for her next CEO role or for board opportunities. Promote readability with written achievement statements and ample white space.

Serena Matthews   serena.matthews@mail.com ▪ 312-245-1234

GREAT PLAINS INTERNET SERVICES, INC., continued

- **Maintained 55% gross margins and 34% EBITDA** during challenging economic and competitive periods.

- **Averaged 15% revenue growth** for 8 consecutive quarters.

- **Slashed telecom costs** by renegotiating leases. Upgraded sales team and retooled social media to support customer acquisition and growth strategies.

U.S. CABLE COMPANY, INC. | Chicago, IL   2005–2013
$600M global B2B provider of IT Infrastructure as a Service

SVP Global Operations (2010–2013)	750 global staff | $350M budget
VP Global Solutions (2008–2010)	600 staff | $44M budget (expense)
VP Operations (2007–2008)	
VP Midwest Region (2005–2007)	

Progressed to increasingly senior leadership roles as the company expanded aggressively through multiple acquisitions and organic growth.

- **Led Global Solutions,** offering managed/virtualized services via Tier 1 Network Backbone and 29 data centers. Grew revenue 12% while scaling operations by $8M yearly through technology enhancements and external partnerships.

- **Provided Professional Services to the company's top 700 global accounts** (Fortune 1000). Grew 6% in one quarter; delivered $23M in annual cost reductions.

- **Merged, integrated, and restructured 3 financially challenged service providers into a $400M nationwide business** offering hosting and consulting services. Improved EBITDA $30M and exceeded revenue goal by 11% while maintaining industry-best customer service.

PRIOR: Dell Computer, Naxos Computer Services, IBM.

PROFESSIONAL PROFILE

EDUCATION	**MBA,** University of Chicago, Chicago, IL **BS,** University of Illinois, Champaign, IL
MEMBERSHIP	National Association of Corporate Directors (NACD) Chicago Entrepreneurship Council
BOARD — Current	Robust Data Center Solutions, LLC | Chicagoland Ventures, Inc. | Women In Technology (Midwest)
— Prior	Great Lakes Technology Systems, LLC | American Cancer Society, Midwest Chapter | University of Chicago Board of Advisors | Greater Chicago Chamber of Commerce
COMMUNITY	Lake Michigan Stewards | Magnificent Mile Historical Commission | Girl Scouts of America, Chicago

RESUME 11: by Wendy Enelow, MRW, CCM, CPRW, JCTC • www.wendyenelow.com

DANIEL R. SUNMAN

DSSUNMAN@YMAIL.COM | 918.526.3902 | WWW.LINKEDIN.COM/IN/SUNMANDS

C-LEVEL EXECUTIVE PROPELLING BREAKTHROUGH PERFORMANCE & FINANCIAL RESULTS

Driving Accelerated Growth & Expansion — Leading Technology Innovation — Delivering High-Quality Services
Building Strong & Sustainable Business Operations — Forging Strategic Alliances & Joint Ventures

Award-Winning Business & Technology Leader who has built numerous successful companies, products, technologies, and organizations throughout the US, Canada, and international markets. Top-flight strategic planning, financial, and organizational leadership talents combined with keen insights into market demand, customer needs, and technology trends. Expert at building sales, service, customer, and partner relationships with top executives at companies worldwide. Talented negotiator.

EXECUTIVE LEADERSHIP QUALIFICATIONS

Strategic Planning & Corporate Vision	P&L Management / Financial & Operations Management
Organizational Design & Development	Technology Design, Development & Commercialization
Mergers, Acquisitions, IPOs & Funding	Global Sales, Marketing & Business Development
Key Account Relationship Management	New Product Launch & Worldwide Market Penetration

PROFESSIONAL EXPERIENCE

President & CEO   2014–Current
AnTEL Corporation – Daytona Beach, FL

Led the successful and profitable transformation of failing, 30-year-old company by developing award-winning, cloud-based, SaaS programs for global insurance industry market and executing a winning business development strategy. Revitalized the entire organization, focused corporate vision and strategic direction, reinvented technology platforms and product/service offerings, and directed sales and marketing teams to peak performance. Full P&L responsibility. Member, Board of Directors.

Sales & Revenue Growth: Far exceeded corporate objectives for sales performance and account capture/retention.
- **Increased recurring revenue 77%** in just 4 years and **total revenue 37.5%** despite intense market competition.
- Negotiated and closed the largest new sale in the company's history – **$15M+ in total contract value (TCV)**.
- **Achieved 21% reduction in service requests, 21% faster close rate, and 60% client engagement plan participation** following implementation of new customer support and account management program.
- **Averaged and sustained 94.5% customer retention rate.**

Financial Performance: Restored the AnTEL Corporation to profitability.
- **Raised millions of dollars in new capital** from private and institutional investors and a major offshore supplier.
- **Completed investment banker process with 3 offers and a successful QoE financial review.**
- **Delivered $2M in annual cost savings** with intelligent on-shore and off-shore staffing/talent management programs.
- Restructured all contracts and licensing terms to reduce risk and **recovered $500K in lost services revenue each year.**
- **Rescued failed $1.5M project and recovered $1M performance bond.**

Technology Development & Commercialization: Created the industry's #1 software solutions platform.
- Reinvented and expanded technology offerings with **60%+ of clients licensing new products** in just 2 years.
- **Orchestrated development of 15 profitable new technology programs** (e.g., claim scoring, predictive analytics) to meet current and projected market demands. **Led successful SOX compliance** and internal system cloud migration projects.
- **Reduced client go-live implementation cycles 50%** through implementation of PMP processes and best practices.
- **Created Risk Management Optimization (RPO) platform** as a unique value proposition and retention strategy for clients.

Organizational Leadership: Rebuilt the company, recruited top talent, and dramatically improved efficiency/productivity.
- **Increased billable revenue 31%** to $220K per FTE with implementation of new staff time reporting systems and practices.
- **Rebranded AnTEL Corporation and product portfolio** and created 30+ digital marketing and lead generation programs.
- **Implemented Salesforce and Pardot solutions,** led redesign of corporate website, and expanded digital footprint.

Strategy: Maximize readability of a great many impressive and relevant achievements by grouping under subheadings for current position, tightening bullet points to 1 or at most 2 lines, and highlighting overarching achievement for each role in a lightly shaded box.

Daniel R. Sunman

Page 2 | DSSSunman@ymail.com | 918.526.3902

C-LEVEL EXECUTIVE / C-LEVEL CONSULTANT – Miami, FL   2000–2014

Delivered a decade of notable achievements as President/CEO/Interim CEO of several emerging and high-growth business ventures. Concurrently, orchestrated high-profile, C-level consulting engagements in partnership with senior operating executives, senior technology teams, Boards, investors, and other stakeholders. Industry experience includes technology, data services, e-learning, energy, and real estate.

- Built Peoples Insurance organization from start-up to operations in 22 key markets and **revenues totaling $140M+.**
- Led strategic planning, financial modeling, and sourcing for **$4M+ solar project** for EnergyTech Corporation.
- Spearheaded acquisition assessments, from due diligence through proposals, market analyses, and documentation, including **$7M acquisition** in claims/risk management industry and **$4M acquisition** in special events industry.
- Collaborated with technology teams and executive leaders to build, commercialize, and market **new e-learning products and software solutions**, including **social networking and self-service kiosk** development projects.

Senior Vice President   1999–2000
INSURANCE SYSTEMS SOLUTION, INC. (ISS) – Miami, FL
($2.8B in annual revenues & one of the world's largest publicly traded company in insurance industry. Subsequently acquired by RTL.)

Recruited by CEO of ISS following acquisition of Sunman Technology Solutions to orchestrate the seamless integration of technology and business operations into their Risk and Claims Division. Facilitated transfer of proprietary technical knowledge, intellectual property, and sales/marketing/business development strategies.

- **Surpassed 2-year revenue growth and earn-out targets by better than 20%.**
- Created robust technology development and sales organization to **expand global reach and industry penetration.**
- Partnered with C-level executive team to plan, strategize, and support the **company's $445M acquisition by ISS.**

President & COO   1990–1999
SUNMAN TECHNOLOGY GROUP, INC. – Miami, FL; Dallas, TX; Phoenix, AZ; Mexico City, Mexico
(Founded through LBO of Donovan & Wright.)

Vaulted company into global market leader with average annual growth of 40% despite intense competition. Set strategic direction and best practices that delivered a commanding market share and numerous industry awards for technology innovation. Secured $12M in funding from VC firm to fuel company growth and position for IPO.

- Delivered extraordinary financial results: **1500 B2B contracts totaling $100M+ in revenue, 40% EBITA,** and an **annual run rate of $225K per FTE** (one of the highest in any company). Earned **98% client satisfaction** ratings.
- Honored with top industry recognition including 2-time **"Product of the Year Award"** from *Risk Management Magazine,* a **"Miami Future 50 Award"** from FL Economic Development, and numerous industry-specific accolades.
- Forged **enduring relationships with key accounts** – Allstate, Archer Daniels, John Hancock, Mayo Clinic, Nordstrom, Starbucks, Sysco, UPS, USAir, and others.
- **Designed, developed, and commercialized new technology platform for global healthcare industry** (North America, Central America, Europe, Middle East) to meet regulatory and JCAHO quality standards for millions of health records.
- Negotiated strategic alliances and partnerships with major industry players (e.g., DNN, KLQ), TPAs, and consulting firms to further **strengthen Sunman's global market presence and rapidly growing revenue channels.**
- **Collaborated with Bank of Miami to position Sunman for premium sale to ISS.** Managed stringent due diligence review, complex negotiations, and sophisticated final transaction. Accepted executive-level opportunity with ISS.

Early Career Highlights: Youngest VP in the history of Donovan & Wright. Led global commercial release of next-generation technology solution, generating $20M+ in profitable new revenues as part of multi-national, multi-industry expansion plan.

EDUCATION: BACHELOR OF SCIENCE (BS) IN BUSINESS ADMINISTRATION – **UNIVERSITY OF FLORIDA**

CHAPTER 5

Sales, Marketing, and Business Development

- Retail Director (Luxury Sales and Marketing)
- Global Sales Executive
- Marketing Executive
- Client Relationship Management Executive
- VP Sales and Marketing
- Division Manager
- Vice President of Marketing
- Global Alliance Executive
- Chief Marketing Officer
- Sales Executive
- Client Services Director
- VP Sales
- Marketing Director

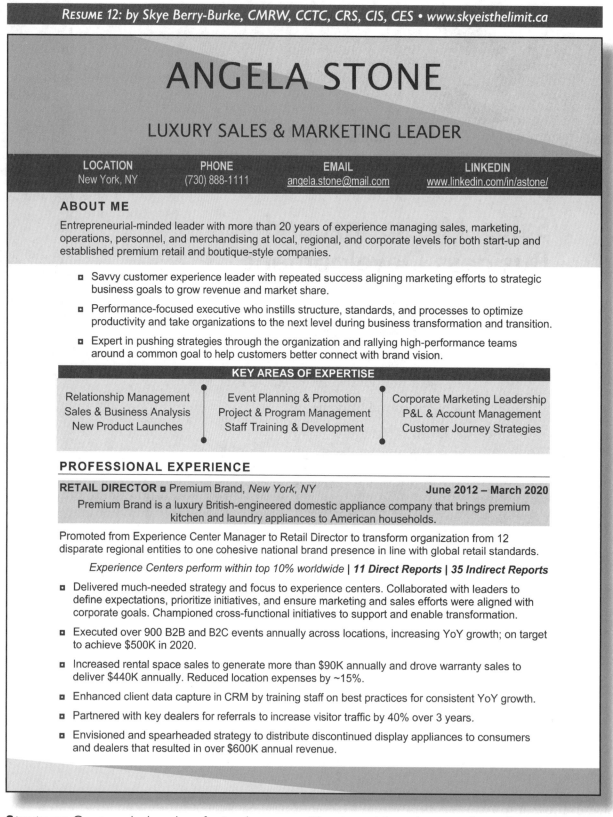

RESUME 12: *by Skye Berry-Burke, CMRW, CCTC, CRS, CIS, CES • www.skyeisthelimit.ca*

ANGELA STONE

LUXURY SALES & MARKETING LEADER

LOCATION	PHONE	EMAIL	LINKEDIN
New York, NY	(730) 888-1111	angela.stone@mail.com	www.linkedin.com/in/astone/

ABOUT ME

Entrepreneurial-minded leader with more than 20 years of experience managing sales, marketing, operations, personnel, and merchandising at local, regional, and corporate levels for both start-up and established premium retail and boutique-style companies.

- Savvy customer experience leader with repeated success aligning marketing efforts to strategic business goals to grow revenue and market share.

- Performance-focused executive who instills structure, standards, and processes to optimize productivity and take organizations to the next level during business transformation and transition.

- Expert in pushing strategies through the organization and rallying high-performance teams around a common goal to help customers better connect with brand vision.

KEY AREAS OF EXPERTISE

Relationship Management	Event Planning & Promotion	Corporate Marketing Leadership
Sales & Business Analysis	Project & Program Management	P&L & Account Management
New Product Launches	Staff Training & Development	Customer Journey Strategies

PROFESSIONAL EXPERIENCE

RETAIL DIRECTOR ▫ Premium Brand, *New York, NY*   **June 2012 – March 2020**

Premium Brand is a luxury British-engineered domestic appliance company that brings premium kitchen and laundry appliances to American households.

Promoted from Experience Center Manager to Retail Director to transform organization from 12 disparate regional entities to one cohesive national brand presence in line with global retail standards.

*Experience Centers perform within top 10% worldwide | **11 Direct Reports | 35 Indirect Reports***

- Delivered much-needed strategy and focus to experience centers. Collaborated with leaders to define expectations, prioritize initiatives, and ensure marketing and sales efforts were aligned with corporate goals. Championed cross-functional initiatives to support and enable transformation.

- Executed over 900 B2B and B2C events annually across locations, increasing YoY growth; on target to achieve $500K in 2020.

- Increased rental space sales to generate more than $90K annually and drove warranty sales to deliver $440K annually. Reduced location expenses by ~15%.

- Enhanced client data capture in CRM by training staff on best practices for consistent YoY growth.

- Partnered with key dealers for referrals to increase visitor traffic by 40% over 3 years.

- Envisioned and spearheaded strategy to distribute discontinued display appliances to consumers and dealers that resulted in over $600K annual revenue.

Strategy: Create a sleek and professional resume with unique deisgn elements that will resonate with the target audience—hiring managers and other authorities in premium and luxury retail goods industries.

ANGELA STONE ◘ Page 2 ◘ 730-888-1111

PROFESSIONAL EXPERIENCE, continued

PROJECT & PRODUCT MANAGER ◘ Premium Chocolate, *New York, NY*　　**April 2010 – June 2012**
Premium Chocolate is a leading source of indulgent chocolate for over 60 years.

Recruited to manage cross-functional teams in roll-out of new products from idea generation to launch. Reported to Executive Vice President and contributed to corporate ecommerce strategy, catalog campaigns, branding, corporate planning, and content generation for marketing purposes.

◘ Led business process improvement projects, including high-visibility SKU reduction project that identified $350K in annual savings.

◘ Managed communication with counsel on intellectual property matters.

◘ Researched competitor products and identified new industry trends. Maximized competitive advantages through new product development that addressed unmet customer needs.

◘ Drafted and produced bi-weekly department report for Executive team that analyzed sales data and provided sales reports and recommendations for product changes.

FOUNDER & MANAGING DIRECTOR ◘ GellyBean Toys, *New York, NY*　　**May 1998 – March 2010**
Specialty toy store recognized as industry leader for its time.

Conceptualized and grew specialty toy store from a small mall booth to 3 high-volume specialty locations. Envisioned and delivered highly differentiated and multi-award-winning, customer-centric, luxury retail experience.

◘ Spearheaded and developed brand identity. Directed creative teams in implementation across all touchpoints, including store design, logo, visual merchandising, marketing collateral, website, and social media platforms.

◘ Established successful merchandising plans and analyzed business results to visualize and modify business plans to achieve goals.

◘ Oversaw and managed all projects from initiation to completion, including site selection, lease negotiation, vendor selection, and oversight of store openings.

◘ Pioneered all front-end to back-end processes—sales, marketing, supply chain and inventory, cost accounting, financial reporting, and human resource policy and procedure.

◘ Awarded multiple "Best Of" retail awards, including Achievement Award for "Best New Store Design."

EDUCATION & TRAINING

Emory Leadership Foundations class | Completion June 2018

Luis Vex Leadership Center Service Excellence Culture Workshop

B.S. MARKETING | 1992
New York University, *New York, NY*

RESUME 13: by Emily Wong, ACRW, CPRW • www.Wordsofdistinction.net

ISABEL SPENCER

Wellesley, MA

(555) 555.555
isabel.spencer@gmail.com
www.linkedin.com/in/isabelspencer

GLOBAL SALES & BUSINESS DEVELOPMENT LEADER

Aggressive Strategy ▶ Targeted Tactics ▶ Market Expansion ▶ Explosive Growth

High-performance leader who mobilizes sales teams to break down geographic boundaries, deliver new revenue streams, and exceed high expectations.

Crusader for emerging technology who inspires channel partners to embrace innovation and deliver results.

Consensus builder adept at cultivating partnerships and building alliances across all business sectors to drive record growth and measurable productivity improvements.

— EXPERTISE that drives success in the delivery of CLOUD SOLUTIONS —

New Market Revenue	Strategic Planning & Implementation	Training & Development
Strategic Partnerships	Key Account Relationship Management	Startups & Turnarounds
New Product Development	Partner Program Development	Consultative Selling
Channel Development	Sales Operations & Processes	P&L & Budget Oversight

SUCCESS HIGHLIGHTS

— Sparked 4.5X surge in key account wallet share, transforming consultancy into a profit center in 2 years.

— Led global team to deliver >$240M in top-line revenue and achieve >200% of quota 3 years in a row.

— Doubled customer base for groundbreaking product, with customers increasing spend 3-fold within a year.

— Gained entry to 15 global markets using a 2-tiered distribution model while increasing profitability 22%.

SENIOR LEADERSHIP EXPERIENCE & RESULTS

Curatica, Wellesley, MA   **2016–Present**
VP OF SALES AND STRATEGIC PARTNERSHIPS

Challenge: Grow customer base for transformative technology with no defined market or category in the face of a business turnaround.

- Enlisted relationship network and led guerilla-marketing campaigns to generate new leads.
- Built trusted partnerships with line-of-business leaders by creating value and a sense of urgency.
- Landed and developed 4 corporate accounts into 6-figure customers.
- **Doubled number of customers and created cross-sell opportunities that ignited a 3-fold increase in customer spend within a year, which led to team surpassing 2017 sales goal.**

Enterprise Cloud Group, Boston, MA   **2013–2016**
DIRECTOR OF SALES & CHANNEL CONSULTING PRACTICE

Challenge: Expand wallet share at major accounts and build a successful consulting services practice.

- Co-developed a consulting practice that encompassed marketing, research, sales, and consulting project delivery for clients that included VMware, HP, and Riverbed Technology.
- Engaged existing outside network and tapped company relationships to uncover pain points, create value, negotiate, and close deals.
- **Drove increase in wallet share by 4.5X for major accounts and exceeded sales targets every year. Transformed consulting practice into a profit center within 2 years.**

Strategy: Extract a major achievement for each sales position and highlight in a shaded box, creating consistency top-to-bottom. Maintain readability, while showcasing many positions and a long career, through concise writing—no paragraph or bullet point longer than 2 lines.

SmartLinks, Boston, MA   **2011–2013**
CLIENT SERVICES DIRECTOR

Challenge: Increase revenue in the face of a limited account base and penetration.

- Identified new entry points, uncovered needs, created value, and closed deals with clients that included Cisco Systems, Dell Inc., Informatica Corporation, Blue Coat Systems, and Sophos.
- Staffed and managed consulting team to deliver projects on time and under budget to all clients.
- **Expanded sales pipeline 4X within 6 months and consistently exceeded annual sales goals. Achieved 100% client-satisfaction rating while managing to profitability.**

Medallion Software, Andover, MA   **2010–2011**
DIRECTOR, GLOBAL CHANNELS & BUSINESS DEVELOPMENT

Challenge: Globally scale up young software company that offered transformational product for which there was no pre-existing demand, while maintaining low cost to market and deliver.

- Developed all aspects of worldwide partner program, including value proposition, partner tiers, and margin structure. Recruited and cultivated distributor relationships, negotiated contracts, and on-boarded.
- Assisted in the creation and implementation of the company's business development strategy.
- Built new partnerships with IBM, BMC, CA, EMC, NetApp, VMware, and Microsoft.
- **Grew deal pipeline 11X within 6 months and increased close ratio 3-fold; increased profitability on all channel sales by 12%; gained entry to 15 new markets through a 2-tiered distribution model.**

CloudOne, Boston, MA   **2006–2010**
NATIONAL CHANNEL SALES MANAGER

Challenge: Quickly scale growth of new storage product through new and existing channels while revitalizing CloudOne's relationship with key business partners.

- Recruited, negotiated contracts, and on-boarded 5 new partnerships.
- Evangelized and educated prospective partners regarding innovative new product. Collaborated on grass-roots sales campaigns
- **Achieved 116% of annual quota and increased wallet share with existing storage partners by 34%.**

Exponet Hosting Service, Boston, MA   **2002–2006**
DIRECTOR OF NORTH AMERICA CHANNEL SALES

Challenge: Grow share in highly competitive market with high expectations for rapid growth.

- Built 7-person team across North America; coached each channel manager in the recruitment, on-boarding, and enablement of local partners; and leveraged partnerships to accelerate sales cycles.
- **Led team to achieve 101% of quota, driving $50M in services revenue—a 24% increase.**

GLOBAL ALLIANCE MANAGER

Challenge: Build out global sales pipeline from ground up.

- Tasked international team of 12 to identify and negotiate new partnerships with Microsoft, Compaq, and Dell to deliver service across emerging markets in Eastern Europe, Southeast Asia, and Latin America.
- Coached strategic partners to modify business processes and compensation methodologies, which fueled motivation, execution, and results.
- **Achieved 200%+ of annual quota 3 years in a row, generating more than $240M in top-line revenue.**

EDUCATION

BACHELOR OF ARTS IN ECONOMICS & MARKETING • **University of Michigan**

Isabel Spencer   Page 2

RESUME 14: by Lisa K. McDonald, CPRW, CSBA • www.careerpolish.com

ARCHIE FITZ

Indianapolis, IN 46000 | 555-555-5555 | archiefitz@gmail.com

AWARD WINNING, NATIONALLY RECOGNIZED SALES PERFORMER, LEADER & INFLUENCER

Changing Mindsets & Driving Profitability as Innovator & Consultative Client Strategy Partner

Steer $83M Revenue Territory | Personal Sales $25M | Retail & Wholesale Accounts

Deliver explosive revenue and territory growth: Leverage market trends and opportunities. **Infiltrate and solidify market dominance**: Drive product launches, competitive trials, brand initiatives, and national marketing campaigns. **Maximize ROI.**

10% GROWTH

Year over Year

vs. 6% Industry Decline

PERSONAL SALES

$25M Revenues

170 Stores

3 Wholesalers – 18 States

TOP 10% IN US

Ranked Nationally in

Sales Among Peers

DIVISION MANAGER

$83M Revenues

900 Accounts

9 Territory Managers

TERRITORIES

Indiana

Illinois

Michigan

Wisconsin

CORE STRENGTHS

Strategic Market Planning & Penetration | High Lead-to-Client Conversion
Product Launches | Territory Growth | Product Presentation & Education | Negotiations
Account Management | Relationship Building | Brand Management | FDA Compliance
Budgeting & Cost Controls | Talent Development | Consumer Behavior Analytics

**See opportunities where others don't.
Act upon them when others can't.**

RESURRECT STALLED TERRITORIES: Revived 4 diverse, complex divisions in 3 years from mediocrity to record-breaking success. Innovated highly potent, repeatable "5P" sales process (presence, product availability, personal selling, promotions, pricing).

ELEVATE CLIENT PROFITABILITY: Guide clients to maximize contract, pricing incentives, and promotions for optimal revenues/market competitiveness with reduced inventory costs. Solidify relationships: Uncover needs, define value propositions, prioritize goals.

INFLUENCE NATIONAL PRACTICES: Transformed haphazard, scattered account communication approach into a transparent all-access system. Method became national SOP. Built correlative product strategy that fueled new revenue streams.

CRUSH GOALS CONSISTENTLY: Post record-breaking revenue and market share increases in heavily regulated and highly competitive market. Outperform in historically negative-trend market fraught with rigorous regulations across all layers of government.

ANALYZE FOR OPPORTUNITY: Develop winning client strategies: Scrutinize market segmentation; volume; taxation; consumer disposition funnel; product tests; and demographic, market-basket, consumer takeoff, and product trends.

CAREER SNAPSHOT

Platinum Plantations, **2012–Present**
> **Senior Division Manager**, 2016–Present
> **Account Manager**, 2014–2016
> **Territory Manager**, 2012–2014

KWI Concepts, **Inside Sales Manager/Crop Planning Specialist**, 2010–2012

EDUCATION & TRAINING

Master of Business Administration (MBA), Stillwater University, 2014
Bachelor of Science (BS), Huntington University, 2010
Critical Selling Skills—*Janek Performance Group* | 7 Habits—*Franklin Covey*

Strategy: Include context and highlight the right information to paint a strong picture of an accomplished sales leader—despite his company's negative social image and down-trending sales.

ARCHIE FITZ

555-555-5555 | archiefitz@gmail.com

PROFESSIONAL EXPERIENCE

PLATINUM PLANTATIONS, 2012–PRESENT

SENIOR DIVISION MANAGER, 2016–Present

Orchestrated surge in profitability, volume, and market share by parlaying personal sales tactics into strategy roadmaps. Developed Territory Managers into high-achieving performers who attain unprecedented results as leaders who inspire their direct peers.

Revenues: $83M | Direct Reports: 9 Territory Managers | Accounts: 900+

Territory: Indianapolis to Fort Wayne/Lafayette to Richmond

- Outperform expectation by coaching Territory Managers (TMs) to lead change, increase portfolio, and overcome market chaos.
- Convert TM mindset from sales to advocate. Spur them to unearth/integrate client's revenue/growth goals into apt programs.
- Elevate TM performance with newly created incubator environment supported by activity-driven coaching and analysis.
- Increase profitability as client Sherpa, guiding clients across contract, pricing, and promotion strategies/execution.
- Transform clients into market movers with just-right product mix/market segment strategies derived from intense data analysis.

ACCOUNT MANAGER, 2014–2016

Elevated marketing-influencing clients and territory performance in high-impact dual role of individual sales agent and leader.

Revenue: $25M | Ranked Top 10% Nationally of Peers | Territory: Wisconsin, Northern Illinois & Michigan

Managed 19 Retail Accounts (170 Store Fronts) & 3 Regional Wholesalers (Distribution in 18 States)

- Saved clients millions in inventory/taxes with strategy that thwarted crippling product tax change from flat-rate to weight-based.
- Architected nationally adopted product-syncing strategy for clients that bred lucrative new revenue streams.
- Reinvented account management strategies for unprecedented success and national adoption.
- Increased competitiveness of accounts by uncovering needs, defining value propositions, and prioritizing business goals.
- Solidified account loyalty by coaching team to transform clients into market influencers using market and competitor analytics.
- Boosted team production, strengthening skills through strategy, programs, and objection-elimination training.

TERRITORY MANAGER, 2012–2014

Transformed four underperforming territories into revenue leaders across all consumer segments forging 'fixer' status.

Revenue: $13M | Recognized Top Performer | Served 100+ Retail Programs | 10% Consistent Growth

Territory: Central Indiana | Client Base: Retail Chain Accounts & Owners

- Reinvented initially assigned territory from dismal performer into a rockstar by reengaging accounts as client partner.
- Duplicated profitability success in 3 years across 4 unique, convoluted, underperforming territories.
- Mastered array of complex retail programs to guide clients in easily adopting and quickly launching lucrative product programs.
- Awarded top performer 2013–2014 based on account growth and talent development.

ADDITIONAL SALES EXPERIENCE:

KWI Concepts, 2010–2012
  Planning Specialist, 2011–2012: *Conditioned $350M of inventory to quality specifications.*
  Inside Sales Manager, 2010–2011: *Supported 2 regional distributors in operations, inventory, and quality.*

RESUME 15: by Debra Boggs, MSM • www.dsprocoaching.com

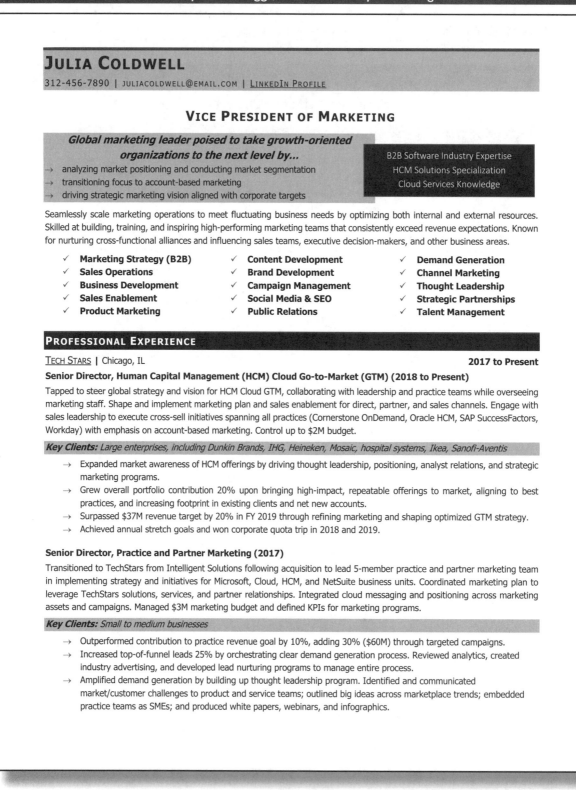

JULIA COLDWELL

312-456-7890 | JULIACOLDWELL@EMAIL.COM | LINKEDIN PROFILE

VICE PRESIDENT OF MARKETING

Global marketing leader poised to take growth-oriented organizations to the next level by...

→ analyzing market positioning and conducting market segmentation
→ transitioning focus to account-based marketing
→ driving strategic marketing vision aligned with corporate targets

B2B Software Industry Expertise
HCM Solutions Specialization
Cloud Services Knowledge

Seamlessly scale marketing operations to meet fluctuating business needs by optimizing both internal and external resources. Skilled at building, training, and inspiring high-performing marketing teams that consistently exceed revenue expectations. Known for nurturing cross-functional alliances and influencing sales teams, executive decision-makers, and other business areas.

✓ **Marketing Strategy (B2B)**	✓ **Content Development**	✓ **Demand Generation**
✓ **Sales Operations**	✓ **Brand Development**	✓ **Channel Marketing**
✓ **Business Development**	✓ **Campaign Management**	✓ **Thought Leadership**
✓ **Sales Enablement**	✓ **Social Media & SEO**	✓ **Strategic Partnerships**
✓ **Product Marketing**	✓ **Public Relations**	✓ **Talent Management**

PROFESSIONAL EXPERIENCE

TECH STARS | Chicago, IL   **2017 to Present**

Senior Director, Human Capital Management (HCM) Cloud Go-to-Market (GTM) (2018 to Present)

Tapped to steer global strategy and vision for HCM Cloud GTM, collaborating with leadership and practice teams while overseeing marketing staff. Shape and implement marketing plan and sales enablement for direct, partner, and sales channels. Engage with sales leadership to execute cross-sell initiatives spanning all practices (Cornerstone OnDemand, Oracle HCM, SAP SuccessFactors, Workday) with emphasis on account-based marketing. Control up to $2M budget.

Key Clients: *Large enterprises, including Dunkin Brands, IHG, Heineken, Mosaic, hospital systems, Ikea, Sanofi-Aventis*

→ Expanded market awareness of HCM offerings by driving thought leadership, positioning, analyst relations, and strategic marketing programs.
→ Grew overall portfolio contribution 20% upon bringing high-impact, repeatable offerings to market, aligning to best practices, and increasing footprint in existing clients and net new accounts.
→ Surpassed $37M revenue target by 20% in FY 2019 through refining marketing and shaping optimized GTM strategy.
→ Achieved annual stretch goals and won corporate quota trip in 2018 and 2019.

Senior Director, Practice and Partner Marketing (2017)

Transitioned to TechStars from Intelligent Solutions following acquisition to lead 5-member practice and partner marketing team in implementing strategy and initiatives for Microsoft, Cloud, HCM, and NetSuite business units. Coordinated marketing plan to leverage TechStars solutions, services, and partner relationships. Integrated cloud messaging and positioning across marketing assets and campaigns. Managed $3M marketing budget and defined KPIs for marketing programs.

Key Clients: *Small to medium businesses*

→ Outperformed contribution to practice revenue goal by 10%, adding 30% ($60M) through targeted campaigns.
→ Increased top-of-funnel leads 25% by orchestrating clear demand generation process. Reviewed analytics, created industry advertising, and developed lead nurturing programs to manage entire process.
→ Amplified demand generation by building up thought leadership program. Identified and communicated market/customer challenges to product and service teams; outlined big ideas across marketplace trends; embedded practice teams as SMEs; and produced white papers, webinars, and infographics.

Strategy: Avoid impression of "stagnation" for this executive, who had joined a startup and remained with it for more than 15 years (1998 to 2017) through several acquisitions and name changes, by showcasing the many ways her role had changed over the years.

JULIA COLDWELL
PAGE 2 OF 2 | 312-456-7890 | JULIACOLDWELL@EMAIL.COM

INTELLIGENT SOLUTIONS (formerly SkySolutions) | Chicago, IL | **2011 to 2017**

Director of Marketing

Recruited to join team to drive marketing strategy, campaigns, and events across US and EMEA for Tribridge HCM practice area following SkySolutions acquisition. Oversaw FTE/contract marketing and creative team. Developed and led analyst relations program. Maintained $2M marketing budget.

Key Clients: *Large enterprises, including Dunkin Brands, Heineken, LinkedIn, Ikea*

→ Conducted post-acquisition brand integration in aggressive 4-month period, including corporate messaging, website development, thought leadership campaign strategy, and social media marketing plan.
→ Elevated revenue pipeline contribution 21% in just 6 months.
→ Drove marketing contribution to revenue by 20% YOY ($2M to $18M) over tenure.
→ Improved reach to channel partner customer base and direct markets through marketing campaigns and events.
→ Coordinated corporate event strategies for US and EMEA markets, with focus on messaging, brand presence, keynote presentations (with clients like Heineken and LinkedIn), booth development, and lead management.

SKYSOLUTIONS | Chicago, IL | **2009 to 2010**

Vice President, Business Development

Challenged to increase business growth for newly established full-service B2B marketing agency focused on healthcare IT industry through pursuing new customers and expanding existing accounts. Formed consultative relationships with customer stakeholders to identify their needs. Designed integrated marketing strategies.

Key Clients: *Healthcare IT businesses, including Allscripts, Carefx, Phytel (now IBM), Aprima, Mediregs*

→ Generated $1M in new business over 8-month period by adding new and growing current accounts.
→ Boosted new account acquisition through strategy planning sessions covering market positioning, campaign concepting, lead management, and resource assignments.
→ Delivered comprehensive rebranding for electronic health record solution provider over ambitious 8-week time frame by directing account team in executing messaging, website, and relaunch campaign.
→ Led 2010 sales campaign for healthcare interoperability provider, working closely with client to plan and manage messaging, HIMSS10 exhibition, product launch, executive special events, microsite development, and advertising.

Earlier Roles with SkySolutions:

Director of Marketing, 2006 to 2009

Director of Marketing and Communications, 2004 to 2006

Senior Manager of Marketing and Sales Programs, 2001 to 2003

Senior Staff Manager, IT Services, 1998 to 2000

EDUCATION & PROFESSIONAL DEVELOPMENT

Bachelor of Arts in English | Northwestern University, Evanston, IL, 1996
Pragmatic Marketing Certified, Level III, 2017

RESUME 16: by Skye Berry-Burke, CMRW, CCTC, CRS, CIS, CES • www.skyeisthelimit.ca

LORI WILLIAMS

loriwilliams@email.com • Ottawa, ON K1P 1P1
613-222-6666 • www.linkedin.com/in/loriwilliams

MARKETING EXECUTIVE with ENTREPRENEURIAL EDGE

Seeking to leverage refreshing and creative branding and business innovation to fuel your organization's product launch.

Award-winning Integrated Marketing Communication Strategist, specializing in connecting vision with innovative digital communication solutions to drive sales, build brand image, and secure customer loyalty.

Purposeful problem-solver able to navigate unfamiliar terrain and achieve success in new industries. Open to relocating or telecommuting.

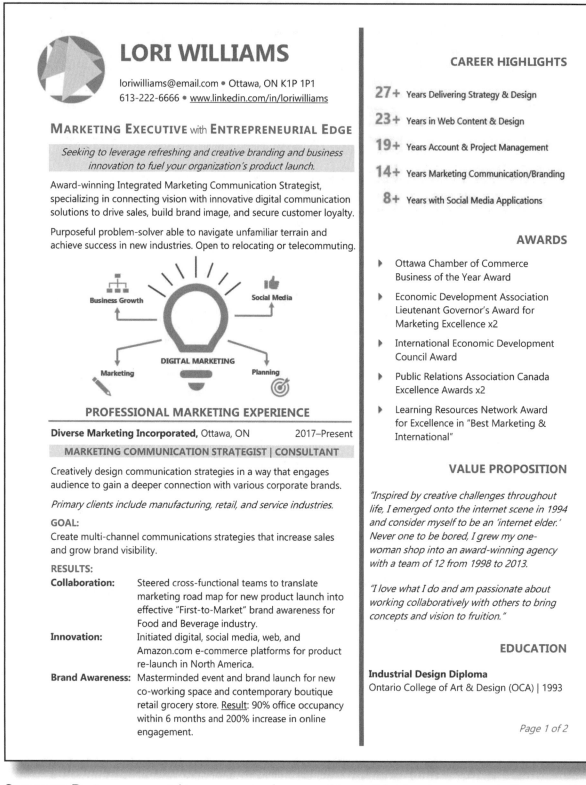

PROFESSIONAL MARKETING EXPERIENCE

Diverse Marketing Incorporated, Ottawa, ON   2017–Present

MARKETING COMMUNICATION STRATEGIST | CONSULTANT

Creatively design communication strategies in a way that engages audience to gain a deeper connection with various corporate brands.

Primary clients include manufacturing, retail, and service industries.

GOAL:
Create multi-channel communications strategies that increase sales and grow brand visibility.

RESULTS:

Collaboration: Steered cross-functional teams to translate marketing road map for new product launch into effective "First-to-Market" brand awareness for Food and Beverage industry.

Innovation: Initiated digital, social media, web, and Amazon.com e-commerce platforms for product re-launch in North America.

Brand Awareness: Masterminded event and brand launch for new co-working space and contemporary boutique retail grocery store. Result: 90% office occupancy within 6 months and 200% increase in online engagement.

CAREER HIGHLIGHTS

27+ Years Delivering Strategy & Design

23+ Years in Web Content & Design

19+ Years Account & Project Management

14+ Years Marketing Communication/Branding

8+ Years with Social Media Applications

AWARDS

▶ Ottawa Chamber of Commerce Business of the Year Award

▶ Economic Development Association Lieutenant Governor's Award for Marketing Excellence x2

▶ International Economic Development Council Award

▶ Public Relations Association Canada Excellence Awards x2

▶ Learning Resources Network Award for Excellence in "Best Marketing & International"

VALUE PROPOSITION

"Inspired by creative challenges throughout life, I emerged onto the internet scene in 1994 and consider myself to be an 'internet elder.' Never one to be bored, I grew my one-woman shop into an award-winning agency with a team of 12 from 1998 to 2013.

"I love what I do and am passionate about working collaboratively with others to bring concepts and vision to fruition."

EDUCATION

Industrial Design Diploma
Ontario College of Art & Design (OCA) | 1993

Page 1 of 2

Strategy: Design an eye-catching resume to showcase this candidate's value as a marketing executive with an entrepreneurial edge. Use dual-column format to place equal emphasis on her skills, awards, and value proposition as well as her practical experience.

LORI WILLIAMS   loriwilliams@email.com • 613-222-6666

ABC Innovation Inc., Telecommute, Ottawa, ON   2013–2016

VP, MARKETING COMMUNICATION & PRODUCT DEVELOPMENT

Recruited to brand ABC and its pioneering geospatial software technology, while simultaneously leveraging founder, Jason Maxx, as a global thought leader in the emerging digital earth industry.

GOAL:

Develop UI/UX design, product marketing, information architecture, and digital integration for the world's first online 3D interactive Digital Earth platform.

RESULTS:

Collaboration: Directed launch execution (media communications, trade shows, content development, and collateral design). Positioned CEO as industry influencer and secured initial $4M corporate investment.

Innovation: Attracted 1,000+ users of web-based analysis and integration tool in less than 3 months, setting ABC technology as global standard.

Brand Awareness: Technology adopted by Canadian Geographic for International Games; implemented in charter schools across Ontario and applied by Federal Geospatial department.

Williams Marketing Group Inc., Ottawa, ON   1998–2013

FOUNDER AND PRESIDENT

Built award-winning marketing group from ground up; grew from a team of 1 to 12 in less than 6 years.

GOAL:

Provide customer intelligence across global product and marketing phases, from ideation to launch and international expansion.

RESULTS:

Collaboration: Consulted on product line/market segment strategy, KPI tracking, B2B and B2C marketing, etc.

Innovation: Orchestrated integrated marketing communication strategy campaign to unite 3 hospitals into 1; attained 80% fundraising goals ($57M) in 1 year. Created direct mail campaign that secured $16M.

Brand Awareness: Captured 500% increase in web hits with award-winning marketing campaign that generated 10% annual student enrollment increase.

Cane & Associates Inc., Ottawa, ON   1994–1997

WEB DESIGNER & PROGRAMMER

Partnered with Google and CBC to lead, design, and program Canada's first award-winning children's educational website: XYZLearning.com.

CLIENT ENDORSEMENTS

"I hired Lori to help me launch my business. Lori is wonderful to work with and exceeded my expectations in increasing my visibility to promote my new business in the community."—S. Walker, XYZ Graphics

"Lori's marketing and communications services really helped my business grow. Her social media marketing skills are exceptional … my recently launched business page delivered new leads and new business in a few short weeks." —W. Smith, Passmore Products

SKILLS & COMPETENCIES

▸ Market Research & Analysis

▸ Product Development & Positioning

▸ Social Media & Digital Strategies

▸ Brand, Identity & Marketing Strategy

▸ P & L, Account & Project Management

▸ Trend Forecasting & Competitive Benchmarking

▸ Advertising Creation & Media Planning

▸ Content Management & Communications

▸ Talent Management & Leadership

▸ Client Acquisition & Retention

▸ Product Launch

▸ Business Turnaround & Rapid Growth

TOOLS & APPLICATIONS

Adobe Suite
Ps ●●●●●●●
Ai ●●●●●●●
Id ●●●●●○○
Ac ●●●●●●○

Social Media
LI ●●●●●●○
TW ●●●●●●●
FB ●●●●●●●
IN ●●●●●●●

Google Products
GA ●●●●●●○
GD ●●●●●●○
GC ●●●●●●●

Microsoft Suite
W ●●●●●●●
PP ●●●●●○○
E ●●●●●●○

RESUME 17: by Wendy Enelow, MRW, CCM, CPRW, JCTC • www.wendyenelow.com

SEAN VARGAS

977-805-9889 | ssvargas3@gmail.com | Dallas, TX | LinkedIn Profile

CLIENT RELATIONSHIP MANAGEMENT EXECUTIVE

International Sales Leadership | Executive Consulting| Account P&L | Cross-Functional Team Leadership

Expert in building and managing multimillion-dollar client relationships that deliver measurable ongoing value. Influence with authority and confidence, establishing critical business relationships with C-level and other top executives and decision makers. Thrive in challenging situations that demand excellence in performance and delivery of aggressive revenue goals.

Diverse industry and market-sector experience globally in Healthcare, Retail, Consumer Products, Banking, Manufacturing, Food & Beverage, Chemical & Petroleum, Hardware & Housewares, and Travel & Transportation.

PROFESSIONAL EXPERIENCE

DELL – US & Worldwide Locations   2001 to Present

High-profile career building and managing some of Dell's most valued customer relationships, leading regional sales and client organizations worldwide, and delivering unprecedented revenue growth. Consistently outperform global competition to position Dell as the preferred solutions provider to industries and companies worldwide. Led sales negotiations and closed multiple client transactions valued at $100M+ throughout Dell career.

Client Director – Aetna Health (Fortune 50) – Connecticut – 2017 to Present
Scope: Aetna has $135B+ in annual revenues | 300K+ employees | 9000+ health clinics nationwide | prescription service provider to major US corporations | full account P&L responsibility

Challenge: To restore and rebuild Aetna Health's business relationship following Dell's divestiture of several top revenue-producing technologies while expanding alliances with Aetna C-level decision makers.

Action: Built powerful relationships with top executives across multiple functions within Aetna, transitioning Dell from IT infrastructure and systems into integrated solutions partner aligned with enterprise strategy.

Results:

- **Generated millions of dollars in new revenues** to Dell through creation of new, high-value revenue streams and business opportunities. Currently projecting 20% growth in new revenues in next 2 years.
- **Expanded Dell's relationship beyond Aetna's IT department** to include partnerships with CHRO (innovative HR analytics solutions), Chief Digital Officer (solutions to support omni-channel strategy to enhance Aetna's customer service and outreach), and Chief Medical Officer (cognitive solutions to combat chronic disease).
- **Built and currently manage/matrix manage** a staff of 10–12 professionals dedicated exclusively to Aetna account in addition to 30+ part-time sales and tech support personnel and 100 project team members.

Client Director – The Home Depot (Fortune 50) – Georgia – 2012 to 2017
Scope: The Home Depot has $75B+ in annual revenues | 175K+ employees | 1200 stores in NA | full account P&L

Challenge: To restore troubled relationship with The Home Depot while simultaneously transitioning from infrastructure and IT sales into higher-value solutions with stronger revenue growth and opportunities.

Action: Earned the trust and confidence of The Home Depot's C-suite and IT executives to introduce new solutions to advance company's operating paradigm and position to achieve/surpass performance goals.

Results:

- **Increased revenues 180%. Sold and delivered the largest transformation project** in client's history with ultimate goal of creating a seamless, multi-channel customer experience. Managed/matrix-managed team of 150+.
- **Enabled 3000% online growth for The Home Depot** by collaborating on next-generation ecommerce site.
- **Introduced solutions that evolved The Home Depot corporate culture,** associate experience, and internal communications, which measurably improved employee retention, productivity, and customer satisfaction.
- **Honored as the "Best of Dell" (one of only 500 in Dell's 350K workforce)** for excellence in delivering client value.

Strategy: Use the Challenge-Action-Results format to clearly define this sales executive's value and contributions throughout a long career with a well-known technology company.

SEAN VARGAS ... 977-805-9889 | ssvargas3@gmail.com   Page 2

Worldwide Client Services Executive – ExxonMobil (Global Fortune 10) – France – 2010 to 2012

Challenge: To expand Dell's services global relationship with ExxonMobil by strengthening client engagement and introducing a new portfolio of consistent and integrated Dell solutions worldwide.

Action: Led worldwide team of business development, sales, and delivery/deployment personnel and resources to meet expanding technology services needs of client organization.

Results:
- **Drove revenue growth of 70% in just 2 years** and positioned Dell as a preferred, top-tier services provider.
- **Delivered new, high-quality services and solutions** to client, allowing them to reduce their total number of suppliers and decrease supplier management requirements, while eliminating Dell's competition.
- **Created consolidated worldwide services agreement and global model** to deliver infrastructure services in each of ExxonMobil's 4 countries (France, Belgium, Italy, US) with an integrated Indian offshore value proposition.

Infrastructure Solutions Leader & Services Transformation Executive – SW Europe – Portugal – 2009 to 2010

Challenge: To drive Dell's services business transformation in Portugal, Spain, France, Italy, The Netherlands, Turkey, Greece, and Egypt and extend into a new global model focused on selling and delivering client-driven infrastructure solutions.

Action: Orchestrated a cross-functional, matrix-managed team of Dell sales, technology, support, and solutions providers to deliver complex customer solutions across multiple markets and industries.

Results:
- **Grew services 20% by expanding and specializing the sales force** while coordinating with Dell development and support teams to create and deploy unique client solutions, further solidifying Dell's leading market position.
- **Honored as one of less than 500 Dell employees worldwide** to receive the 2010 President's Circle Award.

Distribution Sector Leader – Global Technology Services – EMEA – UK – 2007 to 2009
Strengthened regional European business leadership and facilitated cross-functional teams within Dell to develop and deliver fully integrated solutions across the retail, consumer products, and travel and transportation industries.

- **Increased revenues by 40% and created $800M+ of new opportunities** within Europe.
- **Built and expanded key client relationships** with Pepsi, Ralph Lauren, Hershey's, and other key customers.
- **Created strategic partnerships with market leaders** such as Cisco and SAP to design and deploy a joint go-to-market strategy for client engagements across the Europe continent.

SMB & Channels Leader – Global Technology Services – Worldwide – Dell HQ – 2005 to 2007
Leveraged successful US services business model into a global strategy and action plan focused on small and mid-sized clients. Traveled extensively throughout Asia Pacific and Europe to establish low-cost sales channels.

- **Grew services revenues 28%** across all markets globally through creation of new high-volume revenue channels.
- **Won Dell's Profile in Performance Award** for success in new market development, **Hundred Percent Club Award** for outstanding sales performance, and **Team Award** for strong leadership performance.

Highlights of Early Dell Career:
- Increased outbound sales revenues 40% and average transaction 40% for emerging technology ventures.
- Built, trained, mentored, and led teams of up to 90 sales specialists.
- Earned Business Unit Executive, Top Contributor, and Marketing Excellence Awards; Golden Club Honoree.

EDUCATION

BA Degree – University of Texas at Austin – 2001

Dell Professional Development – NextGen for Future Leaders; Services Business Leadership; Leadership Development; Leadership Readiness; Dell Global Sales School Faculty (executive sponsor and mentor for new sales professionals)

RESUME 18: by Kelly Gadzinski, ACRW, CCMC, Registered Corporate Coach • www.kgcareerservices.com

Donald J. Matthews

415-897-6110 ♦ donmatt@gmail.com

Vice President - Sales & Marketing - Rail Transportation

Transformational sales leader with extensive track record of identifying and driving new growth opportunities within the railroad industry, generating multimillion-dollar revenue increases:

United Gear Works	Watlow
Grew new oil & gas business from zero to $4M+ in 1 year.	**Boosted annual sales 65% in 2 years.**

✓ Repeatedly provided strategic leadership to expand into adjacent markets.

✓ Known for breaking down organizational silos and building top-performing sales teams.

✓ Strengthened and communicated brand value through innovative marketing strategies.

✓ Negotiated numerous transportation government contracts and formed exceptional partner relationships.

Leadership Expertise

Strategic Sales Planning & Execution	New Business Development	People & Talent Development
P&L Management & Budgeting	Sales Team Building & Leadership	Entrepreneurial Leadership
Marketing & Brand Strategy	Customer Relationship Management	C-Level Presentations
Key Account Management	Relationship Building & Partnerships	Contract Negotiations

Professional Experience

United Gear Works, Columbus, OH
Major supplier of heavy-duty OEM and aftermarket components for transit, railroad, mining, steel, construction, and general industrial applications.

VP of Sales & Marketing – Transit, Mining, Oil & Gas, Industrial & Locomotive (2019 to present)
Director of Sales – Transit (2016 to 2019)

Hired to lead Transit business unit with $40M annual sales and 10 direct/6 indirect reports. Challenged to ensure continued growth in existing markets while generating new sales in untapped oil & gas market.

Orchestrated and drove strategic plan for massive consolidation of business units that reduced operational redundancies, eliminated superfluous staff, increased customer satisfaction, and boosted revenue. **Promoted to manage all business units within sales organization with $60M total annual sales.**

- Skyrocketed organic growth of oil & gas business through strategic sales leadership, winning $2M new business in 1 year. Formed new business unit to manage rapid growth.

- Built high-performing sales team that grew sales $5M in 4 years.

- Led negotiation of multimillion-dollar settlement with major US transit authority, involving restitution payment and contract expansion that yielded a profitable return.

- Renegotiated contract with largest client, offsetting losses incurred from 30% government-issued tariff.

- Reduced sales quote approval process from 18 days to 24 hours in 12 months through implementation of the USA (understand, simplify, and automate) principle.

- Identified and solidified partnership with European hot works manufacturer, enabling the sale of steel wheels that generated $2M+ new revenue.

Watlow, Littleton, CO
Leading producer of engineered and catalytic heat for oil, gas, nuclear, freight, and transit railroad industries.

Business Development Manager – North America (2013 to 2016)
Collaborated with senior leadership to frame roadmap and strategy to grow business across North America by expanding US Class 1 railroad client base. Recruited, hired, and trained top multilingual sales talent.

Strategy: For this sales executive seeking to remain in the rail industry, highlight that very specific industry experience as well as his strong sales and leadership achievements.

Watlow, continued

- Grew annual sales from $4M to $6M in 2 years by driving expansion into target markets in the US, Canada, and Mexico.

- Relocated division of production from US to Canada, reducing freight costs, increasing margins, and improving customer service to Canadian clients.

- Negotiated multiple transportation government contracts that built sustainable profitability.

- Implemented project workflow system that enhanced operating efficiencies and team productivity.

MJD Industries, Cleveland, OH
Sourcing and distribution of obsolete and legacy transit parts for government-funded authorities.

Founder, President & Sales Manager (2006 to 2013)
Built business from the ground up, growing annual revenue to $800K. Garnered new business by creating and executing comprehensive growth strategy that identified and captured large, international clients. Designed and launched company website that streamlined purchasing process and enhanced overall customer experience.

- Recognized for expertise in locating obsolete and legacy transit parts and advising foreign companies on best means for breaking into US transit market.

- Renegotiated $150K inventory purchasing opportunity to $550K deal with industry-leading multinational transportation company through a detailed market value analysis of each product.

- Attained significant market share from largest competitor by delivering product to Alstrom Transportation that put a critical Boston subway line back into commission.

Motion Motor Services, Columbus, OH
Full-service custom manufacturer and motor repair company with $5M annual revenue.

Sales Manager (1999 to 2006)
Transformed inefficient, disorganized operation into a high-performing team of professionals providing impeccable service company-wide. Identified and introduced process improvements across all facets of the organization—marketing, safety, human resources, accounting, and purchasing. Formulated highly competitive sales strategies that quickly expanded customer portfolio and increased profit margins.

- Grew sales 200% ($2M to $4M) in 5 years through innovative sales and marketing initiatives.

- Refined and revamped company brand by overhauling marketing strategy and hiring top sales talent.

- Boosted productivity 85% through equipment upgrades that significantly reduced labor costs.

- Negotiated sale of business for 150% return in 2006.

PRIOR EXPERIENCE includes selling new and used construction equipment for Frontier Machinery Company and Uhaul Equipment Rental. Attained Top 25 company sales representative ranking out of 350 nationally.

Education

Bachelor of Arts, Ohio University, Athens, OH

RESUME 19: by Lucie Yeomans, CPRW, NCOPE, OPNS, CEIC, JCTC, JCDC • www.yourcareerally.com

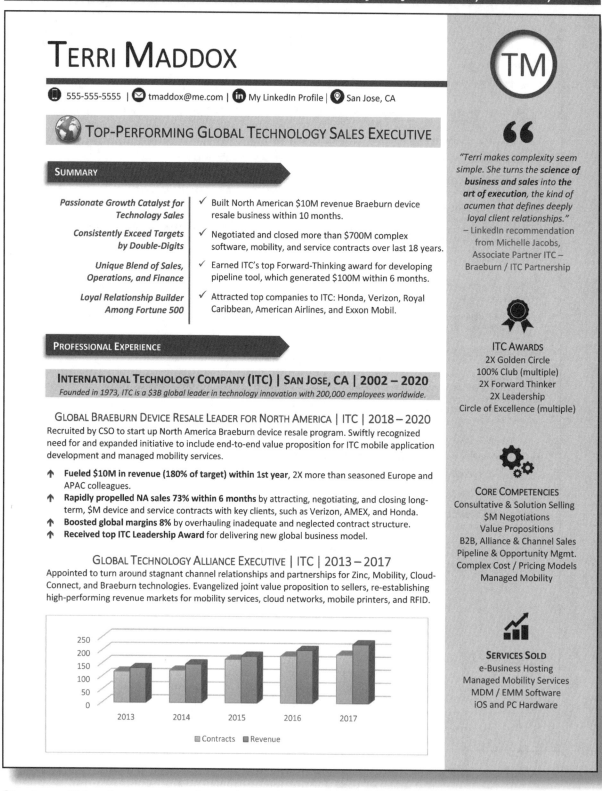

TERRI MADDOX

📱 555-555-5555 | ✉ tmaddox@me.com | in My LinkedIn Profile | 📍 San Jose, CA

🌐 TOP-PERFORMING GLOBAL TECHNOLOGY SALES EXECUTIVE

SUMMARY

Passionate Growth Catalyst for Technology Sales	✓ Built North American $10M revenue Braeburn device resale business within 10 months.
Consistently Exceed Targets by Double-Digits	✓ Negotiated and closed more than $700M complex software, mobility, and service contracts over last 18 years.
Unique Blend of Sales, Operations, and Finance	✓ Earned ITC's top Forward-Thinking award for developing pipeline tool, which generated $100M within 6 months.
Loyal Relationship Builder Among Fortune 500	✓ Attracted top companies to ITC: Honda, Verizon, Royal Caribbean, American Airlines, and Exxon Mobil.

PROFESSIONAL EXPERIENCE

INTERNATIONAL TECHNOLOGY COMPANY (ITC) | SAN JOSE, CA | 2002 – 2020
Founded in 1973, ITC is a $3B global leader in technology innovation with 200,000 employees worldwide.

GLOBAL BRAEBURN DEVICE RESALE LEADER FOR NORTH AMERICA | ITC | 2018 – 2020
Recruited by CSO to start up North America Braeburn device resale program. Swiftly recognized need for and expanded initiative to include end-to-end value proposition for ITC mobile application development and managed mobility services.

↑ **Fueled $10M in revenue (180% of target) within 1st year**, 2X more than seasoned Europe and APAC colleagues.
↑ **Rapidly propelled NA sales 73% within 6 months** by attracting, negotiating, and closing long-term, $M device and service contracts with key clients, such as Verizon, AMEX, and Honda.
↑ **Boosted global margins 8%** by overhauling inadequate and neglected contract structure.
↑ **Received top ITC Leadership Award** for delivering new global business model.

GLOBAL TECHNOLOGY ALLIANCE EXECUTIVE | ITC | 2013 – 2017
Appointed to turn around stagnant channel relationships and partnerships for Zinc, Mobility, Cloud-Connect, and Braeburn technologies. Evangelized joint value proposition to sellers, re-establishing high-performing revenue markets for mobility services, cloud networks, mobile printers, and RFID.

(Bar chart: years 2013–2017 showing Contracts and Revenue)

> ❝ *"Terri makes complexity seem simple. She turns the **science of business and sales** into **the art of execution**, the kind of acumen that defines deeply loyal client relationships."*
> – LinkedIn recommendation from Michelle Jacobs, Associate Partner ITC – Braeburn / ITC Partnership

ITC AWARDS
2X Golden Circle
100% Club (multiple)
2X Forward Thinker
2X Leadership
Circle of Excellence (multiple)

CORE COMPETENCIES
Consultative & Solution Selling
$M Negotiations
Value Propositions
B2B, Alliance & Channel Sales
Pipeline & Opportunity Mgmt.
Complex Cost / Pricing Models
Managed Mobility

SERVICES SOLD
e-Business Hosting
Managed Mobility Services
MDM / EMM Software
iOS and PC Hardware

Strategy: Tailor the resume to align with specific areas of interest for this top-performing sales executive as she seeks her next position. Include numerous unique design elements to demonstrate her ability to capture her audience's interest, just as in sales.

TERRI MADDOX

Page 2 of 2 | 555-555-5555 | tmaddox@me.com

GLOBAL TECHNOLOGY ALLIANCE EXECUTIVE (CONTINUED)

Select Operational Accomplishments

- **Enabled 200+ key ITC sellers** within 6 months.
- **Increased mobility evangelists 33%** in first year, thwarting aggressive global competition.
- **Penetrated untapped Zinc device revenue stream** by collaborating with legal and procurement departments to develop maintenance SOW templates for ITC sellers.
- **Slashed contract completion from 20 to 10 days** by creating maintenance special bid process.
- **Stood up governance models** and global, executive pipeline cadence reviews.

MARKETING AND COMMUNICATIONS OPERATIONS SR. MANAGER | ITC | 2010 – 2013
MARKETING AND COMMUNICATIONS OPERATIONS MANAGER | ITC | 2009 – 2010

Quickly promoted 1 year after being hired as only sales executive to move into marketing operations; recognized for transforming marketing metrics to align with business sales targets.

Performance Snapshot

- ↑ **Generated $100M with initial launch** by leading global team of interns in design, development, and deployment of complex business analytics and pipeline tool worldwide.
- ↑ **Delivered $705M revenue and 57% year-to-year growth** through aggressive promotions.
- ↑ **Realized 11-point improvement** in marketing campaign contribution to ITS revenue.
- ↑ **Drove coverage improvements from 30% to 80%** within 5 months for key marketing programs.

Highest ITC Honors

- 2009, 2012: Leadership Award
- 2010: Forward-Thinking Award (Highest ITC award)

CLIENT SOLUTION EXECUTIVE, E-BUSINESS HOSTING SERVICES | ITC | 2000 – 2009

Established engagement processes and led teams to final contract with industrial and distribution clients for ITC's e-business hosting continuum of services, including colocation, managed services, custom solutions, and Application on Demand (AoD) opportunities.

Performance Snapshot

- ↑ **2009: Influenced $8M e-business** hosting contract extension for BP.
- ↑ **2008: Achieved 107% of $16.5M signings** (TCV) quota.
- ↑ **2005: Finished year with 118% of signings** quota ($24M) and 158% of revenue quota ($2.5M).

Highest ITC Honors

- 2007: ITC 100 Percent Club Winner
- 2006: ITC Golden Circle Award (ITC's highest sales award)
- 2005: ITC Golden Circle Award
- 2003: Risk Taking / Client Satisfaction Award (turned around dissatisfied key customer)

EDUCATION

MBA (Finance Concentration) | UC Davis | Davis, CA
BS in Business Administration (Finance) | Santa Clara University | Santa Clara, CA

BOARD OF DIRECTORS

Board of Directors, Treasurer | Rapid Find Technology | 2016 – Present
Board of Directors, Chairman | AT&I Security Systems | 2010 – Present

"Terri's passion and enthusiasm for business is reflected in her relationships with clients, partners, and team members. She has outstanding sales and leadership skills, consistently making her a top contributor. She is always on the leading edge and is quick to adapt to different areas of the business and learning new skills to serve clients and deliver outstanding results."

– LinkedIn recommendation from Stephen Jost, ITC Sales EVP

PUBLIC SPEAKING
Invited guest speaker for MBA candidates, featuring annual speaking engagements.

UC Davis
University of San Francisco
UC Berkeley
Babson College San Francisco
Santa Clara University

"Terri is a leader who will always ensure that the job gets done no matter what seemingly insurmountable challenges are in the way."

– LinkedIn recommendation from Allison Brown, Director, ITC Partnerships & Alliances at ITC

RESUME 20: *by Louise Garver, ACRW, CERM, CJSS, CPRW, CPBS, CCMC • www.careerdirectionsllc.com*

RYAN MCALISTER

Orinda, CA 94563 | (555) 555-5555 | ryanmcalister@mac.com | <u>LinkedIn</u>

CHIEF MARKETING OFFICER

Software and Cloud Services, including B2B SaaS, Big Data, Martech, and Fintech

Market Strategy & Analytics • Go-To-Market • Corporate Branding • Product Marketing
Product Management • Public Relations • Digital Marketing • ABM • Demand Generation • Lead Generation

Game changer who set the stage for exponential revenue growth, an IPO, and 5 successful exits by defining brand and unique competitive positioning through world-class marketing strategy and execution.

Marketing leader partnering with CEOs to propel recognized enterprise brands: Sybase, Morgan Stanley (MSCI) and VC-backed startups. **Consistently grew revenues and prepared companies for acquisition/IPO** through branding, insightful target market expansion, and go-to-market strategies based on fluency with technical products, customer insights, and analytics. Mobilized company-wide launches, initiatives, and teams with hundreds of professionals. Inspired customer-centric marketing, product development, and sales. Top 5 MBA; BS in computer science.

CAREER MILESTONES

- Initiated cloud strategy and account-based marketing program (ABM) that produced 8-digit revenue growth in just 9 months as CMO at TechOne.

- Drove 8-digit new SaaS product growth in a mature market as CMO at a $350M Fintech company within FIRON (DECI).

- Led 325% CAGR in alliances and promoted to direct all marketing for $100M+ analytics business during Varden's rise from $150M to $1B in 5 years.

EXPERIENCE & IMPACT

CHIEF MARKETING OFFICER   2016–2019

TechOne, San Francisco, CA   *Global leader in email solutions; mid-8-figure ARR*

Recruited to jump-start growth and expand customer base for the B2B enterprise software company. Built an advanced digital marketing function with the full stack of marketing automation, analytics, optimization, attribution, and all processes and technologies required to understand customer behavior and monitor ROI of marketing spend. Grew marketing team from 8 to 16.

➢ **Renamed/rebranded company and launched SaaS API email product that grew $10M+ in 9 months.** Uncovered product/market mismatch and won Board approval to transition from enterprise software to cloud offering.

➢ **Transformed marketing into an ROI-driven, digital organization and primary source of 67% of sales pipeline.**

➢ **Doubled new customer logos in 2 years and dramatically increased the addressable market from $100M to $1B+.** Expanded customer base (LinkedIn, Twitter, Comcast) to smaller and mid-size companies such as banks, publishers, and internet providers.

SR. VICE PRESIDENT / VICE PRESIDENT OF MARKETING & PRODUCT MANAGEMENT   2011–2016

NUCommerce (acquired by Naron for $225M), Agoura Hills, CA (2014–2016)
Sport Portal (acquired by Go Media within 9 months of hire), San Francisco, CA (2013–2014)
Sergen, Inc. (acquired by DataDrive), Santa Clara, CA (2011–2012)

Positioned a series of early/mid-stage VC-backed companies for successful exit/acquisition. Management scope: customer research, value proposition, corporate identity, positioning, product engineering, product launch, demand generation, and pricing. Directed staffs of 4–20. Served as CTO, as needed, and oversaw Agile development process.

Strategy: Position him as a game-changing CMO while avoiding the perception of a "job hopper" by stacking, under a single 5-year time frame, 3 jobs with startups that were quickly acquired.

Ryan McAlister | (555) 555-5555 | Email   Page 2

➢ **Sparked 40% growth for NUCommerce,** partnering with CEO to transform company from a chat provider to a suite of ecommerce conversion marketing solutions. Instituted account-based marketing program, yielding 20% prospect conversion rate. Generated $3M/year of incremental revenue from new products.

➢ **Uniquely positioned Sergen (early-stage analytics company) to avoid 20 competitors in the $500M MySQL data warehouse market. Helped CEO raise $20M capital.** Created brand and built worldwide buzz via social media launch that attracted top customers. Personally sold first 3 customers. Built MRD and 2-year product plan.

➢ **Positioned an advertising tech company (Sport Portal) for quick sale by transitioning software assets into an online advertising SaaS solution rebranded as DataDrive.** Major new customers: Time and CBS Interactive.

CHIEF MARKETING OFFICER / MEMBER OF DECI OPERATING COMMITTEE	**2005–2011**
VICE PRESIDENT OF GLOBAL MARKETING – FIRON (acquired by DECI)	**2003–2005**

FIRON (DECI), Berkeley, CA   *$350M financial services SaaS and data provider*

Upgraded global marketing organization for $150M public risk management software company prior to acquisition by DECI. Led global brand strategy and marketing integration of FIRON into DECI. Grew staff from 14 to 20.

➢ **Generated $2.5M/year of net new revenue captured from largest competitor;** defined and executed channel distribution strategy (partnership with Factset) that halted double-digit customer attrition rate.

➢ **Achieved 8-digit growth for the SaaS product in a mature market;** drove customer research and product-line rationalization that resulted in 50% cancellation reduction and $10M in annual product cost savings.

➢ **Doubled net new business in the hedge fund space** through product refinements that matched market needs.

SENIOR VICE PRESIDENT OF MARKETING	**1999–2003**

Varden, Inc., Mountain View, CA   *#1 enterprise information portal company*

Brought on board as first marketing executive for a startup provider of business intelligence tools. Repositioned and rebranded company as an enterprise information portal (EIP). Leadership scope: product marketing, strategy, alliances, branding, lead generation, and press and analyst relations. Authored S1 filing; developed and participated in roadshow presentations with CEO and CFO; served as the brand's spokesperson and storyteller. Managed/developed staff of 45.

➢ **Propelled company from launch to 10 consecutive quarters of growth and $46M IPO** through marketing, brand, and product leadership for a new category—**earning company Gartner Group Magic Quadrant Leader rank.**

DIRECTOR OF DATA WAREHOUSING AND BUSINESS INTELLIGENCE	**1992–1999**

Sanro (an SED company), Emeryville, CA (1996–1999)   *$1B enterprise software and services company*

Promoted to define, market, and manage flagship data warehousing product; led company's largest product launch that year, coordinating the efforts of hundreds. Oversaw 4 data warehousing products after successful launch. Defined and prioritized product roadmaps. Managed team of 27 in PR, analyst relations, corporate marketing, market research, product management, and product marketing.

➢ **Pioneered and launched industry-leading new product category that ignited 2 years of 100%+ sales growth** for the data warehousing product line and the flagship product (Sybase IQ).

GROUP PRODUCT MANAGER, NEW MEDIA (1993–1996)

Promoted from Senior Product Line Manager & Alliance Manager (1992–1993) to revitalize an underperforming HP channel/product line and **drove revenues from $3M to $55M in 2 years.**

EDUCATION AND CERTIFICATION

Master of Business Administration – Boston University
Bachelor of Science, Computer Science – New York University
Certified Scrum Product Owner – Scrum Alliance, Inc.

Sarah Gottlieb

sarahgottlieb@gmail.com   404-654-4567   LinkedIn Profile

SALES EXECUTIVE

Product & Service Sales ▪ SMB to Fortune 500 C-Suite
Consultative, Relationship-Based Selling ▪ Multi-Year Recurring Revenue Contracts

Uncovering the "why" to build rapport, drive sales, and become a trusted partner in customers' success.

A top performer in every sales role, repeatedly promoted to revive faltering territories and train, mentor, and inspire teams of sales professionals.

✓ **#1 Sales Representative of the Year as a rookie—a first for the company—and repeated in year 2.**
✓ **Consistent President's Club achievement (top 15%) and frequent Diamond Level (top 5%).**
✓ **3-for-3 record of dramatic sales turnarounds in progressively larger territories/regions.**

Expert in every stage of consultative sales—prospecting, uncovering needs and buying motivators, building customer rapport and relationships, proposing the right solutions, closing the deal—and able to quickly build sales skills of underperforming and inexperienced sales reps. **Competitive, collaborative, and wired to reach ever-higher goals.**

PROFESSIONAL EXPERIENCE

AMERICAN ASSISTANCE CORP. *($6.2B publicly traded business services company; NYSE:AMAC)*   2009–Present

DIRECTOR OF SALES, Southeast US (2016–Present) ▪ **TRAINING DIRECTOR, Southeast US** (2014–2016)

Tapped to take on third turnaround challenge in 3 years, focused on staffing, training, and culture shift to deliver best regional results in company history. Promoted to lead Training and then Sales for territory initially comprising 60 sales reps and $180M revenue. Adapted leadership style to Southeastern culture and equipped team to reach aggressive goals by instilling new confidence and competence.

✓ **Sales Results**
- More than doubled territory revenue from $180M to $390M; +20% projected for 2020.
- Sent 20 Sales Partners to President's Club in 2019—more than ever in the history of the Southeast region (all years combined) and 10X number from the region in the prior 2 years.

Revenue $180M to $390M

✓ **Leadership Performance**
- #4 out of 26 Sales Directors and #3 out of 12 Training Directors in company.
- Grew sales force from 60 to 120 reps while reducing turnover from 42% to less than 15%. Recruited for intrinsic sales skills and winning attitude; trained heavily to build skills of both new and existing staff.

SALES MANAGER, Dallas Location (2013–2014)

Delivered rapid sales turnaround, leading strategic sales operations for a team of 11 sales and 2 support staff. Transformed internal culture, restructured sales team, actively recruited new culture-fit talent, emphasized training and mentoring, and achieved results within first quarter—and sustained for year-long tenure and beyond.

✓ **Sales Results**
- Closed sales 11% above goal in first quarter while understaffed by 4 reps.
- Ended year at 32% above goal and 71% above prior year.
- Improved rep productivity 62%.

Team Productivity +62%

✓ **Leadership Performance**
- #2 out of 24 Regional Managers in FY14.
- Sales Manager of the Quarter—Q2, Q3.
- Honed recruiting skills and process to identify and attract talent. Created ideal hiring profile, enabling rapid selection and quick ramp-up.
- Built a stable of high-potential top performers: 4 of 7 have since been promoted.

Strategy: Create a quick read of very impressive and consistent sales achievements by segmenting bullets into small groups, writing concise (mostly 1-line) achievement statements, and adding a graphic that instantly conveys the notable successes of each position.

Sarah Gottlieb   sarahgottlieb@gmail.com ▪ 404-654-4567

SALES MANAGER, FACILITY SERVICES, Amarillo Location (2012–2013)

Promoted to lead turnaround of underperforming sales team, delivered dramatic results in 1 year: +215% sales, +253% sales rep productivity. Inspired, motivated, and mentored team of 8 sales representatives. Trained in fundamental sales skills and set ambitious and unifying team goal: "Every Rep to President's Club … No Rep Left Behind."

✓ **Sales Results**

- Galvanized sales: from 17% under goal (2012) to 77% above (2013).
- 100% of sales team achieved President's Club (top 15% company-wide).

Sales +215% in 1 Year

✓ **Leadership Performance**

- #1 of 36 Managers in the region, 3 out of 4 quarters.
- #1 Sales Manager in the corporation—Q2, Q4, and FY13.
- Diamond Level (top 5%), FY13.
- Transformed underperformers to high-potential sales leaders: 5 of original 7 reps have been promoted and 6 remain with the company.

COPIER SALES REPRESENTATIVE, Houston Location (2011–2012)

Top 5% in sales company-wide for 3 of 4 quarters in first year in Copier Sales. Mastered consultative selling to close multi-year recurring-revenue contracts with businesses from single shop to Fortune 500.

✓ **Sales Results**

- #2 of 140 Sales Reps in Northeast Region.
- President's Club—Diamond Level (top 5% in company)—for 3 quarters and for the year.

#2 in Region, Top 5% in Company

OUTSIDE SALES REPRESENTATIVE, FACILITY SERVICES, Oklahoma City Location (2009–2011)

#1 Sales Representative in the company as a rookie—a first for AMAC. Brought discipline, persistence, and rapport-building skills to the challenge of driving sales of facility products and services to every type and every size of business. Achieved numerous company "firsts" and other distinctions.

✓ **Sales Results**

- Company-wide Rookie of the Year, 2009; reached 187% of requirement for President's Club.
- #1 Sales Representative of the Year, 2009—first time achieved by a rookie at Cintas.
- #1 Sales Representative in the company 2010—2 successive years—first time achieved at Cintas.
- Highest volume ever installed for a Facility Services Sales Representative—2 straight years.
- Singled out by AMAC President to teach winning tactics to representatives across US and Canada.

#1 Sales Rep in Company 2 Straight Yrs

PRIOR

REGIONAL SALES REPRESENTATIVE, Oklahoma Copy Systems, Inc. (2005–2009): Built sales territory from less than $300K to $1.5M+ in 18 months and delivered >20% growth every year thereafter.

EDUCATION
Bachelor of Science, Communications (2005)
UNIVERSITY OF OKLAHOMA, Norman, OK

SLOANE PETERSON

New York, NY 10123 • (212) 867-5309 • sloanepeterson@gmail.com • linkedin.com/in/sloanepeterson

CLIENT SERVICES DIRECTOR | FUTURE VP OF BUSINESS DEVELOPMENT
STRATEGIC BUSINESS DEVELOPMENT—HIGH-IMPACT CLIENT RESULTS

Innovative business executive with 10+ years of experience leading teams to achieve explosive sales for clinical diagnostic laboratory testing services. Proven record of performance in driving new market-share growth, retaining and acquiring new clients, and forging relationships with vendors and executive partners.

✓ **Influential leader with progressive business ideas** and passion for change management to improve processes and impact through effective communication.

✓ **Transformation driver** of major initiative that lowered contract costs 45% and boosted client retention 92%.

✓ **Market growth champion** who captured record $20M contract with a long-targeted account.

✓ **Entrepreneurial spirit in growing teams from the ground up** with big sales wins in less than 18 months.

KEY PROFICIENCIES & AREAS OF EXPERTISE

Strategic & Tactical Planning | Risk Management | Budget Development | Leadership Training & Development |
Process Improvement | Quality Assurance | Profit & Loss Management | Relationship Building | Internal Controls

PROFESSIONAL EXPERIENCE

Director of Client Services | **MERCY ON ME DIAGNOSTICS,** New York, NY (2014–Present)
Regional company with $400M annual revenues, 25 laboratories/offices, and 1,000+ employees.

Direct 166 phlebotomists, 20 account managers, and 15 sales representatives in 19 states. Achieved profit-sharing within 18 months of advancement into senior leadership role.

❖ **Implemented cutting-edge client management software system** that maximized conflict resolution and reduced complaints by 17%.

❖ **Streamlined reporting systems,** resulting in 28% increased client communications across all departments with 14% reduction in employee response time.

❖ **Built and led 150+ member phlebotomy department,** including management team and territory structure, from ground up.

❖ **Overhauled corporate policies and procedures** in 3 key departments: sales, client service, and phlebotomy. Slashed employer turnover rates by 48%.

SUCCESS SNAPSHOT	
92%	Total client retention
45%	Reduced vendor sales contract costs
$340K	Annual company savings
36%	Average revenue growth in first 18 months
#2	Highest achieving sales manager
$20M	Lap Corp deal acquired
$1M	Revenue produced in 2nd year

Regional Sales Manager | **CENTRAL PARK LABORATORY INC.,** New York City, NY (2007–2014)
Start-up laboratory services company with 100+ employees and $15M revenues.

Promoted to Regional Sales Manager from Account Sales Executive after 10 months of hire due to exceptional sales performance. Supervised 10 account executives and led sales team in 4 states with direct reporting to CEO.

❖ **Deployed multi-regional training program** in underperforming areas of 5 counties and 2 states.

❖ **Aggressively pursued competitor clientele** in region where competitor held 95% market share. Captured 40% of market share in less than 1 year.

❖ **Launched 4 new products and seized $750K revenue opportunity** in 8-month span by demonstrating product advantages to competitor clients through consultative sales approach.

❖ **Maintained ranking as #1 Sales & Account Executive** for 10 consecutive months.

EDUCATION

Bachelor of Science in Animal Science, 2007 – North Carolina State University

Strategy: Position this top performer for advancement in her company (note "Future VP" language in headline) by creating a concise 1-page resume with a "success snapshot" that emphasizes key results in an eye-catching format.

Thomas Richards

512.888.6969 | trichards@gmail.com | LinkedIn

Vice President of Sales, Americas

ENTERPRISE SOFTWARE | CYBERSECURITY SOLUTIONS | DIGITAL TRANSFORMATION

High-impact sales leader who elevates team performance, drives exceptional growth, and scales operations for repeatable results.

✓ **Track record of sales transformation and new business growth:** Rebuilt teams and turned around underperforming businesses at Brand Co, Big Co, and New Tech; started up and grew new Brand Co business to $250M in <2 years.

✓ **Committed servant leadership with proven business impact:** Hire, develop, align, and enable teams to deliver complex solutions to demanding enterprise customers. Engage, promote, and retain strong talent.

✓ **Strategic focus and operational excellence:** Identify and focus on core issues/opportunities with maximum impact and align teams to address them. Craft repeatable, scalable processes for sustained high performance.

✓ **Collaboration, internally and externally:** Forge exceptional cross-functional relationships at all levels, including with marketing, support, inside sales, and operations, as well as with customer and channel partners.

✓ **Integrity and authenticity:** Communicate and operate with transparency, accountability, and candor.

SELECT AREAS OF EXPERTISE
VALUE SELLING
TEAM BUILDING & LEADERSHIP
BUSINESS DEVELOPMENT
KEY ACCOUNT MANAGEMENT
CHANGE MANAGEMENT
RELATIONSHIP BUILDING
NEGOTIATION
COMMUNICATION

Experience

New Tech (owned by ABC Co) | 2018–2020

VICE PRESIDENT OF SALES, AMERICAS

Recruited by Chief Revenue Officer (former colleague) to transform the sales strategy and organization and drive business with large and very large customers. ($100M business; 65 direct/130 indirect reports)

- Doubled 7-figure deals, increased 6-figure deals by 58%, and improved renewal rates by 10% YOY; opened several new Fortune 500 accounts.
- Restructured go-to-market strategy to simplify points of interaction, drive efficiency, and improve customer and partner coverage.
- Hired new sales leadership team in North and South America and turned over half of sales force (by design) while retaining key talent.
- Invested in "Value Selling" training pilot for North America staff (sales, marketing, and product management), which became the global standard in 2019.

> ✓ **Doubled 7-figure deals**
> ✓ **Major new logos**
> ✓ **Mgmt and sales team overhaul**

Big Co (acquired by XYZ in 2017) | 2015–2018

VICE PRESIDENT OF SALES, SECURITY, AMERICAS

Recruited by former colleague to lead sales organization, with focus on turning around core business (AProduct) and restructuring the entire organization. ($300M, 80 direct/110 indirect reports)

- Within 1 year, revamped AProduct sales strategy and team, stabilized the business, and returned to single-digit growth after years of double-digit declines.
- Spearheaded a "get well" sales motion to stem defections of existing customers, restructured the team and sales motion to focus on ideal new customers, and systematically executed new plans.

> ✓ **Core business turnaround**
> ✓ **40% new business growth**
> ✓ **Merger integration**

Strategy: Quickly and clearly present this candidate's impressive results in every role through strong bullets, selective bold type, and shaded text boxes that highlight key achievements.

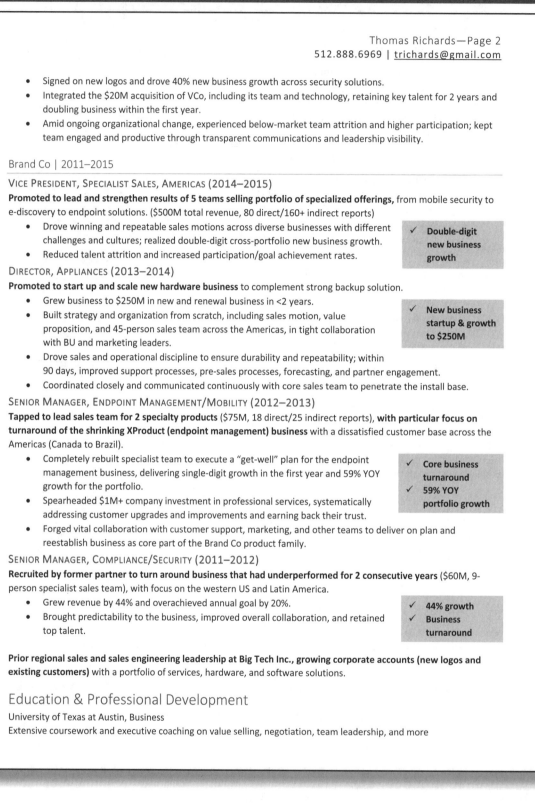

Thomas Richards—Page 2
512.888.6969 | trichards@gmail.com

- Signed on new logos and drove 40% new business growth across security solutions.
- Integrated the $20M acquisition of VCo, including its team and technology, retaining key talent for 2 years and doubling business within the first year.
- Amid ongoing organizational change, experienced below-market team attrition and higher participation; kept team engaged and productive through transparent communications and leadership visibility.

Brand Co | 2011–2015

VICE PRESIDENT, SPECIALIST SALES, AMERICAS (2014–2015)
Promoted to lead and strengthen results of 5 teams selling portfolio of specialized offerings, from mobile security to e-discovery to endpoint solutions. ($500M total revenue, 80 direct/160+ indirect reports)
- Drove winning and repeatable sales motions across diverse businesses with different challenges and cultures; realized double-digit cross-portfolio new business growth.
- Reduced talent attrition and increased participation/goal achievement rates.

> ✓ **Double-digit new business growth**

DIRECTOR, APPLIANCES (2013–2014)
Promoted to start up and scale new hardware business to complement strong backup solution.
- Grew business to $250M in new and renewal business in <2 years.
- Built strategy and organization from scratch, including sales motion, value proposition, and 45-person sales team across the Americas, in tight collaboration with BU and marketing leaders.
- Drove sales and operational discipline to ensure durability and repeatability; within 90 days, improved support processes, pre-sales processes, forecasting, and partner engagement.
- Coordinated closely and communicated continuously with core sales team to penetrate the install base.

> ✓ **New business startup & growth to $250M**

SENIOR MANAGER, ENDPOINT MANAGEMENT/MOBILITY (2012–2013)
Tapped to lead sales team for 2 specialty products ($75M, 18 direct/25 indirect reports), **with particular focus on turnaround of the shrinking XProduct (endpoint management) business** with a dissatisfied customer base across the Americas (Canada to Brazil).
- Completely rebuilt specialist team to execute a "get-well" plan for the endpoint management business, delivering single-digit growth in the first year and 59% YOY growth for the portfolio.
- Spearheaded $1M+ company investment in professional services, systematically addressing customer upgrades and improvements and earning back their trust.
- Forged vital collaboration with customer support, marketing, and other teams to deliver on plan and reestablish business as core part of the Brand Co product family.

> ✓ **Core business turnaround**
> ✓ **59% YOY portfolio growth**

SENIOR MANAGER, COMPLIANCE/SECURITY (2011–2012)
Recruited by former partner to turn around business that had underperformed for 2 consecutive years ($60M, 9-person specialist sales team), with focus on the western US and Latin America.
- Grew revenue by 44% and overachieved annual goal by 20%.
- Brought predictability to the business, improved overall collaboration, and retained top talent.

> ✓ **44% growth**
> ✓ **Business turnaround**

Prior regional sales and sales engineering leadership at Big Tech Inc., growing corporate accounts (new logos and existing customers) with a portfolio of services, hardware, and software solutions.

Education & Professional Development

University of Texas at Austin, Business
Extensive coursework and executive coaching on value selling, negotiation, team leadership, and more

RESUME 24: *by Adrienne Tom, CERM, MCRS, CIS, CES, CCS • www.careerimpressions.ca*

MARK BRYANT

Austin, Texas | 713-777-7123 | mark.bryant@gmail.com

Marketing Director ▪ 20+ Years' Commodity Marketing ▪ Oil & Gas Production
Extract and Maximize Commodity Value to Increase Profitability and Competitiveness

Strategic marketing leader with proven record of determining and enhancing oil & gas commodity value. Champion the solicitation, negotiation, and sale of natural gas, crude oil, and condensate in national markets. Leverage deep market insights and balanced business skills to unearth value opportunities previously undetected. Strong relationship builder.

✓ **Value Creation:** Generated an average of $1.5M in annual revenues over the course of career from the execution of marketing plans, process development, and risk strategies.

✓ **Marketing Strategies:** Developed marketing operations and hedging strategies, for both start-up and established organizations, that boosted business viability and stability.

✓ **Relationship Building:** Fostered extensive industry connections in the LDC and industrial community, including Big Shot Gas Company, Land Corporation, and Potash Inc.

✓ **Commodity Expertise:** Marketed gas, oil, and hydrocarbons across both Western and Eastern US markets. Leveraged land background to provide unique producer insights.

✓ **Business Influence:** Provided direction to senior executives and board of directors on market movements, hedging strategies, acquisitions, and pipeline projects.

> *"Mark is probably one of the sharpest people in business – able to balance relationships with capturing top incremental value."*
>
> *–Vice President, Marketing*

CORE COMPETENCIES

Physical & Financial Trading ▪ Commodity Marketing ▪ Relationship Management ▪ Team Leadership
Contract Negotiations ▪ Performance Management ▪ Market Analysis ▪ Basis Valuation ▪ Transactional Analysis
Executive Communications ▪ Business Development ▪ Risk Assessment & Management ▪ Presentations

LEADERSHIP IN ACTION

BIG TOP PETROLEUM COMPANY – Austin, Texas | 2005 – Present
Upstream oil & gas production company with 200 employees and annual revenues of $800M.

Natural Gas Marketed & Produced:	Condensate and Crude Oil Marketed & Produced:
0.17BCF/day *2004* → **1.0 BCF/day** *2019*	**1,000 BBl/day** *2004*→ **15,000 BBl / day** *2019*

Senior Director, Marketing, 2012 – Present | **Director, Gas Marketing**, 2007 – 2012
Staff Oversight: 2 to 7 | Operating Budget (including compensation): $2.6M

Promoted into progressive positions over 15 years, managing marketing and hedging efforts for all production to increase profitability during periods of growth and change. Currently focused on determining value structure of all production and managing cost control, providing direction and analysis on the market to CFO, CEO, and Board to support business decisions. Negotiate transport, marketing, gathering, and processing arrangements for all commodities across a wide market spectrum. Build effective, long-term relationships with customers across the US. Direct marketing team.

VALUE DELIVERY:

- **Booked $21M in 2019 on 100,000 MMBtu/day of physical transactions** by convincing executives to diminish exposure to demand charges on Major Express Pipeline. Implemented net-back transactions that provided simulated transport between gas source and delivery point.
  - → Took capacity of Major Express Pipeline in 2011 with 0.29 BCFd of capacity and 700,000 MMBtu/day of marketed production, with nearly 50% production burdened by demand charges.
- **Produced $25.5M in revenue** by renegotiating in-field processing. Eliminated costly contracts, extracting value to generate income from processing fees paid to company.
- **Increased transport revenue $8M each year for 6 years** while producing on Major Express Pipeline.
- **Created net incremental value of $1.6M** by selling gas into declining market with a narrowing basis.

Strategy: Use structure and format—shaded boxes and bold headings—to call out key facts and segment rich career achievements into manageable sections. Balance detailed summary section with a powerful endorsement that also adds a human touch.

Mark Bryant | 713-777-7123 | mark.bryant@gmail.com | Page 2

Big Top Petroleum continued...

PROCESS DEVELOPMENT & MARKETING STRATEGIES:

- **Developed marketing program to take advantage of production in new ABC region.** Over a 90-day period built a marketing effort that placed ~65% of production with the ultimate consumer at increased incremental values.
- **Lowered risk and increased assurance on commodity revenues** by creating a process to monitor market exposure and determine creditworthiness of counterparties.
- **Created a framework for executives to effectively initiate and value hedges.** Developed and installed hedging policies and procedures, enabling hedging placement using NYMEX and basis swaps.
- **Shortened timing for connecting wells from 3 weeks to 3 days** while improving connection performance in the field by introducing a more systematic and standardized manner of development.
- **Shifted to reactive market movement approach, on a short-term basis,** enabling pragmatic rig contracts and releases. Developed automated institutional data set to support budgetary decision-making.

Manager, Natural Gas Marketing, 2005 – 2007

Stepped in to manage marketing program, developing and implementing marketing and hedging plans to expand customer base, contracts, and overall commodity value. Provided market analysis and recommendations to CFO. Developed relationships with numerous producers. Initiated and actively traded financial instruments.

HIGHLIGHTS:

- **Expanded customer contracts from original 12 to over 100,** initiating relationships with utilities and industrial end-use customers in a previously untapped western market to grow incremental commodity value.
- **Instituted company's first internal financial hedging policy,** allowing application of financial instruments to effectively hedge exposure to price movements in natural gas, crude oil, and basis.
- **Enhanced marketing and business data accuracy** by securing improved, automated tools and software that reduced errors, effectively captured nominations, and raised performance monitoring.

EARLIER CAREER HISTORY

Dexter Oil Company | Manager, Gas Marketing, 1997 – 2005
Oil Company of California| Senior Gas Marketing Representative, 1992 – 1997

HIGHLIGHTS:

- **Identified and secured new markets for 2 multinational organizations,** placing commodities competitively by prioritizing beneficial markets.
- **Initiated and implemented marketing program** to transition equity production advantage and strategic position on major mid-continent pipes at increased margins into the LDC and industrial market.
- In both companies, **transformed suite of customers from 100% third-party marketers to just 25%.**
- **Captured higher return on value**, increasing commodity price obtained by up to $0.05/MMBtu with the average return at $0.015/MMBtu.
- **Built exploration prospects** into merchantable assets and actively sought out and sold prospects in open market.

EDUCATION

Bachelor of Science, Business Administration – University of Texas

CHAPTER 6

Technology, Engineering, and Science

- Senior IT Lead
- Network Engineering Manager
- VP Technology
- VP Research and Development
- IT Services Manager
- Director of Consulting Delivery
- Telecommunications Director, Internet of Things (IoT)
- IT Director / Senior Program Manager
- Director of Media Operations
- Engineering Manager
- Engineering Business Leader

RESUME 25: *by Lisa K. McDonald, CPRW, CSBA • www.careerpolish.com*

SAM OCEAN

Albany, NY | 555-555-5555 | SamOcean01@gmai.com | www.LinkedIn.com/in/SamOcean

SENIOR IT LEAD DESKTOP SUPPORT SERVICES

Deliver exceptional customer experience. Troubleshoot, diagnose, and resolve complex PC/LAN issues. Mentor team to integrate hardware, software, systems, applications, and solutions that meet client needs and requirements.

BUSINESS VALUE: Multiple-award-winning IT support and operations expert who has repeatedly exceeded corporate and personal goals throughout 20+ year career. Constant learner, invigorated by challenges and meeting the needs of a diverse organization. Excel at working with technology at the client level and spearheading projects that meet client goals. Identify and solve for true end goals through active listening, data collection. and strategic planning.

Client Service & Process Improvement Champion. YOY Meaningful Cost & Time Savings. Annual Benefits:

$63+k Saved	$94+k Cut	1k+ Avoided	40% Boost	44% Surge	18% Slashed
with reverse logistics & Dell paid program	in inventory, parts & labor costs	vendor & contractor hours & costs	in capability with shared tools	in call volume with no added costs/staff	in downtime with pre-emptive program

LEADERSHIP VALUE: Inclusive, shoulder-to shoulder leader. Empower team members through respect, training, mentorship, and collaboration. Inspire, propel staff growth by creating professional development incubator environment.

96% Staff Retention	83% Staff Promoted	6x Award Winner	5 M&As
Over 18-year leadership career for team of up to 8.	into high-level and leadership positions within company	for outstanding performance, leadership, and cost management	Critical in chartering enterprise integrations

EXPERTISE: Customized IT Support | System Deployment | Logistics & Resource Allocation | Customer Service Compliance | Troubleshooting | Process Improvement | Operations | Cloud Environments | Project Management Alliance Building | Leadership | Cost Savings | Compliance | Team Development & Retention | Mergers & Acquisition

Technology: Cosmic Software Distribution & Installation | Remote System Support Tools SSCM, RDP
Operational Systems: Win 7 to Win 10 | Win 311 to Win 10 | Office Suite 2016 | Enterprise MDM | Lync | Skype
Infrastructure: WK: TCP\IP | WK: DHCP, Firewalls, VPN | WK: DNS, Virtualization

CAREER SNAPSHOT:

FIELDS HOLM CORPORATION (Previously Crane Olsen) 1997–PRESENT

Support 6,000 Tier 1 / Tier 2 Clients | Team Size: 8+ | Manage $300,000 Assets & $1M in Inventory

Senior PC/LAN Analyst 4 (2012–Present) | **PC/LAN Analyst 3** (2006–2012)

PC/LAN Analyst 2 (2002–2006) | **Specialist Lead, Assistant Vice President** (1997–2002)

EDUCATION & CERTIFICATIONS

Information Technology Degree, Northerner College
SACM trained | Certifications: A+ | DELL PREMIER | LENOVO SYSTEMS

Strategy: Segment and highlight this candidate's business value and leadership value with a bold design that makes his numerous contributions instantly visible—and avoids typecasting him for his long career with a conservative company not known for IT innovation.

CAREER HISTORY & IMPACT

FIELDS HOLM CORPORATION (Previously Crane Olsen) 1997–PRESENT

Top-ranking leader and founder of specialized technical support team catering to Securities Division and Trading Floor.

Orchestrate team's activities with diagnosis, troubleshooting, installations, logistics, decommissioning, relocation, and imaging. Coordinate new-hire onboarding for hardware, software, operating systems, applications, and networks. Team also supports Technologies Services, Treasury, International, Alternate Lending, and Finance Groups.

Senior PC/LAN Analyst 4 (2012–Present)

$120+k in Costs Savings/Reduction | 100% Data Compliance | Top Performance Awards: Leader & Individual Performer

- Completing Windows 10 deployment and reimaging initiative of 100k+ units; on target to meet 6-month deadline.
- Fuel engineering, network, server deployment, and Helpdesk teams' project success by loaning staff for tasks.
- Assist disaster recovery team in testing functionality and maintaining equipment.
- Provide extensive training to ensure staff maintains highest degree of knowledge and proficiency in equipment imaging/building, Blade technologies (Cloud environment), and reverse logistics.
- Groomed staff for career growth: 15 of 18 promoted to leaders across server and deployment teams.
- Achieved 100% compliance, recording zero data retention violations for desktop/laptop decommissioning process.
- Garnered awards for process reform leadership, staff proficiency maximization, and overall enterprise contribution.

PC/LAN Analyst 3 (2006–2012)

$24k Saved | 44+% Service Capacity | 18% Downtime Cut | Created Zero-Wait Ticket System | Awarded Top Performer

- Configured process improvements that achieved 40% more AV capacity while implementing a zero-wait ticketing system.
- Realized $16k parts/$8k labor cost reduction by performing manufacturer repairs on-site versus outsourcing.
- Boosted call volume capacity 44%, with no additional manpower costs, through operational improvement initiative.
- Cut downtime 18% by conceptualizing and implementing division-wide printer preventative maintenance program.
- Maintained zero compliance risk violations through annual team training on financial-centric compliance requirements.
- Justified department budget needs/spend by creating end-user, production, project, audit, milestones, and staffing reports for executive leadership.
- Guided department through numerous pilot programs, demonstrating capabilities to facilitate enterprise migration.

PC/LAN Analyst 2 (2002–2006)

$10k Saved Annually | 1,000+ Vendor Hours & Costs Eliminated | 4 Consecutive Years No Escalations for 3,000 Clients

- Discovered and introduced Dell on-site paid repair/warranty program for $10k in annual parts/service cost savings.
- Eliminated thousands of dollars in contractor/vendor hours and dollars by inserting staff into IT projects across division.
- Increased operational efficiencies by continually creating and optimizing new procedures and training protocols.

Specialist Lead, Assistant Vice President (1997–2002)

25% Capacity Increase | 100% Customer Service | 5 Years No Escalations | Top Dollar & Star Performance Awards

- Promoted to Team Lead to manage all hardware operations for newly established CIB Securities/Trading division.
- Increased customer support call volume 25% without additional headcount while remaining under budget.

RESUME 26: *by Cheryl Minnick, Ed.D., NCRW, MRW, CCMC, CHJMC, CAA • www.umt.edu*

CHARLOTTE RASMUSSEN

Network Engineering Manager
Technology ▪ Innovation ▪ Transformation

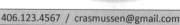

406.123.4567 / crasmussen@gmail.com

GAME-CHANGING TECHNOLOGY INNOVATOR

Innovative Technology is the Core of Business — It Steers Direction and Drives Growth

NETWORK ENGINEERING MANAGER with 15+ years' experience planning, implementing, and supporting existing and next-generation networks to drive revenues, profits, and efficiencies. **INDUSTRY PACESETTER** pioneering transformations, revolutionizing technology, and facilitating decision-making for nationally dispersed telecommunications infrastructure. **AUTHORITATIVE TIER 3 RESOURCE** delivering corporate vision through holistic multiplatform security, compliance, data center, and business transformation expertise, as well as system stability, performance, and operational excellence.

Value Promise	Leadership Successes
Cybersecurity Architecture Software Maintenance & Audits Network Design & Configuration Architecture Development Vendor & Integrator Collaboration Integration & Maintenance Capital Budget Management R&D Trials & Testing Network Infrastructure Strategy Sales Engineering Infrastructure Change Implementation	▪ Designed and led execution of next-generation technology strategy and expanded backbone—reduced operating expenses $5M. ▪ Counseled executives on pioneering innovations and technology strategy to deliver cutting-edge, in-house technical solutions. ▪ Embraced $20M capital and expense budget accountability for data networking and transport equipment. ▪ Wielded technology advances to achieve victories in top- and bottom-line performance and productivity—grew customer base 60%. ▪ Boosted corporate metabolism by igniting passion for change, injecting urgency, and cascading stretch and acquisition targets for quick wins.

PROFESSIONAL EXPERIENCE

SPECTRUM . . . *The nation's largest mutigigabit network providing fiber and ethernet to support end-to-end business and residential communication solutions for voice, data, cloud, and internet services.*

NETWORK ENGINEERING MANAGER, 2017–present
NETWORK ENGINEERING SUPERVISOR, 2013–2017 ▪ DATA NETWORK TECHNICIAN, 2003–2013

Network Engineering Manager

- Lead, manage, schedule, and support Network Engineers, Wireless Engineers, CO/Transport Engineers, and Project Engineers, ensuring customer voice and data networking solutions are developed and implemented.

- Prepare, submit, and administer $2B capital and expense budgets, multi-year action items, and financial plans.

- Solved for the future by creating new process to prioritize data networking projects.

- Documented and archived network designs, problems, and resolutions to provide, coordinate, enhance, and oversee exemplary Tier 3 customer support.

- Delivered legal counsel on process restructure, market expansion, and product line enhancement via acquisitions (Verizon Communications and China Mobile) and broadband infrastructure investment ($150M in 2019).

- Forged communicative relationships with vendors to negotiate and manage contracts and with senior leaders to understand pressing challenges and legacy processes to help maximize corporate success.

> *"Charlie has leveraged her expertise to make Spectrum an industry leader. I seek her insight regularly to maximize our performance."*
>
> *~COO, Spectrum*

Strategy: Enhance a detail- and achievement-rich resume with ample keywords, an attractive graphic, and a powerful endorsement to create a document that is both inviting to read and well suited for robotic scanners.

CHARLOTTE RASMUSSEN   406.123.4567 ▪ crasmussen@gmail.com   Page Two

SPECTRUM, *continued*

Network Engineering Supervisor (Tier 3 Senior Engineering Team), 2013–2017

- Senior member of 10-person team maintaining ISP backbone infrastructure. Set up and monitored BGP peering sessions and traffic at SIX (New York, NY) through router and switch configuration, installation, maintenance, and network monitoring.
- Sub-allocated and maintained IPv4/IPv6 address resources and correspondence with ARIN; assigned subnets and IP pools; provided Tier 3 support fielding Tier 1&2 trouble ticket escalations from technicians.
- Studied revolutionary WAN, security, and firewall technology; worked with VARs and vendors to identify products and solutions for customers' WAN/security data network design, configuration, documentation, and installation.
- Performed customer system performance/issue diagnosis and resolution using Syslogs, Fluke Network, Wireshark Analyzers, and network documentation. Documented design, network problems, and resolution.

Data Network Technician (Tier 2 Support Team), 2003–2013

- Fielded 8K dial-up/DSL customers' calls for network connection and email configuration; installed and troubleshot customers' failing DSL modems and connections; supported technicians with DSL issues/hardware installation.
- Served as Internet Administrator and Data Network Engineer to process customer requests, troubleshoot, and diagnose Tier 1&2 Technicians' escalated internet issues.
- Configured T1 and fractional T1 connectivity in Kentrox CSU/DSU's and American Technologies T1 Integrators to Disco core routers; changed configuration files for email, DNS, ldap, radius, and web servers.

EARLIER CAREER

Technical Engineering Analyst, *Fortune 500 Communications Company, Los Angeles, California, 2000–2003*

Supported 300 school districts in 5 states with computer configuration to access TransACT EduPortal Internet Document Sharing Network and Translation Library of Educational Forms. Provided daily customer need analysis to mold document content, enhance communications, and meet customers' unique needs. Collaborated with decision-makers to manage customers, arrange trainings, and onboard new customers while managing trial TransACT service subscriptions.

EDUCATION & CREDENTIALS

MS in Systems Engineering, University of Southern California, 2007
BS in Data and Decision Science, University of California Los Angeles, 2000

— ▪ ▪ ▪ —

Industry Credentials
Beta Theta Psi, 2017–present
NASBA Center for Public Trust Leadership Certification, 2015
CCNA, Cisco Certified Network Associate ▪ CCNP, Cisco Certified Network Professional
Sun Solaris Part I, 2002 ▪ Sun Solaris Part II, 2002 ▪ UNIX Part I, 2003

RESUME 27: by Alexis Binder, ACRW, MBA • www.greatresumesfast.com

Steven Williamson

555.298.3393 | stevenwilliamson@gmail.com | www.linkedin.com/in/stevenwilliamson

Cleveland, OH 44101

TECHNOLOGY EXECUTIVE
LEADER | "EXECUTION GUY" | TECHNOLOGIST AT HEART

Deliver on complex, high-risk, and high-value products and projects. Combine entrepreneurial instinct, in-depth technical skill, and reputation for developing and motivating cross-functional teams at all levels.

Leadership: Develop sound, concise strategies that move business forward and achieve operational goals. Facilitate productivity by speaking to each team member's individual motivations and bringing everyone together to drive business. Encourage an attitude of "leaning in"; we can get this done collectively.

Project Execution: Implement creative ideas and solutions. Continually deliver revenue-generating projects; increased sales $10M+. Thrive on the chaos of achieving results for multiple simultaneous demands.

Technology Expertise: Established and maintain strong technological knowledge to better inform strategy, project, and partner management initiatives.

AREAS OF EXPERTISE

Team Building ✧ Business Development ✧ Sales Management ✧ Project Management ✧
Concept Development ✧ Partner Management ✧ Purchasing ✧ Negotiation

"Steven has an effective way of bringing people together and keeping them focused on the big picture. He knows how to work through difficult issues and how to use technology to meet the demands of business." — CEO, Flyaway

SELECT CAREER HIGHLIGHTS

Vice President of Technology / Chief Marketing Officer (CMO) | *ManageX* | Cleveland, OH | 2013–Present

Manage $4.4M marketing budget, 50+ manufacturing partner relationships, 58+ technology engineers (nationally located), and a 7-member marketing team.

Architect and implement customers' cloud initiatives, including public, private, and hybrid models with technologies that include AWS, Azure, VMware, and OpenStack. Lead technology-planning and implementation initiatives, including Cloud, Hybrid, and Security environments.

"Steven is an amazing leader, manager, and mentor in one … With his employees, he takes on the task of coaching everyone individually to make them better … With his peers he is a straight shooter … And as if these qualities aren't enough, Steven also has a tremendous technical mind in both hardware and software. Finally, Steven is a business strategist through and through." —John Smith, now R&D Manager at X-IT (worked together for 3 years)

➤ **Increased profits 350%+ within 18 months** as part of executive leadership team by developing a focused strategy.
➤ **Reduced tech-spend $1.5M+ within last 14 months,** while entire executive team reduced operating expenses $4M by executing on developed strategy.
➤ **Grew public awareness** by building and implementing a corporate communications strategy.

Chief Technology Officer (CTO) | Flyaway | Solon, OH | 2009–2013

Spearheaded ideation and creation of the digital platform and mobile apps, while creating a modern and robust technology infrastructure and strategy. Managed cross-functional team of 35 direct reports and project team of 30 domestic and international consultants.

Strategy: Avoid stereotyping this individual as an entrepreneur by omitting his title of "Founder" and using titles that are most relevant to his current goals—and are entirely truthful. In the Summary, use language that reflects the way he speaks about himself (execution guy, technologist at heart).

Steven Williamson | 555.298.3393   Page 2

Oversaw multimillion-dollar technology and product innovation budgets while aligning overall product development and information technology direction. Provided technical architecture, design, and support of all technology projects.

Architected, built, and maintained disaster recovery and business continuity plan. Versed, implemented, and used software development methods, including Agile and SCRUM.

"Steven leads by example as both a technology expert and a senior manager at Flyaway. He has been a true mentor, allowing me to excel on both a personal and professional level. In a short time at Flyaway Steven has built successful IT, product, and software development teams." —Cindy Yukon, now VP of Technology at Globalstar Industries

➤ **Within 5 years**, achieved 6 product launches, a total IT rebuild, an ecommerce platform launch, and creation of the first, cutting-edge audio/e-book service—prior to Amazon, earning industry esteem.

➤ **Doubled sales** by building multiple multimillion-dollar, PCI-compliant ecommerce platforms.

➤ **Grew technologist team** from 3 to 39 within 5 years.

➤ **Boosted revenue 75%** through the development of 4 new products, a current product footprint that still exists.

Microsoft Practice Director | *ManageX* | Cleveland, OH | 2008–2009

Accountable for partner management, partner programs, and customer satisfaction; partners included Microsoft, VMware, and Citrix. Led pre- and post-sale architects tasked with resolving customer-facing projects and problems.

Managed internal technology planning and design for Microsoft and Virtualization products. Implemented customer technical solutions utilizing MSSQL Server, MS CRM, Exchange, and VMware. Advised clients on status of technologies relative to the strategic goals and objectives.

➤ **Built several revenue-generating technology programs** that advanced partner and client relationships.

➤ **Increased sales** from $600K to $1.9M within 1 year.

Senior Director of Technology | Hopenthaler| Cleveland, OH | 2006–2008

Managed multi-location technology teams and facilities, while working closely with 82 portfolio companies. Oversaw all technical business and data systems and projects. Executed all interviewing, hiring, and training—in addition to subsequent planning, assigning, and directing work. Reported to partners (12).

Part of private equity deal teams, including during company-evaluation and venture capital discussions. Assessed technology applications, systems, and ideas for portfolio and potential portfolio companies.

➤ **Within first 9 months**, rebuilt entire infrastructure, including communications, data center, and data repository.

➤ **Reduced turnaround** of required 200+-page quarterly report from 2 weeks to 2 days by automating the process.

➤ **Built portfolio management web app**, which streamlined portfolio company decision making.

Consulting Practice Director | GarnetPC | Cleveland, OH | 2003–2006

Managed 50+ employees and P&L of a $20M products-and-services business unit while developing and expanding partner relationships. Reported to CEO.

➤ **Increased profitability** ~30% and lifecycle management services business 166%, from $1.5M to $4M.

EDUCATION

Master's Certificate in Project Management | *Villanova University* | Villanova, PA
Bachelor's Degree | *Penn State University* | State College, PA

RESUME 28: by Melanie Denny, MBA, CPRW • www.resume-evolution.com

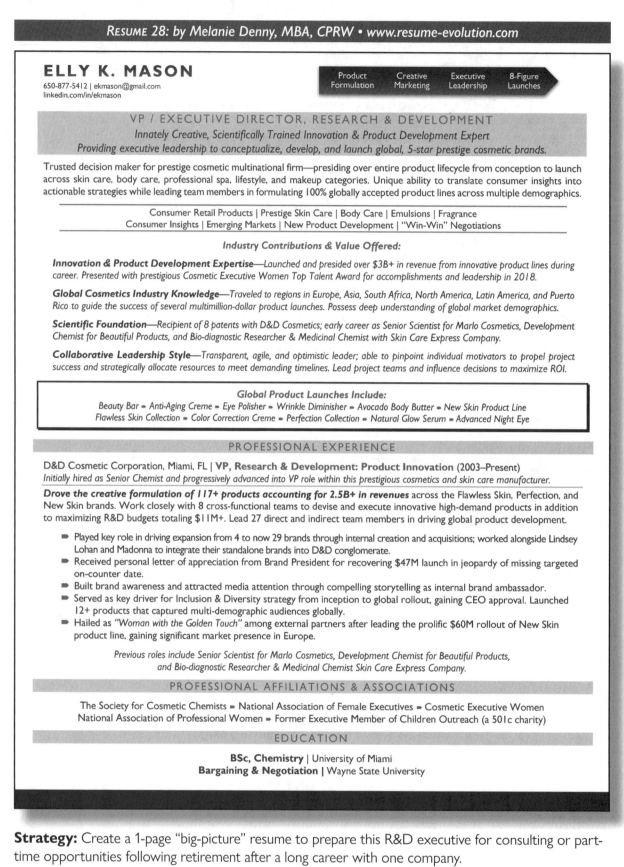

ELLY K. MASON

650-877-5412 | ekmason@gmail.com
linkedin.com/in/ekmason

Product Formulation | Creative Marketing | Executive Leadership | 8-Figure Launches

VP / EXECUTIVE DIRECTOR, RESEARCH & DEVELOPMENT
Innately Creative, Scientifically Trained Innovation & Product Development Expert
Providing executive leadership to conceptualize, develop, and launch global, 5-star prestige cosmetic brands.

Trusted decision maker for prestige cosmetic multinational firm—presiding over entire product lifecycle from conception to launch across skin care, body care, professional spa, lifestyle, and makeup categories. Unique ability to translate consumer insights into actionable strategies while leading team members in formulating 100% globally accepted product lines across multiple demographics.

Consumer Retail Products | Prestige Skin Care | Body Care | Emulsions | Fragrance
Consumer Insights | Emerging Markets | New Product Development | "Win-Win" Negotiations

Industry Contributions & Value Offered:

Innovation & Product Development Expertise—Launched and presided over $3B+ in revenue from innovative product lines during career. Presented with prestigious Cosmetic Executive Women Top Talent Award for accomplishments and leadership in 2018.

Global Cosmetics Industry Knowledge—Traveled to regions in Europe, Asia, South Africa, North America, Latin America, and Puerto Rico to guide the success of several multimillion-dollar product launches. Possess deep understanding of global market demographics.

Scientific Foundation—Recipient of 8 patents with D&D Cosmetics; early career as Senior Scientist for Marlo Cosmetics, Development Chemist for Beautiful Products, and Bio-diagnostic Researcher & Medicinal Chemist with Skin Care Express Company.

Collaborative Leadership Style—Transparent, agile, and optimistic leader; able to pinpoint individual motivators to propel project success and strategically allocate resources to meet demanding timelines. Lead project teams and influence decisions to maximize ROI.

> #### Global Product Launches Include:
> Beauty Bar ▪ Anti-Aging Creme ▪ Eye Polisher ▪ Wrinkle Diminisher ▪ Avocado Body Butter ▪ New Skin Product Line
> Flawless Skin Collection ▪ Color Correction Creme ▪ Perfection Collection ▪ Natural Glow Serum ▪ Advanced Night Eye

PROFESSIONAL EXPERIENCE

D&D Cosmetic Corporation, Miami, FL | VP, Research & Development: Product Innovation (2003–Present)
Initially hired as Senior Chemist and progressively advanced into VP role within this prestigious cosmetics and skin care manufacturer.

Drove the creative formulation of 117+ products accounting for 2.5B+ in revenues across the Flawless Skin, Perfection, and New Skin brands. Work closely with 8 cross-functional teams to devise and execute innovative high-demand products in addition to maximizing R&D budgets totaling $11M+. Lead 27 direct and indirect team members in driving global product development.

- Played key role in driving expansion from 4 to now 29 brands through internal creation and acquisitions; worked alongside Lindsey Lohan and Madonna to integrate their standalone brands into D&D conglomerate.
- Received personal letter of appreciation from Brand President for recovering $47M launch in jeopardy of missing targeted on-counter date.
- Built brand awareness and attracted media attention through compelling storytelling as internal brand ambassador.
- Served as key driver for Inclusion & Diversity strategy from inception to global rollout, gaining CEO approval. Launched 12+ products that captured multi-demographic audiences globally.
- Hailed as *"Woman with the Golden Touch"* among external partners after leading the prolific $60M rollout of New Skin product line, gaining significant market presence in Europe.

Previous roles include Senior Scientist for Marlo Cosmetics, Development Chemist for Beautiful Products,
and Bio-diagnostic Researcher & Medicinal Chemist Skin Care Express Company.

PROFESSIONAL AFFILIATIONS & ASSOCIATIONS

The Society for Cosmetic Chemists ▪ National Association of Female Executives ▪ Cosmetic Executive Women
National Association of Professional Women ▪ Former Executive Member of Children Outreach (a 501c charity)

EDUCATION

BSc, Chemistry | University of Miami
Bargaining & Negotiation | Wayne State University

Strategy: Create a 1-page "big-picture" resume to prepare this R&D executive for consulting or part-time opportunities following retirement after a long career with one company.

RESUME 29: *by Adrienne Tom, CERM, MCRS, CIS, CES, CCS • www.careerimpressions.ca*

MARK DONALDSON
IT Direction & People Development

Dallas, Texas
mark.donaldson@me.com • 214-222-2222
linkedin.com/in/markdonaldson

INFORMATION TECHNOLOGY LEADER
$1.8M+ Cost-Savings ▪ 20%+ Efficiency Gains ▪ High-Performance Teams of 20+

Transform IT processes through continuous improvement initiatives and technology leadership.
Develop cohesive teams to execute on shared IT strategy and vision.

IT LEADERSHIP: Championed the development of strategic technical roadmaps that anticipated and proactively resolved issues. *3-time recipient of Dynamic Leadership Award.*

TRANSFORMATION: Revitalized IT service delivery and operations in multiple organizations. *Turned lowest scoring customer service region into top-scoring region within 1 year.*

PROCESS IMPROVEMENT: Standardized IT work processes and introduced knowledge management process that significantly increased efficiencies and generated cost-savings — *up to $1.8M/annually.*

Technical & Leadership Acumen:

Strategic Business Planning
IT Operations
Team Leadership
Project Management
Vendor Relations & Negotiations
Budget Management
System Development & Enhancement
Infrastructure Management
End User Services

CAREER HISTORY and IMPACTS
BIG BOX SERVICES – DALLAS, TX | 2017 – Present

End User Services Manager
Budget: $2.5M | Supervise: 22 | Teams: Service Management & Service Desk

Stepped in to turn around challenged IT operations and team and implemented standardized ITIL processes to raise efficiency, transparency, and accountability. Continue to manage strategic direction of all IT/ITIL processes, directing two teams. Manage end-user service environment, including vendor management and service desk for 8500 internal customers. Oversee product development, design, and support.

- **Spearheaded the design and implementation of robust, company-wide ITIL processes,** resolving recurring business issues with improved change, incident, and problem management procedures.
    - → **Reduced business-impacting outages 25%.**

- **Restructured service desk team,** implementing cross-training, team building, and efficiency enhancements that eradicated silos, raised morale, and increased shareable knowledge.
    - → **Decreased issue resolution time 50%+.**

- **Increased visibility and transparency of IT operations for executive management,** bringing all IT processes under ServiceNow interface.
    - → **Tied all data into CIO-level dashboard, enabling improved evaluation of IT projects, costs, and resources. Provided accurate data to support company objectives.**

- **Recruited and established dedicated service management team,** developing new ServiceNow platform with Scrum/Agile system development approach.
    - → **Retired multiple legacy systems, consolidating to one platform in less than a year.**

Turned around underperforming team and IT operations:

- ✓ Identified and removed barriers and distractions to boost performance.
- ✓ Instituted team-building activities to foster enhanced communications.
- ✓ Commissioned monthly 360-feedback.
- ✓ Streamlined IT processes and procedures and clarified staff responsibilities.

Strategy: Capture attention in a flash with large impacts (boldly stated in the headline) and continue that trend throughout the resume, with specific achievements presented under each bullet point and highlighted for each position.

Mark Donaldson • 214-222-2222 | Page 2

CAREER HISTORY and IMPACTS continued...

EEE COMPANY – DALLAS, TX | 2015 – 2017
End User Services Manager
Budget: $2.6M | Supervised: 16 | Computer Systems: 3000+

Recruited to direct end-user services and technology for 3500 associates. Led service support, lease and vendor management, purchasing, and device deployment. Managed global ServiceNow strategy. Fostered relationships and spearheaded contract negotiations with large vendors — Microsoft, HP, Verizon, and Dell.

- **Unlocked $400K in annual savings** by renegotiating mobile contract for more than 1000 devices.

- **Reduced cost of leased assets by $200K/year,** overhauling equipment leasing process, improving tracking procedures, replacing leasing vendor, and standardizing system ordering.
  - → **Increased asset recovery and reuse ~20% and achieved 95% return rate.**

- **Boosted value of IT service management,** building a team of dedicated ServiceNow developers to create improved incident and problem management processes and build out a service catalog.
  - → **Generated time savings, improved tracking, and end-user satisfaction with online IT service purchasing catalog — utilized by 75% of the global organization.**
  - → **Increased access and transparency of IT metrics for executive leadership.**

CELLULAR LTD. – CHICAGO, IL | 2005 – 2014
Infrastructure Manager (2011 – 2014) | **Supervisor** (2008 – 2011) | **System Technician** (2005 – 2008)
Peak Budget Oversight: $3.5M | Direct Reports: 18+ | Servers: 700+ | Computer Systems: 1300+

Promoted into positions of increasing responsibility due to performance excellence. Managed all aspects of computer equipment, telephony systems, and customer service for 1800 end users across 120 locations.

Impacts Snapshot:

Combined Cost-Savings	Up-Time Increase	Performance Awards	Reduced Budget
$ 2.6M	13%	4	41%

- **In one year, turned around ineffective team** of 9 regional technicians. Recognized as top 2% of company leadership with 3 Dynamic Leadership Awards in 3 years. Presented Coaches Award in 2007.
  - → **Turned Midwest team from lowest scoring to leading customer service region, across all measurement categories. Positioned team as measurement for the organization.**

- **Generated $1.8M in annual cost savings** in hardware and licensing fees, driving implementation of million-dollar system virtualization using VMWare.

- **Improved system uptime from 96% to 99.99%,** installing proactive monitoring system to analyze and correct issues in real-time.

- **Reduced headcount by 50% while increasing team efficiency,** creating 41% budget savings through streamlined workflows and controlled spending.

EDUCATION & PROFESSIONAL DEVELOPMENT

Master of Science: Business Administration – University of Chicago, 2018
ITIL V3 Foundation Certified, 2015 • Scrum Master Certified, 2015

TECHNICAL TOOLBOX

Expertise across a wealth of systems, processes, and technologies. A sampling includes:
ITIL • Application Development Lifecycle (SDLC) • Scrum Framework • Agile Methodologies
ServiceNow • Remedy Office Suite • VMWare • Citrix

RESUME 30: *by Kelly Gadzinski, ACRW, CCMC, RCC • www.kgcareerservices.com*

VALARIE WESTFALL

416-666-7545 ♦ vwestfall@yahoo.com

TECHNOLOGY DIRECTOR — CONSULTING DELIVERY

Business Analytics ♦ Software Development & Implementation ♦ High-Performance Team Leadership

Transformational technical leader who leverages technology, strategies, and relationships to develop innovative software solutions for large corporations — maximizing performance, quality, and results.

✓ Expert in **managing multiple client engagements** with projects valued up to $1M. Proactively consult and engage with clients to increase confidence, minimize uncertainty, and ensure successful outcomes.

✓ Adept at **bridging the gap between business and technology** to facilitate effective communications and deliver transformative solutions. Drive technology ROI and cost savings through innovation and improvements.

✓ Highly skilled at **motivating teams to embrace new challenges** and work together collaboratively to achieve goals. Inspire others to excel by gaining buy-in, communicating openly, and building mutual respect.

MBA – Case Western Reserve University ♦ Certified Project Management Professional

Signature Strengths

Business-Focused Technology Innovations ♦ Project Leadership & Delivery ♦ C-Suite Presentations ♦ Customer Relations
Software Development Life Cycle (SDLC) ♦ Vendor Management ♦ Contract Negotiation ♦ Budget Management

Professional Experience

Geminize, Indianapolis, IN
Software company integrating data from silos to expose meaningful, business-driving insights on connected data.

Director of Consulting Delivery (2016 to present)
Budget: $3M | 5 direct reports | Startup company

Manage portfolio of projects across multiple Fortune 500 clients to generate useful business insights through deep data analysis. Define client needs and requirements, customizing solutions and ensuring rapid project execution. Challenge and empower team to quickly deliver high-quality analytical insights and results for prestigious retailers. Drive initiatives that identify opportunities for enhanced, more effective sourcing and marketing activities.

- **Boosted annual revenue $1.5M in 5 months** by creating key performance indicators and reports that evaluated the impact of major sales events.

- **Selected by co-founders to run consulting services function.** Generated new business opportunities through increased client engagement, establishing 90-day success criteria and providing exceptional customer service.

- **Saved $100K** by absorbing responsibilities of system administrator, eliminating the need to backfill position. Quickly identified and implemented improvements that enhanced product quality.

StoneEdge, Cleveland, OH
Leading global provider of software solutions for the insurance industry.

Director of Software Engineering (2005 to 2016) & Information Security Officer (2014 to 2016)
Annual Revenue Goal: $4M | Global Team: 6 direct & 20 indirect reports

Oversaw the development, release, and maintenance of web-based applications and solutions for the property-and-casualty insurance industry. Challenged to drive success and business growth in a highly regulated industry during a downward-trending economic cycle. Built a high-performance team that successfully launched multiple $1M+ projects. Set vision and strategy for protecting organization's IT programs from internal and external threats.

Received *Rapids Award* for outstanding commitment to leadership, client relationship management, continuous improvement, and financial effectiveness, setting a gold standard at StoneEdge.

Strategy: Go beyond technical skills and accomplishments to focus on business results and leadership achievements to elevate this resume to the executive level.

VALARIE WESTFALL   416-666-7545 ♦ vwestfall@yahoo.com

<u>StoneEdge</u>, continued

- **Secured $9M (6-year) contract with Progressive Insurance** by leading 12-person global team in the design and implementation of a web-based point-of-sale system within 5 months.

- **Within 9 months, executed $3M highly complex software upgrade project** for high-profile client that involved the consolidation of 2 legacy platforms utilized by diverse work groups.

- **Salvaged $2M contract and restored faith** with client by quickly engaging with expert resources to recover mistakenly deleted data within 72 hours.

- **Demonstrated value to client** by identifying and delivering an alternative hosting solution within 30 days, resulting in $120K savings and compliance with Payment Card Industry (PCI) security standards.

- **Increased client confidence in data protection and integrity** by collaborating with business unit leaders to develop a more mature security posture.

<u>Global Results Systems, Inc.</u>, Pittsburgh, PA
Provider of outsourced solutions for the property-and-casualty insurance industry.

Software Development Manager (2002 to 2005) ♦ **Project Lead** (1999 to 2001)

- **Generated $600K revenue in 6 months** through introduction and delivery of first dot-com project, establishing company as one that builds web-based solutions.

- **Led global team in development of web-based insurance processing system** that increased insurance agent efficiency and improved security of information. Adopted by 900 agents throughout North America within 2 years.

<u>Prior professional experience</u> includes *Contract Programmer* at Vimatex, Inc. (acquired by Honeywell) and *Programmer Analyst* at Branco Systems, deepening knowledge in C++ programming and ERP systems.

Education & Certifications

MBA: Case Western Reserve University, Cleveland, OH

MS Computer Science: Ohio State University, Columbus, OH

BS Physics, Chemistry, and Mathematics: Michigan State University, East Lansing, MI

Certified PMP — Project Management Professional ♦ Certified Neo4j Professional ♦ Data Science with R Language
ITIL V3 Foundation Certificate in Information Technology Service Management

Technical Competencies

C#.NET | R programming language | Python

Neo4j - graph database | SQL Server | Cypher Query Language

MicroStrategy | Java | Visual C++ | Visual Basic | Classic ASP/COM | Visual FoxPro

Visual Studio .NET | CA Agile Central | ASP.NET | JavaScript | JSON | RESTful Web Services

CHEN HILL

chenhill@hotmail.com | www.linkedin.com/in/chenhill

+1 555 818 7147

INTERNET OF THINGS (IOT)
Telecommunications Director

...Demonstrated Success In...

◇ **Commercial Strategy:** Pioneered and directed Commercial and Sales strategy to win one of Hammers IoT's largest IoT deals in history with a European Automotive OEM with total contract value of C$30M+.

◇ **Global Business:** Commercially launched new IoT Products across Europe: Usage Business Insurance, Stolen Vehicle Recovery, NB-IoT, Connected Cabinets, B2C Internet in the Car, and Smart City Partnerships.

◇ **Leadership:** Spearheaded Fone Global IoT worldwide expansion via commercial agreements with Global and Local MNO Partners and Tier 1 Supplier Partnerships.

AREAS OF EXPERTISE

Solution Development	Commercial Management & Support	Commercial Negotiation
Global Enterprise Experience	Strategic Partnerships	Thought Leadership
Product Management	Large & Complex Bid Deal Management	Business Development

"I can honestly say he [Chen] goes out of his way to share his knowledge and experience with his team and better those around him … The nature of our work in the fast-paced world of IoT meant I worked on some complex global opportunities and solutions. I could rely on Chen's composure and experience to ensure a successful outcome"
—Adam West, Head of Global Pricing, Fone Global

PROFESSIONAL EXPERIENCE

HAMMERS COMMUNICATIONS | 2017–Present
Canadian communications and media company operating in the field of wireless communications, cable television, telephone, and Internet connectivity with additional telecommunications and mass media assets.

Head of IoT Commercial Management, Toronto, Canada .... August 2017–Present

Recruited by SVP to senior management position with accountability for IoT Commercial Management and Solutions. Report to Head of IoT sitting within the wider Hammers Enterprise Business Unit.

...Select Highlights...

❖ Launched monthly Regional Sales meetings across Canada with RVPs to review IoT sales performance and financials. Managed closure of incremental $15M of TCV new business in 2019.

❖ Spearheaded Hammers IoT International Global connectivity strategy by creating short-, mid-, and long-term requirements and mechanisms, enabling Hammers to meet the evolving customer business requirements.

❖ Facilitate discussions with Global Partners AT&T, Verizon, Vodafone, Cisco, Amazon, Hammers executives, and other North American technology partners.

❖ Redesigned the IoT Sales commercial framework, introducing fresh commercial methodology that was implemented across IoT Business Unit nationwide.

❖ Administered Commercial and Solutions guidance to IoT Product Managers delivering LTE-M, NB-IoT eUICC, and IoT Partner Programme and implementing go-to-market strategy.

FONE GLOBAL | 2009–2017
British multinational telecommunications conglomerate, predominantly operating services in Asia, Africa, Europe, and Oceania. Fone Global is the ninth-largest telephone operating company by total revenue ($64.5B).

Global Head of IoT Commercial Strategy, Newbury, UK .... May 2015–July 2017

Hand-selected for newly defined role to lead onshore team of 6 Senior Commercial Managers and offshore team of 7 Commercial Managers focusing on global IoT deals across all Industry Verticals & Solutions, Automotive, Vehicle Telematics, Smart Metering, Smart Cities, Internet in the Car, Indirect Channel, and other IoT Verticals.

Strategy: Supplement strong and specific achievements with third-party endorsements that convey this individual's soft skills and leadership talents as well as his technical expertise.

CHEN HILL   +1 555 818 7147 | Page 2

Global Head of IoT Commercial Strategy, continued

...Select Highlights...

❖ Influenced key customer off-site meetings globally, providing market intelligence, commercial insight, and commercial strategy to Global Account Executives.

❖ Supported IoT Expansion Team activity as part of accelerated expansion programme that increased Fone Global IOT's Global Partner footprint.

❖ Won key Automotive deals, including Daimler North America, Ford Europe, Cubic VW (Audi) Europe, Nissan, Panasonic, BMW Bikes, and Honeywell, delivering their Connected Car Programmes (TCV in excess of €400m in 2016 and 2017).

❖ Coached and led Commercial Pricing & Strategy Team (11 FTEs) with responsibility for deals with combined annual TCV exceeding €500m.

❖ Mentored and inspired team to win Usage-Based Insurance deals with Admiral, Wunelli, MCL, and Quixa (TCV €65m) and Key OEM Car Connect Programmes with Porsche, Renault, Nissan Infiniti, and Yamaha Motorbikes (TCV €40m).

❖ Designed commercial strategy and supported go-to-market for new business across vertical IoT industries.

Global IoT Commercial Manager, Newbury, UK ....August 2012–May 2015
IoT Commercial Expert for Global Complex and Strategic Automotive opportunities (Connected Car), developing business cases, defining key commercial propositions, and supporting global account teams with negotiations.

...Select Highlights...

❖ Established Fone Global IoT as #1 in the global marketplace by delivering key commercials / complex business cases, often under extreme pressure. Enabled Fone Global IoT to win several Global Strategic Automotive Customers in an initial 2-year period.

❖ Won deals with combined TCV of €180m, including VW (Audi), Daimler Europe, BMW, and General Motors.

❖ Contributed to key customer off-site meetings and negotiations across Europe as Commercial Lead.

EARLY CAREER

Global Finance Business Partner | Revenue & Systems Accountant, Fone Global, Newbury, UK
Finance Business Partner, Rogers Wealth, London, UK
Finance Analyst, Bodewell Communications, Manchester, UK

"It has been a real pleasure to work with Chen during my time at Fone Global; his commercial knowledge and skill is so impressive. I watched as he built his team, not just in number, but in success and reputation to be world class and highly respected. People want to work with Chen and to learn from him. He also taught me about commercial innovation and how to make deals that are not just competitive, but are compelling, interesting, and future proof."
—Joyce Brone, Business Manager at Fone Global Carrier Services

EDUCATION & QUALIFICATIONS

Executive Management – Fone Global Leadership Essentials Management Programme, May 2016
Bachelor of Science, Information Systems – Leeds Metropolitan University – Achieved highest honours.

CELIA SMITHERS

celia.smithers@mac.com | Seattle, WA 98136 | 555-654-5555 | LinkedIn Profile

TECHNOLOGY EXECUTIVE: GLOBAL FINANCIAL SERVICES
Expert in Digital Transformation

Finance and Technology Executive with 10+ years of success delivering transformational strategies and solutions for large, complex financial institutions.

Value Creator who introduces disruptive technologies and forward-thinking strategies to achieve growth, operational efficiency, and competitive advantage.

Industry Thought Leader and frequent speaker on data migration to the Cloud.

Expertise
- Strategic Planning
- Business Transformation
- Program Leadership
- Client Relationship Management
- Emerging and Disruptive Technologies
- Crisis Management

Signature Achievements

▶ Created new digital transformation practice specialty projecting $100M+ revenue in next 3 years for XYZ Global.

▶ Smoothly executed multiple disruptive business transformations for top-10 global banks.

▶ Delivered the only on-time submission of all major US banks for compliance with new regulations ... in half the time allotted.

▶ Spearheaded BankOne's enterprise-wide OneBusiness transformation, a $42M investment with 30 simultaneous projects.

PROFESSIONAL EXPERIENCE

XYZ Global Technology Services
$100B global business and IT services provider with 300,000 professionals active in 150 countries

Seattle, WA | 2014–Present

Associate Partner, Financial Services Global Consulting (2017–Present)

Promoted to leadership role with broad accountability for revenue generation, engagement delivery, and client relationship management. Blend business knowledge with technology expertise to develop solutions that position large financial entities for the future while solving problems today.

▶ **Generated $35M revenue** in 3+ years; exceeded 2020 revenue target in first quarter.

▶ **Created new practice specialty** in digital transformation—advising companies on business reinvention using advanced and emerging technologies.
   - Built $100M 3-year pipeline with 3 top clients, with enormous expansion opportunities to other clients and industries.
   - Became sought-after speaker for client presentations and industry meetings, sharing strategies for companies to improve speed, agility, and analytics in Cloud environments.

▶ **Spearheaded massive 2-year data transformation program** for a major global bank, streamlining global reporting to achieve 30% reduction in overhead and 28% increase in operational efficiency. Rolled out across 12 countries and consistently met milestones for value delivered.

Senior Manager, Big Data Analytics (2014–2017)

Recruited to XYZ on the strength of large-scale program management experience, leadership skills, and deep technical and banking expertise. Advised CXOs at large global banks on modernizing Finance, Accounting, and Risk operations; solving Big Data challenges; and developing transformation strategies for emerging business imperatives.

▶ **Rescued a major initiative for a top-10 bank.** Stepped in to replace competitor halfway through mandated 18-month time limit for meeting new reporting regulations.
   - Quickly demonstrated program planning/delivery skills plus subject matter expertise to secure the contract for XYZ.
   - Introduced model methodology, an integrated approach that was later adopted by other lines of business at XYZ.
   - Delivered the only on-time successful submission of all of the 10 largest US banks.
   - Secured repeat business from the client and established a dominant position in the risk domain.

▶ **Advised a major global bank on security and privacy solutions** to restore compliance with anti-money-laundering regulations. Prepared client executives for meetings with regulators.

Strategy: Highlight "Signature Achievements" in the summary and provide additional details in the career history to showcase the depth and breadth of this executive's knowledge and experience in digital transformation. Use ample white space and bold type to make document easy to skim.

CELIA SMITHERS

celia.smithers@mac.com | 555-654-5555

Amacord Systems—*$65M technology consulting firm; 500+ employees*   Seattle, WA | 2011–2014

Program Manager

Managed key accounts and relationships with major financial, insurance, and consulting clients. Held full P&L accountability for multimillion-dollar projects.

▶ **Met revenue goals of $25M+ every year,** delivering more than 20 projects annually.

▶ **Managed $85M contract for Bank of America** across 8 leading Cloud environments.

▶ **Collaborated with CIO** to introduce Open Source technology in a major national insurance provider.

BankOne—*$300B retail bank with 39,000 employees*   Seattle, WA | 2006–2011

Project Director, Regulatory Reporting

Spearheaded transformations and upgrades to essential systems and processes related to regulatory oversight and reporting.

▶ **Led massive multi-year Finance and Accounting transformation** to streamline, automate, and eliminate errors from the reconciliation process. Established PMO and partnered with McKinsey team on technology selection, project planning, and implementation.
  – Reduced accounting close period from 45 days to 6 days.
  – Achieved controlled and timely financial reporting by implementing trading systems and accounting sub-ledgers.
  – Streamlined regulatory submissions via modernization of the regulatory reporting platform.
  – Introduced iron-clad methodology to efficiently execute large programs.

▶ **Member of Program Leadership Team for enterprise transformation** of every BankOne business rule, cash flow process, and technology platform to support implementation of a major new initiative, the OneBusiness program that comprised more than 30 large projects running simultaneously and a budget of $42M.
  – Cited for "flawless execution," delivering results on schedule despite tight timeline and intense executive scrutiny.

Prior Positions: **Business Analyst,** CNote Systems (2004–2006); **Java Developer,** Northwest Tech Solutions (2003–2004)

EDUCATION

MBA, Information Systems Management | University of Washington, Seattle, WA | 2011
BS, Electrical Engineering | Carlson University, Seattle, WA | 2003

RESUME 33: *by Laura Smith-Proulx, CPRW, CCMC, NCOPE, COPNS, CPBA, TCCS • www.anexpertresume.com*

ROBERT J. CRANSTON

404.555.3774 - Chicago, IL - RJCranston42@gmail.com - https://www.linkedin.com/in/rjcranston/

SENIOR IT LEADER – EXECUTIVE TECHNOLOGY AUTHORITY

Business Partner Attuned to The Needs of Fast-Growing Enterprises

■ ■ ■

Go-to IT executive, CIO-level leader, and astute business driver behind digital transformation and process efficiencies enabling multimillion-dollar growth. Standardize systems and IT procedures, support complex environments (including healthcare, hospital IT, and manufacturing), and motivate teams to deliver reliable, scalable infrastructures.

> **"Robert's knowledge and expertise are as good as it gets** when it comes to technology. His ability to bridge the gap between IT and the business is highly unusual. He is an incredible asset … among the best I have worked with in IT." — *Supplier Partner Review*

Systems & Operations Optimization - Stakeholder Relations - Restructuring - Team Building & Motivation - Outsourcing
Cost Savings - Emerging Technologies - Change Management - Capacity Planning - Virtualization - IT Turnarounds
Process Improvement - Program & Project Management - Budgets - Strategic Planning - Networking - Vendor Negotiations

Strategic Security, ERP, Infrastructure, & Software Leadership

Accelerated Growth: Supported and enabled 22%+ year-over-year **expansion** with IT infrastructure and network / server changes.

Distribution & Accuracy Improvements: Enabled increased volume with company-wide ERP system that improved performance and service delivery.

Consultative Leadership: Conferred with CEO, CFO, and Board on IT strategies and business case for high-profile changes (including Business Continuity / Disaster Recovery, BYOD, and Mobility) aligned with goals. Built reputation for strong business collaboration and transparency.

Efficient Staffing & Outsourcing: Developed partnerships with **outsourcing vendors** to bolster IT talent and implement complex projects.

Landmark Impact on Efficiency, Modernization & Competitive Edge

⇒ **90-Day Results:** Quickly identified business needs and led modernization to enable rapid growth.

⇒ **95% Virtualization:** Cut costs with VMware infrastructure project.

⇒ **Heightened Productivity:** Embedded Workfront SaaS into Marketing, R&D, and IT for 15%–20% productivity gain.

Professional History

Natural Distribution Enterprises, Ltd. | 2005–Present
Quickly addressed gaps in technology utilization and built viable IT strategy, fueling growth at manufacturer and wholesale distributor in the healthcare and natural foods industry.

IT Director; Senior Infrastructure & Program Leader
Revitalized Technology Approach, Deploying Cutting-Edge Solutions and Driving 166%+ Business Growth

Identified technology-fueled obstacles to growth in first 90 days as senior IT executive with CIO-level authority, enabling company foothold in aggressive natural goods markets. Optimize systems, processes, project methodology, and workflows—revamping infrastructures with premier solutions VMware, PureStorage, Nimble, Juniper, Cisco, Aerohive, ArcticWolf, and ZAP.

Justify upgrades with solid business cases; work closely with stakeholders to meet business needs. Recruit and lead IT reports plus service partners for Security SIEM, ERP, and System Support. Manage $3.6M OPEX spend.

Oversight of All IT Service Management (Helpdesk, Web & Mobile, Apps, Data, & Infrastructure):
SaaS, Social & Mobile Support, Workstations / Endpoints, Devices, Access Control, System Maintenance, End User Support, ERP, SQL Reporting, EDI, B2B Data Exchange, BI, MS Office, Process Improvement, Intranet, Websites, SharePoint, Network Security, Servers, Data Warehouses, Intranet, Mobility, Remote Access, Backup, & Business Continuity

Strategy: Showcase CIO-worthy experiences and achievements (he was already the top IT person at his company but did not have the CIO title) and note his rise through the company as a trusted leader. Illustrate business insight through an endorsement, prominently positioned as part of the summary.

ROBERT J. CRANSTON, SENIOR IT LEADER – PAGE TWO

Natural Distribution Enterprises – IT Director *(Continued…)*

- **Systems Stability & Reliability:** **Boosted IT service delivery, uptime, and fault tolerance**, eliminating outage-prone white-box servers with virtualization, upgrading to Nimble Storage (as beta tester), and converging VMware servers onto HP. Brought storage to ~100TB, with 10:1 server-host ratios simplifying tasks.
  - → Saved up to $10K annually in power and gained better systems protection.

- **Networking & System Upgrades:** Revitalized growth, **turning around stagnant operation** with standardized Dell infrastructure; led virtualization, data networking, and security / storage to current-state technologies.
  - → Added enterprise flash storage (PureStorage and Nimble), Juniper / Cisco networking, Cisco and Aerohive Wifi, state-of-the-art-security (Palo Alto Networks), and managed SIEM (ArcticWolf).

- **ERP Upgrade:** Eased systems bottlenecks with MS Dynamics NAV (replacing MRP), **paving the way for 100% rise in gross revenues** since 2011, plus 10%–15% increase in fulfillment from new KPI and Performance Management reporting. Managed cultural changes and buy-in, plus complex onboarding and customization.
  - → Led integration of embedded EDI processing up to 60% of orders, with significant improvement in inbound PO, supply chain, shipping, and invoicing, plus Process Manufacturing and Data Warehousing.
  - → Resolved deficiencies and enhanced labor utilization, shipping, and distribution cost savings with E-Ship.

- **Collaboration & Project Management:** **Increased accountability to 85% of 30-day** break-fix completion goal; incorporated Workfront for seamless support including Helpdesk request tracking and IT project management.

- **Security Protections:** Incorporated multi-sensor, on-premise endpoint protection and vulnerability management systems for significant reduction in malware and viruses, plus first security policy and metrics.

> **Business-Focused Upgrades**
> - Workfront for Project Management
> - BI System (ZAP) **Integrated With ERP**
> - Email Delivery Improvements/Filtering
> - **IT Integration With PMO**
> - New Data Warehouse & Reporting

- **Business Intelligence:** Added decision-support reporting, executive dashboards, and department reports; led plan for centralized analytics.

- **Website Functionality:** Oversaw changes to B2B and B2C customer-facing sites with Sales and Marketing, adding social media interfaces and directing custom PHP development.

- **Business-Focused Improvements:** **Created bottom-line benefit** with consultative business support, vendor cost savings, top-notch team building, and development of first-time SOPs / OPLs documenting IT processes.

- **Remote Access (US & Canada):** Enabled field sales access to network resources with VPN capability.

SLC Health | 1998–2005

Continually promoted for enhancing systems capacity and security at national healthcare provider, with technology authority for Medical Foundation, Maternity & Surgery Center, and Visiting Nurses Association.

IT Planner; Information Security Analyst; Technical Services Manager
Planned & Rolled Out Epic & Other Medical Care Systems; Supported Growth in Clinic Sites

Handled networking, infrastructure upgrades, security analysis, project management and tracking in MS Project, systems risk assessment, EMR rollout, new site IT systems, and stakeholder relations / education. Planned and implemented WAN and clinical software upgrades, documented project tracking, and managed desktop and server systems. Coached and mentored project teams in responsive support and technical quality.

Other IT Roles: **RCC Medical Group; County of McHenry Info Services**

Education & Technology Training

BS in Business Technology Management (1992)
University of Illinois, Bloomington

Professional Training: Vendor Training & Events Including Mid-Market IT Summit, CIO Summit, & Global Conferences

EMILIO R. TORRES

Director, Media Operations
Media Management & Production | Pre- & Post-Production Services | Media Archives & Libraries
Resource Management | Workflow Improvements | Logistical Support | Client Services & Customer Relations

Strategic and results-driven Media Operations Director with 10 years' experience enhancing business results through staffing, procedural, and technical solutions.

Develop, budget, and implement operating infrastructure for production media asset services. **Build** high-performing teams, delivering staff training and clarifying policies and procedures. **Improve** efficiencies, aligning project and operational resources based on workflows, media systems, file-based technologies, and policies. **Ensure** fiscal responsibility, overseeing project financials and operational expenditures in accordance with business priorities.

Vendor Management
Workflow Development
Financial Management
Employee Leadership
Staff Training & Development
Capacity Management
Change Management
Relationship Development
Contract Negotiations

LEADERSHIP ACCOMPLISHMENTS

- **Planned and oversaw relocation of thousands of assets** while simultaneously providing content in support of daily programming during the B&C and Lifetime merger that affected libraries in NY, LA, and CT.

- **Eliminated inefficiencies and enhanced workflows,** developing a joint collaboration between Media Asset Services, Production Media Operations, and Programming and Marketing partners.

- **Led successful transition to a new corporate-wide asset database,** training the user community on Xytech MediaPulse and executing front-end Systems Administration.

- **Controlled business costs** by managing post-production vendor relationships and negotiating rates and package deals for ongoing and seasonal projects.

- **Collaborated with senior leadership,** developing workflows to meet critical Production, Operations, and Engineering needs as well as client goals and timelines.

- **Turned around a faltering media library,** improving customer satisfaction and staff morale and piloting a new training and development program to increase technological and production support knowledge.

- **Minimized operational downtime** by initiating disaster recovery plans, securing off-site facilities, and leading personnel during a forced emergency closure of the building.

PROFESSIONAL EXPERIENCE

Director, Production Media Asset Services | B&C Networks, New York, NY | 2014–Present
Direct daily business operations and effectively support NY production efforts. Oversee staff development, including training; manage workload; serve as point of communication for corporate and operational decisions, policies, and procedures.

- **Saved $50K** and reduced outstanding assets by creating a flexible and proactive asset review policy.

- **Managed capacity** and client media requirements for materials stored in a limited staging library in New York.

- **Delivered 5% YOY cost reductions,** managing vendor relations and securing preferred rates through negotiation.

- **Managed customer relations and requirements,** monitoring changing client goals, challenges, and timelines.

- **Supported workflows,** registration of assets, and delivery of promotional material from edit to broadcast.

917.123.1234 | New York, NY 10467 | ertorres@gmail.com | linkedin.com/in/ertorres

Strategy: Position this individual for a promotion within his company by emphasizing the breadth of his skills and experience (well beyond what his competitors would have) and subtly aligning him with the company by using its corporate colors in his resume.

EMILIO R. TORRES
Director, Media Operations

PROFESSIONAL EXPERIENCE continued

Manager, NY Media Management & Production Support | B&C Television Networks, New York, NY | 2008–2014

Managed the daily operations of the New York library system, including assigned budget lines, library, and traffic activities for all internal clientele. Forecasted budget lines and managed accruals for Post-Production and Edit Support for International and Promo departments, acting as direct liaison with more than 50 internal and external producers.

- **Streamlined workflow** by analyzing and reconfiguring media-management processes and protocols.

- **Supported i-Mediaflex user needs,** associated file-based strategies, system functionality updates, and work flow.

- **Introduced new digital tools** that speeded and improved delivery of media dub requests for all New York clients.

- **Secured vendors able to accommodate last-minute needs** and emergencies, drawing on industry contacts.

Operational Coordinator, Library Services | MTV Networks, New York, NY | 2004–2008

Supervised library inventory maintenance, interlibrary transfers, and logistical placement on new assets. Coordinated and completed daily library workflow, including inventory circulation, interlibrary transfers, archive cataloging, reference services, tape stock distribution, and duplication.

- **Trained and developed staff librarians** in the areas of departmental policies and library archive database.

- **Disseminated and supervised long-term library projects,** and communicated project status to stakeholders.

SPECIAL PROJECTS

Associate Producer, St John's Spirit of Service Award Biography | B&C Television Networks, New York, NY | 2013 & 2015

- **Coordinated research and documentation** for multiple high-level executives and philanthropists, both receiving award and selected for interview. Assisted in question development, scriptwriting, and pre- and post-production.

- **Conducted on-camera interviews,** engaging talent, friends, and family members of St John's University Spirit of Service Award winners both on location and in B&C Studios.

- **Coordinated graphics,** third-party stills acquisition, animation stand, and production creative for packages.

- **Supervised AVID and FCP edit sessions** in post-production and coordinated final approvals.

EDUCATION

Bachelor of Arts Degree – Mass Communications, Television and Video Production
Minor in Speech Communications
Iona College, New Rochelle NY | 2007

COMPUTER SKILLS

Microsoft Word, Excel, PowerPoint
Mediaflex | iMediaflex | Xytech MediaPulse | WinMLS | ScheduALL
IPV | PPL | PTS | Computron
Visio | Alias

917.123.1234 | 1234 Media Way, Bronx NY 10467 | ertorres@gmail.com | linkedin.com/in/ertorres

RESUME 35: by Louise Kursmark, MRW, CPRW, JCTC, CEIP CCM • www.louisekursmark.com

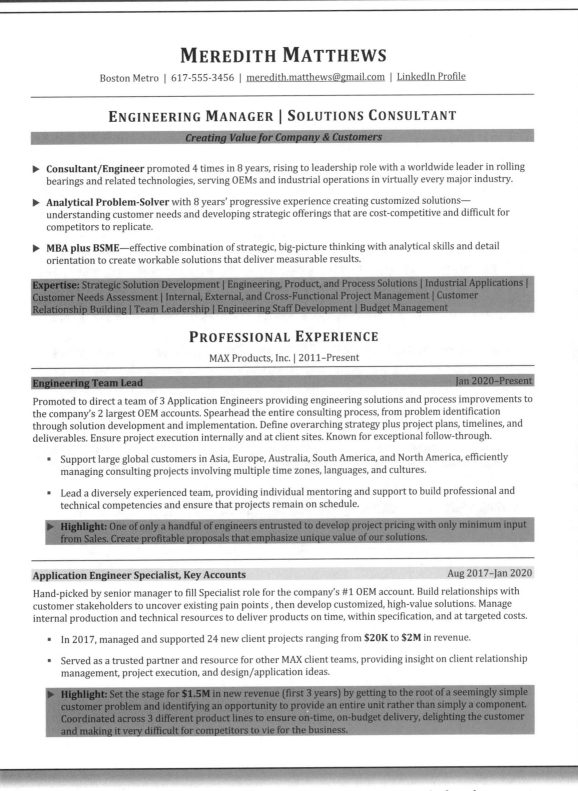

MEREDITH MATTHEWS

Boston Metro | 617-555-3456 | meredith.matthews@gmail.com | LinkedIn Profile

ENGINEERING MANAGER | SOLUTIONS CONSULTANT
Creating Value for Company & Customers

▶ **Consultant/Engineer** promoted 4 times in 8 years, rising to leadership role with a worldwide leader in rolling bearings and related technologies, serving OEMs and industrial operations in virtually every major industry.

▶ **Analytical Problem-Solver** with 8 years' progressive experience creating customized solutions—understanding customer needs and developing strategic offerings that are cost-competitive and difficult for competitors to replicate.

▶ **MBA plus BSME**—effective combination of strategic, big-picture thinking with analytical skills and detail orientation to create workable solutions that deliver measurable results.

Expertise: Strategic Solution Development | Engineering, Product, and Process Solutions | Industrial Applications | Customer Needs Assessment | Internal, External, and Cross-Functional Project Management | Customer Relationship Building | Team Leadership | Engineering Staff Development | Budget Management

PROFESSIONAL EXPERIENCE

MAX Products, Inc. | 2011–Present

Engineering Team Lead   Jan 2020–Present

Promoted to direct a team of 3 Application Engineers providing engineering solutions and process improvements to the company's 2 largest OEM accounts. Spearhead the entire consulting process, from problem identification through solution development and implementation. Define overarching strategy plus project plans, timelines, and deliverables. Ensure project execution internally and at client sites. Known for exceptional follow-through.

- Support large global customers in Asia, Europe, Australia, South America, and North America, efficiently managing consulting projects involving multiple time zones, languages, and cultures.

- Lead a diversely experienced team, providing individual mentoring and support to build professional and technical competencies and ensure that projects remain on schedule.

▶ **Highlight:** One of only a handful of engineers entrusted to develop project pricing with only minimum input from Sales. Create profitable proposals that emphasize unique value of our solutions.

Application Engineer Specialist, Key Accounts   Aug 2017–Jan 2020

Hand-picked by senior manager to fill Specialist role for the company's #1 OEM account. Build relationships with customer stakeholders to uncover existing pain points , then develop customized, high-value solutions. Manage internal production and technical resources to deliver products on time, within specification, and at targeted costs.

- In 2017, managed and supported 24 new client projects ranging from **$20K** to **$2M** in revenue.

- Served as a trusted partner and resource for other MAX client teams, providing insight on client relationship management, project execution, and design/application ideas.

▶ **Highlight:** Set the stage for **$1.5M** in new revenue (first 3 years) by getting to the root of a seemingly simple customer problem and identifying an opportunity to provide an entire unit rather than simply a component. Coordinated across 3 different product lines to ensure on-time, on-budget delivery, delighting the customer and making it very difficult for competitors to vie for the business.

Strategy: Call out a "Highlight" for each position to show a consistent trend of performance in every role in this young manager's career.

MEREDITH MATTHEWS | Page 2   617-555-3456 | meredith.matthews@gmail.com

MAX Products, Inc. | continued

Application Engineer, Aftermarket Accounts   Mar 2016–Aug 2017

Promoted to deliver engineering consulting services to 2 key aftermarket accounts. Brought product and problem-solving expertise to a wide range of customer challenges and created customized solutions to reduce cost, increase throughput, slash production downtime, and replace competitor solutions. Developed and delivered technical training, sales support presentations, and failure analysis reports to customers.

> ► **Highlight:** Addressed a component failure challenge at #1 account that was causing production stoppages every 2 weeks. Recommended and persuaded customer to purchase a significantly higher-priced component by emphasizing long-term value. Overcame resistance to new procedures by taking the time to build relationships at the assembly level. As a result, increased average uptime from 2 weeks to 3 months and earned 3 follow-on opportunities worth **$50K** annually in new business.

Application Engineer, Small/Mid-Sized OEM Accounts   Oct 2013–Mar 2016

Provided technical support to customers and the internal sales team related to product design and selection, prototype and validation testing, product damage analysis, warranty claims, and delivery issues.

> ► **Highlight:** Generated **$250K** in new annual recurring revenue by designing a new machine incorporating an innovative bearing that eliminated frequent downtime and product contamination.

Application Engineer Trainee   Sep 2012–Oct 2013

Recruited from Northeastern into year-long rotational program providing exposure to diverse industries and the complete SKF product line.

EDUCATION

MBA | Boston University, Questrom School of Business, Boston, MA   2019

> ► **Highlight:** Outperformed 5 other teams in capstone project—an engineering challenge to build the most marketable and cost-effective product. Generated $5K sales (5X closest competitor) and 48% profit.

BS Mechanical Engineering | Northeastern University, Boston, MA   2012

> ► **Co-op Rotations:** GE Aviation | Raytheon BBN Technologies | MAX Products

RESUME 36: by Wendy Enelow, MRW, CCM, CPRW, JCTC • www.wendyenelow.com

LAURA A. GREENE

472-342-8822 | lauraagreene@hotmail.com | www.Linkedin.com/in/lagreenega

ENGINEERING BUSINESS LEADER

500+ New Products & New Brands – Consumer Products, Medical Devices, Electronics, Technology

Manufacturing Engineering | Product Development | R&D | Machining | Fixture & Tool Design
Project Management | Process Development | Productivity | Staffing & Training | Regulatory Compliance | P&L

Consistently drive forward innovation, capture new opportunities, optimize business assets and resources, develop new products, craft innovative solutions, and improve machining, tooling, quality, and manufacturing operations. Lead with an entrepreneurial spirit that energizes organizations to surpass milestones and financial objectives. Signature qualifications:

Management Experience:	Strategic Planning, Budgeting, Capital Equipment Acquisition, Outsourcing, Contracts, Supplier Negotiations, Materials & Inventory, Quality, Technology, Team Leadership
Rapid Prototyping Experience:	Prototyping & Mass-Manufacturing Platforms, CNC Programming, Set-Up & Operation, Sheet Metal Fabrication, Part Decoration, Metal Finishing, Plastic Injection Molding
Manufacturing Experience:	Multi-Axis Machining Operations, Manual & Semi-Automatic Fixture Design, Gauging, PLC Programming, Pneumatic & Electro-Mechanical Systems, Micro- & Macro-Plant Layout
Sales & Business Development:	Collaboration with global marketing, sales, and engineering teams to introduce new product concepts focused on design for manufacturability
Facilities Management:	5 new model shop start-ups and expansions; capital equipment acquisition/implementation

PROFESSIONAL EXPERIENCE

Manager – Research & Development ($250K R&D Budget)   2017 to Present

HEALTHCO MEDICAL DIVISION, Baltimore, MD – **Fulfilled/optimized prior investment of $1.2M in tooling.**

Recruited to transition newly established joint R&D Prototype Lab and Advanced Manufacturing Engineering (AME) Machine Shop into a fully integrated, strategically driven business unit to support new product development and manufacturing for $800M medical device company. Partner with operations to identify new product opportunities. Manage 3 labs, OSHA reporting, SDS, PMP training, and HAZMAT handling.

Built sophisticated R&D tooling and machining operation with capabilities that include 2- and 3-axis horizontal turning; 3-, 4-, and 5-axis vertical milling; EDM; grinding; injection molding; unique rapid prototyping (stereolithography (SLA) and 3D printing (3DP)).

- **Capitalized on R&D Prototype Lab by branding and publicizing internal capabilities** across 5 design centers and 4 manufacturing locations throughout the US, China, and Thailand to reduce reliance on third-party contractors.
- **Identified $3M in manufacturing tooling cost savings** through AME, sourcing, and operational changes.
- Created solid **business ecosystem** with standardized processes, systems, training, and protocols.
- **Partnered with** academia to build educational programs to meet workforce needs. Created internship program.

Model Shop Manager   2015 to 2016

LEE DANIELS, INC., Annapolis, MD – **Delivered measurable productivity gains and cost savings.**

Brought in to provide leadership for model shop and manufacturing support for 100+-year-old firearms manufacturer. **Within 6 months, permanently increased capacity,** reduced outsourcing costs, slashed lead time to develop prototypes, and introduced CAD/CAM/CNC. **Implemented first-ever 5S system to expand Six Sigma credentials.**

Strategy: Lead with a strong headline and detailed profile that clearly establish the expertise and value that this executive will bring to her next role. Use bold type strategically to highlight notable achievements and keywords in her job descriptions.

LAURA A. GREENE

472-342-8822 | lauraagreene@hotmail.com | **Page 2**

Founder / Model Shop Director 2010 to 2015

DYNAMIC PROTOTYPES, INC., Dallas, TX – **Developed 300+ unique products each year for 5 consecutive years.**

Founded and directed all operations of specialty model-making company supplying major US corporations (Black & Decker, DeWalt, Healthometer, Memorex, Microdiagnostics, Microsoft, Mr. Coffee, Oster, Q'Straint, Rubbermaid, Sunbeam, Tyco, XM Satellite) in the consumer, medical devices, electronics, and firearms industries.

Held full strategic planning, operating, technical, staffing, project planning, sales/marketing, inventory, maintenance, contracts, purchasing, capital acquisition, and P&L responsibility. Managed model making, prototyping, RP, and related services (e.g., CAD/CAM, CNC programming and machining, molding and casting, fabrication, finishing).

- Invested $250K+ in equipment and inventory to launch venture and achieved **profitability within first year.**
- Planned, designed, laid out, and directed construction of a **state-of-the-art model shop.**
- **Designed and developed new prototype of major component for consumer manufacturing industry.** Reverse-engineered products using manual, optical, and laser scanning technologies while maintaining interchangeability with existing aftermarket products. Designed fixtures and tooling and **reduced machine time by over 70%.**
- Created all **marketing and sales programs,** developed company website, and managed all sales negotiations.

Senior Model Maker / Acting Model Shop Manager 2006 to 2010

CONTEN PRODUCTS, INC., Dallas, TX – **Created/participated in 500+ prototypes and 3D solutions.**

Recruited to new Advanced Innovation Product Development Team following acquisition of Electrolux Household Appliances. Led model making and prototyping of consumer products and appliances for operations worldwide. Managed projects, personnel, equipment, inventory, regulatory compliance, and technology. Worked with design and engineering teams in Mexico and China.

- Introduced new model-making processes (**prototype sheet metal stamping, low temperature metal casting, gold coating, SLS, composite SL, FDM, thermal forming, finishing**).
- Established **world-class outsourcing relationships** and negotiated large-dollar **supplier service contracts.**
- Managed planning, design, and layout for two **new model-making shops** in Texas.

Senior Model Maker – DIGITAL DESIGN ELECTRONICS CORPORATION, Philadelphia, PA 2005 to 2006

Partnered with Industrial Design and Engineering to create conceptual models and develop prototypes for electronic products and components. Implemented new technologies to enhance molding and casting capabilities, expanded vendor channels, and introduced methods to fast-track products through model-making and prototyping.

Manufacturing Engineer – XTLC, Detroit, MI 2003 to 2005

Developed systems, processes, and controls to improve productivity, quality, ergonomics, and safety in 300-person automotive assembly plant. Implemented sensors, PLCs, vision systems, pneumatic, hydraulic, and electric circuits.

EDUCATION

M.S., Manufacturing Engineering, University of Maryland, expected 2021

B.S., Industrial Technology, Emphasis in Model Making, Studies in Manufacturing Technology, 2003
Idaho State University, Boise, ID | Founder, International Association Model Makers (model for chapters nationwide)

Certified Manufacturing Technologist (CMfgT) | GD&T Certification
Technical Training: SolidWorks, MasterCam, Mazak/Mazatrol, SME, AMA, Applied Geometrics, Arburg
Graduate: ProEngineer Level 1 & 2 Training & **Top 5 Finalist for International Design Competition**
Seminars on Kanban, Six Sigma, Micro/Macro Process Control

CHAPTER 7

Finance and Banking

- Executive Director
- Finance Director
- Chief Financial Officer
- Controller
- Risk Manager
- Mergers and Acquisitions Director
- Director of Finance
- Wealth Management/Private Banking Executive
- Chief Risk Officer
- Finance Executive

RESUME 37: by Lucie Yeomans, CPRW, NCOPE, OPNS, CEIC, JCTC, JCDC • www.yourcareerally.com

JEANINE S. MILLER

EXECUTIVE DIRECTOR
FINANCE AND BANKING INDUSTRY LEADER

Nationally respected senior executive with unique combination of astute financial industry prowess, keen economic trend awareness, and disruptive sales strategy expertise.

EXECUTIVE CAREER HIGHLIGHTS

Wells Mutual, Chicago, IL / New York, NY, 2002–2020

Leading global financial services firm and one of the largest banking institutions in U.S., with operations worldwide.

Executive Director, Business Banking Finance   2017–2020

Developed annual volume, balance, and revenue plans for Business Banking Loan Book, totaling $22B+ in outstanding balances and $1B in annual revenue. Led 5 direct reports with oversight of 300+ managers and 2,500+ bankers in field.

NATIONAL SALES
- Fueled new loan origination volumes to $7B annually, highest level in company history. Disrupted status quo among field bankers and management and initiated positive behavior change through extensive, national mentoring, coaching, and training efforts

CORPORATE STRATEGY
- Analyzed market behavior, defined packages for $86M revenue stream, and personally delivered program and key messages to 300+ managers nationwide annually.
- Crafted communication plan for unavoidable regulatory price increase passed on to customer base, reversing typical practice of pushing out cost increases without explanation.

COMPLEX ANALYTICS
- Functioned as corporate point person for evaluating potential effects of adverse economic and financial market conditions, which set strategy and KPs for all national bank branch managers.
- Revealed untapped, multimillion-dollar revenue potential and unique market offerings after partnering with corporate Finance, Risk, and Center for Excellence around Macroeconomics teams to develop highly complex measures.
- Architected and achieved federal approval for quantitative models, in response to Federal Reserve Bank stress-testing requirements for CCAR, ICAAP, and Risk Appetite exercises.

CFO, National Sales, Business Banking, Chicago, IL   2015–2017

Chosen to provide analytic, strategic, and financial support to Business Banking sales organization, consisting of 7 regions, 2,700+ bankers, and 300+ managers serving 600K customers with $65B in deposits, $18B in loans, and more than $2B in annual revenue. Merger combined ~800 bankers in Relationship Managed (RM) channel with ~2,000 bankers in branch channel.

CORPORATE SALES & STAFFING STRATEGY
- Restructured production/sales targets and built annual financial plan to increase accountability among bankers, improve customer service, and align metrics at region, market, and area levels.
- Established monthly analysis, linking revenue growth to banker production and calling activity, resulting in 36% increase in new business and 24% desired attrition.
- Implemented analytics, staffing model, and segmentation projects to evaluate portfolio loads, prospect density, and branch coverage. Corrected alignment for tens of 1,000s of customers to appropriate banker expertise.

CFO, Relationship Managed (RM) Channel, Business Banking, Chicago, IL   2010–2015

Directed strategic and operational management for $1B per year business with $30B in deposits and $12B in credit balances, focused on small- and mid-sized businesses ($3M–$20M annual sales).

CONTACT

(555) 555-5555

jeaninesmiller@gmail.com

Chicago, IL

my Linked in profile

EXPERTISE

$MM Revenue Growth

Analytics

Annual Financial Planning

Business Intelligence

Corporate Strategy

Disruptive Innovation

KPIs

Leadership Development

M&A

National Sales

Risk Management

Reporting

Staffing Models

EDUCATION

BUCKNELL UNIVERSITY

B.S. in Business Accounting

Minor: Economics

Strategy: Segment accomplishments under headings that are both keyword-rich and align with her diverse interests as she pursues a new opportunity. Enhance strong content with a striking yet relatively conservative design that is appropriate for the finance and banking industry.

JEANINE S. MILLER ■ (555) 555-5555 ■ jeaninesmiller@gmail.com
Page 2

CFO, Relationship Managed (RM) Channel (continued)

CORPORATE SALES & REPORTING STRATEGY

- Initiated and created monthly management reporting process to correct glaring inconsistencies and accountability across 9 sales regions and 94 markets. Combined financial results with branch productivity, calling prospecting activity, and credit quality metrics.

CORPORATE STRATEGY HIGHLIGHTS

- Built robust RM staffing model to handle not only RM channel requirements, but also acquisition of and unpredictable growth from former Wells Mutual customers. Used average portfolio size, prospect density, and branch penetration to determine optimal staffing levels in all markets; grew from 0 to 500 bankers.
- Rectified 100s-of-millions of dollars of mismatched commercial retail customers and bankers through collaborative effort with senior banking managers companywide.
- Improved individual productivity per banker and brought banks into corporate alignment by analyzing national, regional, and branch customer base and implementing relevant, market-specific targets for all sales teams. Achieved buy-in to new, more meaningful program through heavy collaboration with bank management.

NATIONAL SALES STRATEGY IMPACT

- Experienced 10% growth year over year (YOY) in existing markets and 30% YOY growth in expansion markets.
- Drove 200+% new customer acquisition growth within first year by changing banker incentive plans to better align with RM Channel strategy.

Vice President – Business Banking Finance | Chicago, IL | 2008–2010
Regional finance manager for Central, Midwest, and East region branch-based business sales organizations.

REGIONAL SALES STRATEGY

- Provided insights and analysis from sales production results to sales force, driving increased acquisition and retention of customers with < $3M annually in sales.
- Researched and analyzed regional business differences, sales strategies for each, and effectiveness of KPIs. Refined data, revamped KPIs, and designed meaningful sales reporting scorecards for regional managers and sales force.

EARLIER WELLS MUTUAL CAREER

Vice President – Finance / Planning and Analysis | Chicago, IL | 2007–2008
Acted as liaison between Corporate P&A and retail businesses, with specific focus on consumer banking, business banking, and insurance businesses. Assisted in building out annual planning and monthly management reporting and outlook processes for Wells Mutual retail businesses. Prepared investor conference and board presentations for senior management.

Vice President – Finance / Controller | New York, NY | 2006–2007
Originated management reporting and planning process for newly launched employee financial services unit.

Vice President – Marketing Analytics | New York, NY | 2002–2006
Managed a team of 8 analysts responsible for optimizing credit card marketing spending to realize highest return on investment while delivering on new account goals of 4M accounts and generating $185M in revenue.

PRIOR EXPERIENCE

Senior Pricing Analyst, Finance | Executive Finance Services, Inc. | Boston, MA

Corporate Strategy Senior Analyst, Global Planning / Analysis Dept. | American Card Co. | Hoboken, NJ

RESUME 38: *by Marjorie Sussman, MRW, ACRW, CPRW • www.linkedin.com/in/marjoriesussmanmrw*

Rick Brent, CFA

212-555-9239 | brent@gmail.com
www.linkedin.com/in/brent

SENIOR FINANCE EXECUTIVE: CONSUMER GOODS

FP&A | BUSINESS PLANNING | GLOBAL ANALYTICS | OPERATIONAL EFFICIENCIES | BRAND VALUE

More than 15 years of Corporate Finance experience – CFO, Finance Director, Controller, and Board Member for multinational enterprises in North America, Latin America, and Asia-Pacific. **Booth MBA** in Finance & Strategy.

- **Executive leader and trusted advisor** in extremely complex industry and macroeconomic conditions.

- **Repeatedly called on to take the reins in crisis situations** to quickly distill complex data into business insights and action that transform, turn around, and establish means to long-term profitability.

PROFESSIONAL EXPERIENCE

WORLDWIDE BRANDS (NYSE: WWB)   New York, Mexico, Wellington | 2006–Present
British multinational; world's leading premium beverage producer; $17.5B revenue, $74B market cap, 180 markets, 28K employees.

Finance Director, Strategic International Initiatives, New York, NY | 2019–Present

Tapped for newly created strategic leadership role, conceiving and executing growth initiatives to expand the company's presence into new international markets. Key growth targets include Latin America and Europe.

- **Growth Strategy:** With executive team, crafted plans and projections to jump-start growth and efficiency in target region 50% in 1 year and 300% in 5 years.

- **Brand Building:** Continue to influence performance of Corona brand as member of Board since 2012.

Chief Financial Officer, Corona, Mexico City, Mexico | 2016–2019

Led finance team in revitalizing the Mexican-headquartered business, reversing a 4-year, 45% decline. Played key role in design and execution of focused 3-tier turnaround strategy in a rock-solid control environment. Member, Corona Board of Advisors (Audit & Governance Committees).

- **Dramatic Turnaround:** Streamlined operations and transformed cost base to improve operating margin and help to restore profitability in export markets after 9 years of losses.

- **Brand Value Creation:** Guided implementation of investment decisions and increased equity in Corona brand by reconnecting with US consumers through event-sponsorship strategy. Elevated Corona to #1 imported beer in the US.

- **End-to-end Efficiency:** Drove company-wide culture change to optimize every dollar spent, and allocated savings to brand growth and long-term investments.

- **Profitable Export Markets:** Changed US distribution to royalty structure, allowing more brand investments and transforming export arm into profit-positive business.

Shareholder Value | Financial Growth

- Grew shareholder equity **35%;** earnings per share **299%;** dividend per share **100%.**

- Grew operating profit **160%;** operating profit margin **201%;** after-tax profit **300%.**

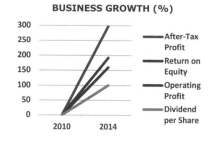

BUSINESS GROWTH (%)

After-Tax Profit
Return on Equity
Operating Profit
Dividend per Share

Strategy: Capture attention with a colorful chart that instantly communicates exceptional results in multiple areas of measurement. Enhance readability with bold introductions to each bullet point.

Rick Brent, CFA   212-555-9239 | brent@gmail.com

WORLDWIDE BRANDS *(continued):*

<u>**Finance Director, Asia-Pacific,**</u> Wellington, New Zealand | 2013–2016

Built and led 20-member team in FP&A for $500M region, increasing transparency and strengthening controls to grow operating profit and margin and create channel integrity.

- **Financial Performance:** Delivered double-digit gains in operating profit and margin through consistent volume growth and innovative pricing strategies, especially in a major wine portfolio.

- **Crisis Management:** Led cross-functional crisis team in stemming $50M financial exposure when major account stopped payment; seized $25M+ of customer's stock and negotiated settlement of the balance with no disruption of business operations.

- **Business Metrics:** Reconfigured metrics on organic performance of distributor depletions rather than distributor sales. Established market-share data in key markets despite the data-poor environment.

<u>**Financial Controller, Asia-Pacific,**</u> Wellington, New Zealand | 2011–2013

Relocated from Toronto to Wellington to establish and staff the control, risk management, financial planning, and reporting structure as company shifted focus from more mature markets to the growth potential of emerging markets.

- **Growth Strategy:** Established groundwork for the region's business to more than double to current level of $1.2B sales and $400M profit in a high volatility and data-poor business climate.

<u>**Partner, Global Business Support Group,**</u> Toronto, Canada | 2008–2011

Supported enterprise-wide projects on strategy and business development, including valuation analysis for acquisition of BevPro business in Ghana; repatriation of trapped currency in Seychelles; monetization of stake in Anheuser Busch; advertising and promotion effectiveness model for North America; and risk mitigation plan to protect IP rights and operations during economic volatility in Venezuela.

<u>**MBA Intern,**</u> Mexico City, Mexico | Summer 2008

During 4-month tenure, executed several projects in Latin American business, most notably performance analysis and value chain recommendation to reverse years of decline in secondary wine brands. Project was extremely well received and led to immediate offer for full-time position upon completion of MBA.

SAMSON WORLDWIDE   New York, NY | 2004–2008
<u>**Manager, Financial Services**</u>

Rapidly promoted from associate to manager of 30+-member team in a Citibank engagement that overachieved on all deliverables and led to a multimillion-dollar add-on engagement.

EDUCATION

Chartered Financial Analyst (CFA)

MBA Finance & Strategic Management: University of Chicago, **Booth School of Business**, Chicago, IL
- Member, Corporate Management & Strategy Group, Entrepreneur & Venture Capital Group

Bachelor of Arts, Business: University of Michigan, Ann Arbor, MI

RESUME 39: *by Emily Wong, ACRW, CPRW • www.wordsofdistinction.net*

Anne-Marie Peterson

555.555.5555

annemariepeterson@gmail.com
www.linkedin.com/in/alexpeterson

CFO | CONTROLLER | CPA

Expert at streamlining corporate acquisitions, scaling for record growth, and expediting the GL closing period.

GAAP • SARBANES-OXLEY TAX COMPLIANCE • SEC DOCUMENTATION • M & A

Senior financial executive with 15+ years of fast-track experience in financial reporting, analysis, forecasting, budgeting, cash management, auditing, and controls for digital, software, and financial organizations.

Transformational leader who reinvigorates companies by restructuring, streamlining, and strengthening financial operations to maximize performance and profitability.

Operations troubleshooter equipped to respond to financial challenges related to turnarounds, acquisitions, and mergers with confidence, determination, and focus in faced-paced environments.

Fixed Assets
Cost Management
Payroll Operations
ERP (Oracle)
AR /AP / GL Account Analysis
Quarterly /Year-End Reporting

PROFESSIONAL EXPERIENCE

VISIOPRINT | Columbus, OH — **2005 – Present**

CFO — 2016 – Present

Oversee team of 50 finance professionals who have accountability for general ledger, fixed assets, inventory, cost management, accounts payable, cash, and payroll operations.

- Promoted to CFO from Assistant Controller within 2 years after successfully leading the acquisition of 5 companies (BabyPrints, Photozip, Origital, MyLife, and YourPublisher).

- Steered company through period of unusually high growth from $500M in 2016 to $900M in 2019.

- Maintained payroll staff of only 3 while overall company headcount grew from 800 to 3.8K.

- Successfully integrated purchase price of all corporate acquisitions.

SENIOR DIRECTOR | ASSISTANT CONTROLLER — 2014 – 2016

Collaborated with ERP team to increase operational efficiency, develop new reports, re-train personnel, develop system processes, and implement new modules/systems.

- Drove all aspects of monthly close process, including BvA analysis and 2nd-level review of JE & BS reconciliation.

- Oversaw quarterly reviews and year-end audit with external auditor, ensuring that all Sarbanes-Oxley (SOX) controls were followed. Developed new SOX controls as needed.

- Reviewed memos and provided footnotes for SEC filings.

- Directed implementation and development of ERP system, ensuring smooth integration of all reporting processes.

- Stabilized AP team and processes after earlier challenges with turnover and fiscal mismanagement.

- Increased operational efficiency by 30% by designing infrastructure to benchmark AP, GL, and payroll processes.

Strategy: Write and structure this candidate's resume to showcase her expertise in key regulatory, and financial affairs and her success in helping guide companies to IPO.

DIRECTOR, SYSTEMS AND COMPLIANCE   2011 – 2014

Oversaw all aspects of SOX 404 governance, ensuring company-wide compliance. Led cross-functional team from accounting, finance, and IT in the evaluation and implementation of best practices for ERP modules.

- Developed 2009 and 2010 SOX audit plan, incorporating AS5 and the COSO framework.

- Introduced and tested 120 controls, resulting in a 98% assessment success rate.

- Slashed overall SOX compliance costs by $350K in 2012 and by $150K in 2013 through additional in-house staffing and testing and collaboration with external auditors to reduce auditor testing.

- Negotiated reduction in auditor fees by 20%.

- Implemented critical patch release adhering to software development lifecycle protocol.

- Established help-desk system and protocol to track and resolve ERP issues. Managed all open issues and implementation of additional modules following initial launch of Oracle.

SENIOR ACCOUNTING MANAGER   2009 – 2011
ACCOUNTING MANAGER   2008 – 2009

Led team of 15 staff and 2 contractors in GL, fixed assets, AP, payroll/equity, and PWC audit.

- Reviewed key contracts and wrote SEC memos for accounting files and discussion with auditor. Project-managed all aspects of first-year accounting SOX 404 compliance.

- Orchestrated Oracle ERP system conversion that included planning, system requirements, SOX process considerations, data conversion, training, QA, reporting, and post-launch issue resolution.

- Managed all aspects of initial public offering (IPO) S-1. Drafted various IPO memos and prepared footnote disclosures for all F-pages.

- Reduced close time from 15 to 10 business days.

PRIOR FINANCIAL EXPERIENCE

SENIOR G/L ACCOUNTANT | Talvis (a CRT Software Co.)   2007 – 2008

- Identified best practices by benchmarking against industry standards and designed process improvements, which led to increase accounting operational efficiencies by shortening the close cycle.

- Integrated Talvis reporting systems (including revenue, AR, and management reporting) with CRT Corp (HQ).

ACCOUNTANT | Deloitte   2005 – 2007

- Led 10 accounting professionals in the execution and review of audit engagements.

- Prepared and reviewed SEC filings of publicly held companies.

EDUCATION/CREDENTIALS

MBA | Anderson School of Management | UCLA

BS, Business Administration, Major: Accounting • **Minor:** Economics | **UC Santa Barbara**

CPA | State of Ohio

Anne-Marie Peterson • annemariepeterson@gmail.com • 555.555.5555

RESUME 40: by Skye Berry-Burke, CMRW, CCTC, CRS, CIS, CES • www.skyeisthelimit.ca

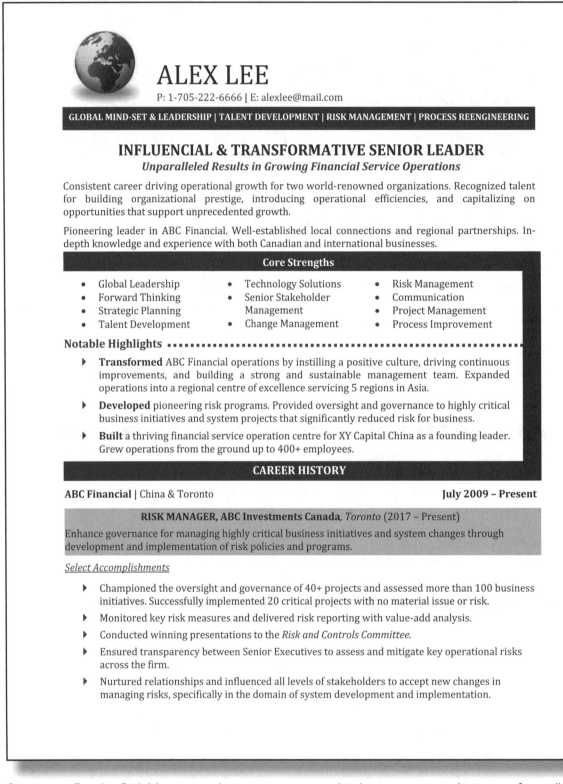

ALEX LEE

P: 1-705-222-6666 | E: alexlee@mail.com

GLOBAL MIND-SET & LEADERSHIP | TALENT DEVELOPMENT | RISK MANAGEMENT | PROCESS REENGINEERING

INFLUENCIAL & TRANSFORMATIVE SENIOR LEADER
Unparalleled Results in Growing Financial Service Operations

Consistent career driving operational growth for two world-renowned organizations. Recognized talent for building organizational prestige, introducing operational efficiencies, and capitalizing on opportunities that support unprecedented growth.

Pioneering leader in ABC Financial. Well-established local connections and regional partnerships. In-depth knowledge and experience with both Canadian and international businesses.

Core Strengths

- Global Leadership
- Forward Thinking
- Strategic Planning
- Talent Development
- Technology Solutions
- Senior Stakeholder Management
- Change Management
- Risk Management
- Communication
- Project Management
- Process Improvement

Notable Highlights ••

▸ **Transformed** ABC Financial operations by instilling a positive culture, driving continuous improvements, and building a strong and sustainable management team. Expanded operations into a regional centre of excellence servicing 5 regions in Asia.

▸ **Developed** pioneering risk programs. Provided oversight and governance to highly critical business initiatives and system projects that significantly reduced risk for business.

▸ **Built** a thriving financial service operation centre for XY Capital China as a founding leader. Grew operations from the ground up to 400+ employees.

CAREER HISTORY

ABC Financial | China & Toronto ⟶ **July 2009 – Present**

RISK MANAGER, ABC Investments Canada, *Toronto* (2017 – Present)
Enhance governance for managing highly critical business initiatives and system changes through development and implementation of risk policies and programs.

Select Accomplishments

▸ Championed the oversight and governance of 40+ projects and assessed more than 100 business initiatives. Successfully implemented 20 critical projects with no material issue or risk.

▸ Monitored key risk measures and delivered risk reporting with value-add analysis.

▸ Conducted winning presentations to the *Risk and Controls Committee.*

▸ Ensured transparency between Senior Executives to assess and mitigate key operational risks across the firm.

▸ Nurtured relationships and influenced all levels of stakeholders to accept new changes in managing risks, specifically in the domain of system development and implementation.

Strategy: For this Risk Manager seeking a promotion within his company, set him apart from all other candidates through a striking design and emphasis on broad expertise and exceptional achievements.

Alex Lee | 1-705-222-6666 | alexlee@mail.com | Page 2

HEAD OF OPERATIONAL DEVELOPMENT, ABC Financial International, *China* (2016 to 2017)

Led project team to deliver regional initiatives, management reporting, system enhancements, and user acceptance tests to meet global and regional goals across Asia operations.

Select Accomplishments

▶ Created and implemented a standard project management framework for Asia operations. Established a function of system enhancements and user acceptance tests.

▶ Reduced regulatory and reputational risks by delivering the Global Program to identify gaps in complying with ABC Financial Corporate and local country regulations.

▶ Implemented and supported various global and regional projects, such as Client Experience NPS (net promoter score) Program, Global Efficiency Enhancement Program, China New Business Development Initiative, and the Hong Kong Business Suitability Program.

HEAD OF HONG-KONG OPERATIONS, ABC International, *China* (2011 to 2016)

Led Asia retail operations centre; implemented business initiatives and end-to-end service delivery. Managed more than 150 processes in relation to account services, client trading, bank reconciliation, fund data maintenance, and quality assurance. Serviced 5 Asian regions.

Select Accomplishments

▶ Reinforced and influenced a culture of continuous improvement with ongoing training and reward programs; resulted in a strong, dedicated, and sustainable management team.

▶ Built the Hong Kong Operations Knowledge Database and Management Operating Platform; recognized as winning solution by leadership team.

▶ Developed innovative Investment Dealing System; improved productivity by 30% and significantly reduced financial risk.

XY CAPITAL | China   **2005 – 2011**

VICE PRESIDENT | CHIEF OPERATIONS OFFICER AUTO FINANCE (2009 to 2011)
OPERATIONS MANAGEMENT MANAGER (2008 to 2009) | CUSTOMER SERVICE MANAGER (2007 to 2008)
TRANSITION MANAGER (2005 to 2007)

Select Accomplishments

▶ Formed multiple strategic partnerships to lead the auto finance joint venture business initiative.

▶ Led the Underwriting Department of 240 staff and established credit card operations center development plans and management policies.

▶ Established a customer service call-centre from start-up; grew from 3 staff to 50 within 1 year.

▶ Improved service quality processing cycle time from 9 to 4 days.

▶ Steered the CMMI L5 (Capability Maturity Model Integration) certification project, setting XY Capital apart as the global leader for IT service delivery.

EDUCATION & PROFESSIONAL DEVELOPMENT

MASTER'S IN ENGINEERING | Wuhan University, China | 2003
BACHELOR'S IN ENGINEERING | Jiangsu University, China | 2000

BUSINESS ADMINISTRATION ADVANCED DIPLOMA
Development Management University, Singapore | 2005

<u>Additional Training</u>: Chartered Investment Manager, Canadian Securities Institute (in progress) | Business Edge Management Program, University of Sault Ste. Marie (2018) | Canadian Securities Course, Canadian Securities Institute (2017) | Project Management Professional, PMI (2011)

RESUME 41: by Melissa Orpen-Tuz, CPRW • www.greatresumesfast.com

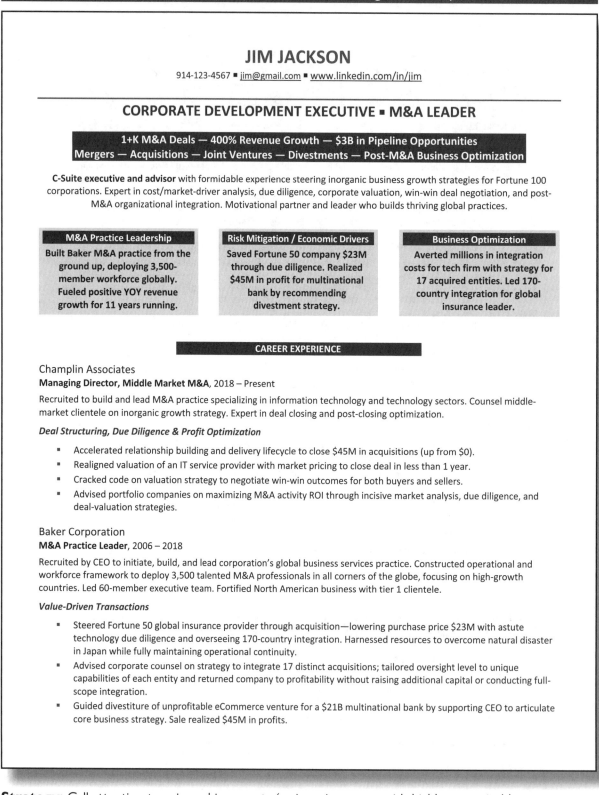

JIM JACKSON

914-123-4567 ▪ jim@gmail.com ▪ www.linkedin.com/in/jim

CORPORATE DEVELOPMENT EXECUTIVE ▪ M&A LEADER

1+K M&A Deals — 400% Revenue Growth — $3B in Pipeline Opportunities
Mergers — Acquisitions — Joint Ventures — Divestments — Post-M&A Business Optimization

C-Suite executive and advisor with formidable experience steering inorganic business growth strategies for Fortune 100 corporations. Expert in cost/market-driver analysis, due diligence, corporate valuation, win-win deal negotiation, and post-M&A organizational integration. Motivational partner and leader who builds thriving global practices.

M&A Practice Leadership	Risk Mitigation / Economic Drivers	Business Optimization
Built Baker M&A practice from the ground up, deploying 3,500-member workforce globally. Fueled positive YOY revenue growth for 11 years running.	Saved Fortune 50 company $23M through due diligence. Realized $45M in profit for multinational bank by recommending divestment strategy.	Averted millions in integration costs for tech firm with strategy for 17 acquired entities. Led 170-country integration for global insurance leader.

CAREER EXPERIENCE

Champlin Associates
Managing Director, Middle Market M&A, 2018 – Present

Recruited to build and lead M&A practice specializing in information technology and technology sectors. Counsel middle-market clientele on inorganic growth strategy. Expert in deal closing and post-closing optimization.

Deal Structuring, Due Diligence & Profit Optimization

- Accelerated relationship building and delivery lifecycle to close $45M in acquisitions (up from $0).
- Realigned valuation of an IT service provider with market pricing to close deal in less than 1 year.
- Cracked code on valuation strategy to negotiate win-win outcomes for both buyers and sellers.
- Advised portfolio companies on maximizing M&A activity ROI through incisive market analysis, due diligence, and deal-valuation strategies.

Baker Corporation
M&A Practice Leader, 2006 – 2018

Recruited by CEO to initiate, build, and lead corporation's global business services practice. Constructed operational and workforce framework to deploy 3,500 talented M&A professionals in all corners of the globe, focusing on high-growth countries. Led 60-member executive team. Fortified North American business with tier 1 clientele.

Value-Driven Transactions

- Steered Fortune 50 global insurance provider through acquisition—lowering purchase price $23M with astute technology due diligence and overseeing 170-country integration. Harnessed resources to overcome natural disaster in Japan while fully maintaining operational continuity.
- Advised corporate counsel on strategy to integrate 17 distinct acquisitions; tailored oversight level to unique capabilities of each entity and returned company to profitability without raising additional capital or conducting full-scope integration.
- Guided divestiture of unprofitable eCommerce venture for a $21B multinational bank by supporting CEO to articulate core business strategy. Sale realized $45M in profits.

Strategy: Call attention to prior achievements (major wins, some with highly recognizable company names) in the summary to be certain they are not overlooked. Provide details of the earliest positions but avoid over-emphasizing dates by tucking them next to the job titles, not at the right margin.

JIM JACKSON

914-123-4567 ▪ jim@gmail.com ▪ Page 2 of 2

Baker Corporation—continued

- Provided advisory services to construction materials company CEO that resulted in unwinding planned acquisition after technology and operational due diligence uncovered millions in hidden costs.
- Championed post-acquisition technology and operational optimization to position aerospace company for sustainable revenue and strong corporate performance.
- Orchestrated joint venture partnerships to expand Baker's capabilities, delivering sound corporate governance and financial models to protect corporate position.

Organizational Leadership & Operational Excellence

- Created and maintained $400M annually in pipeline opportunities ($3B throughout tenure).
- Propelled positive YOY compound annual growth rate (CAGR) for 11 consecutive years, 70% of which represented sustainable revenue.
- Closed $100M in cross-sector M&A services within 1 year.
- Hired and trained cadre of professionals to drive a high-quality engagement delivery cycle and support global client strategy development, execution, and oversight.
- Created rigorous M&A training that earned approval as a Baker-certified program.
- Personally delivered $15M in M&A services upon client request.

Perfect Solutions, Inc.
Chief Executive & Managing Director, 1999 – 2006

Founded and directed professional services consulting practice focused on M&A, divestment, and joint venture initiatives. Advised clients on financial and operational optimization strategies.

Corporate Development Strategy & Execution

- Cultivated and sustained relationships with global Fortune 100 companies, specializing in medical device and pharmaceutical clients.
- Built thriving practice from scratch to $10M in annual revenue and negotiated sale to Baker.

The J.M. Group, Inc.
Executive Vice President & Chief Operating Officer, 1988 – 1999

Co-founded and led M&A-focused professional services firm. Hired and developed 100-member team. Developed and oversaw execution of highly effective operating model, market growth strategies, and internal practices.

Strategic Inorganic Growth | M&A Leadership

- Spearheaded acquisition of Boston-based scientific R&D organization and served as CEO, reengineering business model to deliver high-impact, go-to-market strategies and propelling 400% revenue growth.
- Brokered sale to Big Four consultancy after building revenue from zero to $85M.

***

*Previous experience in the **United States Air Force**, specializing in military intelligence and covert operations.*

EDUCATION

Executive Master of Business Administration (EMBA) | Cambridge Institute of Technology

Master of Business Administration (MBA), Finance–Master of Science (MS), Economics | University of Michigan

Bachelor of Science (BS), Mechanical Engineering | University of Oregon

Warren Adaris

Bethesda, MD • 413.239.4551

warren.adaris@gmail.com • LinkedIn

DIRECTOR OF FINANCE & OPERATIONS – CORPORATE & NONPROFIT

- ⊙ **Finance Executive** with over a decade of proven experience delivering effective and relevant financial planning and analysis while executing multiple operational priorities for organizational budgets of up to **$25 million**. Specific expertise with nonprofit sector.

- ⊙ Known as a **problem solver** accomplished at analyzing complex financial data, **controlling costs,** and implementing solutions in fast-paced, high-pressure environments. Skilled at integrating technology and **automating processes** to enhance long- and short-range financial planning.

- ⊙ Adept at working as part of a cross-functional team or autonomously. Known for clear, concise and consistent cross-functional **communication** with stakeholders at all levels, including C-suite executives.

CORE COMPETENCIES

Strategic Planning • Financial Analytics • Performance Metrics • Reporting Automation • Accounting
Business Cases • Operational Process Improvement • Financial Management Planning Tools • Digital Strategy
Cost Reductions • IT Compliance & Audit Support • Data Management & Visualization • Donor-Funded Budgets
Ad Hoc Reporting • General Ledger Software Systems • Tableau

PROFESSIONAL EXPERIENCE

DIRECTOR, FINANCE & ADMINISTRATION – *Fitness DC*   2016 – Present; Washington, D.C.
Standardize financial and business operations, overseeing 112 employees while implementing measures to increase revenue and control costs.

- Achieved **46%** first-year revenue increase by reviewing and redefining service pricing structure of fitness programs and marketing promotions.
- Drove **38%** revenue gain in year two by spearheading development of new Sweat DC fitness program.
- Kept operating expense at **16%** under budget by implementing new, more efficient accounting system.
- Reduced accounts receivables by **95%** through customer relationship management, developing productive relationships and defusing conflict.

FINANCE OFFICER – *National Science Administration*   2009 – 2016; Washington, D.C.
Led nonprofit business planning, financial, budgeting, and procurement activities for multiple programs with budgets of up to **$25M**.

- Uncovered fraudulent diversion of **$1.2M** to employee, resulting in investigation and financial policies overhaul. Sought out by external accounting team for advice on controls and due diligence.
- Increased copy-center revenue from **$1.7M** to over **$3M**, adjusting pricing based on usage analysis.
- Provided financial and planning leadership for new, high-profile **$2.3M** multi-year grant-driven program, The Science Initiative, ensuring effective representation of science and scientists in television and film and establishing science resource support for entertainment.

PREVIOUS POSITIONS as **BUSINESS MANAGER** for *Education Publications, Inc.*, **DIRECTOR OF BUSINESS OPERATIONS** for the *Washington Group,* and **BUSINESS MANAGER** for *New York Dispatch*.

EDUCATION

BACHELOR OF BUSINESS ADMINISTRATION – *The George Washington University*   Washington, D.C.

Strategy: Facilitate a transition back to the nonprofit sector with a format that puts equal emphasis on corporate and nonprofit roles. Use bold type to call attention to numbers in the accomplishment bullets, providing proof of achievements and evidence of future value.

RESUME 43: by Louise Kursmark, MRW, CPRW, JCTC, CEIP, CCM • www.louisekursmark.com

SIOBHAN ADAMS CFP®, CRPC®, RFC®, CLU®

Greater Los Angeles | 213-332-9988 | siobhanadams@gmail.com

SENIOR EXECUTIVE: FINANCIAL SERVICES INDUSTRY
WEALTH MANAGEMENT | PRIVATE BANKING | INVESTMENTS

Strategy | Sales | Client Experience | P&L | Risk Management | Business Transformation
Cross-Business Partnerships | Sales Team Recruitment | Coaching and Mentoring | Team Leadership

✓ **Growth Driver** who consistently builds top-performing teams and creates a culture that values collaboration and a differentiated client experience. Transformed 2 sales regions from lowest tier to **top 5** in the company.

✓ **Thought Leader** in practice management, conceiving innovative strategies and programs that are adopted company-wide.

✓ **Inspirational Manager** who recruits, develops, and integrates diverse individuals into cohesive, highly skilled teams united around shared vision and purpose.

✓ **Business Partner** collaborating across segments to drive efficiency, client capture, and results for the entire business ecosystem.

PROFESSIONAL EXPERIENCE

Western Investments (Division of Western Financial)   2001–Present
Western Investments, offering financial planning and advisory services through the retail branch network, is an arm of Western Financial ($400B AUM, 6th-largest financial institution in the US).

SENIOR VICE PRESIDENT | REGIONAL SALES MANAGER, Los Angeles — Western Investments | 2015–Present

Recruited to rebuild Western Investments' underperforming "Spotlight Market." Currently manage $794M AUM and a team of 17 Advisors and 4 support staff delivering investment advice and financial planning services across 13 retail regions/172 branches.

✓ **Sales Performance**

- Elevated region from **#31** to **#3** in revenue in 3 years, earning 2019 Bravo award as one of company's top 5 RSMs.
- Added **$2.9M** to P&L and **$212M** in net advisory assets since 2015.
- Delivered consistent growth and outperformed ever-rising sales goals:

	P&L Contribution	Revenue to Plan	Advisory Growth Goal
2019 Results	155.75%	103%	123%
2010 Projections	146.5%	105%	120%

> Advisory AUM +157% to $314M

✓ **Team Leadership and Inspiration**

- Transformed business model from transactional to consultative, driving fundamental shifts in sales strategy, client relationship building, and talent management. Created common culture of purpose and performance.
- Rebuilt the sales team, recruiting 11 new Financial Advisors (**80%**) in the first year and coaching/mentoring in consultative selling, risk management, and the fundamentals of financial planning. In 2019, team was **#1** in financial planning proficiency, scoring **92.31%** vs. company average of **55.5%**.
- Developed the market's first million-dollar producer, who increased revenue **73%** to **$1M+** in first year (2015).

✓ **Strategy and Innovation**

- Crafted an innovative business plan to drive growth along all 4 pillars of Western's central strategy. Following great success in Los Angeles region, plan was launched nationwide.
- Designed standardized sales management process to align bank leadership with Financial Advisors to jointly build pipeline and capture emerging household growth opportunities. Process was subsequently rolled out across the retail branch network.
- Tapped to join the RSM Advisory Council, a small team of cross-functional business leaders providing insights to senior leadership to solve emerging business challenges.

> 2 programs expanded company-wide

✓ **Company Leadership and Recognition**

- One of 5 selected annually company-wide to attend prestigious CBA Executive Banking School, a 3-year leadership development program for high-potential leaders in the banking industry (2018–2020).
- Recruited by Regional President to join the board of an Employee Business Resource Group.

Strategy: Emphasize numbers and results—in bullet points, in a table, in bold print, and in call-out boxes—to make this executive's achievements jump off the page. Segment numerous achievements into easily skimmed sections with keyword headings.

SIOBHAN ADAMS | Page 2   213-332-9988 | siobhanadams@gmail.com

VICE PRESIDENT | REGIONAL SALES MANAGER, Northern California | 2013–2015

Elevated region from #38 to #5 in revenue in 1 year. Drove collaboration with business line leaders to market Western Investment capabilities throughout the bank channel.

✓ **Sales Performance**

- Increased YOY sales revenue **16%** to **$5M+.**
- Produced **$750K** in additional annual recurring fee revenue, adding more than **$54M** in net advisory assets in one year.
- Star Performer winner, 2013—top 5 RSMs in the company.

✓ **Recruitment, Coaching, and Development**

- Recruited, on-boarded, and coached 7 new Financial Advisors in first 6 months.
- Built a cohesive, high-performing team.

✓ **Business Leadership**

- Embraced the challenge of managing P&L—a new imperative for RSMs. Added thousands to the bottom line, without diminishing coverage or service, by identifying and eliminating underutilized real estate and telephone expenses.
- Invited to speak at the company's first RSM meeting. Educated peers on cost-saving strategy that subsequently delivered more than **$1M** annual savings to the company.

> Revenue +16% YOY to #5 in company

ASSISTANT VICE PRESIDENT | FINANCIAL ADVISOR, Sacramento, CA | 2010–2013

Rose rapidly to top performance by building strong relationships with clients and with bankers at multiple branches in the region. Collaborated with business partners to work as unified team to advance referral flow and improve client experience. Managed a team of 11 licensed bankers.

✓ **Sales Performance**

- Champion Award nominee, 2009—Western's top sales honor.
- Star Performer, 2008—top 10% of Advisors in the company.

✓ **Leadership**

- Mentor to new advisors—requested by SVP to coach fellow Financial Advisors to strengthen skills in problem solving, business development, relationship management, and sales.

> Top 10% sales company-wide

RETAIL INVESTMENT OFFICER, Fresno, CA | 2003–2006

Built new business by selling the value of financial advisory services in preparing for the future. Coached, mentored, and developed 7 licensed bankers. Held compliance and oversight responsibilities, requiring earning Series 24 license.

BANK BRANCH MANAGER, Fresno, CA — Western Bank | 2001–2003

Accountable for branch sales performance and operations, including compliance. Led vigorous training and development programs to build staff sales skills and customer service expertise. Rose to **#1** in the region in deposit growth (**+60%**) and was rapidly promoted to pilot new retail investment program and build out licensed financial services at the branch level.

EDUCATION

MBA | 2004
Bachelor of Science in Business Administration | 2002
California State University, Fresno

PROFESSIONAL CERTIFICATIONS AND LICENSES

- CFP — Certified Financial Planner
- CRPC — Chartered Retirement Planning Counselor
- RFC — Registered Financial Consultant

- CLU — Chartered Life Underwriter
- FINRA Licenses — Series 4, 6, 7, 24, 53, 63, 65
- Life, Health, and Variable Contracts insurance licenses

RESUME 44: by Lucie Yeomans, CPRW, NCOPE, OPNS, CEIC, JCTC, JCDC • www.yourcareerally.com

DOUGLAS R. DeLISE

✉ dougdelise@gmail.com 📱 (555) 555-5555 in https://www.linkedin.com/in/dougdelise/ 📍 Denver, CO

BUSINESS-FOCUSED FINANCE VICE PRESIDENT AND CPA

Instinctively quick to adapt to dynamic situations and strategically lead teams to award-winning results.

Rewarded for consistently delivering results:

- After 2010 company merger and 2-in-a-box Controller role, chosen to lead both rapidly growing organizations as sole Controller of $1B company.
- Selected to serve as 1 of 14-member Operating Committee, executing company strategy and critical issue response; 1 of only 5-member 401(k) and Profit Sharing Committee to strategize with and guide the Plan.
- Awarded 1 of only 15 Presidential Awards for timely execution of tax strategy.
- Go-to Ernst & Young Senior Accountant for 1st-year and high-profile audit engagements; chosen for innate ability to recognize, prioritize and balance client needs versus job requirements.

| Operational Excellence |
| Team Development |
| Strategic Acumen |

Reputation for positively affecting change:

- Steered $250M capital redemption, saving tens of millions of dollars in taxes.
- Repeatedly recruited and built loyal, high-performing teams with low attrition.
- Reduced bad debt from $1.1M to $0.1M after establishing internal controls in direct-store-delivery (DSD) organization.
- Ran corporate customer pricing and vendor bill-back system implementation; went live with zero issues.

Strategy • M&A • Business Integrations • System Implementations • Team Development • IFRS • Financial Close
Big 4 Public Accounting • Reporting • Budgeting • Forecasting • Treasury • Credit • Lean Process • SAP

EXPERIENCE

AMERICAN FOODS CO. | DENVER, CO | 2016–PRESENT
$23B food company and leading foodservice distributor, partnering with ~250K chefs, restaurateurs, and foodservice operators.

Division Vice President, Controller (2018–Present)

Appointed by new CFO after company merger and shared controller position to manage 5 direct reports, lead 100+ person organization, collaborate with/report to parent company executives, and oversee multifaceted operations, including financial and cost accounting, treasury, credit, reporting, forecasting, planning, DSD administration, and warehousing.

Initiate and lead multimillion-dollar cost/tax savings and performance improvement programs.

- Drove highest internal audit scores in company history by establishing best practices for internal controls in DSD organization in areas of route settlements, inventory, fixed assets, expense reporting, credit, and accounts receivable.
- Headed $250M capital redemption and cash pooling implementation for U.S. entities, saving tens of millions of dollars in taxes. As a result, awarded 1 of 15 Presidential year-end awards for 2019.
- Directed financed organization through vendor recall with full recovery of $3.5M loss from vendor.
- Improved working capital days and free cash flow by increasing days payable outstanding (DPO) by 40%.

Strategic thought leader, delivering results by leveraging industry knowledge and simplifying complexity.

- Key member of U.S. Opportunities Project charged with integrating $110M fast-growing sister company into American Foods' operating model and capturing thousands in synergies.
- Led steering committee through key initiatives, including SAP Human Capital Management and Payroll Implementation, as well as High Jump Sales Application Implementation, on time and under budget.
- Author quarterly president's letter and operating analysis for executive committee and board of directors.

Consistently recognized as an industry leader.

- Selected as 1 of 100 out of 79,000 employees globally to participate in first year of **Stanford's Executive Leadership Program** and then to participate in **MIT Leadership Program.**
- Chosen to serve as 1 of 5 members on 401(k) and Profit Sharing Advisory Committee and 1 of 7 members on Executive Operating Committee responsible for company strategy and critical issue response.

Strategy: Create an achievement-rich resume with just enough "flash" to be differentiating yet appropriate for the relatively conservative field of finance.

DOUGLAS R. DELISE

Page 2 | ✉ dougdelise@gmail.com | 📱 (555) 555-5555

AMERICAN FOODS CO., CONTINUED

American Foods Controller (2016–2018)

Managed 40+ member team responsible for financial and cost accounting, budgeting, forecasting, and payroll, representing $600M in annual revenue.

- Developed and guided highly motivated team to total savings of $50M+ (67% more than projected by Boston Consulting Group) through M&A, post-merger integration, and synergy initiatives.
- Streamlined accounting close procedures to meet the company's 2-day close requirement and 3-week annual close requirement within extremely tight deadline, allowing on-time M&A press release.

NEW DAIRY COMPANY | DENVER, CO | 2010–2016

$2.8B regional food service distribution company that markets consumable products, commercial food service equipment, and tabletop accessories.

Corporate Finance Manager – Contracts and Pricing (2012–2016)

Rapidly promoted to Corporate Finance Manager, reporting directly to Corporate Controller, Procurement Services (who reported to the President/CEO) and directed team of 12. Managed implementation of customer contracts related to pricing, vendor deviations, incentives, order guides, custom invoicing, audits, and reporting.

- Maximized gross profit with 99% accuracy rate.
- Generated $10M in revenues through a school-bid system.
- Spearheaded a Lean project, implementing school commodity net-off-invoice system, that resulted in a $250K benefit.

Accounting Manager, Illinois Foods Division (2010–2012)

Managed $32M in accounts payable, implemented workflow and document imaging, analyzed and simplified sales tax policies and procedures, and directed team of 6.

- Slashed operating costs 32% and increased efficiencies 48% through major redesign and automation of A/P workflow.
- Saved division $1.8M by initiating partnership with IT to implement electronic A/P workflow and document imaging solution. (Leading to promotion as Corporate Finance Manager.)
- Updated payment selection process, increasing delayed payments by $3M while maintaining 100% cash discounts.
- Delivered 28% efficiency gain in procurement services by leading and managing a tracking system conversion.

ANCHORS MARINAS | CONTROLLER | DENVER, CO | 2008–2010

$15M marina management company, managing boat storage, boat rentals, restaurants, and stores.

Restructured and reduced month-end close procedures and monthly financial reports 50%. Administered year-end audits and authored financial statements. Implemented cash projection tool, capital expenditure policies, and point of sale (POS) systems.

BIG 4 PUBLIC ACCOUNTING EXPERIENCE

Deloitte & Touche LLC, Chicago, IL | Senior Accountant | 2006–2008
Ernst & Young LLC, Chicago, IL | Senior Accountant, Assurance and Advisory Services | 2004–2006

EDUCATION

Bachelor of Science in Business Administration and Accounting | Southern Illinois University | Carbondale, IL

CERTIFICATIONS & PROFESSIONAL AFFILIATIONS

Certified Public Accountant (CPA), State of Colorado
Member, Finance Executives International
Colorado Society of Certified Public Accountants

REBECCA TRIPLETT

Mobile: 613-909-8821   linkedin.com/in/rebtriplettcfo   RebTrip209@gmail.com

CHIEF FINANCIAL OFFICER

Astute Financial, Business & Technology Leadership
Master of Professional Accountancy | CPA | PMP | Six Sigma Black Belt | Big Four

Senior finance executive and key member of executive teams driving revenue growth for companies in diverse industries and circumstances—startup, turnaround, and high growth. **Financial and business strategist** focused on delivering quick and sustainable results for shareholders, owners, and private equity (PE) investors.

Hands-on operational leader with extensive project, process, and reengineering expertise. Consistently drive positive transformation, simplification, and improvement through Six Sigma and PMP principles.

Collaborative team builder who instills purpose and mission in a diverse and multigenerational workforce.

PROFESSIONAL EXPERIENCE

PARTNER & INTERIM CHIEF FINANCIAL OFFICER (CFO)   2019 to Present
CASPERSON PARTNERS, LLC *(Technology consultants to mid-size firms)* | San Jose, CA

Recruited to provide senior financial leadership to preeminent consulting group of 75 former Fortune 500 CIOs working with Fortune 500 corporations, privately held companies, PE firms, and government agencies.

- **Consulting with CEOs, CIOs, and other senior executives** to share financial and accounting process expertise for the implementation of multimillion-dollar technology systems.
- **Spearheading the design and implementation of a replicable process** to productize and leverage the firm's go-to-market services.

CHIEF FINANCIAL OFFICER (CFO)   2016 to 2019
DISCOVER RECOVERY *(Agency serving Fortune 500 clients; $65M annual revenues; 180 staff)* | Santa Clarita, CA

Member of 6-person executive team leading PE-backed mid-size company through a period of rapid growth.

- **Enabled $1.1M revenue growth** in just 6 months by implementing advanced analytics technology system that "graded" collectability of Discover's 5M+ debtors.
- Refreshed accounting systems and processes to help drive **46% business growth** during 3-year tenure.
- Renegotiated long-term debt portfolio and **reduced cost of capital by 11%** ($350K annual savings).
- **Slashed $425K from annual cost** of IT services while **increasing internal customer satisfaction 20%.**
- Leveraged **Lean Six Sigma** to streamline operations and reporting. **Cut monthly closing cycle 50%.**

CHIEF FINANCIAL OFFICER (CFO) & FOUNDING PARTNER   2013 to 2016
CUSTOM SOLUTIONS AUDIT, LLC *(CFO/CIO/project management consulting firm)* | Denver, CO

*Provided executive-level financial leadership as **Interim CFO** for key client engagements with:*

- MARKS ASSOC. ($24M SaaS and technology manufacturing). Led financial affairs as company transitioned from start-up to product launch to **100% revenue growth in 1 year and 7% profit margin.**
  - Secured PE funding; renegotiated $3M term debt, slashing interest rate 45% ($200K annual savings).
  - Project-managed installation of 14 ERP modules in 4 months and saved $125K in labor and SW costs.
  - Saved an additional $120K/year through Six Sigma projects in operations and product management.

Strategy: Describe context and scope of each position in a shaded box to clearly distinguish from bullet-point achievements. Throughout, write tight copy that allows important and differentiating information to stand out.

CUSTOM SOLUTIONS AUDIT - *Continued*

- GLASER HEALTHCARE ($17M provider). Renegotiated debt to defer potential bankruptcy and developed 1-, 3-, and 5-year plans to support continued operations. **Won approval from 2 PE firms and bank.**
- DENVER WOODS ($25M manufacturer). Reengineered key manufacturing operations to boost efficiency and keep pace with rapid growth. **Slashed costs $400K and improved product delivery 12%.**

CHIEF INFORMATION OFFICER (CIO)   2009 to 2013
MXR FINANCIAL SERVICES *($220M+ BPO, financial services, and debt recovery firm; 4500 staff)* | Denver, CO

Senior Technology Executive tasked with creating a viable technology infrastructure to support internal demand, customer needs, and long-term growth. Managed $20M budget, 6 reports, and 135-person team.

- **Facilitated 70% revenue growth and $1.4M+ savings** by upgrading data and voice systems, networks, and technologies. Implemented cloud computing, CISCO VOIP call center solution, and 3 e-commerce systems that processed 2M call center transactions monthly. **Reduced call handling time 29%.**
- Constructed **business intelligence and data warehousing** system to support 20M consumer accounts.
- Led first successful SAS70 audit, enabling MXR to retain its Fortune 100 clients (**$50M in contracts**).
- **Salvaged $5.1M PeopleSoft ERP project** and restored continued rollout and enhancements.

SENIOR VICE PRESIDENT (SVP) & CHIEF INFORMATION OFFICER (CIO)   2004 to 2009
ALLY CORPORATION *(NASDAQ: ALY; $2.4B revenues; 40K employees; 60+ locations)* | Chicago, IL

Recruited to lead the expansion of technology infrastructure to support 37% annual growth for an industry leader in BPO call centers and global provider of communication and network infrastructure systems. Accountable for $72M P&L and 12 direct reports leading a team of 400 employees and contractors.

- Drove customer-focused technology solutions that contributed to **300% revenue growth** ($350M to $1.4B) over 5 years and an **increase in market cap of $1.7B.**
- Built fault-tolerant 24/7 e-commerce, call center, and cloud-computing technologies that **processed 42 B-C customer transactions** annually ($750M in annual revenues).
- **Expanded technology footprint** from 12 US sites to 40 locations worldwide as part of global expansion.

*Launched professional career with **Andersen** (Big Four) and advanced to **Manager** within 2 years. Subsequently held Director and C-level positions serving major clients in **energy** and **telecommunications.***

EDUCATION

Master of Professional Accountancy / BBA – Management	UNIVERSITY OF SOUTHERN CALIFORNIA
Certified Project Management Professional (PMP)	PROJECT MANAGEMENT INSTITUTE
Lean Six Sigma Black Belt (LSSBB)	COLORADO STATE UNIVERSITY
Certified Public Accountant (CPA) – Current	CALIFORNIA & COLORADO

PROFESSIONAL AFFILIATIONS

Association for Corporate Growth | CA & CO Society of CPAs | AICPA | Turnaround Management Association

William Hall

917-545-7766 • hall@gmail.com
Long Island City, NY 11101

Chief Operations Officer/Chief Risk Officer

Executive Profile

- **OPERATIONAL EXCELLENCE** – Excel at creating the vision for and building operational infrastructures that systematize processes, eliminate redundancies, reduce costs, and create corporate accountability.

- **RISK ACCOUNTABILITY** – Skilled at inaugurating initiatives to ensure compliance, mitigate corporate exposure and risk, minimize financial hardship and loss, assess client creditworthiness, and ensure integrity of company product mix.

- **THOUGHT LEADERSHIP** – Serve as key senior management team member on 20 corporate steering committees that affect every part of the business, including audit and regulatory examinations, technology, security, deal commitments, new products, and trade execution.

Operational Leadership Snapshot

• Risk & Control Metrics	• Business Continuity Planning	• Merger Readiness Assessments
• Loss Events Data Collection/Review	• Privacy/Records Management	• Audit & Regulatory Coordination
• Vendor Risk Assessments	• Fraud/Information Security	• Corporate Governance
• Sarbanes Oxley (SOX) Coordination	• Market Risk/Credit Exposure	• Business/Product Review

Professional Experience

BNP PARIBAS BANK, New York, NY   **2099 to Present**

SVP & SENIOR OPERATIONAL RISK OFFICER	New York, NY	2014 to Present
SVP OF OPERATIONAL RISK MANAGEMENT	Freeport, NY	2012 to 2014
SVP OF BROKERAGE OPERATIONS	Freeport, NY	2009 to 2012

Recruited to create the firm's inaugural operational risk team to track, analyze, and report operational risk and manage $1B in daily risk exposure. Established risk hierarchy, metrics, and reporting for the bank and its major business units to trim operational expenses by 40% and save millions of dollars. Grew team to core functional area with $7M budget and staff of 30. Member of and subject matter expert for multiple internal steering committees tasked with supporting the corporate infrastructure and delivering superior ROI to stakeholders. *Key milestones include:*

- **REGULATORY COMPLIANCE** – Managed liability, regulatory, and reputational issues and achieved FINRA, OCC, and Basel II compliance by creating an internal database to track losses and pinpoint breakdowns in the process. Built processes to report $100K+ losses within 48 hours and developed monthly reporting to mitigate risk.

- **CREDIT EXPOSURE** – Partnered with treasury services group to systematize processes around reviewing credits, credit limits, and compliance.

- **LOSS PREVENTION** – Trimmed loss revenue from 3% to 0.5%, exceeding corporate expectations by 200% and saving millions of dollars versus historical losses. Introduced a novel initiative that tied individual bonuses for top 200 executives in firm to loss prevention performance.

- **BUSINESS/PRODUCT REVIEW** – Launched a product team to consolidate existing sales products, manage integrity of product mix, review new products' underwriting and fee structures, and assess performance of products.

- **TECHNOLOGY PROJECT AUDITS** – Review close to 500 technology projects and service-level agreements with 1,000+ vendors to keep mission-critical projects on track and to allocate necessary funding.

LEADERSHIP SOUND BITES

- Recruited to BNP as one of the youngest Senior Vice Presidents in the firm.

- Began career at BNP managing 70% of the operations for BNP Securities despite no previous brokerage experience.

- Voted by peers as #1 functional staff within the business.

- Convinced 95% of staff to relocate from Freeport to New York City following BNP merger.

Continued…

Strategy: Combine tight, well-written content with structure/design features that make this resume easy to skim and easy to read—and easy for readers to understand the value this finance executive offers.

William Hall

917-545-7766 • hall@gmail.com
Page 2

BNP PARIBAS BANK

- **OPERATIONAL QUALITY ASSURANCE** – Key member of executive information security investment committee charged with auditing client reporting and creating QA processes. Currently developing an integrated portal to ensure consistent reporting and achieve regulatory compliance.

- **BUSINESS CONTINUITY/DISASTER RECOVERY** – Consolidated disaster recovery sites and recycled PCs to better use resources with no increase in costs.

- **MERGERS/OPERATIONAL INTEGRATIONS –** Championed and rolled out a risk management tool to track events, milestones, and readiness assessments in conjunction with merger activity.

- **OPERATIONS REENGINEERING –** Created the operational transformation to support straight-through processing for BNP Securities; saved $1.2M in year one while increasing capacity in several areas by 500%. Achieved objectives by conducting one-on-one meetings with brokers at 100 branches, tightening processes, and redeploying staff without increasing headcount.

ABN-ANRO GROUP, New York, NY   2004 to 2009

PROJECT MANAGER OF OPERATIONAL ANALYSIS, 2007 to 2009

Developed/analyzed sales and operational metrics. Launched IT cost center and installed data platform that monitored the group's telephony and other computer networks for the company's start-up secured credit card business.

- Trimmed $750K off internal maintenance costs by developing a new IVR application that automated customer service tasks and decreased need for service center staff.

- Increased performance 97% by reengineering the back-office management system.

SALES MANAGER, HOME EQUITY GROUP, 2005 to 2007

Managed sales for the company's start-up home equity loans business.

- In just 4 months, designed and rolled out an online loan processing system.

- Implemented a troubleshooting system that automated trend analysis and general reporting features. Constructed the group's first contact management system.

- Managed a 24/7 IT center handling 3,000+ calls per day.

OPERATIONAL ANALYST, 2004 to 2005

Managed process improvements, including an automated call system and back-office fulfillment process for the bank's cell phone service.

LEADERSHIP SOUND BITES
- One of the youngest managers in the company's history.
- Recruited and hired staff of 40+ sales people and 2 managers.

Education

B.S., Business Administration, New York University   2003

RESUME 47: by Wendy Enelow, MRW, CCM, CPRW, JCTC • www.wendyenelow.com

ALLISON GRACESON, JD, CPA

832-549-9412 | alligraceson@yahoo.com | Galveston, TX 77090

ENERGY AND OIL & GAS INDUSTRY EXECUTIVE | CORPORATE COUNSEL | FINANCE EXECUTIVE
CORPORATE COUNSEL & LITIGATION EXPERT | BUSINESS STRATEGIST | FINANCE & CAPITAL MARKETS LEADER | HR EXECUTIVE
CORPORATE SECRETARY | BOARD MEMBER & ADVISOR | TALENTED & FEARLESS NEGOTIATOR | BOLD DECISION-MAKER

Mergers & Acquisitions	Intellectual Property
Joint Ventures & Strategic Alliances	Team Building & Leadership
Corporate Governance	Contracts Management
Securities & SEC Reporting	C-Suite Relationship Management
Risk Management & Mitigation	Board Presentations & Relations

PROFESSIONAL RECOGNITION

GALVESTON 50 (TOP WOMEN IN C-SUITE POSITIONS), National Diversity Council (2019)
COVER STORY FEATURE, 4 Leading Women General Counsels, *Legal-Business Magazine* (Nov/Dec 2017)
FINALIST, BEST CORPORATE COUNSEL AWARD, *Galveston Business Journal* (2015)

PROFESSIONAL EXPERIENCE

RTD-MOBILE GEOPHYSICAL COMPANY – Galveston, TX & Dubai, UAE   2015–Present
Global provider of geoscientific data products/services to oil & gas industry. $2B market cap.

SENIOR VICE PRESIDENT, GENERAL COUNSEL, SENIOR HR DIRECTOR & CORPORATE SECRETARY (2019 to Present)
SENIOR VICE PRESIDENT, GENERAL COUNSEL & CORPORATE SECRETARY (2018 to 2019)
VICE PRESIDENT, GENERAL COUNSEL & CORPORATE SECRETARY (2015 to 2018)

Member of 9-person Senior Executive Committee that achieved and sustained profitability, strong cash flow, and no debt despite turbulent market and economic conditions throughout NA's oil and gas industry. Helped to make difficult business decisions regarding assets, resources, and personnel to ensure long-term success.

Leadership responsibility is vast with emphasis on legal affairs, M&A, credit facilities, SEC filings, audit reporting, corporate governance, risk, corporate compliance, and HR. Manage 4 attorneys and paralegal.

SIGNATURE ACHIEVEMENTS:

- **Reinvigorated passive legal organization into a vibrant and valuable partner.** Changed perception of legal as a business disruptor into a vital business partner to support global expansion and mitigate legal and economic risk. Empowered legal staff with autonomy and decision-making authority.

- **As the only executive in the corporation with previous divestiture experience,** stepped up to manage 2 financially critical and time-sensitive transactions. Instantly boosted profitability and met financial goals.

- **Elevated SVP and General Counsel roles** by earning trust, demonstrating value, and sharing multidisciplinary expertise to become a vital partner to global Board of Directors (US and UAE).

- **Partnered with UAE GC on critical litigation matters,** including years-long investigation and trial for a complicated tax-related matter and successful conclusion of several other matters.

- **Evaluated potential acquisitions and provided expert legal and financial expertise to accelerate corporate growth.** Selected candidates and structured, negotiated, and closed deals ($15M–$200M).

- **Hand-picked by CEO for senior HR leadership role** (effective 2020) to rebuild and revitalize organization and deliver similar success as achieved in legal department.

Strategy: Start with a summary that consists entirely of keywords and positions this executive for several different leadership roles within the oil & gas industry. Detail distinguishing "signature achievements" for her most recent positions and just briefly summarize older roles.

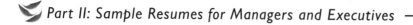

ALLISON GRACESON, JD, CPA

832-549-9412 | alligraceson@yahoo.com

DRANKIRK SERVICES, INC. – Galveston, TX   2009–2015
Publicly traded company (NYSE: DRK) providing specialty contracting to electric power, natural gas, pipeline & telecom

VICE PRESIDENT & GENERAL COUNSEL *(10 attorneys & 7 professional support staff)*
Allied with Board of Directors, C-suite executives, senior management, and key operating managers within the organization to provide expert legal, M&A, negotiations, risk management, and financial expertise.

- **Led $900M merger of publicly traded competitor and numerous other acquisitions and investments** – powerline and pipeline construction and equity investment in JV operating midstream assets in SW US.
- **Personally negotiated $450M+ in credit facilities, convertible subordinated notes, and redemption.**
- **Introduced more aggressive litigation strategies,** enforced non-competes, and settled multiple wage and hour class-action lawsuits. Maintained strong winning record in both legal negotiations and court proceedings.
- **Demonstrated superb negotiation skills by devising creative solutions** to structure complex transactions, eliminate roadblocks, and bring deals to close.
- **Launched comprehensive analysis of acquisition candidates and expansion partners,** including FCPA compliance, to penetrate African market. Negotiated with senior business and government leaders.

BROWN GORDON TAYLOR & LAWSON LLP *(formerly Kingston & Martin, LLP)* – Galveston, TX   2005–2009
SENIOR COUNSEL. Senior transactional attorney primarily for energy industry clients for 2 large international law firms. Built and retained impressive client portfolio based on strong corporate law and legal firm experience. Served as lead Attorney on M&As and divestitures, securities offerings, and corporate governance.

ATECHPRIME CONSULTING SOLUTIONS, INC. *(formerly Glasgow Partners, Inc.)* – Dallas, TX   2002–2005
DIRECTOR – CORPORATE STRATEGY & DEVELOPMENT. Spearheaded aggressive M&A program for Business Strategy & Development Group of publicly traded global IT consulting firm, including key role in $1B acquisition of Metamor. Led complex M&A transactions – selection, legal, financial negotiations, SEC filings, and closings.

CUTHBERT & COHEN, LLP – Dallas, TX   1998–2002
ASSOCIATE – BUSINESS DIVISION. Built thriving legal practice (M&A, project financings, debt and equity offerings, securities) based on prior corporate experience in business, finance, law, and oil and gas.

ACCOUNTING EXPERIENCE: CPA – 7 years: 2 as **PUBLIC ACCOUNTANT** and 3 as **AUDITOR** with May Consulting.

EDUCATION & PROFESSIONAL LICENSES

JD, UNIVERSITY OF DALLAS LAW CENTER, Dallas, TX
Summa Cum Laude; Graduated #1 in Class of 300; Managing Editor, Dallas Law Review

BBA – ACCOUNTING, SOUTHERN TEXAS UNIVERSITY – *Summa Cum Laude; Member of 3 Honor Academic Societies*

LICENSES: State Bar of Texas; Certified Public Accountant (TX)

BOARD AFFILIATIONS

GALVESTON AREA'S WOMEN CENTER – BOARD DIRECTOR, FINANCE COMMITTEE CHAIR (2017-Present)
Raised $1M+ as Leadership Campaign Chair (2016-2017)

GALVESTON CITY MUSEUM – BOARD MEMBER, FINANCE COMMITTEE MEMBER (2015-Present)

CHAPTER 8

Operations and Manufacturing

- Operations Manager
- Director Environmental Health and Safety
- Logistics and Supply Chain Executive
- VP Manufacturing
- Director of Operations
- Senior Manager, Manufacturing
- Senior Buyer
- Chief Purchasing Officer
- Chief of Staff
- Chief Operating Officer

RESUME 48: *by Andrea Adamski, CPRW • www.writeforyoukc.com*

Peter Urgalis

St. Ludger, MO • 572.739.2568 • purgalis@gmail.com

OPERATIONS MANAGER – LOGISTICS & CONTINUOUS IMPROVEMENT ANALYSIS EXPERTISE

- ◉ Customer-focused, award-winning operations manager with over a decade of progressive experience, ensuring **continuous process improvement** and **safety and revenue gains** across **950,000** sq. ft. of space, overseeing staff of **250+** and annual budget of up to **$12M**.

- ◉ Adept and adaptable problem solver known for implementing best practices and proactively, quickly, and effectively anticipating and resolving issues. Decisive leadership in operational analysis, planning and development, P&L management and logistical project management.

- ◉ Outstanding collaborator acknowledged for providing logistical assistance and guidance across diverse cross-functional departments and operational levels. Two-time winner of **Facility Manager of the Year.** Eligible for Department of Energy (DOE) Q-level security clearance. Willing to travel.

CORE COMPETENCIES

Operational Process Improvements & Recommendations • Logistical Project Management • Customer Service
Operational Data Analysis • Integrated Supply Chains • Inbound & Outbound Shipping • Receiving & Transportation
Environmental Monitoring Program Reporting • Safety Programs, Regulations & Procedures • Inventory Management
Regulatory Compliance: Federal, State, Local, DOT & DOE Regulations • Regulatory Compliance Training

OPERATIONS MANAGEMENT EXPERIENCE

MULTIPLE PROMOTIONS to positions of increasing responsibility as a career employee of **SUNSHINE DISTRIBUTION CENTER** in Charleston, Missouri.

OPERATIONS MANAGER, DRY & PERISHABLE OPERATIONS SHIPPING & RECEIVING   2016 – Present
Manage daily operations for both dry and perishable warehouses with nearly **1M** total square feet and combined annual budget of **$12M**. Direct P&L, business plan, safety, quality assurance, training, retention, human resources, communications, and internal investigations.

Supervise, schedule, and track production of **250** staff and 9 salaried managers receiving, filling orders, and shipping **200,000+** cases of merchandise daily. Ensure continuous improvement, safety, and on-time delivery across 500-square-mile territory serving 110 Superstores and 73 Sunshine Membership Clubs.

- • Consistently exceeded production goals:

	2017	2018	2019
Dry Warehouse	104.3%	107.9%	110.7%
Perishable Warehouse	100.1%	111.2%	112.9%

- • Reduced perishable warehouse turnover by **20.5%** and dry warehouse turnover by **13.3%** over 3 years, producing steady year-over-year reductions during tenure to date.

- • Dry goods receiving team ranked **first** in production out of 53 grocery distribution centers in 2019. Additionally, the team is exceeding 500 days without a medically treated accident and fast approaching the 2-year milestone for **zero** medically treated accidents.

- • Perishable shipping team achieved safety milestone of exceeding one year with **zero** medically treated accidents in 2019.

Strategy: Draw immediate attention to production achievements via a table that anchors page 1 of this concisely written 2-page resume for a senior manager with 15 years of experience.

OPERATIONS MANAGER, PERISHABLE OPERATIONS SHIPPING & RECEIVING   2012 – 2016
Managed daily operations for **450,000**-square-foot perishable goods warehouse within **$6M** annual budget, supervising staff of **100+** and 5 salaried managers. Controlled and minimized loss for quick turnaround for inventory that included a heavy percentage of perishable items—flowers, refrigerated/frozen food, and produce.

- Achieved an **11.7%** reduction in medically treated accidents over one year.

- Realized a **9.4%** increase in productivity over one year.

OPERATIONS MANAGER, DRY OPERATIONS SHIPPING & RECEIVING   2019 – 2012
Oversaw **$3M** annual budget, **500,000**-square-foot dry goods warehouse, and **80** staff.

- Selected as **Designated Super User**, integral to transition from antiquated, paper-based to electronic freight-tracking system. Completed the implementation— including equipment set up and testing and training for **50+** users—within expedited **45**-day timeline with **zero** incidents/revenue loss.

- **Promoted** to Operations Manager based on superior performance in prior Area Manager role, receiving **Facility Manager of the Year Award** twice, in 2005 and 2009.

PREVIOUS POSITIONS as Area Manager for *Sunshine Distribution Center*, **STORE DIRECTOR & ASSISTANT MANAGER** for *Fidelity Foods, Inc.*, and **RADAR OPERATIONS SPECIALIST, PETTY OFFICER** for *United States Navy*.

CERTIFICATIONS / TRAINING

SEXUAL HARASSMENT TRAINING – *Sunshine*   2018

HAZARDOUS MATERIAL MANAGEMENT, CLEANUP & DISPOSAL – *Sunshine*   2017

GENERAL AWARENESS & SITE SECURITY – *Department of Transportation*   2015

LABOR RELATIONS – *Sunshine*   2014

EDUCATION

BACHELOR OF SCIENCE, BUSINESS ADMINISTRATION – *Eastern Missouri State University*   Warrentown, MO

Peter Urgalis • 572.739.2568 • purgalis@gmail.com

RESUME 49: by Abby Locke, MRW, CCMC, CPBS, MBA • linkedin.com/in/abbymlocke-mba

BARBARA L. STANFORD

2700 Banner Drive, NE, Washington DC 20018
Telephone: 202-696-0040 / Email: bstanford@aol.com / Cellular: 202-709-5019

SENIOR MANAGEMENT

Environmental Health & Safety ▸ Facilities Management ▸ Technical Services

Bringing World-Class Performance and Compliance to Manufacturing and Production Operations
Infusing global manufacturing operations with advanced, state-of-the art engineering solutions that streamline processes, curtail hazardous waste costs, and elevate environmental and safety standards.

EXECUTIVE PROFILE

Unwavering success record in devising manufacturing and plant operating strategies that eliminate redundancies, automate processes/systems, increase production output, and deliver productivity, quality, and efficiency gains.

Impressive career history of developing award-winning initiatives and engineering solutions that generated a net total of $34.5 million.

Proven reputation for designing cutting-edge manufacturing facilities and implementing continuous improvement processes that revolutionize environmental safety and health regulation standards.

Notable Career Achievements & Milestones

* Architected environment, health, and safety programs and policies that became **"benchmark"** and **"world-class"** models that were fully adopted throughout the Smart Razors Company.

* Expanded Smart Razors' product portfolio/annual revenues by developing 6 new products while simultaneously **containing $650,000 in production and operation costs.**

* Engineered and **designed a $2.5 million, environmentally friendly, state-of-the-art manufacturing facility** that became primary prototype for future facility developments at the Smart Razor Company.

* Optimized manufacturing operations to **efficiently generate more than 1 billion products (Paper Buddy)**, a monumental feat for the first time in the division's history.

* Earned **National Safety Council's prestigious Sweepstakes Trophy** for maintaining the best safety records and programs for 7 straight years, an unmatched feat in the manufacturing industry

EXECUTIVE PERFORMANCE HIGHLIGHTS

The Rubber Guys, North America
DIRECTOR, Environmental Health & Safety – San Jose, CA
2017–present

Hand-picked by North American Operations to oversee the overall compliance of 13 manufacturing, distribution, and R&D operations in Mexico, Canada, and US. Charged with recruiting, hiring, and training a qualified environmental health and safety (EHS) team. Conducted additional safety and awareness training for up to 5,000 employees.

▸ **Environmental Health & Safety Management:** Decreased occupational injuries 400% by developing and implementing world-class EHS and risk management policies, programs, and practices.

▸ **Cost Reduction & Savings:** Identified $3.5 million reductions in worker compensation costs through business-wide checks-and-balances systems.

▸ **Facilities & Logistics Management:** Delivered $5.8 million in savings by strategically managing the closures of company's California and Wisconsin manufacturing facilities.

Strategy: Build a strong Executive Profile that brings impressive and record-setting achievements to the forefront. Use important keywords to introduce bullet points within each job listing.

BARBARA STANFORD   **PAGE TWO**

DIVISION MANAGER, Technical Services – San Jose, CA (2015–2017)

Retained as a key executive member of transition team following The Rubber Guys' acquisition of the Stationery Product Group, a division of Smart Razor Company. Challenged to execute 100-day operational plan and fully integrate manufacturing operations for Paper Buddy products. Managed environmental health and safety standards for entire operations.

▸ **Asset Management:** Verified more than $120 million in company assets, processes, and equipment transfers to support division's sale to The Rubber Guys.

▸ **Environmental Health & Safety Programs:** Collaborated with Los Alamos Lab to implement state-of-the-art technology that purged hazardous materials from production operations. Efforts resulted in a "Clear Air Award" from California's South Coast Air Quality Management District.

▸ **Manufacturing Engineering:** Realized $4.75 million in annual cost savings by orchestrating relocation strategy to transfer environmentally challenged manufacturing facility to new facility in Mexico.

Smart Razors Company, San Jose, CA   1999–2007
DIVISION MANAGER, Technical Services (2013–2015)

Promoted to lead and direct all engineering and facilities management activities for Stationery Products Group. Integrated technology/engineering solutions that produced efficient, cost-effective operating processes. Performed routine audits of company's facilities in China, India, and Mexico.

▸ **Strategic Planning & Direction:** Demonstrated expert technical and administrative leadership role in responding to natural disaster; salvaged materials and restored business to normal operations in only 2 weeks.

▸ **Operations Reengineering:** Reduced annual hazardous waste 12% and captured $4 million in savings by instituting effective operational standards.

▸ **Manufacturing Technology Integration:** Introduced state-of-the-art air pollution control technologies and innovative engineering solutions that reduced factory air emissions 90% and saved company $250,000.

▸ **Cost Savings & Avoidance:** Shrunk annual utility and energy expenses more than $2 million by renegotiating vendor contracts/purchases and instituting energy conservation policies.

▸ **Customer Relationship Management:** Increased and maintained customer satisfaction rating to more than 98% by establishing customer awareness programs and customer focus strategies.

MANAGER, Chemical, Environmental & Safety Engineering (2018–2013)

Tasked with revamping and restructuring manufacturing facility plagued with poor health and environmental safety standards. Assumed directive to streamline operations, eliminate occupational hazards, and decrease levels of manufacturing waste and air emissions.

▸ **Turnaround Management:** Upgraded division's safety and manufacturing standards to highest, best-performing operations in entire company while generating $1.2 million in savings.

▸ **Manufacturing & Operations Reengineering:** Reduced operating costs by $1.4 million and lowered occupational and environmental hazards by incorporating $2.5 million in equipment and process improvements.

EARLY COMPANY EXPERIENCE: Delivered significant contributions to company's revenue growth and production output through **Manager of Engineering & Maintenance** and **Project Engineer** positions. Top position achievements included **triple-digit increases** in process, equipment, and operational efficiencies.

EDUCATION

BS, Chemical Engineering – University of Michigan, Ann Arbor, MI

John Fixer, MBA, LCB

(213) 555-1212 • jfixer007@gmail.com • Long Beach, CA

International Logistics & Supply Chain Executive

Global-Scale Leadership and Transformation
Worldwide Supply Chain Management, Transportation, and Procurement
Compliance • Third-Party Logistics (3PL) • Strategy • Policy Development

➢ Leadership and transformation of Fortune 500-scale global logistics networks and companies to $869M.
➢ Licensed US Customs Broker. Compliance subject matter expert. Mitigated 7-figure risk. Familiar with CTPAT.
➢ Led $600M organization through US Customs Audits and Anti-Dumping Investigation.

More than 15 years of senior management experience in Logistics, Transportation, Supply Chain, and Key Account Management. Worldwide supply chain experience: North America, Asia, Europe, South America, and Australia. MBA and continuing study toward APICS CPIM credential. Known for collaboration and vision as well as strategy and daily performance management.

Technologies: SAP ECC 6.0 and MacPac, Ariba, SharePoint, ShipERP, 3PL OM portals

Professional Experience

ACME CORPORATION (2014 to Present)
$869M global supplier of high-performance engineered materials.

Director, Global Logistics: All domestic / international transportation and logistics at 33 locations worldwide.

➢ **Redesigned company's worldwide logistics system.** Standardized processes and documentation across the enterprise and reduced cost 10% by implementing new transportation management system. Simultaneously improved information security, governance of data, and reporting/audit capabilities.

➢ **Developed strategy to improve capacity planning, equipment utilization, and inventory management at 3 manufacturing sites.** Oversaw implementation of Manufacturing Execution System powered by SAP production planning (PP) and material management (MM) modules, delivering real-time metrics of plant efficiency. **Projected annual savings/efficiency gains up to $8.5MM.**

➢ **Consolidated onto global single-source carrier,** reducing small parcel carrier spend 15%, lowering claims 30%, and improving on-time delivery 10% (to 97%).

➢ **Developed precious-metal transportation policy and risk-shift strategy adopted by Acme worldwide.** Collaborated with business units and carriers to implement new policy.

➢ **Led Acme Logistics and Professional Services through $50M acquisition with zero delay in customer on-time deliveries.** Analyzed and mitigated potential sources of disruption.

Global Category Manager for Professional Services: $60MM procurement and contracting for HR, IT, finance, marketing, legal, and environmental health and safety services.

➢ **Produced $5M savings on $60M annual spend** by developing and executing category strategy.

➢ **Negotiated significant cost reductions:** 80% savings on enterprise CRM ($210K), 55% savings in print equipment and services ($205K), and 20% reduction in life and disability insurance costs ($285K).

OMNILINE INTERNATIONAL (2012 to 2014)
$439M multinational company with $30M annual freight spend.

Global Logistics and Compliance Manager. Strategic leadership, policy development, and process improvement for all domestic and international freight, compliance, and warehousing worldwide. Liaison with US Customs on all trade-related matters.

➢ **Identified and mitigated massive risk to company (millions of dollars in fines and penalties)** by proactively executing compliance initiative with US Customs and Border Protection.

➢ **Aligned logistics practices and goals of 9 subsidiaries worldwide with those of headquarters.**

➢ **Achieved 31% savings ($450K annually)** and improved efficiencies on international inbound transportation.

Strategy: Showcase the incredible magnitude of this executive's work—global, Fortune 500-scale logistics and hundreds of millions of dollars of value driven—by defining his impact in specific, quantifiable terms in every section of the resume.

John Fixer, MBA, LCB

(213) 555-1212 • jfixer007@gmail.com • Long Beach, CA

Continued

- ➤ **Invented statistical sampling audit method approved by US Customs,** streamlining audit processes and saving hundreds of thousands of employee hours.
- ➤ **Delivered 37% cost reduction on northbound shipments from Mexico** by increasing subsidiary freight utilization.
- ➤ **Produced immediate 75% reduction in warehouse pick/put-away time** by upgrading inefficient layouts.

RADIX INTERNATIONAL CORPORATION (2006 to 2012)

$600M manufacturer of products that guard and protect some of the world's most sensitive electrical and electronic equipment.

Global Trade and Compliance Manager/International Customer Service Manager. Global supply chain operations with $110M COG, including all imports and exports; $5M domestic inbound, third-party logistics (3PL) partners worldwide; and 11 distribution centers in North America, Asia, Europe, South America, and Australia. Seven direct reports.

- ➤ **Established first Compliance department in company's 93-year history.** Conducted on-site internal compliance audits and training in 6 countries.
- ➤ **Successfully led $600M organization through US Customs Audits and Anti-Dumping Investigation.** Led negotiation of tariff disputes, mitigating more than $100K.
- ➤ **Negotiated and finalized $2.5MM global freight-forwarding bids, saving $750K annually.**
- ➤ **Launched duty drawback program, recovering $110K+ worldwide in duties and taxes each year.**
- ➤ **Conceived and implemented cross-department country of origin and Harmonized Tariff data integrity project** for 36,000 SKUs involving multiple systems and countries.

TRANSPORT, INC. (subsidiary of Omnicorp) (2005 to 2006)

Leading provider of drayage services in the United States.

Account Executive. Development of sales territory encompassing 5 intermodal terminals and 2 states. Full-cycle B2B sales to import/export accounts: initial prospecting, lead qualification, closing, account maintenance, account retention.

- ➤ **Won multiple high-value accounts: Dollar Store, Little Tikes, Kenmore, and Procter & Gamble.**

OFFICE SUPPLIES, INC. (2001 to 2004)

International Logistics Coordinator. Global supply chain with Fortune 100-level volume: 10,000+ containers/year supplying inventory to 1,000 retail locations. International freight spend of $11M.

Education, License, and Training

Master of Business Administration, Executive Management specialization, California University
Bachelor of Arts in Economics, University of California Los Angeles
Licensed Customs Broker, United States Customs and Border Protection (CBP) (2010)
Enrolled in APICS CPIM Exam preparation (APICS CPIM Learning System)
Karrass Effective Negotiating

Professional Memberships

Council of Supply Chain Management Professionals (CSCMP), Institute for Supply Management (ISM)

RESUME 51: by Louise Garver, ACRW, CERM, CJSS, CPRW, CPBS, CCMC • www.careerdirectionsllc.com

WILLIAM T. PARKERSON

Cedar Grove, NJ 07009   parkersonw@gmail.com   (732) 599-4481

PLANT / OPERATIONS / GENERAL MANAGEMENT EXECUTIVE

Multi-site manufacturing plant/general management career building and leading high-growth, transition, and start-up operations in domestic and international environments with annual revenues up to $680M.

CORE COMPETENCIES

Manufacturing Leadership—Strong P&L track record with functional management experience in all disciplines of manufacturing operations • Developing and managing operating budgets • Spearheading restructuring and rationalization of plants and contracted distribution facilities • Initiating lean manufacturing processes, utilizing SMED principles • Establishing performance metrics and supply-chain management teams.

Continuous Improvement & Training—Designing and instituting leadership enhancement training program for all key plant management • Instituting Total Quality System (TQS) process in domestic plants to promote the business culture of continuous improvement • Leading ISO 9001 certification process.

New Product Development—Initiating plant-based "New Product Development Think Tank" that developed 130 new products for marketing review, resulting in the successful launch of 5 new products in 2019.

Engineering Management—Overseeing corporate machine design and development teams • Developing 3-year operating plan • Directing the design, fabrication, and installation of several proprietary machines • Creating project cost-tracking systems and introducing ROI accountability.

PROFESSIONAL EXPERIENCE

BEACON INDUSTRIES, INC., Maspeth, NY (2012–Present)
Continuous promotion to executive-level position in manufacturing and operations management during periods of transition/acquisition at a $680M Fortune 500 international manufacturing company. Highlights include:

Vice President of Manufacturing (2015–Present)

Senior Operating Executive responsible for the performance of 7 manufacturing/distribution facilities for company that experienced rapid growth from 4 plants generating $350M in annual revenues to 14 manufacturing facilities with revenues of $680M.

Charged with driving the organization to becoming a low-cost producer. Established performance indicators, operating goals, realignment initiatives, productivity improvements, and cost-reduction programs that consistently improved product output, product quality, and customer satisfaction

- **Saved $13M annually** by reducing fixed spending 11% and variable overhead spending 18% through effective utilization of operating resources and cost-improvement initiatives.

- **Cut workers' compensation costs 40%** ($750,000 annually) by implementing effective health and safety plans, employee training, management accountability, and equipment safeguarding. Led company to achieve recognition as "Best in Industry" regarding OSHA frequency and Loss Workday Incident rates.

- **Reduced waste generation 31%,** saving $1M in material usage by optimizing manufacturing processes as well as instituting controls and accountability.

- **Enhanced customer satisfaction 3%** during past year (measured by order fill and on-time delivery percentage) through supply-chain management initiatives, inventory control, and flexible manufacturing practices.

- **Trimmed manufacturing and shipping-related credits to customers from 1.04% to 0.5%** of total sales, representing annual $1.8M reduction.

- **Decreased total inventories 43%** through combination of supply-chain management, purchasing, master scheduling, and global utilization initiatives.

Strategy: Bring out core competencies with a detailed and keyword-rich introduction. Support these areas of strength with notable achievements called out in the chronological work history.

WILLIAM T. PARKERSON – (732) 599-4481 – Page 2

General Manager, Northeast (2012–2015)

Assumed full P&L responsibility for 2 manufacturing facilities and a $20M annual operating budget. Directly supervised facility managers and indirectly 250 employees in a multi-line, multicultural manufacturing environment. Planned and realigned organizational structure and operations to position company for high growth as a result of acquiring a major account, 2 new product lines, and 800 additional SKUs.

- **Reduced operating costs $4.5M** through consolidation of 2 distribution locations without adverse impact on customer service.

- **Started up 2 new manufacturing operations,** closing 1 plant and integrating acquired equipment into existing production lines; achieved without interruption to customer service, 2 months ahead of target, and $400,000 below budget.

- **Increased operating performance by 15%** while reducing labor costs by $540,000.

- **Reduced frequency and severity of accidents by 50%** in 3 years, contributing to a workers' compensation and cost-avoidance reduction of $1M.

- **Decreased operating waste by 2%** for an annual cost savings of $800,000 in 2 manufacturing facilities.

- **Maintained general management and administrative cost (GMA) at a flat rate** as sales grew by 25% annually over 3 years.

ROMELARD CORPORATION, Detroit, MI (1998–2012)
Division Manufacturing Director (2008–2012)

Fast-track advancement in engineering, manufacturing, and operations management to division-level position. Scope of responsibility encompassed P&L for 3 manufacturing facilities and a distribution center with 500 employees in production, quality, distribution, inventory control, and maintenance.

- **Delivered strong and sustainable operating gains:** Increased customer fill rate by 18%; improved operating performance by 20%; reduced operating waste by 15%; reduced inventory by $6M.

- **Justified, sourced, and directed the installation of $10M** in automated plant equipment.

- **Implemented and managed a centralized master schedule** for all manufacturing facilities.

- **Reduced annual workers' compensation costs by $600,000.**

- **Created Customer Satisfaction Initiative program** to identify areas of concern; implemented recommendations, significantly improving customer satisfaction.

Prior Positions: Manufacturing Manager (2006–2008); Plant Manager (2005–2006); Engineering Manager (2003–2005); Plant Industrial Engineer (1998–2003).

EDUCATION & PROFESSIONAL DEVELOPMENT

Bachelor of Science in Manufacturing Engineering
Syracuse University, Syracuse, NY

Continuing professional development programs in
Executive Management, Leadership, and Finance

RESUME 52: Wendy Enelow, MRW, CCM, CPRW, JCTC • www.wendyenelow.com

MATTHEW LOCATELLI

910-655-3420 ◆ mattlocatelli@gmail.com ◆ LinkedIn Profile

MANUFACTURING OPERATIONS MANAGEMENT | PROGRAM & PROJECT MANAGEMENT

Facility Operations & Business Management | Industrial & Manufacturing Engineering
Earned-Value Management Program Tracking | Business Planning, Staffing & Budgeting
Supply Chain Management/MRP Processes | Lean+10x & Six Sigma | Productivity & Process Improvement
Quality Assurance, CMMI & ISO 9001 | Risk Management | Program Management | Motivational Team Leadership

PROFESSIONAL HONORS & DISTINCTION

2015 Luther King – Martin Marietta Defense, Space & Security (BDS) Award
2013 Martin Marietta Network & Space Systems (N&SS) Employee Engagement Award

Active DoD TS/SCI Security Clearance (through 2021)

PROFESSIONAL EXPERIENCE

MARTIN MARIETTA – Electronics & Information Solutions (E&IS), Rochester NY   2015 – Present
Acquired Beta ST, Inc., a wholly owned subsidiary of Harris Tech Corporation, in 2015

Senior Manager – Rochester Operations – 150-Person Workforce ($42M Annual Sales)

- **Increased throughput 400%** on $100M Ship Advanced Signal Equipment program within first 6 months. Introduced daily product meetings, line-of-balance schedule tracking, and metrics-driven performance improvement.

- **Achieved $1.7M in Lean+10x savings** and won 2015 Luther King corporate award for innovation in defense, space, and security. Delivered strong results through continuous improvements in yield, labor reduction, and throughput.

- Directed market-based affordability initiatives with strong results: **group utilization >95%; management ratios >20:1;** employee involvement team cost savings exceeding plan with average employee grade level below qualifications.

- **Exceeded financial plan for 4 consecutive years** and on-plan for 2020/21. Manage P&L for spares, repairs, and depot programs ($10M in annual revenue; 25% profit margin) that have consistently executed on schedule and on/under budget.

- Established Employee Involvement (EI) program **that delivered $585K in cost savings in 1st year**, contributed on multiple EI teams as manager/facilitator, and won 2013 Network & Space Systems (N&SS) Employee Engagement award.

RADIAN TECH, INC. – Wholly Owned Subsidiary of Westinghouse Electric Corporation, Pittsburgh, PA   2008 – 2015
$400M leading developer of R2XD4 systems & technologies

Director of Operations – 95-Person Workforce ($300M Annual Sales)

- **Directed $300M annually** in contracts for command, control, communications, computer, combat, intelligence, surveillance, and reconnaissance programs for products transitioning from development to prototype to production.

- **Increased throughput and build rates for Garner Systems product line by 800%+** through facility investment/expansion, new process development, manpower planning, and resource acquisition/allocation.

- Utilized Lean Six Sigma methodologies to increase efficiency, reduce cost, introduce best practices, and improve quality across all programs. Most notably, **delivered 76% reduction on $500M, multi-year, Navy Ship System contract.**

- Provided operational leadership for key **business development activities, proposals, client presentations, and negotiations.**

Strategy: Pack numerous keywords and distinguishing credentials into a concise summary section, followed by an experience section that features tightly written bullet points with achievements emphasized in bold.

MATTHEW LOCATELLI

910-655-3420 ♦ mattlocatelli@gmail.com ♦ LinkedIn Profile
Page 2

LAMITAN-PVI, INC. – ELECTRONICS MANUFACTURING SERVICES, Philadelphia, PA   2005 – 2008
$11B telecommunications giant that acquired Dover Tech Tri-Solution's manufacturing facility in Raleigh

Manufacturing Engineering & Quality Manager – 600-Person Workforce ($400M Annual Sales)

- Directed complete manufacturing engineer support services, process development, quality, test engineering, and new product introduction — **2000+ product assemblies, 8 key customers, and 58 direct reports.**

- Introduced 41 telecom assemblies (RF & Digital CDMA) on schedule, **contributing $70M in annual revenue.**

- Delivered **$3.6M in savings** through labor cost reductions and floor space/workflow and process optimization.

DOVER TECH TRI-SOLUTIONS, INC. – CONSUMER PRODUCTS, Raleigh, NC   2002 – 2005
$1.2B telecommunications and cell phone division

Senior Program Manager – 114-Person Manufacturing Team ($275M+ Annual Sales)

- Led successful industrialization for DTT18-2 and R4LX, the smallest D-AMPS phone packages offering dual-band and dual-mode technology. Program **generated $275M+ in annual revenue with 30%+ profit margin.**

- **Increased capacity from 3700 units/day to 6000 units/day** to meet explosive market demand.

DOVER TECH TRI-SOLUTIONS, INC. – PRIVATE RADIO SYSTEMS, Durham, NC   2000 – 2002
$600M manufacturer of advanced radio technologies for global market applications

Production Manager – 17-Person Manufacturing Team ($75M Annual Sales) – 2001 – 2002

- Achieved/surpassed all cost, quality, and scheduling objectives throughout entire 2-year tenure.

- **Improved PRISM HP and IPE radio cumulative yields 25% and 46%,** respectively, through Six Sigma quality initiatives.

- **Reduced production costs 35%** through implementation of Lean Manufacturing methodology.

Industrial Engineer – RMAF Final Assembly ($100M Annual Sales) – 2000 – 2001

- Standardized assembly processes that **reduced rework 35% and improved product quality 28%.**

- Won 2001 Management Award for **25% reduction in cycle time and $100K savings in parts handling costs.**

EDUCATION & PROFESSIONAL DEVELOPMENT

MASSACHUSETTS INSTITUTE OF TECHNOLOGY
Bachelor of Science (BS), Industrial Engineering – 1997

MARTIN MARIETTA CORPORATION
Program Management | Employee Involvement | Lean+10x | Aerospace Industry Manufacturing Seminar (AIMS) Supplier Management Training | Business Development Process Rollout | Export Controls | Proposal Training | PM/QA

RESUME 53: by Louise Kursmark, MRW, CPRW, JCTC, CEIP, CCM • www.louisekursmark.com

Rafael Pérez

305-678-8765 | rafaelperez@mac.com | www.LinkedIn/com/in/rafaelperez

Global Operating Executive / Project Manager

Consistently delivered exceptional quality and profitability in managing complex, logistically challenging construction projects around the world.

Transformed troubled operations to top performers.

Structured and negotiated innovative alliances and complex project contracts that delivered win-win outcomes.

> Manufacturing Operations
>
> Plant & Production Startups
>
> Profit & Performance Gains

Industries: Pharmaceutical | Health & Beauty | Automobile | Telecommunications | Bulk Paper
Languages: Bilingual English/Spanish | Conversational Portuguese

Professional Experience

JACOBS ENGINEERING GROUP (NYSE:JEC) | 1998–Present
Global engineering and construction services contractor; $15B annual revenue.

Director of Caribbean Operations, Miami, FL | 2016–Present

Challenged to improve operating performance and implement standardized practices throughout $75M Caribbean Basin operation—a rapid-growth area with primary concentration in engineering and construction (grassroots and retrofit) for pharmaceutical and biotech companies. Key clients include Pfizer, Takeda, Astra-Zeneca, Merck.

Profit Performance
- Averaged 30% gross profit annually—double projections.

Project Leadership and Execution
- Completed all projects on or ahead of schedule, with record profitability and in full compliance with Jacobs' exceptional quality standards and with stringent FDA requirements for pharmaceutical manufacturers.
- Rescued a $25M project that had fallen dangerously behind schedule. Successful project completion led to $120M in new projects from client without a competitive bid process.
- Overhauled the project execution process, instituting rigorous standardized practices for first time in region.
- Directed implementation of integrated technology systems (communication, cost, scheduling, accounting).
- Relocated 4 operations from Puerto Rico to other Caribbean locations in the immediate aftermath of Hurricane Maria. Drove rapid re-start and achieved zero missed deliveries.

Director of Operations, Jacobs South America, Sao Paulo, Brazil | 2014–2016

Launched Jacobs's South American operation: Developed and executed business strategy and oversaw growth from startup to $90M annual revenue. Managed operations, construction engineering services, and support for regional projects. Clients included Ford, Intel, Takeda, and Procter and Gamble.

Strategy and Startup
- Overcame bureaucratic obstacles to gain official registration required for business startup in Brazil. Succeeded in obtaining rare dual registration for Jacobs as both construction and engineering services company.

Strategy: Add a bold graphic at the top to quickly identify 3 key areas of expertise. In the experience section, segment strong achievements under meaningful headlines to reinforce this executive's value and track record.

Rafael Pérez | 305-678-8765 | rafaelperez@mac.com

CONTINUED

- Conceived, researched, negotiated, and executed a strategic alliance with the largest full-service engineering firm in Argentina. Expanded project capabilities for both companies and enabled the capture of key contracts.
- Devised an innovative contract labor arrangement that reduced permanent labor costs and contributed significantly to profitability.

Project Leadership and Execution

- Completed a $250M project for Ford, ahead of schedule and under budget, and delivered a manufacturing plant that has since become Ford's global benchmark for project process and construction quality.

Director of Business Operations, JPG Operating Company, Cincinnati, Ohio | 2013–2014
Director of Business Management, JPG Operating Company | 2012–2013

Directed all business activities for joint Jacobs–Procter and Gamble alliance that built P&G health & beauty care and disposable paper products facilities worldwide during period of rapid growth. Challenged to maximize profit while delivering on all project components and meeting rigorous requirements for quality and customer satisfaction.

Profit Performance

- Outperformed all expectations for financial performance and profit; exceeded profitability of all other Jacobs operations by 100%.
- Conceived and put in place a unique "no overhead" arrangement that guaranteed profitability while delivering value and benefit to the client. System has since been adapted for use with other key clients who have major, ongoing projects.

Strategic Leadership

- Developed highly accurate global forecasting system using client data that enabled us to maintain core staff competencies for rapid deployment once P&G made "go" decision on new plant construction.

Project Manager / Project Director | 2017–2012

Executed complex construction projects for Jacobs clients worldwide. Key clients included Procter and Gamble, Apple, and Scientific Atlanta.

Project Leadership and Execution

- Initiated the hiring of local nationals rather than expatriate Americans for major projects in China and Thailand. Improved profitability by $1.8M on one project alone; also benefited project through increased knowledge of local customs, language, and culture. Practice has become the preferred method for all Jacobs projects in Asia.
- Executed P&G project in China on schedule through innovative labor-force arrangement that required extensive negotiation with government officials.

Controls Manager—Cost Engineer—Controls Engineer | 1998–2017

Education / Additional

Bachelor of Science in Mechanical Engineering | 1997
University of Maryland

United States Air Force | 1992–1998
Honorably Discharged

Sandra O'Hara, CPM

203-367-9870 • sandraohara@yahoo.com

PURCHASING MANAGER

Global Sourcing • Supplier Management • Outsource Manufacturing • Continuous Cost Reduction

Certified Purchasing Manager with extensive experience sourcing/procuring industrial materials from international vendors. Familiar with import/export regulations, adroit at vendor negotiations, and skilled at "getting the right part at the right time."

Team player who works easily with all departments, from manufacturing and engineering to sales. A flexible, significant contributor in startups and established companies.

- Supplier Management
- Cost Controls
- Import/Export
- Vendor Selection
- Pricing
- Product Development
- Contract Negotiation
- Inventory Control
- Quality Improvement

EXPERIENCE AND ACHIEVEMENTS

EX-O LASER CORPORATION, Norwalk, CT: *Largest US manufacturer of high-powered industrial CO2 lasers, with offices in the US and Belgium and agents around the world.*

Department Manager/Senior Buyer, 2013–Present
Provided purchasing expertise through significant company growth and evolution, adding responsibilities and adapting to accommodate new products and materials, new manufacturing methods, new corporate ownership, and relentless drive for cost reduction.

Lead a professional purchasing organization (3 direct reports) with a focus on correct vendor selection and continuous cost reduction through vendor partnering, advanced methodologies, and skillful negotiations.

Purchase all manufacturing services, parts fabrication, and assembly outsourcing; negotiate and implement vendor contracts; interface with engineering and manufacturing; analyze cost and value of current and new product designs; ensure compliance with US export regulations; work with customs brokers.

- Managed **58%** of total company spend of **$5.3M** in 2019.
- Launched continuous cost-cutting efforts, partnering with suppliers to drive down costs annually.
- Identified and captured savings opportunities by negotiating exclusive vendor contracts:
  - Saved **12%** on ball-bearing purchases and gained security of consigned on-site inventory.
  - Reallocated multiple parts to same vendor for **50%** cost reduction.
- Oversaw implementation of Kanban automated inventory system that generated **$50K** cost savings and increased inventory turns from **4** to **12** while warehouse staff fell by **50%.**
- Saved **$90K** in first year, **$273K** by year 3, by contracting overflow assembly work to outside manufacturer.

Buyer, AMPAC Seals (*Acquired by Ex-O Laser in 2013*), 2010–2013
Established a solid vendor base for commodities during company startup when garnering supplier contracts was a challenge. Procured all commercial parts, services, and electronic components, closely coordinating with manufacturing to determine JIT needs. Created the company's first inventory control system.

Draftsman/Designer, AMPAC Seals, 2008–2010
Crafted design and layout of mechanical systems and components, detailing, and material lists while company transitioned from startup R&D to product manufacturer.

EDUCATION – PROFESSIONAL CERTIFICATIONS – AFFILIATIONS
Certified Purchasing Manager (CPM)–Institute for Supply Management (ISM)
Member–New England Chapter, ISM
Certificate in Mechanical Drafting–Delahunty Institute, Jamaica, NY

Strategy: Showcase her steadily expanded role as the company she joined more than 10 years ago grew from startup and was acquired by a much larger global organization.

RESUME 55: by Kelly Gadzinski, ACRW, CCMC, RCC • www.kgcareerservices.com

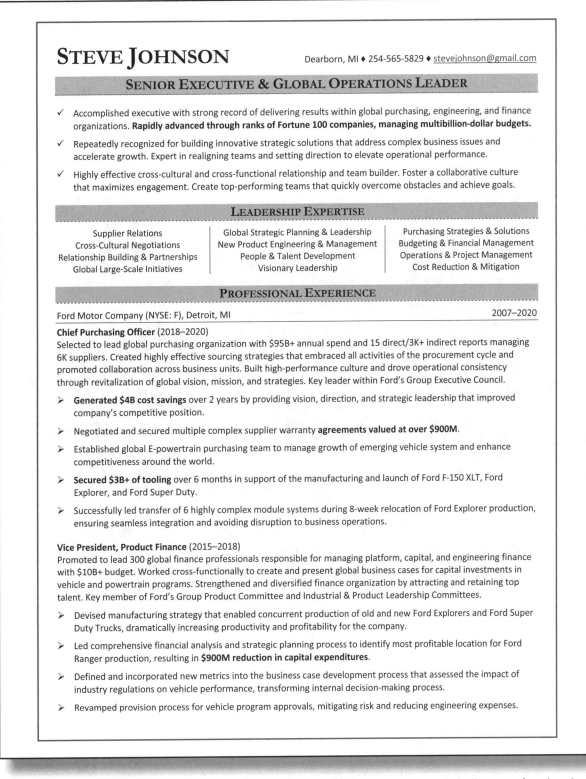

STEVE JOHNSON

Dearborn, MI ♦ 254-565-5829 ♦ stevejohnson@gmail.com

SENIOR EXECUTIVE & GLOBAL OPERATIONS LEADER

✓ Accomplished executive with strong record of delivering results within global purchasing, engineering, and finance organizations. **Rapidly advanced through ranks of Fortune 100 companies, managing multibillion-dollar budgets.**

✓ Repeatedly recognized for building innovative strategic solutions that address complex business issues and accelerate growth. Expert in realigning teams and setting direction to elevate operational performance.

✓ Highly effective cross-cultural and cross-functional relationship and team builder. Foster a collaborative culture that maximizes engagement. Create top-performing teams that quickly overcome obstacles and achieve goals.

LEADERSHIP EXPERTISE

Supplier Relations	Global Strategic Planning & Leadership	Purchasing Strategies & Solutions
Cross-Cultural Negotiations	New Product Engineering & Management	Budgeting & Financial Management
Relationship Building & Partnerships	People & Talent Development	Operations & Project Management
Global Large-Scale Initiatives	Visionary Leadership	Cost Reduction & Mitigation

PROFESSIONAL EXPERIENCE

Ford Motor Company (NYSE: F), Detroit, MI   2007–2020

Chief Purchasing Officer (2018–2020)
Selected to lead global purchasing organization with $95B+ annual spend and 15 direct/3K+ indirect reports managing 6K suppliers. Created highly effective sourcing strategies that embraced all activities of the procurement cycle and promoted collaboration across business units. Built high-performance culture and drove operational consistency through revitalization of global vision, mission, and strategies. Key leader within Ford's Group Executive Council.

➢ **Generated $4B cost savings** over 2 years by providing vision, direction, and strategic leadership that improved company's competitive position.

➢ Negotiated and secured multiple complex supplier warranty **agreements valued at over $900M.**

➢ Established global E-powertrain purchasing team to manage growth of emerging vehicle system and enhance competitiveness around the world.

➢ **Secured $3B+ of tooling** over 6 months in support of the manufacturing and launch of Ford F-150 XLT, Ford Explorer, and Ford Super Duty.

➢ Successfully led transfer of 6 highly complex module systems during 8-week relocation of Ford Explorer production, ensuring seamless integration and avoiding disruption to business operations.

Vice President, Product Finance (2015–2018)
Promoted to lead 300 global finance professionals responsible for managing platform, capital, and engineering finance with $10B+ budget. Worked cross-functionally to create and present global business cases for capital investments in vehicle and powertrain programs. Strengthened and diversified finance organization by attracting and retaining top talent. Key member of Ford's Group Product Committee and Industrial & Product Leadership Committees.

➢ Devised manufacturing strategy that enabled concurrent production of old and new Ford Explorers and Ford Super Duty Trucks, dramatically increasing productivity and profitability for the company.

➢ Led comprehensive financial analysis and strategic planning process to identify most profitable location for Ford Ranger production, resulting in **$900M reduction in capital expenditures**.

➢ Defined and incorporated new metrics into the business case development process that assessed the impact of industry regulations on vehicle performance, transforming internal decision-making process.

➢ Revamped provision process for vehicle program approvals, mitigating risk and reducing engineering expenses.

Strategy: Create a resume with a classic layout that establishes contexts and challenges of each role, highlights notable achievements, and displays a progressive 25-year career.

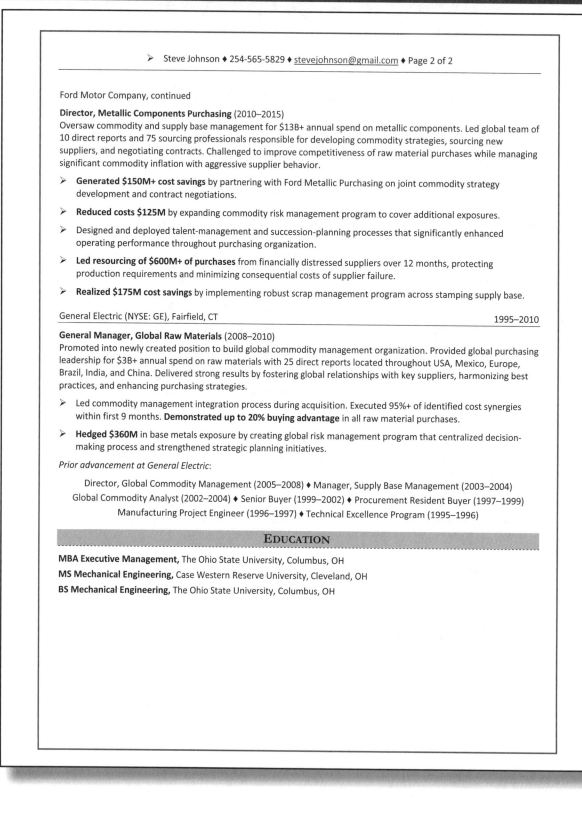

➢ Steve Johnson ♦ 254-565-5829 ♦ stevejohnson@gmail.com ♦ Page 2 of 2

Ford Motor Company, continued

Director, Metallic Components Purchasing (2010–2015)
Oversaw commodity and supply base management for $13B+ annual spend on metallic components. Led global team of 10 direct reports and 75 sourcing professionals responsible for developing commodity strategies, sourcing new suppliers, and negotiating contracts. Challenged to improve competitiveness of raw material purchases while managing significant commodity inflation with aggressive supplier behavior.

➢ **Generated $150M+ cost savings** by partnering with Ford Metallic Purchasing on joint commodity strategy development and contract negotiations.

➢ **Reduced costs $125M** by expanding commodity risk management program to cover additional exposures.

➢ Designed and deployed talent-management and succession-planning processes that significantly enhanced operating performance throughout purchasing organization.

➢ **Led resourcing of $600M+ of purchases** from financially distressed suppliers over 12 months, protecting production requirements and minimizing consequential costs of supplier failure.

➢ **Realized $175M cost savings** by implementing robust scrap management program across stamping supply base.

General Electric (NYSE: GE), Fairfield, CT   1995–2010

General Manager, Global Raw Materials (2008–2010)
Promoted into newly created position to build global commodity management organization. Provided global purchasing leadership for $3B+ annual spend on raw materials with 25 direct reports located throughout USA, Mexico, Europe, Brazil, India, and China. Delivered strong results by fostering global relationships with key suppliers, harmonizing best practices, and enhancing purchasing strategies.

➢ Led commodity management integration process during acquisition. Executed 95%+ of identified cost synergies within first 9 months. **Demonstrated up to 20% buying advantage** in all raw material purchases.

➢ **Hedged $360M** in base metals exposure by creating global risk management program that centralized decision-making process and strengthened strategic planning initiatives.

Prior advancement at General Electric:

Director, Global Commodity Management (2005–2008) ♦ Manager, Supply Base Management (2003–2004)
Global Commodity Analyst (2002–2004) ♦ Senior Buyer (1999–2002) ♦ Procurement Resident Buyer (1997–1999)
Manufacturing Project Engineer (1996–1997) ♦ Technical Excellence Program (1995–1996)

EDUCATION

MBA Executive Management, The Ohio State University, Columbus, OH
MS Mechanical Engineering, Case Western Reserve University, Cleveland, OH
BS Mechanical Engineering, The Ohio State University, Columbus, OH

RESUME 56: by Adrienne Tom, CERM, MCRS, CIS, CES, CCS • www.careerimpressions.ca

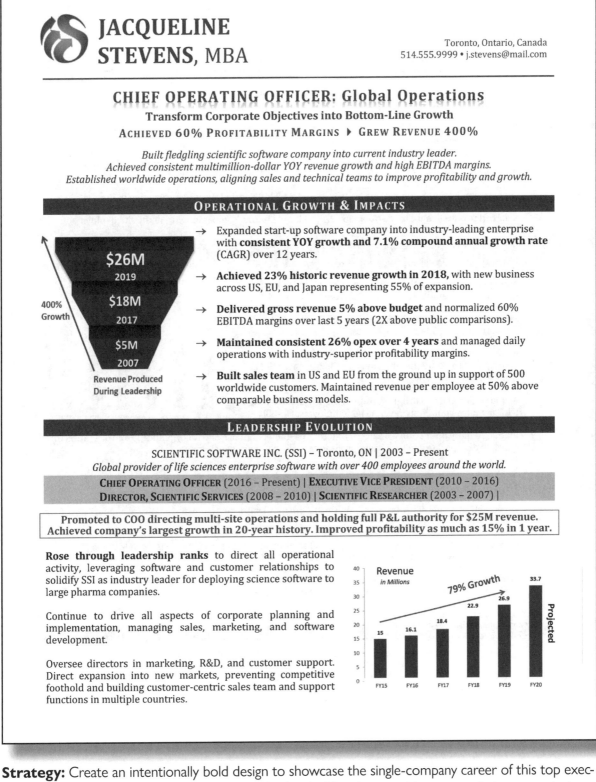

JACQUELINE STEVENS, MBA

Toronto, Ontario, Canada
514.555.9999 • j.stevens@mail.com

CHIEF OPERATING OFFICER: Global Operations
Transform Corporate Objectives into Bottom-Line Growth
ACHIEVED 60% PROFITABILITY MARGINS ▶ GREW REVENUE 400%

Built fledgling scientific software company into current industry leader.
Achieved consistent multimillion-dollar YOY revenue growth and high EBITDA margins.
Established worldwide operations, aligning sales and technical teams to improve profitability and growth.

OPERATIONAL GROWTH & IMPACTS

$26M
2019

$18M
2017

$5M
2007

400% Growth

Revenue Produced During Leadership

→ Expanded start-up software company into industry-leading enterprise with **consistent YOY growth and 7.1% compound annual growth rate** (CAGR) over 12 years.

→ **Achieved 23% historic revenue growth in 2018,** with new business across US, EU, and Japan representing 55% of expansion.

→ **Delivered gross revenue 5% above budget** and normalized 60% EBITDA margins over last 5 years (2X above public comparisons).

→ **Maintained consistent 26% opex over 4 years** and managed daily operations with industry-superior profitability margins.

→ **Built sales team** in US and EU from the ground up in support of 500 worldwide customers. Maintained revenue per employee at 50% above comparable business models.

LEADERSHIP EVOLUTION

SCIENTIFIC SOFTWARE INC. (SSI) – Toronto, ON | 2003 – Present
Global provider of life sciences enterprise software with over 400 employees around the world.

CHIEF OPERATING OFFICER (2016 – Present) | **EXECUTIVE VICE PRESIDENT** (2010 – 2016)
DIRECTOR, SCIENTIFIC SERVICES (2008 – 2010) | **SCIENTIFIC RESEARCHER** (2003 – 2007) |

Promoted to COO directing multi-site operations and holding full P&L authority for $25M revenue.
Achieved company's largest growth in 20-year history. Improved profitability as much as 15% in 1 year.

Rose through leadership ranks to direct all operational activity, leveraging software and customer relationships to solidify SSI as industry leader for deploying science software to large pharma companies.

Continue to drive all aspects of corporate planning and implementation, managing sales, marketing, and software development.

Oversee directors in marketing, R&D, and customer support. Direct expansion into new markets, preventing competitive foothold and building customer-centric sales team and support functions in multiple countries.

Revenue *in Millions*

79% Growth

15 (FY15) 16.1 (FY16) 18.4 (FY17) 22.9 (FY18) 26.9 (FY19) 33.7 (FY20, Projected)

Strategy: Create an intentionally bold design to showcase the single-company career of this top executive. Include comparisons to competitors and other highly relevant achievements that communicate her value.

Jacqueline Stevens, MBA • 514.555.9999 • j.stevens@mail.com | Page 2

Scientific Software Inc., continued...

ENTERPRISE VALUE & REVENUE EXPANSION
Drove revenue growth in alignment with corporate objectives, achieving EBITDA and profitability goals...

✓ Outperformed revenue expectations, successfully **growing global revenue an average of 4% per year over past 6 years**. Accomplished what no other industry competitor has achieved.

✓ **Exceeded revenue growth in new market areas 26%** over the last 4 years, consistently achieving aggressive growth targets.

✓ Expanded customer and market share in both US and EU, with **new business representing 50% of growth revenue** from FY14 to FY18.

✓ Orchestrated recent company sale to US investor for $220M, **quadrupling enterprise value**.

✓ **Secured product as main platform** for 92% of large pharma companies with multi-site deployments.

OPERATIONAL EXCELLENCE & EFFICIENCY
Established efficient and effective worldwide operations, raising business visibility and competitive placement...

✓ **Managed daily operations with superior profit margins.** Improved profitability (EBITDA) 13% from FY17 to FY18.

✓ **Maintained consistent 24% opex** for last 3 years despite 30% growth in number of employees.

✓ Increased operational efficiency and productivity, maintaining **revenue per employee at 50% greater** than similar public companies.

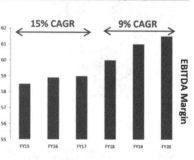

✓ Acquired European distributor, **improving top-line revenue $1.5M** while maintaining revenue per employee of $500K.

✓ **Managed daily operations** in sales, marketing, customer support, and R&D, guiding group of 11 directors to achieve corporate goals for sales, profitability, and software development.

STAFF & BUSINESS LEADERSHIP
Fostered highly productive teams and drove forward business strategies...

✓ **Hired and trained 60% of current global support and sales team**, raising quality of support scientists and sales team to achieve closing rate of 62%.

✓ Created onboarding program to ensure critical sales training skills remained sustainable during enterprise growth. **Improved sales readiness time 55%.**

✓ Created and managed execution of corporate objectives that established company as leader and only profitable company in industry. **Presented regularly to board of directors**.

EDUCATION & PRESENTATIONS

Master of Business Administration (MBA) – *McMaster University*
Bachelor of Science, Chemistry – *McMaster University*
Delivered over 500 presentations to PhD and C-suite customers across Canada, US, EU, and Japan

MBA, Strategy

BSBA, Marketing
Concentration

Alan Kozak

555-555-1111 | alankz@gmail.com | LinkedIn

Strategic Business and Operations Leadership

Dynamic **business and operations strategist** with diverse background, demonstrating a nimble ability to become productive in different environments – oil and gas, retail, clean energy, and digital media.

Experienced account manager and business strategist in $multimillion products and services, leveraging **keen ability to network to build lucrative, resilient relationships** with partners and executives.

➔ Favor **defendable disruptive strategies** that assure **profitability.**

➔ **Synthesize up-down details** to create holistic, effective, and sustainable future-focused solutions.

➔ Display an ability for **near-instant rapport to influence executives, clients, and staff.**

Expertise: Build strategic partnerships ➔ Report key metrics with forecasts to profitability ➔ Compose and present influential executive-level presentations ➔ Negotiate agreements ➔ Create best-in-class client experience ➔ Promote products and services ➔ Manage projects, operations, and systems

Professional Experience

ENERGY STORAGE INC. | Buffalo, NY | 2017–Present
Utility-scale energy storage start-up has multiple projects in various development phases in North America and Australia.

Chief of Staff (2019–Present) | **Operations Manager** (2018–2019) | **Business Development** (2017–2018)

Overall Contributions: Contributed to company's growth, scaling operations from 5 to 35 staff and developing market position from start-up to growth phase, repeatable business model to utility scale.

- **Chief of Staff:** Support leadership team with strategic counsel in governance issues and project and program management; execute governance programs; create documents, project timelines and control; conduct training in building engaging, influential presentations.
  - o Provide executive assistance to CEO; execute plans on behalf of CEO, COO, CP Finance, and SVP Engineering; liaise with AU client's GM, Directors, and technical and business teams.
  - o Represented company as panelist, AU conference, on topic of future of energy storage.
  - o Member of weekly executive-level Corporate Governance Strategy meetings; prepare and share dashboards and reports tracking deliverables and resolution of identified issues.

- **Operations Manager:** Introduced project controls and analysis, working with technical and business development teams to drive accountability into project management. Led procurement for $10M project, addressing contract details, iterations, regulations, and tracking.

- **Business Development:** Supported transition from repeatable business to large utility-scale customizations requiring financial analysis and planning, engineering and development. Set up tools to support long cycle account development. Oversaw financial controls, accounting, HR, and analysis.

DIGITAL MEDIA | Chicago, IL | 2015–2017
National leader in digital media applications across property management, retail, financial, and restaurants.

Account Manager

Skills: Business strategy, business model generation, project management, relationship building; 2 direct reports

- Tripled creative revenue with effective P&L ownership of largest client by media revenue; collected data and presented analytics. Liaised with mall management and client executives in $multimillion deals.
- Rescued stalled projects valued at $3.5M, winning over major clients, effectively repairing and re-instilling trust with C-level executive, reviewing business models, and overhauling quality.

Strategy: Communicate this executive's brand as a disruptive thought leader through language, achievements, and activities highlighted throughout his resume. Overcome potential concerns regarding several short-term positions by introducing them with a brief mention of industry downturn.

555-555-1111 | alankz@gmail.com | Page 2 of 2

SKIS & BIIKES | Chicago, IL | 2013–2015
City's largest private sporting goods retailer.

General Manager

Skills: Product knowledge and sales training, customer experience improvements, operational efficiencies.

- Managed 4 supervisors and 2 managers leading ~36 staff conducting sales and operations; oversaw staff performance and sales and customer relationship training; monitored revenue goals.
- Led by example, achieving top-5 sales producer status. Empowered independent decision making that improved performance, culture, and customer satisfaction
- Launched point-of-sale computer system.

Held series of short-term roles, which were eliminated as the oil and gas industry stalled and layoffs ensued:

Technical Account Representative | PIPING SPECIALITIES | Houston, TX | 2011–2013
Serving nuclear, mining, and chemical industries, company is distributor of industrial chemical-handling equipment.
Skills: Financial modeling, business intelligence analysis, presentations, research, scorecards.
- Supported C-suite decisions by building excellent financial models, conducting business intelligence analysis, and creating reports. Delivered technical presentations to engineers and procurement teams at Canada's largest engineering, procurement, and construction or EPC companies.

Business Development | LONESTAR OIL | Houston, TX | 2009–2011
Skills: New market expansion, revenue generation, new product introduction, technical market research.
- Achieved 7% net new revenue by conducting technical market research analysis, creating a strategy, and building strategic partnerships, decisively influencing executive decision to execute new product offering.

Account Manager | OIL ENTERPRISE INC. | Houston, TX | 2007–2009
Skills: Research, market penetration strategy, cross-functional team leadership, product commercialization.
- Researched, developed market penetration strategy, and led cross-functional team of 17 sales and engineering staff in commercialization of new category technology (oilfield drill bits).

SAVANNA PETROLEUM INC. | Houston, TX | 2002–2007
Global oilfield services company with 3rd largest rig fleet in Texas.

Investor Relations and Account Manager

Skills: Cross-functional team leadership, international bids and contracts, sales generation, cost reduction.

- Led product team that identified international bid potential. Assembled cross-functional team – finance, sales, procurement, safety – in analysis and improvement of complex international bids to overcome internal resistance and ultimately secure $202M 5-year contract in Australia.
- Increased YoY sales by 18%–28%.
- Generated 8% above-industry equipment utilization and maintained margins; contributed to fleet tripling as industry declined 12%.

Education

Carter School of Business, Texas University	Master of Business Administration	2017
• Strategy concentration/part time accelerated program	
MBA Finance Association	2016
• Financial model-building course specific to Carter MBA graduate students	
Carter School of Business, Texas University	Bachelor of Science in Business Administration	2001
• Marketing concentration	

Professional & Competitive Activities

- → Co-author of customer experience design article published by American Marketing Association, 2019
- → Speaker & un-conference participant, #LeanEnterpriseNY – Corporate & Process Innovation, 2018
- → MBA Hackathon Case Competition – winner of "People's Choice" category, 2017

RESUME 58: *by Adrienne Tom, CERM, MCRS, CIS, CES, CCS • www.careerimpressions.ca*

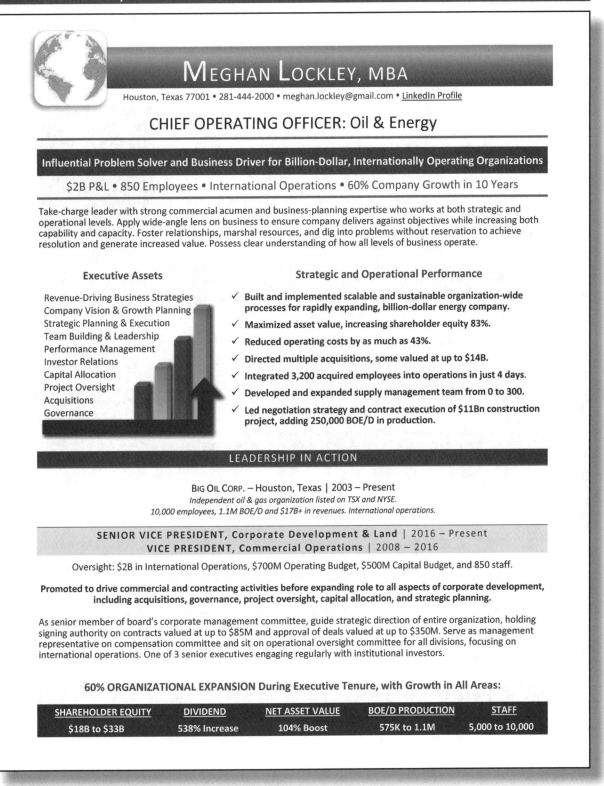

MEGHAN LOCKLEY, MBA

Houston, Texas 77001 • 281-444-2000 • meghan.lockley@gmail.com • LinkedIn Profile

CHIEF OPERATING OFFICER: Oil & Energy

Influential Problem Solver and Business Driver for Billion-Dollar, Internationally Operating Organizations

$2B P&L • 850 Employees • International Operations • 60% Company Growth in 10 Years

Take-charge leader with strong commercial acumen and business-planning expertise who works at both strategic and operational levels. Apply wide-angle lens on business to ensure company delivers against objectives while increasing both capability and capacity. Foster relationships, marshal resources, and dig into problems without reservation to achieve resolution and generate increased value. Possess clear understanding of how all levels of business operate.

Executive Assets

Revenue-Driving Business Strategies
Company Vision & Growth Planning
Strategic Planning & Execution
Team Building & Leadership
Performance Management
Investor Relations
Capital Allocation
Project Oversight
Acquisitions
Governance

Strategic and Operational Performance

✓ Built and implemented scalable and sustainable organization-wide processes for rapidly expanding, billion-dollar energy company.

✓ Maximized asset value, increasing shareholder equity 83%.

✓ Reduced operating costs by as much as 43%.

✓ Directed multiple acquisitions, some valued at up to $14B.

✓ Integrated 3,200 acquired employees into operations in just 4 days.

✓ Developed and expanded supply management team from 0 to 300.

✓ Led negotiation strategy and contract execution of $11Bn construction project, adding 250,000 BOE/D in production.

LEADERSHIP IN ACTION

BIG OIL CORP. – Houston, Texas | 2003 – Present
Independent oil & gas organization listed on TSX and NYSE.
10,000 employees, 1.1M BOE/D and $17B+ in revenues. International operations.

SENIOR VICE PRESIDENT, Corporate Development & Land | 2016 – Present
VICE PRESIDENT, Commercial Operations | 2008 – 2016

Oversight: $2B in International Operations, $700M Operating Budget, $500M Capital Budget, and 850 staff.

Promoted to drive commercial and contracting activities before expanding role to all aspects of corporate development, including acquisitions, governance, project oversight, capital allocation, and strategic planning.

As senior member of board's corporate management committee, guide strategic direction of entire organization, holding signing authority on contracts valued at up to $85M and approval of deals valued at up to $350M. Serve as management representative on compensation committee and sit on operational oversight committee for all divisions, focusing on international operations. One of 3 senior executives engaging regularly with institutional investors.

60% ORGANIZATIONAL EXPANSION During Executive Tenure, with Growth in All Areas:

SHAREHOLDER EQUITY	DIVIDEND	NET ASSET VALUE	BOE/D PRODUCTION	STAFF
$18B to $33B	538% Increase	104% Boost	575K to 1.1M	5,000 to 10,000

Strategy: Inspire a "wow" effect with sharp and meaningful graphics and bold emphasis on strong achievements. Create further impact through tight writing that is loaded with keywords.

Meghan Lockley, MBA • 281-444-2000 • meghan.lockley@gmail.com | Page 2

Senior Vice President / Vice President at Big Oil Corp., continued...

Organizational Growth:

- **Grew net asset value from $40 per share in 2008 to $82 per share in 2016.**
  - → Spearheaded negotiation and integration efforts of major $14B acquisition.
  - → Helmed multifunctional effort to integrate 3,200 acquired employees into operations just 60 days from deal announcement to closing.
- **Expanded company operations despite unpredictable energy industry climate** by bringing together internal and external groups to work cohesively on building and executing a vision and solidifying organizational structure and processes.

2016 Acquisition:
20% Revenue Growth
35% People Increase
25% Production Expansion

Operational Improvement:

- **Reduced operating costs 43% within international division, generating $520M in free cash flow per year.** Drove performance improvements across reliability, project execution, and cost control.
- **Improved company compensation support from 81% to 95% in 1 year.** Revamped long-term incentive compensation and vesting of options.

Commercial Operations:

- **Resolved $1.2B insurance claim, recovering 90% of payments in under 1 year.** Spearheaded strategy development and negotiation of final claim with international, mutual, and captive insurance companies.
- **Championed creation and development of high-level supply management team,** growing from 9 to 300 members to support construction of $11B greenfield construction project that grew oil production by 250,000 BOE/D.

BIG OIL CORP. – Houston, Texas

MANAGER, Commercial Operations | 2003 – 2008

Rejoined organization to drive joint venture relationship management and introduce commercial resource and supply management function to one of the industry's fastest-growing companies. Directed royalty income and eventual sale of large portion of royalty assets. Managed corporate and captive insurance companies. Oversaw 55 staff.

- **Built one of the strongest commercial teams in the industry.** Developed and hired cross-functional resources to champion all aspects of commercial resources during time of phenomenal expansion.
- **Secured and maintained one of the lowest insurance costs in the industry, despite 10X organizational growth.** Fostered strong relationships with lead syndicates and consistently delivered to plan.

MIDSTREAM INC. – Houston, Texas | 1998 – 2003
Jointly owned local gas-processing organization with 3 major sour gas processing facilities with 800 MMSCFD processing capacity. 250 field employees and 35 head-office staff.

PERFORMANCE DELIVERY DIRECTOR, Oil & Gas

Stepped into this newly formed joint venture to drive creation and implementation of corporate plan. Quickly pivoted strategy from monetizing assets to formulating standalone operating company after major merger. Managed relationships with working interest partners and asset customers. Directed team of 5.

- **Developed corporate strategy focused on delivering operating results and gaining partner and customer support.** Laid foundation for expanding pipeline infrastructure, which increased throughput.
- **Resolved significant partner disputes and conflicts.** Directed partner communications and coordinated effort that built credibility and secured support for necessary infrastructure and operational expansion.

EDUCATION

Master of Business Administration (MBA) – University of Texas
BSc, Geophysical Sciences, with Honors – University of Texas

CHAPTER 9

Health Care

- Administrative Manager
- Chief Operating Officer
- Vice President
- Executive Director
- Chief, Medical Readiness
- Senior Vice President
- Research Coordinator
- Vice President of Benefits
- Health System CEO
- Executive Vice President

SAMUEL BASH

510-972-3454 | Sam.Bash@gmail.com | Berkeley, CA 94701

NATIONAL DIRECTOR
Leading transformative change in healthcare delivery

Healthcare executive and champion of strategic growth who has streamlined business processes across a large hospital system, improved care, and delivered bottom-line results through visionary leadership.

- **Identify and optimize opportunities for organizational excellence.** Built Care Coordination Command Center in-house from the ground up in under 2 years.
- **Lead and motivate cross-functional teams**. Recipient of coaching and team impact awards for leadership/contributions in diverse, multi-disciplinary teams.
- **Cultivate key relationships within all levels of the healthcare system.** Partner with C-suite executives and serve on national advisory committees.

Expertise
Project Management
Negotiation
Strategic Planning
Healthcare Operations
Data Analysis
Team Building

Professional Experience

Alma Health, Berkeley, CA   2016–Current

ADMINISTRATIVE MANGER

Advance and execute system-wide initiatives in partnership with C-suite executives to strengthen the organization's market position and accomplish strategic goals. **Spearhead outcome-focused growth strategies** that increase access to care, maximize system efficiency, and reduce healthcare costs.

Impact: Led teams that reduced costs by $5M+ and expanded access to quality care via new care models.

Innovative Care Models
National Solution Center | Care Coordination Command Center (C4)
- Formalized organizational structure, services, best practices, and budget for new National Solution Center in alliance with VP of Patient Access.
- Spearheaded C4 from vision to operation in **18** months, re-imagining hospital delivery systems from clinical communication to telemetry and patient experience/access.
- Built C4 entirely in-house with no additional resources. Standardized care and protocols through infrastructure creation and staff training.

Process Improvements
- Led state-wide online scheduling program rollout (In-Quicker), influencing **350** physicians to join platform; **34%** of **8,400+** appointments new to providers in **5**-month period. Adding 4 new care areas in 2020.
- Standardized language and patient scheduling/care in PHS rebuild. Homogenized procedure time, prep, and intake across facilities. Increased efficiency with new search filter and uniform procedure categories.

Business Operations
- Garnered **$3M** impact following **$7M** loss in graduate residency program via financial restructuring.
- Reduced operating budget by **$2M** for the 2019 fiscal year through physician/staff restructuring and contract renegotiations in nationally acclaimed sports performance program.

Strategy: Assist this executive to gain a promotion at his current organization by showing leadership skills in 3 key areas—innovative care models, process improvement, and business operations—as well as his ability to collaborate with C-suite executives.

SAMUEL BASH

Page 2

510-972-3454 | Sam.Bash@gmail.com | Berkeley, CA 94701

Professional Experience [cont.]

Pharma and Co., Louisville, KY   2002–2016

SENIOR HOSPITAL ACCOUNT SPECIALIST   2007–2016

Directed hospital business development for Central and Southeast Kentucky territories. Developed disease-state management programs and protocols, securing product access and positioning for diabetes and cardiovascular products. Cultivated key relationships within all levels of the healthcare system.

Impact: Created a district-wide sales analytical tool assessing territory needs and sales trends while directing 9 new product launches/reissues and hospital conversions.

- Exceeded portfolio sales goals from **108%–120%** to plan as an annual top **25%** sales performer.
- Increased product accessibility and coverage through insurance payer negotiations.
- Converted **6** hospitals from competitor to Pharma product as MVP of Hospital Training Class (2010).
- Front-runner in prescription sales as **#1** in Midwest/**#4** in the nation during the first year of new prescription sales responsibility (2011).

SALES REPRESENTATIVE | AREA SALES TRAINER   2002–2007

Neuroscience sales executive marketing **6** products to primary care and pediatric physicians in Central Kentucky. **Promoted to Area Sales Trainer** where developed training programs for **10** district managers and **120** sales reps. **2x recipient of monthly coaching champion award.**

Impact: Led 2 product launches, achieving rapid market penetration, and created 2 key training programs that advanced product knowledge and selling skills across the region.

- **3x winner of "Peer Award,"** nominated by **3** different teams in **5** years.
- Conducted **4** major trainings annually re: disease stat, product knowledge, and sales. Identified regional training needs and developed custom situational workshops. Coached sales reps 1:1.
- Trained **30** new hires and **6** new trainers. Contributed to first field-based new-hire training curricula.
- Surpassed annual/quarterly sales goals, consistently **ranking in top 5%–12% in sales** among **520** reps.

Education & Professional Affiliations

University of Louisville
Master of Health Administration (MHA), 2016 | **Master of Business Administration** (MBA), 2001

California University
Bachelor of Business Administration (BA), 1995

Cystic Fibrosis Foundation, Board Member (California Chapter)
American College of Healthcare Executives, Member (California Chapter)

DAVID A. WILLIAMS

Orange County, CA   dwilliams@mailnet.net   (714) 336-8998
LinkedIn.com/in/davidawilliams

COO / VICE PRESIDENT / EXECUTIVE DIRECTOR
Expertise in Multi-Facility Health and Fitness Organizations

Operations and Sales Executive with a track record of increasing sales and profits, turning around underperforming locations / regions, and leading expansion for multi-unit operations with up to $10M in annual revenues (both profit-driven and non-profit). Consistently exceeded goals, sales plans, and turnaround objectives for each employer.

Expert in analyzing existing operations and implementing the necessary strategies and formal business practices to improve profit performance, grow membership sales, and increase retention rates. Proven financial and business acumen combined with practical experience and formal training in health and fitness. Strong educational foundation with MA and BBA degrees. Areas of strength include:

- Multi-Unit Operations Management
- Budgeting / Expense Control
- Sales Management / Sales Training
- Marketing / Sales Promotions

- Business Development
- Fitness Program Development
- New Facility Design / Opening
- Staff Leadership / Motivation

PROFESSIONAL EXPERIENCE

ORANGE COUNTY COMMUNITY HEALTH AND FITNESS ORGANIZATION — Tustin, CA   2018–Present
(Non-profit organization offering sports, aquatics, and fitness programs for member families)

Vice President, Health and Fitness

Hired to orchestrate an aggressive turnaround for the region from a $1.2M loss to sustainable net gains within 2 years. Hold full responsibility for the planning, staffing, and operating performance of 6 locations with 200+ employees, 18,000+ members, and $5.5M in annual revenues.

Broad scope of accountability includes day-to-day operations, revenue performance, membership sales, staff training, program development implementation, and customer service. Supervise 6 facility directors and 18 program managers. Develop and manage a $5.5M program budget. Provide leadership to capital campaign and facility design phase for 2 new locations with a $20M budget.

- **Turned region around from a $1.2M loss to a projected positive net in 2 years.**
- **Grew new membership sales from 3,500 in 2018 to more than 7,000 YTD in 2020.**
- **Increased revenue from personal training programs more than 100% within one year.**
- **Strengthened member-retention rate to 70% across all locations through improved customer service.**
- **Improved lead generation 15% by designing a prospect-management / tracking system.**

T.S. FITNESS / EMERALD GYM – locations in TX and SC   2013–2018
(Operator of fitness clubs in 2 states)

Chief Operating Officer

Senior operations manager with full responsibility for day-to-day facility operations, sales, accounting, human resources, and fitness programs for a newly established company with 3 facilities, 60–80 full- and part-time staff, and $2.5M in annual sales.

Strategy: Avoid a dense appearance by breaking fairly detailed position descriptions into multiple short paragraphs, then creating high-impact, tightly written, 1- or 2-line bullet points that highlight strong results for every position.

David A. Williams   Page 2   (714) 336-8998

<u>T.S. FITNESS / EMERALD GYM</u> *(continued)*

Established formal business practices and standardized sales and operations processes across all locations to support continued growth and expansion.

- **Grew profits more than 20% each year.**
- **Developed and implemented formal sales procedures that resulted in a 20%–30% increase in new memberships each year.**
- **Increased personal-fitness and group-fitness revenues more than 50% per year.**
- **Developed new business by establishing relationships / alliances with corporate and allied health providers.**

<u>MEGA FITNESS / MEGA GYM</u> — Houston, San Antonio, and Dallas, TX   2010–2013
(Operator of fitness clubs with $10M in annual revenues)

Vice President, Sales and Operations

Led operations, sales, staff training, and fitness programs for 12 Mega Gyms with nearly 100,000 members and up to $10M in combined annual sales. Provided leadership and direction for 250+ sales and fitness staff, 12 general managers, and 4 regional managers in a rapidly growing organization. Worked closely with general managers of each location, providing guidance in maximizing sales and increasing member-retention rate while reducing expenses.

- **Delivered double-digit sales growth each year.**
- **Maintained member retention rate at more than 70%.**
- **Launched a comprehensive fitness and nutrition program, which included more than 200 personal trainers.**
- **Contributed to design and pre-sale phases for 5 new facilities.**

<u>FORT BEND GENERAL HOSPITAL</u> — Needville, TX   2007–2010
(A 150-bed community hospital)

Director, Business Development

Directed business-development activities to revitalize an older hospital in an industrial suburb of Houston. Developed and coordinated promotions, community-relations activities, and special programs for physician recruitment.

- **Built a local Preferred Provider Organization (PPO) from scratch to more than 10,000 participants. Model was duplicated at other Houston-area hospitals.**

EDUCATION

SOUTHWEST TEXAS STATE UNIVERSITY — New Braunfels, TX
- **Master of Arts, Kinesiology,** GPA 4.0 (2007)
- **Bachelor of Business Administration,** Cum Laude (2005)

Available to travel and/or relocate

COOL J. DAVIES ▪ 312-555-6666 ▪ coolj@mail.com ▪ LinkedIn Profile

Strategic Leader — Healthcare Practice Administration & Operations Management

OPTIMIZING ➡ Operations ➡ Staff Readiness ➡ Service Delivery ➡ Patient Experience

- Highly effective leader with **15 years of expertise directing various operational aspects of large medical treatment facilities and leading sizeable clinical and administrative teams** to efficiently provide medical and administrative services to high volumes of patients.

- Accomplished project manager, overseeing **multimillion-dollar budgets and service enhancement projects to align healthcare services and delivery to evolving healthcare trends**.

- Operations expert who proactively **analyzes, identifies, and implements cost-saving systems and functional improvements and enforces compliance** while maximizing capabilities and resources to guarantee favorable outcomes.

Core Competencies
- ☑ Healthcare Operations
- ☑ Project Management
- ☑ Strategic Planning
- ☑ Staff Leadership
- ☑ Contract Management
- ☑ Compliance & Quality
- ☑ Medical Response Plans
- ☑ Budget Management
- ☑ Training & Development

Professional Experience

United States Air Force
Air Base, USA | 11/2014–Present

Chief, Medical Readiness   04/2016–Present

Direct medical readiness operation of 135 clinical personnel providing healthcare services to 27,000 patients. Identify and initiate technological upgrades, training, and procedural modifications to improve operations and staff capabilities needed to provide adequate responses on military installation and during humanitarian efforts and conflicts. Sustain and deploy high-quality medical teams across 19 specialty areas to deliver $31M in annual healthcare services. Lead, train, coach, and develop 3 employees and coordinate and facilitate leadership training and development for 45 leaders. Develop reports, analyze metrics, and revise medical readiness plans for emergency management, disease containment, and installation responses.

Highlighted Contributions

- ☑ **Operations Management:** Discovered severe staffing deficit in clinical operations. *Result: Increased medical support and services 51% by promptly ramping up staffing levels and adding 100 team members.*

- ☑ **Project Management:** Spearheaded critical data compilation and circulation efforts for 75 medical facilities feeding pertinent information to 8 occupational health clinics linked worldwide. *Result: Supported key initiatives implemented from large-scale program focused on improving healthcare services, delivery, and outcomes for 9.4 million patients across the world.*

- ☑ **Leadership: Served** as interim manager of alternate medical operation with 49 employees. *Result: Site named #1 out of 9 medical sites for achieving 100% compliance training.*

- ☑ **Project Management:** Mobilized 84 clinical team members to support $2M communal event for an anticipated 75,000 attendees.

Chief, Medical Information Systems   11/2014–04/2016

Oversaw $10M network operation consisting of 20 servers across 7 medical treatment facilities supporting 15,000 patients. Aligned daily operations and 14 team members with Department of Defense (DoD) information security and assurance practices and regulations governing electronic protected health information (ePHI). Facilitated staff training and coached 9 team members on information security policies and procedures for medical treatment facilities.

Highlighted Contributions

- ☑ **Project Management:** Led 3 12-member project teams through combined $17.5M software and network infrastructure improvements. *Result: Stabilized medical systems supporting 55,000 patients and $31M in healthcare services.*

- ☑ **Medical Systems Stabilization:** Restored system outage within 24 hours. *Result: Facilitated prescription fulfillment services for 44,000 patients.*

Strategy: Translate military experience to language that works in civilian environments and highlight exceptional results to position this healthcare leader for success once he leaves the Air Force.

COOL J. DAVIES ■ 080-5555-6666 ■ coolj@mail.com ■ Page 2

United States Air Force
Air Base, Abroad | 10/2013–11/2014

Chief, Patient Administration
Supervised 16 contractors and confirmed tasks were completed in compliance with multi-year, billion-dollar medical services contract. Led team in performing patient administration functions for 8 medical treatment facilities and coordinating $900K in inpatient and outpatient healthcare services for 900 patients. Developed reports and analyzed metrics on bed availability, staffing, dental health, and medical care. Adhered to Department of Defense information security and privacy regulations.

Highlighted Contributions

☑ **Program Management:** Earned Contracting Officer's Representative (COR) Certification and *effectively managed $3.6M contract over 4-week period* during staffing shortage.

☑ **Compliance:** Assessed site compliance against operating standards for medical programs. *Result: Discovered and corrected 8 deficiencies and achieved 98% compliance rate.*

☑ **Quality Management:** Inspected pharmaceutical inventory to identify safety violations. *Result: Removed expired pharmaceuticals and secured funding for replacement medications.*

United States Air Force
Air Base, USA | 01/2010–09/2013

Manager, Education & Training
Administered training programs covering 28 specialty areas and 500 military, civilian, and contract personnel. Audited 25,000 personnel training records to verify basic life support (BLS) certifications and collaborated with 55 training providers to coordinate recertification training. Trained 45 team members on how to effectively implement life-saving strategies during critical and non-critical incidents on military installations and during humanitarian efforts and conflicts.

Highlighted Contributions

☑ **Compliance:** Identified training deficiency that hindered operational compliance and medical team readiness to administer medical services to 22,000 patients. *Result: Immediately implemented appropriate training procedures and reinstated medical group readiness in less than 30 days.*

☑ **Quality Management:** Piloted unit's self-inspection program to proactively meet inspection standards. *Result: Received 100% rating during mandatory health services inspection.*

☑ **Operational Efficiency:** Streamlined patient intake process by merging medical groups and staff to collectively perform the functions. *Result: Reduced number of hours required to perform work functions by 30%.*

Education & Certifications

Master of Business Administration in Strategic Leadership
Bachelor of Science *(Summa Cum Laude)* in Health Sciences / Health Care Management
Trident University International

Associate of Applied Science in Health Care Management
Community College of the Air Force

Certified Contracting Officer's Representative (COR) | Professional Manager Certification
First Aid & CPR Certified

Technical Systems & Regulatory Knowledge

The Joint Commission Accreditation Standards | Accreditation Association for Ambulatory Health Care **(AAAHC) |** Aeromedical Evacuation | Electronic Medical Records (EMR) | Composite Health Care System (CHCS) | MilPDS (Military Personnel Data System) | Aeromedical Services Information Management Systems (ASIMS) | Electronic Protected Health Information (ePHI**)** TRICARE Operations & Patient Administration Functions | Health Insurance Portability and Accountability Act (HIPAA) Department of Defense COMPUSEC/1 | Military Health System | Microsoft (Word, Excel & PowerPoint)

10 Awards & Commendations ~ Available Upon Request

VICTORIA CHANG

victoria.chang@gmail.com • 555-456-7890 • LinkedIn.com/in/VictoriaChang

SENIOR EXECUTIVE—MEDICAL AND PHARMACY SERVICES

| Sales & Marketing | ➡ | Operational Efficiency | ➡ | Aggressive Growth | ➡ | Acquisition & Expansion |

Strategic and visionary leader who played an integral role in leading 2 healthcare services organizations to top revenue and profit performance while delivering exceptional customer service and satisfaction.

Well qualified in all areas of executive leadership, with hands-on experience in operations, sales and marketing, and technology. Managed the successful integration of 10 mergers and acquisitions. Created a common brand image and unified teams of people who embodied the organizational vision and customer mission.

- Operational VP during rapid and massive growth of PharmaCare from $23M to $1.1B in revenue.
- Regional SVP for the one of the most profitable and customer-focused operations in the company.
- Driver behind growth of small pharmacy into dominant regional provider of contract services to LTC market.

EXPERIENCE AND ACHIEVEMENTS

PharmaCare Corp. (NYSE:PCC), Los Angeles, CA   2007–Present
$2.6B company, one of the nation's largest providers of medical supply and pharmacy services to the long-term-care market.

SENIOR VICE PRESIDENT, SOUTHWEST REGION, 2015–Present

SNAPSHOT: Transformed region from declining performance to top national status in revenue, profitability, customer satisfaction, and cost control.

Assumed leadership of Southwest region after MedCap acquisition doubled company size; region was experiencing stagnant revenue, declining profits, and significant loss of its prime LTC customer base. Drove improvement initiatives across the full scope of operations for nearly $100M region, with full accountability for sales, finance (P&L), clinical services, and operations.

- **Turnaround Leadership / Revenue & Profit Performance:** Rebuilt the organization, strengthening management, sales, and operations/administrative teams and deeply instilling core values of customer service and efficient operations. Achieved impressive performance gains across the board:

	2016	2019	Improvement
Revenue	$42.6M	$96.0M	+225%
Operating Income	$2.6M	$9.2M	+353%
Customer Base (# beds)	19,017	23,661	+124%

- **Sales, Market Positioning, Training & Customer Service:** Built sales focus and competency at all levels of the organization through effective training and constant communication/reinforcement.
  - Reduced sales staff from 8 to 2 while more than doubling revenues.
  - Drove sales growth toward high-quality customers and preferred payor mix to increase income 225% with only a 25% increase in customers.
  - Elevated region from last to #1 in the company in customer satisfaction.
  - Built brand image, customer loyalty, and retention by initiating "The PharmaCare Difference" strategy complete with tagline, branding program, and integrated marketing efforts.

- **Finance, Operations & Technology Leadership:**
  - Implemented multidiscipline CRM program (Sales Logix) that provides instantly accessible information for every aspect of business performance. Customized off-the-shelf program for specific healthcare/LTC environment.
  - Centralized billing operations to improve both performance and efficiency. Reduced days sales outstanding 62%, from 132 days to 51; achieved the lowest bad-debt ratio in the company.

Strategy: "Snapshot" each position to give a high-level view of impressive results, share specific achievements in sections that are introduced with keyword headlines, and leave sufficient white space to keep this detail-rich resume readable.

VICTORIA CHANG   victoria.chang@gmail.com • 555-456-7890 • LinkedIn.com/in/VictoriaChang

SENIOR VICE PRESIDENT, PHARMACY OPERATIONS, 2011–2015 | VICE PRESIDENT, PHARMACY OPERATIONS, 2007–2011

SNAPSHOT: Led organization through dynamic expansion—doubling in size every year through active acquisition strategy and organic growth.

Provided strategic and hands-on guidance to smoothly integrate operations, expand services, grow revenue and profitability, and gain efficiencies. Managed pharmacy, purchasing, clinical operations, and sales/marketing support.

- **Revenue Performance:** Oversaw operations as organization grew to more than 25X its original size—from $23M, 9,000 beds (FY07) to $1.1B, 245,000 beds (FY15).

- **Strategic Leadership:** Member of senior management team creating and executing merger/acquisition strategy, including due diligence; actively engaged in evaluating, purchasing, and integrating 10 companies with their resultant impact on business growth and geographic expansion. Highlights include:

– 2007	Southwest Medical	Added $13M, 10,000 beds in Southwest
– 2009	Desert Healthcare	Added $8M
– 2011–2012	Omega Drugs, BlueCare	Grew West Coast region
– 2014	Community Care	Expanded business to home infusion
– 2015	MedCap	More than doubled annual revenue; expanded to national operation

- **Technology:** Standardized operating procedures and technology platforms across the organization. Implemented X-Fact LTC system and managed technology conversions for each acquisition.

- **Marketing/Branding:** Managed operational aspects of remarketing/rebranding following organizational **name** change and creation of the nationwide PharmaCare brand in 2014.

- **Sales:** Worked closely with sales and marketing teams to integrate newly acquired businesses. Guided sales teams during contract negotiations and authorized final approval of all agreements.

Masterson Drug Company, Phoenix, AZ   1997–2007
DIRECTOR, CONTRACT PHARMACY SERVICES, 2000–2007

SNAPSHOT: Grew fledgling long-term-care pharmacy operation from a single site to a prominent regional player in the emerging industry—55 dispensing sites servicing 18,000 beds.

Assumed leadership of new operation following its acquisition and developed the strategy, services, programs, and operating policies to achieve rapid growth and healthy profitability. Fully accountable for all facets of sales, marketing, operations, and finance.

- Grew revenues from $500K to $14MM in 10 years and created one of the company's highest profit centers.
- Negotiated all purchasing contracts for equipment and supplies.
- Improved efficiency and accountability by designing and implementing computer applications for pharmacy distribution and customer reports.

PHARMACY MANAGER, RETAIL OPERATIONS, 1999–2000 | PHARMACIST, 1997–1999

EDUCATION / LICENSURE

Bachelor of Science in Pharmacy   University of Arizona College of Pharmacy
Professional State Licensure   Arizona | New Mexico | California

Walter Preston

Columbia, MO • 573.229.7459 • wpreston@gmail.com • LinkedIn Profile

HEALTHCARE EXECUTIVE / SR. VICE PRESIDENT / COO – FORTUNE 500 EXPERIENCE

⊙ Accomplished senior healthcare executive with over a decade of demonstrated experience increasing profits by up to **52%**, turning around underperforming businesses, and leading expansion for multi-unit operations at multibillion-dollar Fortune 100 and 500 healthcare services companies.

⊙ Keen understanding of pharmacy operations and surgical supply industry; core background in operations, sales, and marketing. Commitment to healthcare industry includes holding 2 **surgical supply patents**.

⊙ Forward-thinking, strategic leader who influences others to think differently, raise the bar, and consider **alternative solutions** while remaining cognizant of all factors. International business acumen, successfully negotiating strategic sourcing relationships and partnerships with companies in **China** and **Germany**.

CORE COMPETENCIES

Revenue & Profit Growth • Market Share Growth • Healthcare Markets • Medical & Surgical Supplies
Pharmaceuticals • Strategic Planning & Analysis • Change Management • Process Management
Financial Planning • Lean Six Sigma (LSS) • Operations Management • Sales Management • Quality Assurance
Supply Chain Management • Regulatory Compliance • Standard Operating Procedures (SOPs)

HEALTHCARE EXECUTIVE EXPERIENCE

SR. EXECUTIVE VICE PRESIDENT — *Chain Pharmaceuticals*   2018–Present; Atlanta, GA
Hired to relaunch *Inco* brand to aggressively grow market share. Direct P&L, strategic planning, sales, marketing, customer service, staffing, regulatory compliance, and operating performance of *Inco* with **60+** associates, **5,300+** customers, and **$22M** in annual revenues. Direct reports include VPs of administration, professional services, sales, and marketing and one financial analyst. Collaborate with and solicit buy-in from other C-level executives.

Select Accomplishments:

♦ Delivered a **52% increase** in year-over-year profit from 2018 to 2019; trending toward similar results in 2020.

♦ Increased top-line sales by **50,000** prescriptions per month. Raised customer service score **36%** in 12 months.

♦ Fostered strategic company relationship with the **International Consortium of Pharmacists** and the **National Compounding Pharmacists** organization.

GENERAL MANAGER — *Evercare*   2016–2018; Springfield, MO
Directed and mentored a team of **312** associates and **12** direct reports in the production, promotion, and sale of pharmaceutical products and services for **3,000+** customers. Formulated short- and long-term strategic plans and budgets based on corporate growth objectives. Promoted and implemented the process for joint commission of both long-term care and infusion pharmacies.

Select Accomplishments:

♦ **Saved $1.2M annually** by reducing courier costs and **$60K per month** by cutting overtime in first 18 months.

♦ Decreased annual operating expenses **21%** through restructuring operations and reducing full-time employees (FTEs) from 240 to 219.

Strategy: Start with a headline that announces the level of his experience with Fortune 500 companies and continue with a strong profile, extensive list of core competencies (keywords), and chronological work history that highlights strong accomplishments.

PRESIDENT & CEO / COO — *ATL Medical*   2014–2018; Columbia, MO
Hired to provide a new strategic direction, leading company in a total transformation from a small, family-owned business to a global provider of healthcare products. Introduced LSS process improvement enterprise-wide while building an inside telesales and customer service team to generate leads. Secured financing for and globally launched new product campaign.

Select Accomplishments:`

♦ Delivered the **highest shareholder return** in the company's **16**-year history.

♦ Saved **$5.2M** annually through restructuring of existing outsourcing and logistics partnerships and contracts, including new international partners in Europe and China.

♦ Increased sales by **43%** and reduced labor by **28%** within the first year. Reduced operating expenses by **35%** year-over-year through warehouse consolidation initiative.

♦ **Co-invented and patented** a disposable hospital curtain product; exceeded initial forecasted sales by **49%**.

SR. VP, OPERATIONS VP, QUALITY & PROCESS IMPROVEMENT — *Geneva Scripts*   2012–2014; Kansas City, MO
Directed the most profitable portion of the mail-order pharmacy business—order processing, fulfillment, and call center. Restructured and realigned 4 departments for higher productivity and better cost control. Built LSS organization, including hiring and training professionals from entry-level managers up to senior directors with green and master black belts.

Select Accomplishments:

♦ Boosted the department's conversion rate from **85% to 92%** within 12 months.

♦ Saved **$2.3M** annually and improved customer service by executing switch of interactive voice response (IVR) vendors.

♦ Cut costs a total of **$20M** by employing LSS techniques enterprise-wide.

PREVIOUS HEALTHCARE MANAGEMENT POSITIONS at *Bluebird Health* in Provo, Utah, and *Strategy Health* in Denver, Colorado: **SR. VICE PRESIDENT OF OPERATIONS**, **SALES MANAGER,** and **DIRECTOR OF OPERATIONS**.

EDUCATION

BACHELOR OF SCIENCE, BUSINESS ADMINISTRATION — *Eastern Kansas State University*   Lawrence, KS

Walter Preston • 573.229.7459 • wpreston@gmail.com

RAJ AGARWAL

raj.agarwal@mail.com   312-654-4567   LinkedIn Profile

SENIOR HEALTHCARE EXECUTIVE
Operations Management | Business Outsourcing | Product Line Management | General Management

---

Catalyst for positive change and growth, defining success through people, process, and product.

High-impact executive with exceptional record of success orchestrating and delivering consistent and measurable breakthroughs in business outsourcing selection and management, revenue and profit growth, market and customer expansion, operating cost reductions, and productivity and efficiency gains.

Change agent and consensus builder who champions aggressive advancements in products and services to maintain competitive edge in the marketplace. *Expertise includes:*

Customer-Driven Management

➜ **Salvaged credibility with clients and business associates** by creating a provider service recovery plan that dramatically improved customer service, call center response time, and problem resolution.

Organizational Realignment & Engineering

➜ **Achieved buy-in across organizational lines** to deliver member acquisition plan, sustainable operating model, and shared business processes, successfully meeting crucial deadline for installation of $225M Medicare product.

➜ **Led timely installation of $6M Oracle CRM application,** rescuing faltering project and revitalizing team. Deployment to 300 end users required extensive change management, process redesign, resource modeling, and training.

➜ **Generated $100M savings over 3 years,** leading RFP assessment team in selection of new pharmacy vendor.

Advanced Product Development

➜ **Accelerated transaction processing to 1M in first 2 years** and saved thousands in administrative costs by developing and implementing a suite of web-based e-health provider products.

PROFESSIONAL EXPERIENCE

MIDWEST HEALTH CARE (MHC), Evanston, IL   2009–Present

Vice President of Benefits, Product & Market Performance (2015–Present)
Challenged to drive the development and adoption of new commercial products, including vendor negotiations and benefits compliance with regulatory agencies in 3 states. Built a highly regarded organization that has become a valued resource for key initiatives across the enterprise.

Organizational Leadership:
- Manage $4M budget and 40-member staff, strategically leveraging resources in support of organization's goals.
- Instilled customer-focused culture that produces effective cross-functional teamwork and innovative thinking.

Growth & Expansion:
- Drove accelerated development and implementation of a crucial Medicare product that strengthened market presence and sustained a multimillion-dollar business line in a highly competitive market; worked closely with key leaders to garner resources, remove roadblocks, and achieve critical milestones for installation and migration of 20,000 members in just 7 months.
- Expanded market coverage to western Michigan by adding innovative products and services, including most recently a tiered network product for the Illinois Group Insurance Commission.

Performance & Process Improvement:
- Brought company to 100% benefits compliance by redesigning work processes and teams.
- Renegotiated $3M fulfillment contract for member materials, generating a $1M savings in 18 months.
- Restructured and revitalized product implementation team to average 4 new product installations per year—always meeting or beating schedule and budget goals.

Strategy: Ensure that key achievements are not overlooked by highlighting them in the summary. In the experience section, divide bullets into easily skimmed groups under headings that reiterate skills and value.

RAJ AGARWAL <u>raj.agarwal@mail.com</u> • 312-654-4567

MHC, continued

Vice President of Provider Operations (2011–2015)
Recruited to position based on extensive background in hospital operations, physician relations, sales, and service. Oversaw all operations and services, including training and communications, for 33,000 providers in a 4-state region.

Organizational Leadership:
- Managed $12M budget and 135 full-time employees who served as primary administrative interface with the plan.
- Oversaw contract fulfillment for EDI, claims, configuration, and provider call center, administering $26M budget and managing 200-member outsourced staff.
- Instrumental contributor to MGC turnaround strategy by integrating services and instituting cost-saving measures in areas of provider service, claims processing, and headcount reduction.

Performance & Process Improvement:
- Improved all measures of provider service claims processing and business processes; recovered $60M in cash advances to providers.
- While growing transaction volume, downsized staff by 40%, working closely with personnel through the transition.

Director of Corporate Development (2009–2011)
Managed new business development team during market assessment and acquisition of 2 organizations, including due diligence and operations integration.

Organizational Leadership:
- Led transfer of all Medicaid business to Midwest Community Health Plan.
- Led operations integration efforts for Healthy Midwest, a wholly owned subsidiary of Midwest Health Center.

BLUE CROSS BLUE SHIELD, Chicago, IL   2005–2009

Director of Network Management, National Sales Division (2007–2009)
Recruited, hired, and supervised 10-member professional and support staff, consistently exceeding targets for productivity and efficiency to successfully meet operating and financial goals.

Product Line Manager (2005–2007)
Administered P&L responsibility for $200M product line for the pharmacy, child health, and student markets. Created and directed a 6-month project that successfully launched an innovative child health insurance product.

CHICAGO WEST MEDICAL CENTER, Melrose Park, IL   1995–2005

Vice President of Strategic Planning & Community Relations
Fast-track promotion from original hire as Planning Analyst to final position of Vice President, with interim roles as Manager of QA and Director of Social Services. Recruited to each successive position based on consistent contributions to productivity, excellence, and efficiency improvement.

Organizational Leadership:
- Key member of Senior Administrative Negotiating Team in merger with South State Hospital.
- Developed business plan that included acquisition of new technologies, recruitment of additional physicians, and a tertiary hospital alliance for teaching and training programs.
- Strengthened community relations to win support for $12M building program, previously strongly opposed.

Performance & Process Improvement:
- Won DON approval for expansion of 4 units; completed project on budget and ahead of schedule.
- Integrated Social Service and Utilization Review Departments into a program nationally acclaimed for its success.
- Developed medical staff quality and utilization improvement plan to achieve JCAHO accreditation.

EDUCATION | CERTIFICATION | LEADERSHIP DEVELOPMENT

M.H.A., Northwestern University, 2001
B.A., Sociology *(summa cum laude),* Loyola University, 1995
Project Management Certification, University of Chicago, 2013
Leadership Development Program, Northwestern University, 2015

RESUME 65: *by Adrienne Tom, CERM, MCRS, CIS, CES, CCS • www.careerimpressions.ca*

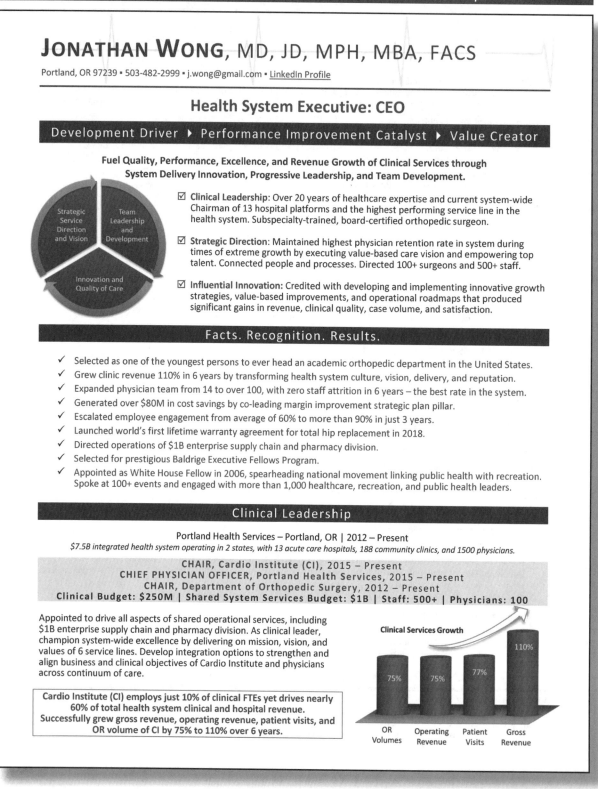

JONATHAN WONG, MD, JD, MPH, MBA, FACS

Portland, OR 97239 ▪ 503-482-2999 ▪ j.wong@gmail.com ▪ LinkedIn Profile

Health System Executive: CEO

Development Driver ▶ Performance Improvement Catalyst ▶ Value Creator

Fuel Quality, Performance, Excellence, and Revenue Growth of Clinical Services through System Delivery Innovation, Progressive Leadership, and Team Development.

☑ **Clinical Leadership:** Over 20 years of healthcare expertise and current system-wide Chairman of 13 hospital platforms and the highest performing service line in the health system. Subspecialty-trained, board-certified orthopedic surgeon.

☑ **Strategic Direction:** Maintained highest physician retention rate in system during times of extreme growth by executing value-based care vision and empowering top talent. Connected people and processes. Directed 100+ surgeons and 500+ staff.

☑ **Influential Innovation:** Credited with developing and implementing innovative growth strategies, value-based improvements, and operational roadmaps that produced significant gains in revenue, clinical quality, case volume, and satisfaction.

Facts. Recognition. Results.

✓ Selected as one of the youngest persons to ever head an academic orthopedic department in the United States.

✓ Grew clinic revenue 110% in 6 years by transforming health system culture, vision, delivery, and reputation.

✓ Expanded physician team from 14 to over 100, with zero staff attrition in 6 years – the best rate in the system.

✓ Generated over $80M in cost savings by co-leading margin improvement strategic plan pillar.

✓ Escalated employee engagement from average of 60% to more than 90% in just 3 years.

✓ Launched world's first lifetime warranty agreement for total hip replacement in 2018.

✓ Directed operations of $1B enterprise supply chain and pharmacy division.

✓ Selected for prestigious Baldrige Executive Fellows Program.

✓ Appointed as White House Fellow in 2006, spearheading national movement linking public health with recreation. Spoke at 100+ events and engaged with more than 1,000 healthcare, recreation, and public health leaders.

Clinical Leadership

Portland Health Services – Portland, OR | 2012 – Present
$7.5B integrated health system operating in 2 states, with 13 acute care hospitals, 188 community clinics, and 1500 physicians.

CHAIR, Cardio Institute (CI), 2015 – Present
CHIEF PHYSICIAN OFFICER, Portland Health Services, 2015 – Present
CHAIR, Department of Orthopedic Surgery, 2012 – Present
Clinical Budget: $250M | Shared System Services Budget: $1B | Staff: 500+ | Physicians: 100

Appointed to drive all aspects of shared operational services, including $1B enterprise supply chain and pharmacy division. As clinical leader, champion system-wide excellence by delivering on mission, vision, and values of 6 service lines. Develop integration options to strengthen and align business and clinical objectives of Cardio Institute and physicians across continuum of care.

Cardio Institute (CI) employs just 10% of clinical FTEs yet drives nearly 60% of total health system clinical and hospital revenue. Successfully grew gross revenue, operating revenue, patient visits, and OR volume of CI by 75% to 110% over 6 years.

Clinical Services Growth

OR Volumes 75% | Operating Revenue 75% | Patient Visits 77% | Gross Revenue 110%

Strategy: Succinctly summarize a very robust career, using lean content and a creative format to convey valuable information quickly. Note footnote at bottom of page 2 that promises more of the details that might be found in a traditional medical CV.

Jonathan Wong, MD, JD, MPH, MBA, FACS | Page 2

Portland Health Services Leadership Achievements & Impacts:

COST SAVINGS DELIVERY:
Pharmacy: $10M
Medical Devices: $16M
IT Reorganization: $6M
Supply Chain: $50M

- **Delivered $80M in system services and supply chain cost reductions**, co-leading and executing effort to streamline operations.

- **Consolidated 32 departments into 5 clinical institutes,** gaining buy-in to streamline care continuum, improve patient care focus, and enhance governance.
  - ✓ Elevated employee engagement scores to 90%+ satisfied/very satisfied.

- **Positioned clinical services as industry leader,** boosting community reputation and patient satisfaction through forward-thinking processes, improvement initiatives, industry partnerships, and strategic leadership efforts.
  - ✓ Developed and introduced roadmap with value-based care focus and high degree of staff participation.
  - ✓ Championed initiative to establish world's first total hip replacement warranty, a 2-year journey.
  - ✓ Produced $4M in cost savings, reorganizing supply chain to consolidate delivery and management.

- **Increased physician satisfaction from 60% to 100% while sustaining productivity growth,** instilling processes to raise engagement and encourage autonomy.
  - ✓ Maintained highest retention rate in system despite highest department growth.
  - ✓ Empowered team to make decisions, providing resources and recognition to improve workplace culture.
  - ✓ Improved KPIs, such as time to be seen (from 40% to 90%) and fill rate (from 45% to 95%).

University of California Health Science Center – Los Angeles, CA | 2003 – 2011
$500M academic medical center with 27 clinical sites, 705-bed Level 1 academic trauma hospital, and 5,000+ faculty and staff.

ASSOCIATE PROFESSOR, Department of Orthopedics, 2009 – 2011
ASSOCIATE DIRECTOR, Orthopedic Residency Program, 2004 – 2011
CHIEF, Division of Orthopedic Trauma Care, 2004 – 2011
ASSOCIATE MEDICAL DIRECTOR, Trauma One Center, 2003 – 2011

As Chief of Orthopedic Trauma Division, directed orthopedic academic program and clinical operations comprising 50% of all faculty and staff. Established highly specialized orthopedic trauma division designed to maximize efficiency and enhance patient outcomes. As Associate Professor and Associate Director of Orthopedic Residency Program, supervised 46 residents, ensuring achievement of all academic requirements.

Additional, Notable Experience

Chair: Surgical Suite Governance Board, Portland Health Services, 2017 – Present
Member: Cardio Institute Health System Physician Council, 2017 – Present
Board Member: American Medical Political Action Committee (MPAC), 2016 – Present
Member: Board of Directors, Keystone Accountable Care Organization, 2012 – Present
Baldrige Executive Fellow, 2016 | White House Fellow, 2006

Education

Master's in Business Administration – Booth School of Business, University of Chicago, 2017
Doctor of Medicine – California University of Science and Medicine, 1997
Juris Doctor (JD/MPH Program) – California Western School of Law, 1995
Master's in Public Health (JD/MPH Program), Health Law – California University, 1995
Bachelor of Arts – Pomona College, 1990

More information about my post-graduate medical training, public service, community service, fellowships and awards, journal activities, honors, and publications available upon request.

RESUME 66: *by Louise Kursmark, MRW, CPRW, JCTC, CEIP, CCM • www.louisekursmark.com*

Brendan McNulty

617-555-3456 • brendan.mcnulty@mac.com • LinkedIn Profile

Healthcare Senior Executive: Sales & Account Management

Industry Leader | Revenue & Profit Driver | Expert in the Art of Account Management

- Managed **$5B P&L** and strategic nationwide accounts for the **#1** healthcare company in its segment.
- Delivered double-digit revenue increases via new business development and **97%** client retention.
- Built Account Management function that helped drive early-stage health benefits company to **$100M** revenue.
- Recognized for ability to get to the heart of each client's needs and build exceptional partner relationships.

Client Cultivation & Business Retention	New Business Development	Strategic Planning
Profit & Performance Improvement	P&L & Operations Management	Negotiations
Account Management Best Practices	Team Leadership & Collaboration	Executive Presentations

Professional Experience

Pharma-Ben (formerly Pharm Health Solutions), Boston, MA   2004–Present

$100B+ Fortune 100 company, the largest pharmacy benefits organization in the US

VICE PRESIDENT / GENERAL MANAGER, 2017–Present

$5B P&L • 400 nationwide accounts • 5M+ insured • 5 direct, 40 indirect reports

Selected to lead vastly expanded National Service Group business following acquisition—doubled scope of responsibility and added critical new accounts including the "crown jewel" SEI Trust. Melded Pharma-Ben and Pharm Health account teams into one cohesive team of top performers. Instilled best practices of consultative sales, client relationship building, and long-term account management.

- Outperformed profit goal by at least **10%** every year by landing new business and partnering/consulting to build programs meeting clients' specific needs.
- Achieved **97%** client retention.
- Secured 3-year renewal (with 4th option year) of **#1** account.
- Introduced clients to biopharmaceutical advances and new drug therapies; helped create guidelines to manage costs while delivering needed benefits.
- Managed **RFP** process and negotiations for both new and renewing contracts.
- Continued to lead **Benefits Advisory Council** (now in its 12th year) and build invaluable relationships at executive level in healthcare and service industries.

New Profit Dollars

VICE PRESIDENT / GENERAL MANAGER, Pharm Health Solutions, 2009–2017

$3B P&L • 100+ nationwide accounts • 3M insured • 10 direct, 40 indirect reports

Hand-picked to build and lead newly formed Key Accounts/National Service Group with challenge to grow revenue, profits, and brand recognition through dedicated account management and upselling of entire product line. Created highly effective strategy for identifying prospects, managing RFPs, winning new business, securing renewals, and infiltrating within accounts to drive business growth.

- More than doubled the division:

	Revenue	Accounts	Insured
2017	**$3.0B**	**100**	**3M**
2009	**$1.4B**	**50**	**1.1M**

- Secured key wins with jumbo accounts – unions serving **200K** to **500K** members in varied service industries. Retained **100%** of strategic accounts, inking multi-year contracts at renewal time.
- Conceived, launched, and chaired **Benefits Advisory Council,** an innovative program that twice each year brings together up to 40 strategic clients for a 2-day brain trust retreat. Brainstorm healthcare challenges and solutions, provide opportunities for leaders to network, and offer access to corporate CEO.

Strategy: Use a table and a chart to highlight impressive results throughout this executive's career in pharmacy benefits sales and account management. Put all numbers in bold so they jump off the pages.

Brendan McNulty   617-555-3456 • brendan.mcnulty@mac.com

Pharma-Ben, continued

NATIONAL ACCOUNT EXECUTIVE, 2006–2009

$500M revenue • 3 direct reports • strategic accounts including Raytheon, IBM, GE, Pfizer

Promoted to manage strategic business in the Northeast Region.

- Increased sales **20%–30%** by creating programs that incentivized clients to convert to generic medications.
- Achieved **80%** retention of key accounts.
- Chosen as 1 of just 20 managers nationwide to participate in intensive, year-long **Emerging Leaders Program** (3 days/month out of office). Transformed leadership/management skill set and gained notice of top executives, leading to rapid promotion to challenging new VP role.

DIRECTOR OF MARKETING, 2005–2006

Recruited to launch health management program to large employers, managed care organizations, and labor unions nationwide.

- Effectively created adjacent market outside traditional prescription benefit management business.
- Grew from **0** to **10** clients in **15** months, contributing **$100K** in incremental revenues.

Caretakers, Inc., New Haven, CT   2003–2005

#2 nationwide in demand management • 2M+ members in managed healthcare entities (PPOs, HMOs, large employer groups)

EXECUTIVE DIRECTOR, CUSTOMER SERVICE, 2004–2005
DIRECTOR, ACCOUNT MANAGEMENT, 2003–2004

Recruited when the company had just 6 clients and a robust pipeline but lacked the strategy, process, people, and leadership needed for professional account management. Built the Account Management function from the ground up, then expanded role to encompass leadership of integrated customer and account service functions for 71 clients (2.5M individuals) as the company grew to $100M revenue.

- Held oversight responsibility for company's entire book of business. Personally managed 3 largest accounts representing more than **30%** of revenue.
- Maintained **95%** account renewal rate, the highest in company history and far outpacing **88%** industry average.
- Generated **$1M+** in incremental revenue through strategies to sell add-on services to existing accounts.
- Drove operating improvements: Saved **$500K** via vendor consolidation, reengineered reporting and customer information functions, and efficiently managed **$1.5M** annual spend for company client communications.

Prior: Advanced from finance/accounting positions into line management with CVS, Woonsocket, RI.

Education
BS BUSINESS ADMINISTRATION
University of Connecticut, Storrs, CT

AMIKA ABASE

413-456-5543 | amika.abase@gmail.com | LinkedIn Profile

HEALTH CARE INDUSTRY EXECUTIVE – EXPERT IN STRATEGIC PLANNING & MARKETING
POST-ACUTE CARE | LIFE CARE | SKILLED CARE | HOME CARE | HOSPITAL CARE
POPULATION HEALTH | ACCOUNTABLE CARE ORGANIZATIONS

MBA – HEALTH CARE ADMINISTRATION | BOARD OF DIRECTORS EXPERIENCE | EXECUTIVE CONSULTANT

More than 20 years of success crafting strategic solutions and creating profitable new lines of business within the increasingly complex health care landscape. An expert in shaping policy, prioritizing strategies, building new programs and services, improving quality of care, increasing revenues, and decreasing operating costs.

Pioneered true innovations in care delivery, risk taking, reimbursement, branding, and organizational leadership.

PROFESSIONAL EXPERIENCE

EL CERRITO HEALTH SYSTEM, El Cerrito, CA   2002 to Present
Community-based integrated health delivery system with 1 hospital, 4 home health agencies, and 5 long-term care and residential facilities serving 100K+ patients annually

Executive Vice President – Strategic Planning, Marketing, HR & Life Care (2016 to Present)
Senior Vice President – Planning, Marketing & Home Care (2009 to 2016)
Vice President – Planning & Marketing (2002 to 2009)

*Member of 12-person management committee, including executive leadership team, that led organization through long-term change, expansion and diversification, **delivering revenue growth of 180%+.***

Scope of Leadership Responsibility

Most-senior Strategic Planning, Marketing, Human Resources, and Life Care Executive, leading 5 VP and Director reports in 4000-employee organization with $375M annual budget. Partner with board, medical chiefs and chairs, C-level executives, and senior management for health system's strategic plan, annual priorities and proposed joint ventures. **Manage system's most profitable division with 8%+ operating margin.**

CAO of Life Care Division (1100 beds and $70M annual budget) offering independent living, personal care, skilled nursing, and short-stay rehabilitation. Provide executive-level strategic and planning leadership to tactical operations teams.

COO of Active & Retirement Living Corporations (planned community with 800 units – townhomes, condominiums, and independent living), a joint venture with for-profit development company.

Senior Marketing Executive orchestrating brand development, reputation management, and advertising for health care, home care, and life care organizations.

Senior VP who led corporate and business line operations for $35M homecare and hospital organization.

Strategy: Provide 2 discrete sections for the current long-term job—one outlining extensive scope of responsibility, the other notable contributions—to create a logical flow and provide context for the many things this executive has been involved in and has accomplished.

AMIKA ABASE

413-456-5543 | amika.abase@gmail.com | LinkedIn Profile

Notable Achievements & Contributions – El Cerrito Health System

- Spearheaded the creation of Life Care Division's Short-Stay Rehabilitation Program, which has grown to approximately 100 beds at 2 facilities. Delivered outcomes better than both state and nationwide averages, decreasing readmissions 36% and reducing length of stay 25%.
- Involved in regional Accountable Care Organization (ACO), in collaboration with 4 other provider organizations, participating in MSSP to better manage care and divide risk with other insurers.
- Created innovative strategies and business plans to grow revenues and cut expenses while improving quality of patient care as Centers for Medicare and Medicaid Services (CMS) and insurers focus on cost reduction.
- Profitably transitioned home care business from cost reimbursement to prospective pay as mandated by CMS. Restructured operations, introduced 24x7 centralized call management system, and reduced 20 FTEs.
- Collaborated with risk partner (Bay Area Health) to provide direct admissions to short-term care services, successfully substituting skilled care for hospital care at much lower cost.
- Innovated new training programs to expand skill level of nursing professionals to meet changing health care delivery paradigm as focus shifts to providing more intensive services in skilled care environments.

CALIFORNIA CARE CENTERS, Oakland, CA   1993 to 2002
(Regional health care system with 6 hospitals and a total of 1179 beds)

Director of Planning & Market Research (2000 to 2002)
Senior Corporate Planner (1996 to 2002)
Special Projects Coordinator (1995 to 1996)
Operations Analyst (1993 to 1995)

Fast-track promotion through increasingly responsible positions in strategic and business planning. Collateral responsibility as **Health Care Consultant** on engagements with for-profit management services subsidiary.

- Designed, launched and managed first-ever physician referral service to support entire health system.
- Prepared fully funded $73M CON application for hospital replacement and expansion.
- Led a series of operational audit and cost-containment programs. Assisted with acquisition integration.
- Identified and evaluated new business opportunities to drive long-term growth in highly competitive market.

EDUCATION

MBA – Health Administration – University of San Francisco
BS – Health & Physical Education – University of California, Berkeley

PROFESSIONAL & LEADERSHIP AFFILIATIONS

- **Board Director & Management Committee Member,** Bay Area Health League (2015 to Present)
- **Board Director, Executive Committee Member & Finance Chair,** Maternal Care Coalition (2010 to 2018)
- **Member,** Forum of Executive Women (2015 to Present)
- **Member,** Society for Health Care Strategy and Market Development (1998 to Present)
- **Member,** Health Care Strategists (2014 to 2019)

CHAPTER 10

Human Resources and Organizational Development

- Talent Acquisition & Diversity Leader
- Chief Talent Officer
- Head of Organizational Performance
- Human Resources Director
- Business Partner
- Human Resources Director
- VP Human Resources
- Chief Human Resources Officer
- Chief Learning Officer

SERENA SANTIAGO

Atlanta, GA 30306 • 914-420-6570 • santiagoser@aol.com • LinkedIn Profile

SENIOR STAFFING EXECUTIVE

Talent Strategy, Acquisition & Leadership: Pfizer, Novartis, Pittsburgh Gazette, UPS

Quality-Driven, Cost-Effective Recruiting Throughout North America, Europe, and the Pacific Rim. MBA Degree.

Strategic Talent Acquisition Executive recognized for success in building global staffing models and reducing time-to-hire and cost-to-hire for all organizations while consistently exceeding expectations for quality of hire. Successful collaborator and partner to other senior executives to meet operational staffing needs worldwide. A big-picture thinker with achievements in employment branding, M&A integration, HRIS, diversity, and vendor management.

- **10K Annual New Hires.** Created novel talent acquisition strategies to attract new hires worldwide for Pfizer's diversity-focused recruitment and staffing programs.
- **46% Growth in Employee Volume.** Brought Sandoz staff to 2200 in IT, HR, finance, science, research, sales, and support functions while reducing turnover 10%+.
- **$1M+ Search Firm Cost Savings.** Designed focused staffing strategy to deliver huge cost savings to Novartis.
- **Innovative Social Media Strategies.** Attracted top talent by leveraging social media and web presence to strengthen employee branding for The Pittsburgh Gazette.

PROFESSIONAL EXPERIENCE

GLOBAL LEADER – TALENT ACQUISITION & DIVERSITY   2016 to Present

PFIZER PHARMACEUTICALS (*$10B medical technology manufacturer with 45K employees*) – Atlanta, GA

Recruited by Spencer Stuart to join Pfizer in 2012. Declined that opportunity and recruited for the 2nd time in 2014. Accepted challenge to redefine talent acquisition strategy, design world-class global staffing processes, introduce advanced technologies, and implement critical diversity initiatives to facilitate continuous improvement. Manage a team of 10 direct reports in a 200-person department.

Cost-to-Hire -60%

- **Created staffing model that delivers 10K+ new hires yearly. Positioned Pfizer as "employer of choice."**
- **Reduced cost-to-hire 60%+** and **decreased time-to-hire 45%+.**
- **Captured $15M in savings** over 3 years by restructuring and rebidding contingent worker program.
- Standardized recruiting and hiring from **18 different models into 1 single process.**
- Improved departmental **customer survey scores from 70% to 90% in 1st year.**
- Orchestrated implementation of **Workday solutions:** ATS cloud and mobile-enabled recruiting for worldwide markets; global talent acquisition dashboard with regional metrics for senior managers.

SENIOR DIRECTOR – STAFFING & OPERATIONS   2012 to 2016

SANDOZ, INC. (*$900M biotech company with growth from 1800 to 5000 employees in 4 years*) – Atlanta, GA

Built first-ever talent acquisition organization for fast-growing company (20% annual increase with 2nd most successful drug launch in US history). Created best-in-class-sourcing strategies and scalable recruitment and metrics-driven staffing models to meet growth demand with the very best candidates for the organization.

Cost-per-Hire -50%

- **Reduced cost-per-hire 50%** with online presence, social media outreach, and referral sources. Decreased reliance on contingent recruiters and orchestrated development of LinkedIn and Facebook pages.
- **Cut days-to-hire 30%** with preferred vendor list and new recruiting alliances.
- Created new executive recruiting function with predictable processes that **improved service level 50%.**

Strategy: Balance left-margin graphics—showing a trend of top performance in every position—with succinct, clear, powerful bullet points that emphasize quantifiable results.

SERENA SANTIAGO • Page 2   914-420-6570 • santiagoser@aol.com • LinkedIn Profile

SENIOR DIRECTOR – STAFFING & OPERATIONS – GROW-TECH, INC. (continued)

- **Implemented new Applicant Tracking System (ATS)** with improved metrics and reporting.
- Streamlined immigration processes, created relocation department, and expanded college recruiting.

DIRECTOR – GLOBAL STAFFING   2006 to 2011

NOVARTIS (*$85M pharmaceutical research & manufacturing division*) – Pittsburgh, PA

Recruited to Novartis as part of new management/executive team brought in to turn company around, rebuild brand, and recapture market share. Crafted cost-effective recruiting and staffing models for employees, managers, and senior executives worldwide. Managed $15M budget, 5 recruiting managers, and 15 indirect reports supporting operations in 135 countries (with 50% of leadership in overseas locations).

Staffing Costs -15%

- **Orchestrated placement of 1000+ new hires** throughout North America, Europe, and the Pacific Rim.
- **Reduced staffing costs 15%** and **interview-to-hire ratio from 3 to 1.**
- **Decreased search firm volume 82%** and **saved $1.2M in annual hiring costs.**
- Managed complex **post-acquisition workforce integration** processes and standardization.
- **Improved intern conversion rate 47%** to further accelerate and strengthen talent base.

DIRECTOR – STAFFING   2003 to 2006

THE PITTSBURGH GAZETTE (*$2B+ in annual revenue with employees in the US & Europe*) – Pittsburgh, PA

Designed and launched recruiting initiative that freshened brand to connect with next-generation leadership as The Gazette moved into digital technology. Devised creative sourcing strategies to meet hiring shortfalls.

Time-to-Fill -37%

- **Cut time-to-fill 37%** (93 days to 58 days) with new messaging, marketing, and outreach.
- **Created innovative college internship and recruitment programs** targeted to top-tier business schools.
- **Drove Chairman's diversity initiative** with new dashboard showing cultural representation by business and highlighted underrepresentation of key populations to be targeted recruitment candidates.

DIRECTOR – STAFFING   2000 to 2003

FIRST FINANCIAL PARTNERS (*$18B in revenue with employees throughout the US*) – Princeton, NJ
Promoted from Manager of Staffing to Director within first year of hire. Managed $5M budget and 25 direct reports across 4 US locations. Met high-volume staffing and training needs with innovation and creativity.

Cost-per-Hire -50%

- Conceptualized and launched recruitment plan to **attract 800 new hires within 8 months.**
- **Reduced cost-per-hire 50%** by redesigning sign-on bonus program and other key recruiting functions.
- **Addressed $13M annual knowledge loss** by understanding and resolving issues related to high turnaround among women and minorities.

Early Professional Career: Promoted rapidly through increasingly responsible **operations management and HR generalist positions with UPS.**

EDUCATION

Master of Business Administration (MBA) – Rutgers University
Bachelor of Arts (BA) – Labor Relations – Rutgers University
Executive Studies at Center for Creative Leadership | Six Sigma Green Belt Certification

RESUME 69: by Louise Kursmark, MRW, CPRW, JCTC, CEIP, CCM • www.louisekursmark.com

CHRIS CASTIGLIONE

503-555-6712 • chriscastiglione@mail.com • LinkedIn Profile

CHIEF TALENT OFFICER — SENIOR HUMAN RESOURCES EXECUTIVE
Building Organizational Value by Strengthening People, Process & Performance

- **HR Leader:** Transformed and currently lead Talent and HR organization for a $200M business with a high proportion of in-demand strategic, analytical, and technical talent.

- **Business Executive:** Led $11M P&L organization, nearly doubling size in 3 years while sharpening focus on talent management.

- **Continuous Improvement Driver:** Spearheaded organization-wide initiatives and cross-functional teams to elevate performance and deliver measurable value to clients and company.

PROFESSIONAL EXPERIENCE

Sun Media | One of world's largest communications groups

Portland, OR • 2012–Present

▶ EVP/CHIEF TALENT OFFICER, 2016–Present
Member of 10-person executive team driving goals and development of Sun Media. Scope includes Talent Management, Talent Acquisition, HR Systems & Operations, Benefits (Shared Service), Compensation; 20 HR professionals.

<u>Chosen to lead HR for newly combined Sun Media</u>—with challenge to build a Talent Management organization that supports new CEO's vision and organizational growth goals. Drove a strategic transformation of HR culture and function from transaction-oriented to people- and talent-focused.

- **Rebuilt Talent and HR organization,** expanding from 7 to 20 professionals to support new initiatives and 23% annual growth rate of the business.

- **Revamped onboarding, performance management, and learning and development**—simplifying processes and making talent development the focal point. Quickly delivered measurable gains:
  - 5-fold increase in training hours—including new soft-skills program and new eLearning options
  - 21% growth in internship program and pipeline
  - 32% jump in employee engagement and satisfaction
  - 24% reduction in turnover of high-performing/high-potential employees

- **Brought talent acquisition in-house and built a nimble, efficient capability.**
  - Slashed outside recruiting fees by $600K annually.
  - Reduced time-to-hire by 17 days.
  - Piloted social-media recruitment and outreach to 8 key universities.

- **Realigned organizational model** to better reflect emerging needs and industry standards. Redefined roles and hierarchy, defined competency expectations, standardized and updated all job descriptions, and conducted compensation analysis.

- **Upgraded HR processes, systems, and data management** to improve efficiency, reduce error-prone manual operations, and create a scalable platform. Implemented new applicant-tracking and onboarding tools. Began rolling out new payroll, benefit, and talent management modules (to be completed by Q3 2020).

▶ SVP MEDIA INTEGRATION, 2016
Change management initiative, leading operational integration across US and Canada.

<u>Led integration of all offline and online media operations,</u> melding different cultures, capabilities, and organizational systems under the new nameplate of Sun Media.

- **Spearheaded comprehensive review of current state**—revealing siloed responsibilities, duplication of efforts, and cultural divisions.

- **Developed new operating model** and responsibility matrix for the organization across each capability and level. Mapped staffing requirements and allocations.

- **Pioneered new education and cross-training curriculum** and rolled out company's new strategic approach to all staff.

Strategy: Focus on recruitment, talent management, and other HR-related accomplishments for this executive who had transitioned from business leadership to talent and human resources management and wants to continue on that trajectory.

CHRIS CASTIGLIONE   503-555-6712 • chriscastiglione@mail.com

▶ **SVP/MANAGING DIRECTOR, Sun Digital,** 2012–2016
$11M P&L and direct oversight of agency operations in Portland plus satellites in Los Angeles and Chicago—85+ total staff.

Promoted to the Sun Digital executive leadership team, with management responsibility for $150M in billings.

- **Drove $4.5M in new business** and expanded headcount 44%.
- **Focused on talent recruitment and development** as the critical factors in continued growth and creative excellence.
  - Launched employee recognition program to celebrate extraordinary customer service, effort, and innovation.
  - Improved recruiting efficiency by implementing candidate and referral tracking tools.
  - Strengthened employee communications to foster transparency, engagement, and alignment with goals.
- **Led US task force to define and implement talent initiatives around recruitment, staff development, and retention.** Components included entry-level training and career pathing; talent assessments and calibration activities; and standardization of promotion criteria, reporting relationships, and competency evaluation guidelines.

Mar-Tech, Inc. | Global marketing and technology agency   Portland, OR • 2005–2012

▶ **VP MARKETING,** 2007–2012 • **ASSOCIATE DIRECTOR,** 2005–2007
$7M P&L, 8 direct reports, teams of 50+ cross-functional specialists.

Led account management and client relationships with Microsoft, Amazon, and other marquee clients.

- **Planned and managed cross-channel marketing programs** that delivered exceptional results for clients.
- **Developed and delivered training on CRM best practices** at 11 Time Warner Cable divisions in 5 states. Managed employee communication regarding new CRM interface.

Deloitte | Big 4 professional services firm   Boston • 1997–2005

▶ **MANAGER/CHIEF OF STAFF, Strategic Risk Services,** 2003–2005 • **ASSOCIATE/SENIOR ASSOCIATE,** 1997–2003
Marketing communications, recruiting, role definition, workforce planning, staffing management, budgets; 40+ staff.

One of 4 chosen to launch and lead new practice focused on organizational development and design, process management, and change management in the context of operational risk management and internal controls.

- **Grew the organization** from startup to 43 individuals.
- **Exceeded annual revenue targets by 50%** each year.

EDUCATION

MBA, Marketing Concentration | University of Oregon, Lundquist College of Business, Portland, OR—Summa Cum Laude   2002
BA, Economics | Reed College, Portland, OR—Honors Program   1997

Daniel da Silva

London, United Kingdom
daniel.dasilva@gmail.com • +44 20 555 5555 • LinkedIn.com/in/danieldasilva

SENIOR HUMAN RESOURCES EXECUTIVE / STRATEGIC BUSINESS PARTNER

Delivering transformational HR leadership to drive success of international growth initiatives in FMCG and Pharma / Consumer Health industries

Proactive and business-minded HR leader with a dynamic 15-year career steering organisations through complex transitions and building an empowered and talented workforce in cross-cultural environments within highly competitive consumer products and pharmaceutical / healthcare industries.

Proven expertise in defining organisational structure and human capital requirements to align HR functions with business goals, providing the catalyst to optimise performance, enhance productivity, and drive revenue and profit growth. Articulate communicator and highly skilled negotiator. Fluent in English and Portuguese (native); intermediate Spanish.

CORE COMPETENCIES

• Talent Management	• Strategic Planning / Business Analysis	• Business Partnering
• Succession Planning	• Executive Committee Membership	• Organisation Design
• Staffing & Recruitment	• Due Diligence / Divestiture	• Corporate Restructuring
• Compensation & Benefits	• Human Capital Requirements Planning	• HR Risk Assessment

PROFESSIONAL EXPERIENCE & ACCOMPLISHMENTS

PHARM-GLOBAL CONSUMER HEALTH, London, UK   2010–Present
(Privately held subsidiary of Pharm-Global Worldwide, Pharm-Global Consumer Health is a world leader in the research, development, manufacture, and marketing of pharmaceutical self-medication brands.)

> **Head of Organisational Performance** (London; 2017–Present)
> **Head of Human Resources, Europe** (London; 2014–2017) Directed team of 8–10.
> **Head of HR Processes, Europe** (Lisbon; 2010–2014) Directed team of 6–9.

Rapidly promoted through a series of increasingly strategic HR business partner roles to drive regional and global change initiatives during period of complex organisational restructuring. Consistently successful in HR director-level and specialist roles with significant contributions in the areas of strategic workforce planning, headcount reduction, talent management, business partnering, and organisational development.

Key player in meeting bottom-line profit objectives in challenged economic market. As Member of Senior Executive Team for Pharm-Global Consumer Health worldwide, collaborate with senior leadership in designing HR solutions to support business objectives in the areas of brand planning, marketing, finance, strategic planning, and business plan development.

Notable Achievements:

> ➢ **Business Partnering & Organisational Design:** Developed and executed HR headcount reduction strategy for operating plan that was instrumental in 12-month turnaround of Pharm-Global Consumer Heathcare business in the UK, following 8-year decline. Reduced headcount 10% YOY, resulting in 15% profit improvement in a shrinking market.

> ➢ **HR Infrastructure Development / Staffing & Recruitment:** Transformed HR infrastructure at London headquarters office of 900 with 11 entities. Redesigned staffing and recruitment function, re-negotiated agency fees, and shifted recruitment focus to internal and web-based systems. Reduced time-to-hire by 10% and cut agency expenses 50%, achieving overall cost savings of 80%.

> ➢ **Talent Management:** Implemented succession planning and internal recruitment measures for Lisbon organisation of 120 to secure top talent pipeline during the largest reorganisation in company history. Achieved target performance metrics of 70 / 30 within 18 months.

> ➢ **Workforce Design and Realignment:** Conducted due diligence and workforce realignment following business unit divestiture. Saved £1 million, met headcount objectives, and ensured attainment of P&L target.

Strategy: Stack multiple positions with the same company into a single section to avoid repeating similar job descriptions and instead focus on notable achievements.

Daniel da Silva – **Page Two**
daniel.dasilva@gmail.com • +44 20 555 5555 • LinkedIn.com/in/danieldasilva

PHARM-GLOBAL CONSUMER HEALTH, *continued*

➢ **Employee Relations / Vendor Management:** Transformed inefficient, audit-critical HR function in London into reliable, structured, and risk-averse organisation within 12 months. Delivered cost improvement of £1 million p.a. through cost-effective vendor management and reduction of legal cases by 70%.

➢ **Organisational Performance Assessment:** Implemented strategies and HR programs that improved communication engagement results by 6 basis points on average across all HR categories, outperforming results of previously administrated substandard Pricewaterhouse Coopers global survey.

➢ **HR / Business Integration:** Spearheaded cross-functional HR / business planning process throughout Euro Zone market, using functional dialogue methodology to ensure HR / business alignment for workforce planning, competency development, and budget planning. Introduced process to all Pharm-Global European HR leaders.

➢ **Retention and Risk Assessment:** Designed and implemented workforce planning and retention strategy using risk-value matrix. Improved employee retention through 25% reduction of voluntary turnover at corporate HQ.

IBERIAN CONSUMER PRODUCTS (ICP), Global Corporate Headquarters, Lisbon, Portugal   2006–2010
(Global consumer products company and world leader in the household health and personal care sectors)

Compensation & Benefits Director – Top 400 Executives (2008–2010)
Special Project Manager (2008)
Human Resources Manager, Western Europe (2006–2008)

Excelled in strategic HR leadership roles and was selected for special project with global scope.

Notable Achievements:

➢ **Compensation & Benefits / Business Partnering:** Developed variable bonus plan for top 400 executives, laying groundwork for 200% increase in new product development project pipeline that delivered significant incremental net revenue and gross margin improvement.

➢ **Compensation & Benefits / Vendor Management:** Replaced global tax provider and managed transition in 6 months, delivering immediate 3.6mGBP impact, 10% cost savings, and major improvement in service delivery.

FRANCISCA PRODUCTS, Lisbon, Portugal   2000–2006
(Manufacturer of adhesive products)

Human Resources Manager

➢ Generalist role with an operational focus. Managed staffing and recruitment, employee relations (commercial, supply, labour), and HR administration / payroll (PAISY).

EDUCATION & PROFESSIONAL DEVELOPMENT

University of Coimbra, Portugal

➢ Baccalaureate 2000; Post-Graduate Specialisation in Organisational Development, 2002

Numerous corporate-sponsored training and leadership development programs in management development, coaching and mentoring, change management, 360° feedback, global project management, and negotiations.

RESUME 71: by Emily Wong, ACRW, CPRW • www.wordsofdistinction.net

BEATRICE RANDAZZO, SPHR

Minneapolis, MN

555.555.5555 | beatrice.randazzo@gmail.com

www.linkedin.com/in/beatrice.randazzo

STRATEGIC BUSINESS PARTNER & HUMAN RESOURCES LEADER

TRUSTED ADVISOR to senior management and human-centered **CHANGE AGENT** who develops organizational initiatives that accelerate achievement of business goals with an eye on the bottom line. Expertise includes:

Compensation Planning	Leadership Development	Employee Relations
Succession Planning	Employment Law & Compliance	Function Reorganization
Reduction in Force	Strategic Workforce Planning	Performance Management
Pipeline Management	Executive Coaching	Change Management

Career Highlights

▶ Eliminated **$12M** in labor costs while leading a **$45B** sales organization through a post-merger restructure.

▶ Slashed executive search agency fees by **>$500K** in one year by building a talent pipeline for key positions.

▶ Saved **$460K** in hiring costs by streamlining new graduate relocation and onboarding process.

▶ Reduced expenses by **$240K** in one year by replacing vendor and negotiating new agency commission rate.

PROFESSIONAL EXPERIENCE

FINNEY DRUG COMPANY ▪ Minneapolis, MN   2012–Present

DIRECTOR | HR BUSINESS PARTNER ▪ 2015–Present

Develop strategic partnerships with operational leaders through coaching and counseling that lead to career progression, professional development, and individualized performance management.

▪ Eliminated $12M in labor costs through strategic RIF while co-leading $45B 10K-employee sales organization through post-merger restructure.

▪ Partnered with cross-functional business leaders to design and launch first rotational program with the end goal of developing agile talent that could easily pivot between roles.

▪ Conducted compensation equity analysis on 700 exempt positions to identify internal pay inequities. Reduced attrition 50% by re-negotiating all salary bands.

▪ Partnered with regional sales VPs to identify performance strengths and weaknesses of 26 senior directors and designed—in collaboration with senior directors—individual development plans.

HR CONSULTANT ▪ 2015
SENIOR HR GENERALIST ▪ 2014–2015
HR GENERALIST ▪ 2012–2014

Delivered employee relations, succession/workforce planning, performance management, and compensation planning services for 600+ sales and account managers.

▪ Developed compensation plan that was later rolled out as standard practice across the organization.

▪ Coached senior management on developing and administering individual development plans.

▪ Conducted organizational reviews to aid management in identifying training deficits. Designed new training program that led to conflict resolution and improved operational efficiencies.

▪ Realigned/restructured sales and account management team post Medco merger to support a reduced budget and new business strategies.

Strategy: Convey this HR professional's "superpower," her ability to seek out and eliminate unnecessary costs—a skill that was recognized and rewarded throughout her career.

Beatrice Randazzo ▪ 555.555.5555 ▪ beatrice.randazzo@gmail.com ▪ Page 2

ST. LUKE'S CHILDREN'S HOSPITAL ▪ Minneapolis, MN   2010–2012
TALENT ACQUISITION CONSULTANT

Partnered with senior management of assigned business groups and provided career mapping, coaching, and talent succession planning for 800+ clinical and non-clinical employees.

- Introduced and implemented first summer intern program to source talent pipeline.
- Developed and executed human capital strategies that supported business objectives.
- Led efforts to promote employee engagement through the Hospital Leadership Council, acting as co-facilitator for monthly meetings that focused on organizational change management.

LARAMIE DRUG ▪ West Orange, NJ   2009–2010
CONTRACT RECRUITER

Partnered with R&D management to lead their strategic staffing and workforce planning efforts supporting 1K+ employees globally. Advised directors, managers, and staff on policies, procedures, and employment law.

- Partnered with client groups to identify and address global business and human capital issues.
- Forged partnerships with universities to source talent and established pipelines by region to cut expenses. Streamlined new graduate relocation and hiring program, saving the company $460K in costs.
- Conducted job evaluations and market rate comparisons to formulate accurate job descriptions.

KAISER PHARMACEUTICAL COMPANY ▪ Fort Lee, NJ   2007–2009
SENIOR SOURCING SPECIALIST

Recruited to build R&D talent pipeline for specialty pharmaceutical company. Successfully sourced active and passive candidates for hard-to-fill director-and-above positions in pharmaceutical, clinical, sales, and marketing.

- Championed AIRS integration to ensure Kaiser was OFCCP compliant and created best practices for the staffing department to ensure ongoing compliance.
- Slashed executive search agency fees by >$500K in one year by building internal talent pipeline for key positions through training and development programs.
- Earned the *Driving Change Award* for designing and implementing grassroots new-hire referral program.

CALVIN MANUFACTURING ▪ Fort Lee, NJ   2006–2007
RECRUITER

Managed full-cycle recruitment process while partnering with hiring managers to develop new strategies for recruiting top talent for hard-to-fill engineering positions.

- Performed compensation reviews for new graduates and built business case for revised salary grade.
- Re-negotiated vendor fees with outside agencies to ensure competitive rates. Saved $240K in first year.

MERCK & CO. ▪ Kenilworth, NJ   2002–2005
TRAINING & DEVELOPMENT COORDINATOR

Supported talent acquisition and training/development functions of global R&D organization.

- Co-designed and implemented summer intern program for up to 100 college students and managers annually to broaden their educational experience and build corporate bench strength for future talent needs.

EDUCATION & PROFESSIONAL TRAINING

B.S., Business, RUTGERS UNIVERSITY, New Brunswick, NJ—2002
SPHR | HRCI—2016

RESUME 72: by Tammeca Riley, CPRW, CRS-MCT • www.infinitepotentialresumes.com

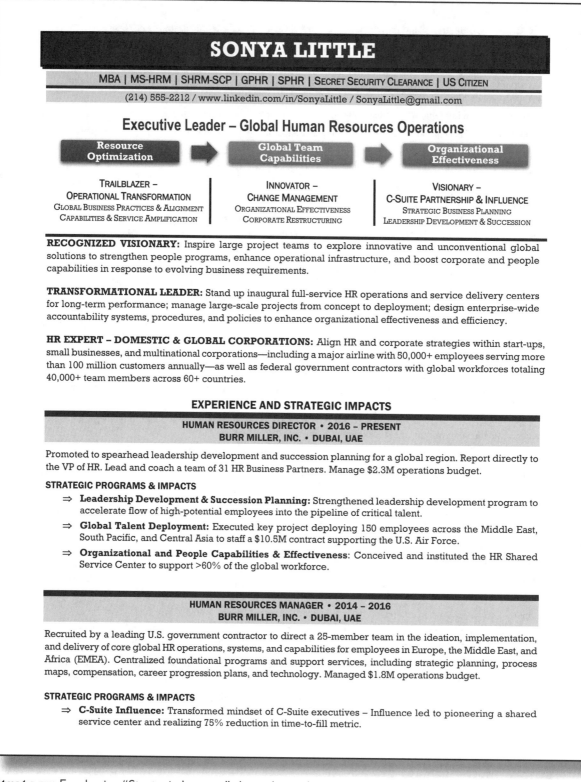

SONYA LITTLE

MBA | MS-HRM | SHRM-SCP | GPHR | SPHR | SECRET SECURITY CLEARANCE | US CITIZEN

(214) 555-2212 / www.linkedin.com/in/SonyaLittle / SonyaLittle@gmail.com

Executive Leader – Global Human Resources Operations

Resource Optimization	Global Team Capabilities	Organizational Effectiveness
TRAILBLAZER – OPERATIONAL TRANSFORMATION	INNOVATOR – CHANGE MANAGEMENT	VISIONARY – C-SUITE PARTNERSHIP & INFLUENCE
GLOBAL BUSINESS PRACTICES & ALIGNMENT CAPABILITIES & SERVICE AMPLIFICATION	ORGANIZATIONAL EFFECTIVENESS CORPORATE RESTRUCTURING	STRATEGIC BUSINESS PLANNING LEADERSHIP DEVELOPMENT & SUCCESSION

RECOGNIZED VISIONARY: Inspire large project teams to explore innovative and unconventional global solutions to strengthen people programs, enhance operational infrastructure, and boost corporate and people capabilities in response to evolving business requirements.

TRANSFORMATIONAL LEADER: Stand up inaugural full-service HR operations and service delivery centers for long-term performance; manage large-scale projects from concept to deployment; design enterprise-wide accountability systems, procedures, and policies to enhance organizational effectiveness and efficiency.

HR EXPERT – DOMESTIC & GLOBAL CORPORATIONS: Align HR and corporate strategies within start-ups, small businesses, and multinational corporations—including a major airline with 50,000+ employees serving more than 100 million customers annually—as well as federal government contractors with global workforces totaling 40,000+ team members across 60+ countries.

EXPERIENCE AND STRATEGIC IMPACTS

HUMAN RESOURCES DIRECTOR • 2016 – PRESENT
BURR MILLER, INC. • DUBAI, UAE

Promoted to spearhead leadership development and succession planning for a global region. Report directly to the VP of HR. Lead and coach a team of 31 HR Business Partners. Manage $2.3M operations budget.

STRATEGIC PROGRAMS & IMPACTS

⇒ **Leadership Development & Succession Planning:** Strengthened leadership development program to accelerate flow of high-potential employees into the pipeline of critical talent.

⇒ **Global Talent Deployment:** Executed key project deploying 150 employees across the Middle East, South Pacific, and Central Asia to staff a $10.5M contract supporting the U.S. Air Force.

⇒ **Organizational and People Capabilities & Effectiveness**: Conceived and instituted the HR Shared Service Center to support >60% of the global workforce.

HUMAN RESOURCES MANAGER • 2014 – 2016
BURR MILLER, INC. • DUBAI, UAE

Recruited by a leading U.S. government contractor to direct a 25-member team in the ideation, implementation, and delivery of core global HR operations, systems, and capabilities for employees in Europe, the Middle East, and Africa (EMEA). Centralized foundational programs and support services, including strategic planning, process maps, compensation, career progression plans, and technology. Managed $1.8M operations budget.

STRATEGIC PROGRAMS & IMPACTS

⇒ **C-Suite Influence:** Transformed mindset of C-Suite executives – Influence led to pioneering a shared service center and realizing 75% reduction in time-to-fill metric.

Strategy: Emphasize "Strategic Impacts" throughout the resume to illustrate value to the business as well as diversity of experience. Include an "Educational Sabbatical" listing to explain a 2-year gap in employment.

(214) 555-2212 / **SONYA LITTLE** / SonyaLittle@gmail.com

⇒ **Organizational and People Capabilities & Effectiveness:** Installed a call-center operation and recruited 7 team members to ramp up recruitment of foreign nationals – 60% of company's global workforce.

⇒ **Global Talent Acquisition Strategy:** Strategized and directed rapid recruitment and mobilization of foreign nationals. Filled 40% of critical vacancies within 90 days and saved $500K in expenses over 3 months by executing an integrated and optimized workforce planning strategy.

⇒ **People Influence:** Inspired team to champion > 50% of the international recruitment and staffing efforts.

EDUCATIONAL SABBATICAL • 2012 – 2014
FULL-TIME MBA / MS STUDENT

Attained dual graduate degrees while volunteering as the Transition Support Counselor for the Dallas HR Management Association – Job Link, and Director of Communication for University of Texas SHRM Chapter.

SR. HUMAN RESOURCES BUSINESS PARTNER • 2005 – 2012
KBR, INC. • DUBAI, UAE

Hired by a global technology, engineering, procurement, and construction company to strategize and augment capabilities of 25K-employee workforce and operations in 40 countries. Orchestrated full HR operations, services, and support for 60+ managers and executives throughout the Middle East and Asia. Supervised 32 global team members across 19 countries, as interim HR Manager.

STRATEGIC PROGRAMS & IMPACTS

⇒ **Project Management:** Directed project team in designing and executing project focused on functional and efficient document retention practices that saved the federal government $2.5M.

⇒ **Organizational Efficiency:** Increased ROI between 15% and 20%, gaining 30% over expected corporate objectives and outcomes. Surpassed target compliance audit rate, achieving 97% and 43 out of 50 error-free system implementations.

PRIOR POSITIONS
DELTA AIR LINES | SANFORD SERVICES, INC. | MAX SYSTEMS

Progressed through HR roles—including Staffing Associate, Talent Executive, Learning and Development Leader, and HR Director—with a major U.S. airline, a regional services firm, and a technology startup.

EDUCATION | PROFESSIONAL CREDENTIALS & MEMBERSHIPS | QUALIFICATIONS

University of Texas
MBA in Global Business
M.S. in Human Resource Management
B.S. in Human Resources

SHRM-SCP CERTIFICATION • Society for Human Resource Management (SHRM)

SPHR and GPHR CERTIFICATIONS • Human Resources Certification Institute (HRCI)

Society for Human Resource Management (SHRM)

⇒ **Project Management / Accounting:** RationalPlan, MS Project, and Costpoint

⇒ **Business Intelligence Tools:** Crystal Reports, Oblix, SQL Programming (Build Queries), and Oracle

⇒ **Applicant Tracking Systems (ATS) & HRIS:** iCIMS, Taleo, Kenxa, SAP, and Workday

⇒ **Productivity Tools:** Microsoft (Word, Excel, Access, Visio, Publisher, and SharePoint

⇒ Global Employment Law

PAGE 2

RESUME 73: *by Stephanie Clark, MRW, MCRS • www.newleafresumes.ca*

BRENDAN ROBERTS

B.A. | C.P.H.R. | C.H.R.L.

Leverage HR as strategic business partner

EXECUTIVE HUMAN RESOURCE LEADERSHIP

218.511.1111 | roberts@xmission.com
Linkedin.com/in/brendanrobertsHR

HR INFRASTRUCTURE & PLANNING | PROGRAM CREATION | BUSINESS PARTNERSHIP | CHANGE MANAGEMENT

Leadership Profile: **17+ years of managing/directing HR programs that facilitate business growth**

Multi-faceted HR professional, strategic partner, and collaborative executive leadership team member. Leverage blend of business savvy, influential communications, and visionary leadership to drive HR, organizational, and bottom-line financial performance.

Support organizational growth through strategic and scalable functions; champion organization's competitive status by attracting and retaining talented staff; identify opportunities and drive continuous improvement.

 Overall, as an HR strategist, my goal is to keep an organization competitive for future viability. From talent acquisition, performance, and retention to policy compliance, labor relations, and health and safety – every facet must work together to further orizational and business goals."

Core Skills & Competencies

Team Leadership | Strategic Planning | Training & Development | Multi-site Operations | Project Management

Communications | Merger & Acquisition | Financial Management | Succession Planning | Labor Management

Payroll / Benefits / Health and Safety | Recruitment/ Performance/ Retention | Policy/Process/Systems Design

PROFESSIONAL EXPERIENCE

VENUE HOLDINGS LTD. | Salt Lake City, Utah | 2004—present
Award-winning real estate company with assets >$3B in commercial, industrial, and residential properties.

Vice President, Human Resources   2015–present
Promoted to new role to support aggressive growth and acquisition; in addition to HR, given accountability for payroll, office services, and training and development. Also accountable for health and safety across organization.

- **Major Project:** Member, senior leadership planning team, determining staffing, scaling, budget, and resourcing to facilitate 6-month commercial properties acquisition and facility management project.

- **Launch of company's 1st HRIS:** Supported aggressive growth, issuing RFPs and assessing scalable platform; earned accolades from CFO for "best roll-out, hands down of project of this magnitude."

- **Continuous Improvement:** Streamlined payroll to align with core values of integrity and service; introduced performance reviews to align strategic corporate objectives to each employee.

- **Competitive Retention Strategy:** Addressed turnover of up to 20% in a division through a variety of strategies: communication, engagement survey, individual development plans, and others.

Strategy: Paint a formidable picture of results, accomplishments, and versatility by emphasizing the business impacts this HR executive has delivered throughout his career. Substantiate his value with a third-party testimonial in the summary.

Brendan Roberts |281.511.1111 | broberts@xmission.com

VENUE HOLDINGS LTD.

Director, Human Resources   2010–2015

Reported to President and COO; established company's first Human Resources division; provided hands on management and strategic leadership for 200+ employees across 2 provinces during aggressive growth cycle.

- **Established HR functions**: Aligned policies with culture and needs of organization; introduced comprehensive policy review and development to close gap on compliance issues; leveraged compensation as competitive market strategy; negotiated 20%+ savings on benefits package and better returns on executive and staff pensions; ensured customer service and other training for excellence.

- **Focus on people**: Developed adaptable in-house talent pool by creating process for identifying high performers and educating managers on value of cross-training and skill development. Significantly reduced turnover. Standardized transparent recruitment process using best practices.

- **Focus on future**: Introduced succession plans and programs for knowledge transfer, implementing and operationalizing Senior Management succession plan.

REAL ESTATE INTERNATIONAL | Vancouver, BC, Canada   2003–2010

Leading global real estate services organization, consistently ranked among The Global Outsourcing 100 top businesses and the World's Best Outsourcing Advisors.

Manager, Human Resources, Corporate Canada

Reported to VP, Operations, and Chief Human Resource Officer, Global. Accountable for Canadian HR strategies and design and implementation of HR programs and policies. Contributed to Executive Committee meetings; ran annual HR workshops at 3-day management training event; participated in IT leadership initiative. Managed $1.5M budget and 6 HR professionals across Canada.

- Built Canadian HR platform to provide consistent and standardized HR fundamentals to 1100 employees in 12 offices across Canada, soliciting input and conducting surveys to create benchmarks.

- Slashed staff turnover by 50% through compensation and strengths-based career path development.

- Led HR's due diligence through major merger and acquisition and participated in several others.

TRANSOLUTION – OLYMPIC TRANSPORTATION | Salt Lake City, Utah   2001–2003

Manager, Human Resources for Olympic Transportation

Joined project after its launch. Led or contributed to several strategic teams, worked within several collective agreements, met tight timeline, and facilitated a 30% increase in ridership with minimal staff increase.

- **Successful results measured by**: Achieved unions' cooperation with Letters of Understanding, without penalty; received positive press coverage—without exception; and received letters of commendation from the State representative, as well as the Mayor.

EDUCATION

CPHR and CPHR BC & Yukon (2005)   Diploma, HR Management | BCIT, Business Administration
Bachelor of Arts | Simon Fraser University   Management Training | Leadership Assessment | TELUS

RESUME 74: by Louise Garver, ACRW, CERM, CJSS, CPRW, CPBS, CCMC • www.careerdirectionsllc.com

SUSAN B. ALMANN

914-271-5567 | sbalm345@gmail.com | LinkedIn Profile

STRATEGIC HUMAN RESOURCES EXECUTIVE

Multinational Organizations | Medical Equipment and Manufacturing Industries

Proactive business partner to senior management, guiding the development of performance-driven, customer-driven, and market-driven organizations. Proven effectiveness in providing vision and counsel to steer organizations through periods of accelerated growth and economic downturn.

Expertise in all generalist HR functions and initiatives:

Recruitment & Employment Management … Leadership Training & Development … Benefits & Compensation … Reorganization & Culture Change … Merger & Acquisition Integration … Union & Non-Union Employee Relations … Succession Planning … Expatriate Programs … Long-Range Business Planning … HR Policies & Procedures

PROFESSIONAL EXPERIENCE

MARCON MANUFACTURING COMPANY, Peekskill, NY
Vice President, Human Resources (2014–Present)

Challenge: Recruited to create HR infrastructure to support business growth at a $30 million global manufacturing company with underachieving sales, exceedingly high turnover, and lack of cohesive management processes among business entities in U.S. and Asia.

Action: Partnered with President and Board of Directors to reorganize company, reduce overhead expenses, rebuild sales, and institute solid management infrastructure. Established HR with staff of 5.

Results:
♦ Renegotiated cost-effective benefit programs that saved $1.5 million annually.
♦ Reorganized operations and facilitated seamless integration within parent company of 150 employees from two recent acquisitions.
♦ Reduced sales-force turnover to nearly nonexistent and upgraded quality of candidates hired by implementing interview-skills training and management-development programs. Results led to measurable improvements in sales performance.
♦ Recruited all management personnel, developed HR policies, and fostered team culture at new Malaysian plant with 125 employees.
♦ Initiated business reorganization plan, resulting in consolidation of New York and Virginia operations for $6.5 million in cost reductions.

BINGHAMTON COMPANY, New York, NY
Director, Human Resources & Administration (2011–2014)

Challenge: Lead HR and Administration functions and staff that supported 1,600 employees at $500 million medical equipment manufacturer. Contribute to company's turnaround efforts, business unit consolidations, and transition to focus on consumer products.

Action: Established cross-functional teams from each site and provided training in team building to coordinate product development efforts, implement new manufacturing processes, and speed products to market. Identified cost-reduction opportunities; played a key role in reorganization initiatives that included closing union plant in Texas and building new plant in Georgia.

Strategy: Use a Challenge-Action-Results format to clearly illustrate experience and achievements in key areas that impact an organization's business performance well beyond HR.

SUSAN B. ALMANN • PAGE 2

Director, Human Resources & Administration, continued...

Results:
- Instituted cross-functional team culture that provided foundation for successful new product launches and recapture of company's leading edge despite intense market competition.
- Spearheaded flawless integration of two operations into single, cohesive European business unit, resulting in profitable turnaround.
- Restructured and positioned HR organization in the German business unit as customer-focused partner to support European sales and marketing units.
- Initiated major benefit cost reductions of $3 million in first year and $1 million annually while gaining employee acceptance through concerted education and communications.

ARCADIA CORPORATION, New York, NY
Director, Human Resources (2007–2011)
Assistant Director of Human Resources (2005–2007)

Challenge: HR support to corporate office and field units of an $800 million organization with 150 global operations employing 4,500 people.

Action: Promoted to lead staff of 10 in all HR and labor relations activities. Established separate international recruitment function and designed staffing plan to accommodate rapid business growth. Negotiated cost-effective benefits contracts for union and non-union employees.

Results:
- Oversaw successful UAW, Teamsters, and labor contract negotiations.
- Established and staffed HR function for multimillion-dollar contract with U.S. government.
- Introduced incentive plans for field unit managers and an expatriate program that attracted both internal and external candidates for international assignments in the Middle East.
- Resolved HR issues associated with two business acquisitions while accomplishing a smooth transition and retention of all key personnel.
- Restructured HR function with no service disruption to the business while saving $1.5 million annually.

EDUCATION

M.B.A., Cornell University, New York, NY
B.A., Business Administration, Amherst College, Amherst, MA

AFFILIATIONS

Society for Human Resource Management
Human Resource Council of Albany

RESUME 75: by Melissa Orpen-Tuz, CPRW • www.linkedin.com/in/melissaorpentuz

Rhonda Gray

401-123-4567 ▪ rhonda@gmail.com ▪ www.linkedin.com/in/rhonda/

SENIOR HUMAN RESOURCES EXECUTIVE

Leading Change & People-Centric Strategies for High-Growth Organizations
Best-in-Class Human Capital Initiatives — Business-Aligned Solutions — Service Delivery Optimization

Senior business partner who shapes and oversees delivery of human capital solutions that support fast-moving enterprises in attracting, retaining, and rewarding top talent. Organizational strategist able to introduce processes, tools, and systems that optimize the employee experience. Top performer who consistently exceeds customer and partner expectations.

Partnership Strategy ▪ Talent Development & Management ▪ Employee Relations ▪ Legal Compliance
Workforce Planning ▪ Performance Management ▪ New Business Ventures ▪ Multi-Location Leadership

ACHIEVEMENT SNAPSHOT

Strategic Business Leadership: Played crucial role in establishing and integrating new partnerships, operating models, and business lines for forward-thinking enterprise that tripled in size in 4 years (from 12 locations in 2015 to 36 in 2019).

Organizational Change Management: Steered process of articulating company values, garnering enterprise-wide buy-in for strategic solutions aligned with business needs and growth goals.

Employee Lifecycle Excellence: Built flexible, robust HR solutions and programs to create a thriving culture and become an employer-of-choice for a talented, diverse workforce.

LEADERSHIP & EXPERIENCE HIGHLIGHTS

CRONDEN | Warwick, RI   2008 – Present
Privately owned family of companies with a diversified national presence through innovative public-private partnerships with the military, higher education, and the public sector. 900 employees across 35 offices and partnering facilities.

CHIEF HUMAN RESOURCES OFFICER (2016 – Present)

Ascended to executive leadership role in a high-growth, agile organization. Lead 12-member corporate team spanning talent strategy, organizational design, employee and labor relations, benefits and compensation, payroll, and HRIS.

- **Change Management:** Guided business leaders through organizational transitions to reinforce company culture and secure executive endorsement for value-differentiating HR programs.

- **Organization Design:** Strategized with senior leaders to create and introduce an organizational structure that maximizes flexibility, eliminates roadblocks, and encourages inclusivity.

- **Employee Engagement & Retention:** Oversaw design and implementation of tailored, flexible onboarding, performance management, recognition, and benefits and compensation programs.

- **Strategic Business Advising:** Championed unique employee experience to prospective partners and charted path forward post-award to drive seamless service delivery.

- **Diversity & Inclusion:** Designed inaugural organization-wide diversity and inclusion strategy to optimize innovation and deepen employee engagement for a multi-location, multi-business-line workforce.

- **Talent Acquisition:** Reengineered recruiting and hiring model to empower functional leaders to own the process and partner with HR on instituting best practices that enhance the client experience.

- **New Business Development:** Joined company owner and CFO on investment committee to offer recommendations on new business pursuits, ensuring alignment with corporate strategy and growth goals.

- **Labor Relations:** Negotiated union contract for company's first foray into a unionized environment to pave the way for positive employee relations throughout a $307M partnership with Indiana University.

Strategy: Lead with strengths—showing how in-tune this executive is with the business, introducing bullets with relevant keywords, and focusing on her approach to constructing people-centric programs and relationships. Omit Education section to avoid calling attention to her lack of a college degree.

Rhonda Gray

401-123-4567 ▪ rhonda@gmail.com ▪ www.linkedin.com/in/rhonda/

CRONDEN | Warwick, RI   continued

DIRECTOR | HUMAN RESOURCES BUSINESS PARTNER (2010 – 2016)

Earned 2 promotions during rapid growth phase and quickly evolving organizational landscape. Oversaw HR operations at 6 military locations and 10 campus locations. Led 5-member geographically dispersed HR team.

- **Strategic HR Leadership:** Played key role in transforming organizational perception of HR from personnel administration to fully integrated business partners and advisors.

- **Business Growth Initiatives:** Tapped to launch and integrate 2 new business lines (Cronden Stormwater and Cronden Higher Ed) and advise senior leaders on attracting and retaining talent in a start-up environment.

- **Talent Development & Management:** Infused strategic business decisions with a people-centric approach to technology investments, program design and development, and employee retention strategies.

HUMAN RESOURCES MANAGER (2008 – 2010)

Hired as 2nd on-site HR manager for newly established public-private partnership for federal government housing communities. Provided day-to-day HR leadership for Fort Jameson's 130 employees in Ohio and Fort Mandon's 60 employees in Pennsylvania. Partnered with corporate headquarters to align local efforts with enterprise goals.

- **Multi-Location HR Leadership:** Established first on-site HR presence for 2 locations.

- **Employee Experience:** Facilitated entire employee lifecycle for 190 staff including talent acquisition, benefits and compensation, talent development and retention, and employee relations and engagement.

- **Leadership Development:** Advised management on employee relations and employment law compliance.

- **Program Planning & Execution:** Partnered with corporate HR staff to develop enterprise-wide human resources initiatives and steered local customization and execution.

THE FANCY HOTEL, INC. | Aurora, CO   1994 – 2007

779-room hotel and resort with 185K square feet of meeting space and 1,700 employees. Longest-running consecutive winner of the AAA 5-Diamond and Forbes Travel Guide 5-Star Awards.

ASSISTANT DIRECTOR, HUMAN RESOURCES | DIRECTOR OF RECRUITMENT

Earned multiple promotions during tenure. Led and developed 16-member team. Oversaw employee services, talent acquisition, and risk management functions. Advised leadership on attracting and retaining top talent.

- **Employee Services & Relations:** Oversaw student and employee housing for the international recruitment program's 240-unit student and employee housing community.

- **New Business Integration:** Facilitated seamless incorporation of newly acquired hotel property to deliver unified, consistent employee experience across multiple locations.

- **Talent Acquisition Strategy:** Developed and oversaw innovative talent acquisition tactics to build an international workforce in high-volume, seasonal hiring environment.

- **Partnership Development:** Forged mutually beneficial alliances with trade and hospitality educational institutions to generate pipeline of candidates.

- **Operations Management:** Excelled in leadership development program for rising managers, ascending through management roles in housekeeping and recruiting.

COMMUNITY ENGAGEMENT & AFFILIATIONS

Volunteer ▪ Fund Cancer Walk | The Orange School | Westerly Veterans Administration Medical Center
Member, Local & National Organizations ▪ Society for Human Resources Management (SHRM)

RESUME 76: by Louise Kursmark, MRW, CPRW, JCTC, CEIP, CCM • www.louisekursmark.com

MARCO CIMINO

313-555-2211 | marco.cimino@mac.com | LinkedIn Profile

TALENT DEVELOPMENT EXECUTIVE
Future-Focused Leadership of Learning & Development Organizations
Leader Development | Employee Engagement | Organizational Development | Innovative Learning Models

Strategic Leader — Innovator and Builder — Trusted Advisor
dedicated to creating high-impact programs that meet current and emerging business needs.

Chief Learning Officer of the Year Nominee, 2020 | Key contributor in **"Best Place to Work"** recognition, 2019

PROFESSIONAL EXPERIENCE

AERO-TECH COMPANY, Detroit, MI | *$1B company, a leading provider of technology to the space industry*   2008–Present

Chief Learning Officer

Recruited to lead the Learning and Development Division of mission-driven organization that is dedicated to advancing the aims of space exploration. Manage $7M annual budget, 25 staff, 60+ vendors, and classroom and on-demand learning programs for 9,000 employees.

Aligned Learning and Development initiatives with strategic goals of the business, introduced metrics and data-driven decision-making, pioneered effective programs for all levels of employees, and delivered measurable, high-impact results.

LEADERSHIP DEVELOPMENT

- **Leadership Competency Models:** Developed the first organization-wide models that described leadership performance in concrete, behavioral terms. Launched 360-degree feedback and needs assessments to identify critical competency gaps and created 3 new programs to drive competency and performance gains among 3 levels of leaders.

  | **91%** Strong belief in value of programs |

- **Leadership Development:** Designed and delivered intensive programs to build competencies and develop leadership talent for the organization. Customized programs to meet needs of specific sub-groups.

- **Job Shadowing:** Doubled participation and reduced costs of program that pairs junior staff with senior leaders to explore potential careers.

TECHNICAL SKILLS DEVELOPMENT | EMPLOYEE ENGAGEMENT

- **Strategic Technical Training:** Designed transparent, data-driven annual process for prioritizing training requirements to meet ever-expanding needs within highly engineering/technology-driven company. Replaced 30%–40% of programs annually to keep pace with emerging needs.

- **Engineering Expertise:** Developed models, assessments, and 3 distinct development programs to continuously strengthen the organization's #1 core competency of aerospace engineering..

  | **91%** Satisfaction **96%** Learning useful to project work |

- **Program and Resource Development:** Built extensive curriculum and vast library of resources to facilitate and augment classroom and on-demand training.

- **Employee Assimilation:** Orchestrated process to inform, integrate, and inspire new hires during their first 6 months.

ORGANIZATIONAL DEVELOPMENT | STRATEGIC PLANNING | BUSINESS CONSULTING

- **Strategic Planning:** Designed the first formal strategic framework for the company. Articulated mission, vision, values, goals, and objectives and created blueprint for each year's strategic planning process.

- **Executive Alignment:** Engaging leaders at all levels, brought key management processes (R&D, budgeting, business planning, performance management, compensation) into alignment with the strategic planning process.

- **Voice of the Customer:** Designed and launched first "voice of the customer" data collection process, which became a standard measure in the company's annual operating plan.

- **Consulting:** Served as trusted advisor to senior executives and consultant on all major change initiatives. Managed in-house OD consultants working with business leaders and teams to address challenges and achieve strategic goals.

Strategy: Break up achievements from long tenure into clearly defined groups introduced with relevant keyword headings, and highlight quantified results in shaded boxes at right. Minimize details of early career in OD and quality to maintain a strong focus on talent development.

MARCO CIMINO

313-555-2211 | marco.cimino@mac.com

MIDWEST TELECOM, Detroit, MI | *$30B telecommunications company*   2003–2008

Senior Manager, Organizational Development, 2005–2008
Senior Consultant, Organizational Development, 2003–2005

Joined team of experienced OD professionals to build state-of-the-art internal consulting practice. Served as Practice Leader for process improvement, benchmarking, and mergers/acquisitions. Managed 2 direct reports, 10 indirect reports, and external vendors.

- **Highlights:**
    - ✓ Led a strategic planning process for Human Resources to establish goals, objectives, and measures of success.
    - ✓ Identified root causes of IT turnover and recommended strategies to increase retention.
    - ✓ Researched trends, success rates, common pitfalls, and best practices in M&A and created management guides for achieving full value from a deal.

LAKE SYSTEMS GROUP, Detroit, MI | *IT and systems solutions provider*   1997–2003

Director, Quality Improvement & Organization Development, 2000–2003
Director, Quality Improvement, 1999–2000
Manager, Quality Improvement, 1998–1999
Human Resource Specialist, 1997–1998

Introduced Total Quality Management (TQM) to the company and advanced to become chief architect for TQM and organizational development.

EDUCATION

MA in Organizational Behavior, WAYNE STATE UNIVERSITY | 2006
BS with Honors in Psychology, Cum Laude, UNIVERSITY OF MICHIGAN | 1997

PROFESSIONAL AFFILIATIONS

Organizational Development Network | Association for Talent Development
Society for Human Resource Management

CHAPTER 11

Hospitality and Entertainment

- Venue Manager
- Restaurant General Manager
- Club General Manager
- Hotel General Manager
- Hotel Group Executive
- Vice President, Reservations
- Hospitality Area Director
- Travel and Tourism Industry Executive
- Vice President and Head of Programming
- Chief Marketing Officer, Media Entertainment

RESUME 77: by Georgia Adamson, MRW, ACRW, CPRW, CJSS, CERM, NCOPE
• www.asuccessfulcareer.com

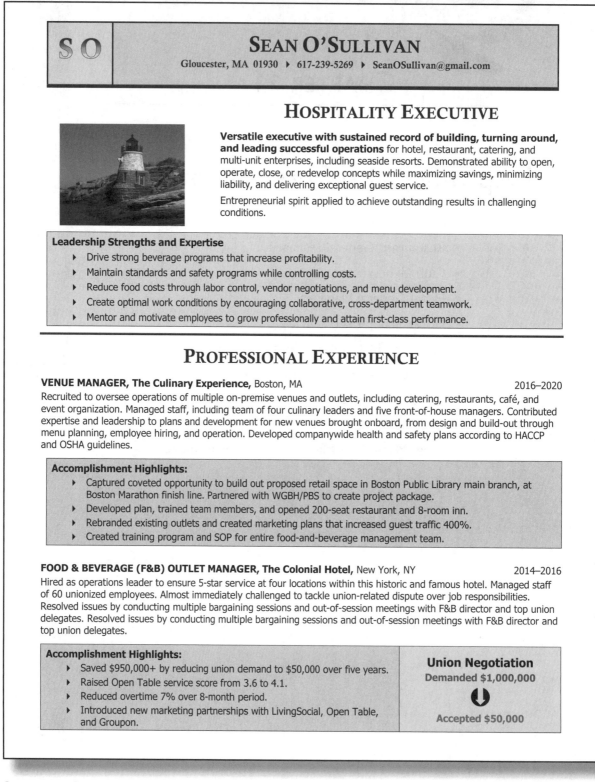

SEAN O'SULLIVAN

Gloucester, MA 01930 ▶ 617-239-5269 ▶ SeanOSullivan@gmail.com

HOSPITALITY EXECUTIVE

Versatile executive with sustained record of building, turning around, and leading successful operations for hotel, restaurant, catering, and multi-unit enterprises, including seaside resorts. Demonstrated ability to open, operate, close, or redevelop concepts while maximizing savings, minimizing liability, and delivering exceptional guest service.

Entrepreneurial spirit applied to achieve outstanding results in challenging conditions.

Leadership Strengths and Expertise
▶ Drive strong beverage programs that increase profitability.
▶ Maintain standards and safety programs while controlling costs.
▶ Reduce food costs through labor control, vendor negotiations, and menu development.
▶ Create optimal work conditions by encouraging collaborative, cross-department teamwork.
▶ Mentor and motivate employees to grow professionally and attain first-class performance.

PROFESSIONAL EXPERIENCE

VENUE MANAGER, The Culinary Experience, Boston, MA   2016–2020

Recruited to oversee operations of multiple on-premise venues and outlets, including catering, restaurants, café, and event organization. Managed staff, including team of four culinary leaders and five front-of-house managers. Contributed expertise and leadership to plans and development for new venues brought onboard, from design and build-out through menu planning, employee hiring, and operation. Developed companywide health and safety plans according to HACCP and OSHA guidelines.

Accomplishment Highlights:
▶ Captured coveted opportunity to build out proposed retail space in Boston Public Library main branch, at Boston Marathon finish line. Partnered with WGBH/PBS to create project package.
▶ Developed plan, trained team members, and opened 200-seat restaurant and 8-room inn.
▶ Rebranded existing outlets and created marketing plans that increased guest traffic 400%.
▶ Created training program and SOP for entire food-and-beverage management team.

FOOD & BEVERAGE (F&B) OUTLET MANAGER, The Colonial Hotel, New York, NY   2014–2016

Hired as operations leader to ensure 5-star service at four locations within this historic and famous hotel. Managed staff of 60 unionized employees. Almost immediately challenged to tackle union-related dispute over job responsibilities. Resolved issues by conducting multiple bargaining sessions and out-of-session meetings with F&B director and top union delegates. Resolved issues by conducting multiple bargaining sessions and out-of-session meetings with F&B director and top union delegates.

Accomplishment Highlights:
▶ Saved $950,000+ by reducing union demand to $50,000 over five years.
▶ Raised Open Table service score from 3.6 to 4.1.
▶ Reduced overtime 7% over 8-month period.
▶ Introduced new marketing partnerships with LivingSocial, Open Table, and Groupon.

Union Negotiation
Demanded $1,000,000
⬇
Accepted $50,000

Strategy: Capture immediate attention with striking visuals while keeping readers interested with strong and relevant achievements.

SO   SEAN O'SULLIVAN
Gloucester, MA 01930 ▸ 617-239-5269 ▸ SeanOSullivan@gmail.com

FOOD & BEVERAGE SUPERVISOR, High Stakes Hotel, Reno, NV   2013–2014

Drove key actions for F&B team during launch of 392-room luxury hotel. Organized logistics to obtain off-site training space for staff and to load equipment for 23-story hotel, including five food-and-beverage outlets, banquet rooms, and spa.

> **Short Deadline
> 5-Star Hotel Launch**

Achieved on-time opening despite receiving required certificate of occupancy only three days before grand opening. Hotel earned 5-star rating from Forbes and AAA.

WINE DIRECTOR/MANAGER, Rotisserie by Broadview Group, New York, NY   2012–2013

Managed daily operations for landmark Manhattan restaurant that grossed $500,000 in monthly sales. Oversaw complex wine programming with list of 5,000+ bottles. Monitored and managed weekly and monthly beverage inventories. Partnered with general manager to maintain 21% beverage cost. Developed monthly wine-training program to enhance staff knowledge.

Accomplishments included decreasing daily operating expenses 2% with 70% flow-through, creating award-winning beverage program, and initiating popular happy hour in midtown Manhattan.

EDUCATION

▸ **Bachelor of Science in Hotel Administration, Major in Hospitality Management,**
University of Massachusetts, Amherst, MA
▸ **Associate Degree in Culinary Arts,** New England Culinary Institute, Montpelier, VT

CERTIFICATIONS

▸ ServSafe®
▸ Alcohol Awareness
▸ American Heart Association Heart-Saver/First Aid

▸ TIPS® (Training for Intervention ProcedureS)
▸ Massachusetts Allergen Awareness
▸ Massachusetts Crowd Control
▸ Choke Saver

RESUME 78: *by Anita Radosevich, CPRW, IJCTC, CEIP • www.careerladdersinc.com*

James E. Hansen

Danville, California 94526• (530) 779-9004 • jamesehansen@gmail.com

HOSPITALITY / FOOD SERVICE MANAGEMENT

Guest Relations | Service Management | Budget Management

FOOD AND BEVERAGE MANAGER offering 15+ years' combined experience in general management, sales, and marketing for full-service hospitality operations. Catalyst for change, transformation, and performance improvement. Respond rapidly and appropriately to changing circumstances. Consistently increase service standards, quality, and profitability. **Core competencies include:**

❑ Menu Planning/Pricing	❑ Service Enhancements	❑ Project Management
❑ Organizational Development	❑ Revenue Growth	❑ Marketing Strategies
❑ Public Relations Skills	❑ Inventory & Cost Control	❑ Revenue Projections
❑ Vendor Sourcing/Negotiations	❑ Turnaround Strategies	❑ Cross-Functional Team Training
❑ P&L Budget Accountability	❑ Food Sanitation Practices	❑ Staff Supervision/Motivation

─────────────────**Career Highlights**─────────────────

MANAGEMENT & ADMINISTRATION

- Proven track record in turnaround management through close attention to budget administration, organizational structure, and staff supervision and development.

- Combine leadership and management skills to maximize assets in both vendor relations and corporate growth — quickly resolve problems that hinder progress or create disputes.

- Exceed employer expectations with "above and beyond" focus on guest satisfaction and retention, strict attention to quality service, and consistent applications of extra effort.

- Highly skilled in managing budgets above $5 million.

SALES & MARKETING

- As Director of Sales, worked cooperatively with sales staff and set up appropriate distribution networks for product nationwide; expanded network reach to distributors and sales staff; rapidly expanded market penetration and grew revenue.

- Delivered presentations to groups for large-scale product promotion of Nicolini Winery.

- Gained exposure globally for company's marketed product.

─────────────────**Professional Experience**─────────────────

DOMINIC'S, Redding, California   2015–Present
General Manager (2018–Present)
General Manager, Yolo County Fairgrounds, Davis, California (2015–2018)

Establish operating and financial goals for food and beverage operations of several venues. Report directly to the Vice President. Supervise and evaluate 1,500+ staff. Review and assist in the development of menus and marketing plans with appropriate department heads.

- Structured and developed 3 different budgets for increased flexibility.

- Increased profit margins 7% through operational improvements and efficiencies.

- Grew sales revenues in Ventura, Yolo, and Sacramento Counties.

…Continued…

Strategy: Focus on food service management to position this executive for his current career interests, but convey strong achievements from prior management career to open him up for multiple opportunities.

James E. Hansen   Page Two

Professional Experience, Continued

MARINA RESORT, Sacramento, California   2008–2015

Director of Food and Beverage

Charged with budget management for nightclub/restaurant. Streamlined catering, concerts, and special events. Recruited, supervised, trained, and scheduled staff. Oversaw scheduling, inventory management, and menu development. Maintained daily and annual sales records.

CATERINA'S SPAGHETTI HOUSE, Davis, California   2006–2008

Bartender / Customer Service

Acted as Event and Entertainment Coordinator during holidays, weekends, and special events.

MARINA RESORT, Sacramento, California   2005–2006

Club Manager

Oversaw event planning and coordination.

WAREHOUSE CONCERT SERIES, Davis, California   2004–2005

Special Event Coordinator

Coordinated and supervised concert beer sales for the Fish Market and Petra's Restaurants at the Warehouse Concert during popular rock-band performances.

NICOLINI WINERY, Napa, California   1998–2004

Director of Sales and R & D

Brought on board as the driving force to spearhead rapid, profitable growth. Vigorously pursued strategic partnerships to build visibility and support product. Developed progressive marketing and negotiated exclusive contracts with 176 distributorships.

—Professional Development—

Seminars: General Management, Dale Carnegie — Leadership and Presentation Training

Marketing Development Expertise: New Client Development, Territory Management, Key Account Management, New Product Introduction, and Sales Presentations

Certification: California Food Certification

Military: United States Marine Corps, Honorable Discharge
Leadership Training, Noncommissioned Officers' School

RESUME 79: by Louise Kursmark, MRW, CPRW, JCTC, CEIP, CCM • www.louisekursmark.com

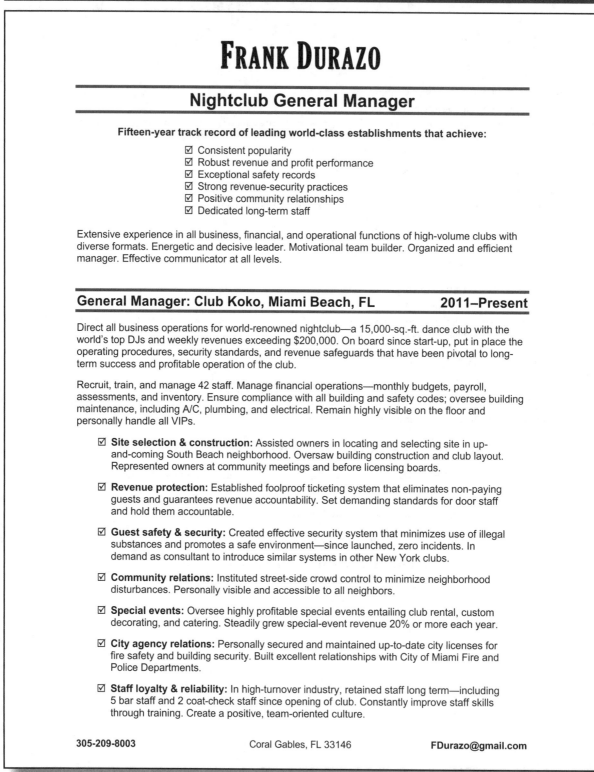

FRANK DURAZO

Nightclub General Manager

Fifteen-year track record of leading world-class establishments that achieve:

- ☑ Consistent popularity
- ☑ Robust revenue and profit performance
- ☑ Exceptional safety records
- ☑ Strong revenue-security practices
- ☑ Positive community relationships
- ☑ Dedicated long-term staff

Extensive experience in all business, financial, and operational functions of high-volume clubs with diverse formats. Energetic and decisive leader. Motivational team builder. Organized and efficient manager. Effective communicator at all levels.

General Manager: Club Koko, Miami Beach, FL   2011–Present

Direct all business operations for world-renowned nightclub—a 15,000-sq.-ft. dance club with the world's top DJs and weekly revenues exceeding $200,000. On board since start-up, put in place the operating procedures, security standards, and revenue safeguards that have been pivotal to long-term success and profitable operation of the club.

Recruit, train, and manage 42 staff. Manage financial operations—monthly budgets, payroll, assessments, and inventory. Ensure compliance with all building and safety codes; oversee building maintenance, including A/C, plumbing, and electrical. Remain highly visible on the floor and personally handle all VIPs.

- ☑ **Site selection & construction:** Assisted owners in locating and selecting site in up-and-coming South Beach neighborhood. Oversaw building construction and club layout. Represented owners at community meetings and before licensing boards.

- ☑ **Revenue protection:** Established foolproof ticketing system that eliminates non-paying guests and guarantees revenue accountability. Set demanding standards for door staff and hold them accountable.

- ☑ **Guest safety & security:** Created effective security system that minimizes use of illegal substances and promotes a safe environment—since launched, zero incidents. In demand as consultant to introduce similar systems in other New York clubs.

- ☑ **Community relations:** Instituted street-side crowd control to minimize neighborhood disturbances. Personally visible and accessible to all neighbors.

- ☑ **Special events:** Oversee highly profitable special events entailing club rental, custom decorating, and catering. Steadily grew special-event revenue 20% or more each year.

- ☑ **City agency relations:** Personally secured and maintained up-to-date city licenses for fire safety and building security. Built excellent relationships with City of Miami Fire and Police Departments.

- ☑ **Staff loyalty & reliability:** In high-turnover industry, retained staff long term—including 5 bar staff and 2 coat-check staff since opening of club. Constantly improve staff skills through training. Create a positive, team-oriented culture.

305-209-8003   Coral Gables, FL 33146   FDurazo@gmail.com

Strategy: Present a strong list of qualifications in all relevant areas in an easy-to-skim format and tight, high-impact copy.

FRANK DURAZO

Page 2

Security & Event Consultant | 2013–Present

Coordinate DJ events and record-label parties for New York's annual New Music Summit. Highlights:

- ☑ **Funk It Up**—Bring in expert team to provide security oversight for popular event drawing 6,000 fee-paying guests.

- ☑ **Def Records**—Direct operations for record-label publicity events and DJ showcases.

Manager: Parrott's Porch, Key West, FL | 2009–2011

Turned around unprofitable, inefficient, poorly managed facility and created a lucrative restaurant/ nightclub that was so successful, owners invested in South Beach club (Club Koko) and brought me on as GM from day one.

- ☑ **Operational turnaround:** Revamped entire operation for better efficiency; replaced 90% of staff; introduced new computer system for cash registers and office functions; instilled strict operational policies and procedures. Transformed lax operation to consistently profitable "tight ship."

- ☑ **Safety and security:** Implemented and maintained new security practices for bar, nightclub, and restaurant.

- ☑ **Entertainment:** Brought in popular DJs and bands that boosted attendance year round.

Manager: Casa Robles Nightclub, Boca Raton, FL | 2004–2009

Worked in all areas of nightclub operations, beginning as busboy and advancing to manager of 25,000-sq-.ft. establishment with 1,800-patron capacity.

Managed stock and ordered inventory. Handled all employee payroll accounts. Hired and trained staff at every level. Managed special events as well as day-to-day functions of the club.

Licenses / Certifications / Technical Skills

- ☑ Miami Fire Department certifications: Fire Drill Conductor, Maintenance, Public Assembly.

- ☑ Miami Health Department License for Food Service.

- ☑ Certified auto mechanic—sheet metal work, fabrication, and installation.

- ☑ Former union carpenter—scaffolding and rigging experience on high-rises.

- ☑ Licensed refrigeration and air conditioning technician—electrical and plumbing experience.

- ☑ Florida Real Estate License. Managed commercial property with zero tenant loss.

305-209-8003 | Coral Gables, FL 33146 | FDurazo@gmail.com

RESUME 80: *by Wendy Enelow, MRW, CCM, CPRW, JCTC • www.wendyenelow.com*

LILIA CHEN, CCM

980-421-9855 ... LiliaChenCCM@yahoo.com ... http://www.linkedin.com/in/LiliaChenCCM... San Francisco Metro

PRIVATE CLUB MANAGER | HOSPITALITY EXECUTIVE | GENERAL MANAGER
Deliver Strong & Sustainable Operational & Financial Gains
Build Consensus, Community & Collaborative Club Culture
Strengthen Commitment to Member Services & Quality

San Francisco-based Club Manager with 15+ years of experience managing high-profile private clubs for distinguished clientele. Impressive track record of performance by combining operational expertise with innovative programming and an unwavering commitment to the service and satisfaction of all members. Talented trainer/team builder/business leader.

Extensive network of influential professional, political, and community contacts throughout the Bay Area.

PROFESSIONAL EXPERIENCE:

THE DELOREAN CLUB – San Francisco, CA   2018 to Present
$4.5M annual revenue ... 447 member families ... 80 employees ... 8 direct reports

GENERAL MANAGER——————————————————————————————

Recruited by President and Board of Directors to revitalize The DeLorean Club and restore it to a position of prominence and relevance. Challenged to meet new debt obligation by driving strong revenue growth, providing decisive leadership, strengthening member relations, and introducing the finest in quality and service standards.

Identified and capitalized on every opportunity to increase revenues, minimize costs, and upgrade member services and outreach. Recruited talented management team, retrained existing staff, and built new Club culture recognizing excellence across all quality, performance, and member relations metrics.

➢ **Raised member dining participation and private events revenue 50%** in just 18 months.
➢ **Grew non-F&B revenue 22%** by increasing membership and dues and expanding sports and youth programs.
➢ **Delivered the highest membership levels in the Club's 75-year history.** Enabled 2 initiation fee increases in 3 years and the first dues increase in 6 years (while retaining 100% of membership). Approaching wait list.
➢ **Hired world-class team of tennis coaches**, significantly expanded youth tennis and summer camp programs, and engaged younger audiences as a key market differentiator for long-term, sustainable membership growth.

CLUBAMERICACORPORATION *(largest operator of private clubs in the world)* – **San Francisco, CA**   2007 to 2018

Returned to ClubAmerica at the request of executive management to provide operational leadership to several of its most prominent clubs. Excelled in turning around stagnant and non-performing operations, introducing member-centric quality and service standards, upgrading culture, and achieving aggressive revenue goals.

Honored with 5 prestigious corporate awards: Circle of Excellence (3); Super Star (1); Rising Star (1) during tenure.

GENERAL MANAGER & COO – **THE BAY AREA CLUB** – 2013 to 2018——————————————————
$4M annual revenue ... 1000 member families ... 55 employees ... 6 direct reports

Accepted top management position at one of SF's oldest private clubs (founded in 1902) to address key member, facility, and revenue challenges. Strategically aligned, and won support of, all-volunteer Board and Committee.

➢ **Partnered with ClubAmerica to relocate to new prime location** (from 60-year-old, below-market lease) and drove double-digit membership growth in $3.7M newly renovated clubhouse.
➢ **Restored Club to prominence** and repositioned on growth trajectory. Won the 2018 Performance Excellence Award (significant design in hospitality) and honored as "Best Business Lunch" in SF Magazine.

Strategy: As well as strong achievements, bolded to capture immediate attention, include additional details such as board affiliations and personal activities to add value and interest to this executive's resume.

LILIA CHEN, CCM

980-421-9855 ... LiliaChenCCM@yahoo.com   Page 2

GENERAL MANAGER – THE SF-OAKLAND MEMBER CLUB – 2010 to 2013
$9M annual revenue ... 2800 member families ... 130 employees ... 9 direct reports

➤ **With minimal interruption to members and services, led a logistically complex, $4M renovation** of all restaurants/F&B outlets, athletic areas, and locker rooms. Met/surpassed all project milestones.

GENERAL MANAGER – THE ELLENSPOINT CLUB – 2008 to 2010
$4M annual revenue ... 1000 member families ... 60 employees ... 8 direct reports

➤ **Drove ranking from #65 to #5 out of 80 ClubAmerica properties nationwide** (based on revenue, cost, quality metrics, and member retention). Led massive culture-change effort to meet performance targets and delivered consistently positive employee and member survey results showing highest satisfaction ratings.

F&B DIRECTOR – THE DONOVAN-FIELDS CLUB promoted to THE VARSITY CLUB (2007 to 2008)

THE ALT FOOD COMPANY – Oakland, CA   2003 to 2007

FOUNDER & GENERAL MANAGER

Identified market opportunities in downtown Oakland and launched 2 new F&B ventures (lunchtime venue targeting corporate clients; 160-seat, quick-serve restaurant concept). Managed large-scale property renovation, created menu, staffed/trained, and directed daily operations. Successfully negotiated and closed $500K SBA loan.

TRES CHIC RESTAURANT CORP – San Francisco, CA   1997 to 2003
Promoted from GENERAL MANAGER (staff of 60) to REGIONAL TRAINING MANAGER of all management and general management personnel for 13 restaurant locations. Opened 2 new, top-performing restaurants.

THE DELOREAN CLUB *(largest operator of private clubs & resorts in the US)* – San Francisco, CA   1993 to 1997
Promoted rapidly to SERVICE DIRECTOR for front-of-the-house operations at Academy Club and SF Metro Club.

EDUCATION:

BS – HOTEL & RESTAURANT MANAGEMENT – University of San Francisco – 1993
GRADUATE – Center for San Francisco's Future Leadership Forum – 2015
CERTIFIED CLUB MANAGER (CCM) – Club Managers Association of America – 2019

BOARD AFFILIATIONS:

BOARD DIRECTOR – Chinese-America Foundation – 2018 to Present
BOARD DIRECTOR – Club Manager Association of America (SF Chapter) – 2014 to Present
PRESIDENT – Chinese-American Chamber of Commerce (SF Chapter) – 2013 to 2018

NOTABLE CONTRIBUTION: Led successful transition of SF Chapter of Chinese-American Chamber of Commerce into Chinese-American Foundation (leading bilateral foundation promoting high-impact exchanges between the US and China) to expand organization's reach and resources in business, education, and culture/arts. Rallied and won the trust/support of membership and board to restructure association and lead into the future.

PERSONAL PROFILE:

Student Private Pilot License | Certified Scuba Diver | Founder – International Wine & Cheese Association
Fluent English | Native Chinese

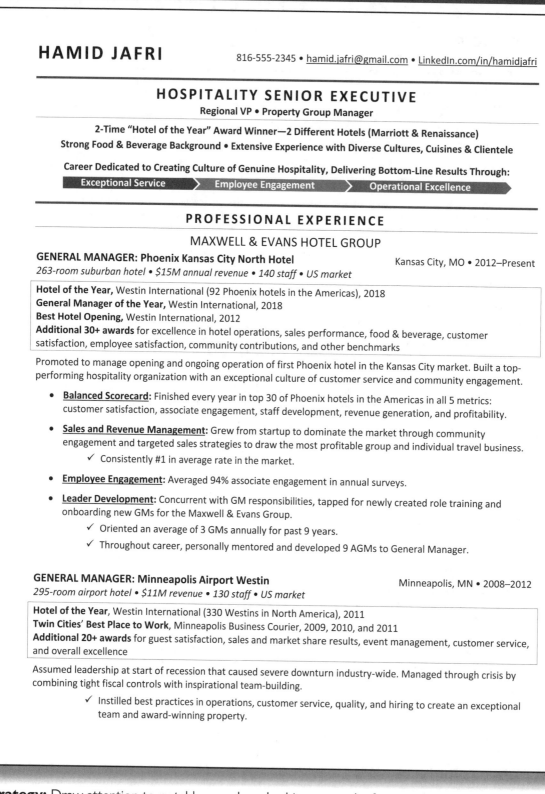

RESUME 81: by Louise Kursmark, MRW, CPRW, JCTC, CEIP, CCM • www.louisekursmark.com

HAMID JAFRI

816-555-2345 • hamid.jafri@gmail.com • LinkedIn.com/in/hamidjafri

HOSPITALITY SENIOR EXECUTIVE
Regional VP • Property Group Manager

2-Time "Hotel of the Year" Award Winner—2 Different Hotels (Marriott & Renaissance)
Strong Food & Beverage Background • Extensive Experience with Diverse Cultures, Cuisines & Clientele

Career Dedicated to Creating Culture of Genuine Hospitality, Delivering Bottom-Line Results Through:

Exceptional Service → **Employee Engagement** → **Operational Excellence**

PROFESSIONAL EXPERIENCE

MAXWELL & EVANS HOTEL GROUP

GENERAL MANAGER: Phoenix Kansas City North Hotel   Kansas City, MO • 2012–Present
263-room suburban hotel • $15M annual revenue • 140 staff • US market

> **Hotel of the Year,** Westin International (92 Phoenix hotels in the Americas), 2018
> **General Manager of the Year,** Westin International, 2018
> **Best Hotel Opening,** Westin International, 2012
> **Additional 30+ awards** for excellence in hotel operations, sales performance, food & beverage, customer satisfaction, employee satisfaction, community contributions, and other benchmarks

Promoted to manage opening and ongoing operation of first Phoenix hotel in the Kansas City market. Built a top-performing hospitality organization with an exceptional culture of customer service and community engagement.

- **Balanced Scorecard:** Finished every year in top 30 of Phoenix hotels in the Americas in all 5 metrics: customer satisfaction, associate engagement, staff development, revenue generation, and profitability.

- **Sales and Revenue Management:** Grew from startup to dominate the market through community engagement and targeted sales strategies to draw the most profitable group and individual travel business.
  - ✓ Consistently #1 in average rate in the market.

- **Employee Engagement:** Averaged 94% associate engagement in annual surveys.

- **Leader Development:** Concurrent with GM responsibilities, tapped for newly created role training and onboarding new GMs for the Maxwell & Evans Group.
  - ✓ Oriented an average of 3 GMs annually for past 9 years.
  - ✓ Throughout career, personally mentored and developed 9 AGMs to General Manager.

GENERAL MANAGER: Minneapolis Airport Westin   Minneapolis, MN • 2008–2012
295-room airport hotel • $11M revenue • 130 staff • US market

> **Hotel of the Year**, Westin International (330 Westins in North America), 2011
> **Twin Cities' Best Place to Work**, Minneapolis Business Courier, 2009, 2010, and 2011
> **Additional 20+ awards** for guest satisfaction, sales and market share results, event management, customer service, and overall excellence

Assumed leadership at start of recession that caused severe downturn industry-wide. Managed through crisis by combining tight fiscal controls with inspirational team-building.

- ✓ Instilled best practices in operations, customer service, quality, and hiring to create an exceptional team and award-winning property.

Strategy: Draw attention to notable awards and achievements by framing them within a box at the start of each position description. Avoid dense text in every section of the resume, from a crisp and eye-catching summary through a progressive 20-year career in hospitality.

HAMID JAFRI

Page 2 • 816-555-2345 • hamid.jafri@gmail.com

GENERAL MANAGER: University Inn & Conference Center   South Bend, IN • 2006–2008
139-room conference hotel • $7M annual revenue • 120 staff • US market

Maxwell & Evans Award of Excellence, 2007

In first General Manager role, focused on performance benchmarks in key result areas to drive operational excellence. Reported directly to 9-member Board of Directors for the University-owned hotel.

ASSISTANT GENERAL MANAGER: Radisson Hotel Dubuque   Dubuque, IA • 2004–2006
257-room downtown hotel • $9M annual revenue • 140 staff • US market

Radisson President's Award, 2005

HYATT INTERNATIONAL HOTELS

DIRECTOR OF FOOD & BEVERAGE: Hyatt Regency Saipan   Saipan, Micronesia • 2003–2004
325-room resort • 13 outlets • $14M annual f&b revenue • 181 staff • Japanese, Korean, Chinese, US market

DIRECTOR OF FOOD & BEVERAGE: Hyatt Regency Saujana   Kuala Lumpur, Malaysia • 2002–2003
387-room conference resort and country club • 13 outlets • $11M annual f&b revenue • 276 staff • Malaysian market

ASSISTANT DIRECTOR OF FOOD & BEVERAGE: Grand Hyatt Resort of Fiji   Suva, Fiji • 2001–2002
455-room resort • 10 outlets • $13M annual f&b revenue • 232 staff • Japanese, Korean, Chinese, US market

Pre-Opening Assistant Director of Food & Beverage

RESTAURANT MANAGER: Hyatt Regency Boston   Boston, MA • 2000–2001
CORPORATE MANAGEMENT TRAINEE: Hyatt Regency Boston   Boston, MA • 1999–2000
264-seat fine dining revolving restaurant • $3M annual f&b revenue • 44 staff • US business/tourist market

Pre-Opening Team of Hyatt Regency Cambridge during this assignment

PRIOR

Positions as **Chef Patissier, Chef de Partie,** and **Apprentice Chef** in Liverpool, London, and the Channel Islands.

EDUCATION

BSc (Hons) in Hotel and Catering Management: University of Leeds, England
HND in Hotel, Catering, and Institutional Management: Westminster College, England
City and Guilds Chef Qualifications: Liverpool Technical College, England

Gallup High-Performance Management Workshop
Gallup Talent-Based Hiring / StrengthsFinder Assessment / Associate Opinion Survey

---

BOARD AND INDUSTRY LEADERSHIP

Board Member, Missouri Hotel & Lodging Association, 2018–Present
President, Tourism Commission, Kansas City Convention & Visitors Bureau, 2016–Present

RESUME 82: *by Louise Kursmark, MRW, CPRW, JCTC, CEIP, CCM • www.louisekursmark.com*

ROXANNE TAYLOR

212-555-6543   www.LinkedIn.com/in/RoxanneTaylor   roxanne.taylor@mail.com

SENIOR EXECUTIVE: HOSPITALITY / TRAVEL INDUSTRY

20 Years of Top Performance with One of the World's Leading Hospitality Brands:
Driving Revenue Growth – Pioneering Revenue Management – Improving Call-Center Performance

Innovative executive who translates ideas and concepts into revenue and market share. Change leader repeatedly successful in developing world-class teams that rapidly engage and respond to diverse business and customer demands.

Strong experience identifying and aligning people and technology to deliver products, programs, team efficiency, and cost savings in the areas of distribution, call centers, revenue management, customer data integration, and CRM. Broad leadership capacity and proven ability to manage multiple concurrent roles and responsibilities.

Revenue & Market Share Growth ▪ Strategic & Tactical Planning ▪ Organizational Restructuring ▪ Cost Reduction & Control
Yield Management Optimization ▪ Hotel Pricing Concepts ▪ Technology & Project Management
Revenue Management ▪ Reservations ▪ Electronic Distribution ▪ Call Centers

PROFESSIONAL EXPERIENCE

HOSPITALITY HOTELS   2000–2020

Progressive high-profile leadership roles with one of the nation's preeminent hospitality companies, directing Rooms, Reservations, Revenue Management, and strategic corporate initiatives. Performance highlights include:

- Built Hospitality's Revenue Management function from the ground up, propelling 4 straight years of market-share growth.
- Delivered Hospitality's first consolidated view of global customer data.
- Transformed reservations call center from underperformer to #1 globally ranked and revenue-producing asset.

VICE PRESIDENT, RESERVATIONS   New York, NY, 2018–2020

Promoted to manage global reservations and drive development of a CEO priority: a global customer data management system to create Hospitality's first-ever consolidated customer snapshot. Built consensus and earned executive-level buy-in for the enterprise-wide change initiative. Propelled both immediate findings and long-term strategic plan.

Challenge: Derive single view of customer value for the global corporation and create systems/processes to disseminate findings across the enterprise.

Actions:
- Drove dual initiatives—delivering first consolidated reports to CEO in 180 days and simultaneously orchestrating long-term strategic plan to create the systems, processes, and protocols to deliver relevant customer information to each point of customer contact globally.
- Selected vendors, managed contracts and budgets, and orchestrated smooth system integration and data output.
- Fully assimilated all North America and International Reservation systems, call center applications, SOPs, and service delivery standards in 10 global call centers.

Results:
- Hospitality's **first** global unified view of customer value—producing surprising results and arming leadership team with reliable data for strategic decision making.
- **5%** reduction in call-center operations costs through shortened hours—without diminishing service quality.
- **21%** drop in reservation system fees.

VICE PRESIDENT, REVENUE MANAGEMENT   New York, NY, 2014–2018

Hand-picked to assume newly created role and build Hospitality's first Revenue Management organization—while retaining all responsibilities as VP Central Reservations. Developed new operation from the ground up, from strategic plan through system development, deployment, migration, and integration across the Hospitality enterprise.

Challenge: Maximize potential of 60,000 rooms and $5B in revenue. Develop new aspect of company culture to embrace Revenue Management.

Strategy: Use Challenge-Actions-Results format to clearly define scope and achievements of each position—as well as notable firsts and measurable performance improvements.

212-555-6543   ROXANNE TAYLOR   roxanne.taylor@mail.com

VICE PRESIDENT, REVENUE MANAGEMENT   *continued*

Actions:
- In 14 months built industry-competitive Revenue Management organization: 15 corporate staff, 105 hotel revenue managers.
- Guided system development, providing key input on pricing and availability strategies.
- Created 3-tier training program to build expertise in leadership, pricing, distribution, analytics, and systems.

Results:
- **4** consecutive years of market-share growth.
- **30%** reduction in turnover of hotel revenue managers.
- Seamless integration of **150** multi-brand hotels into Central Reservations with zero disruption to core brands.

VICE PRESIDENT, CENTRAL RESERVATIONS   Kansas City, MO, 2009–2014

Transformed lackluster reservations operation to top-performing, revenue-generating service center providing heightened levels of service to all Hospitality callers and outsourced services to third-party reservation providers. Held full executive authority for entire North American call center, reservations operations, and related technology—700 associates, $2B revenue.

Challenge: Improve service, lower costs, boost revenues, minimize turnover, and secure data.

Actions: Orchestrated total restructuring of the reservations operation.
- Drove a rapid action plan to hire and train 100 new associates.
- Launched a management leadership and mentoring program.
- Created self-directed teams to instill ownership for service levels, scheduling, and team performance.
- Implemented a call-gating system.
- Developed initial disaster recovery plan to safeguard $2M in daily revenue.

Results
- **#1** worldwide ranking among leading hotel chains in cost-of-sale, as rated by independent source (up from **#4**).
- **20%** reduction in turnover.
- **33%** drop in hotel reservation costs with 6% increase in average rate and conversion.
- **5%** savings in net costs through third-party service provision.
- Restoration of service levels to Hospitality callers.

CORPORATE DIRECTOR, ROOMS   Kansas City, MO, 2005–2009

Advanced through the ranks to highly visible corporate role with direct accountability for front-desk service, technology, management recruiting and staffing, new hotel openings, and procurement.

Challenge: Raise low levels of front-desk customer service in high-turnover industry.

Actions: Introduced company's first all-inclusive front-desk training program. Incorporated multimedia eLearning for efficiency and cost control.

Results: **42%** improvement in front-desk customer service.

PRIOR POSITIONS WITH HOSPITALITY CORPORATION   2000–2005

Executive Assistant Manager—Rooms / Rooms Manager / Project Manger—Hotel Openings
Front Office Manger / Assistant Executive Housekeeper / Management Trainee

EDUCATION

MBA – CORNELL UNIVERSITY, Johnson School of Business, New York, NY
BS Hotel Administration – CORNELL UNIVERSITY, Ithaca, NY
Kellogg Executive Education – Pricing Strategies and Tactics, KELLOGG SCHOOL OF MANAGEMENT, Chicago, IL

RESUME 83: *by Louise Kursmark, MRW, CPRW, JCTC, CEIP, CCM • www.louisekursmark.com*

Karl Wendt

karlwendt@gmail.com • +49 12 3456 7890
Skype: karlwendt • linkedin.com/in/karlwendt

GLOBAL HOSPITALITY EXECUTIVE
Profit Performance • Turnaround • International Expansion • Revenue Management

25 Years in Corporate & Hotel Management –
Driving Profit Growth & Delivering Results in 17 Cities, 11 Countries, 4 Continents
Karlsbad International • AAA 5-Diamond & 4-Diamond • Multi-Brand Properties • Luxury Brand Experience

Culturally versatile executive who thrives on steep challenges and has proven success in multiple roles, unusual circumstances, and diverse regions (Asia, Americas, EMEA). Exceptional team builder able to convey vision and create sense of common mission. Native German, fluent English, basic French and Spanish.

- Revenue Management
- Strategic Leadership
- Development Planning
- Acquisitions & Integrations
- Rebranding & Restructuring
- Cost Controls & Contingency Planning
- Hotel Openings
- RevPar & GSI Improvements
- Crisis Problem-Solving

PROFESSIONAL EXPERIENCE AND ACHIEVEMENTS

KARLSBAD HOTELS INTERNATIONAL • Worldwide, 1995–Present
Leading German company operating 330 hotels in 37 countries on 4 continents • €1.3B annual revenue

MANAGING DIRECTOR, Karlsbad Cinque Terre   Italy, 2018–Present
Delivered rapid performance gains at one of the company's premier resorts: 918 suites, 14 restaurants, 16 bar properties; 14-member management team; 1,500+ total employees. Full P&L responsibility.

- Improved YOY financial performance in every area of measurement:

EBITDA	GOP	RevPar	Total Revenue
+51%	+29%	+23%	+$83M
	(Obj.: +12%)		(2020 Proj: +$94M)

- Built a cohesive leadership team, improved communication, and created a leaner operating structure.
- Achieved **$5M** in incremental revenue by revitalizing up-selling programs and incentives.
- Earned numerous "firsts," awards, and improved rankings:
  - Best company hotel in Market Matrix (88% combined), 2018
  - AAA 5-Diamond Award, Casa Karlsbad, 2019 (top 0.2% of 30,000 reviewed)
  - #1 Family Hotel, TripAdvisor, January 2020
  - #5 Hotel, Trip Advisor, November 2019

SENIOR VICE PRESIDENT AND GLOBAL BRAND AMBASSADOR   Germany, 2014–2018
Led company transition from region to brand in 14-country EMEA region, representing €250M revenue, 51 hotels, 18,000 rooms, and 13,000 staff. Developed brand genesis, established new international SOP, and implemented new revenue strategies to reinforce own web and distribution channel. Traveled extensively to secure brand expansion.

- Delivered financial gains year after year:

	2015	2016	2017	Q1 2018
EBITDA	+0.3%	+1.2%	+7%	+3%
RGI	108.8%	110.1%	110.7%	106%
RevPar	+1.2%	+2%	+4.8%	+11.4%

- Saved **€3.2M** through region-wide cost contingency plan and **€4.2M** through lease renegotiations.
- Restructured **€20M** capital investment plan.
- Drove revenue from karlsbad.com up **40.7%** to **€62M** for the region.

Karl Wendt • karlwendt@gmail.com • +49 12 3456 7890   Page 1 of 2

Strategy: Showcase the progressive career of this executive (25 years with one of the world's leading hotel companies) and use tables and bold type to highlight his many notable achievements in locations around the world.

KARLSBAD HOTELS INTERNATIONAL • continued

EXECUTIVE VICE PRESIDENT, SOUTH AMERICA Argentina, 2011–2014
Opened Karlsbad's first hotel in Argentina and exceeded all performance expectations for $59M region comprising 10 hotels (3,675 rooms, 5,500 employees) in 5 countries and 8 cities. Created improvement plans based on unique needs of each property and culture.

- Achieved impressive year-over-year performance gains:

GOP	RevPar	Total Revenue
+7.3% ($0.8M)	+9.4% ($6.2)	+10.49% ($5M)

- Increased loyalty program membership **203%** to 180,000.
- Led the region to the #1 GOP per room in the company.
- Awarded "Best International New Opening" from International Hotel Association.

GENERAL MANAGER, KARLSBAD SHANGHAI China, 2008–2011
Delivered exceptional results during period of global economic recession.

- Delivered **47%** GOP and set a company record for highest GOP/month (**70%**).
- Achieved the best GSI scores in the company, 2009–2010.

PRIOR ROLES WITH KARSLBAD Worldwide, 1995–2008
General Manager, Karlsbad Sydney, 2004–2008
Resident Manager, Karlsbad Melbourne, 2002–2004
Resident Manager, Karlsbad Mexico City, 2000–2002
Resident Manager, Karlsbad Berlin (Flagship Hotel), 1997–2000
Assistant Manager, Karlsbad London, 1995–1997

EDUCATION

BS in Hospitality Management Cologne Business School, Germany, 1995
Revenue Management, Human Resources (Staffing and Selection) Cornell University, Sydney, 2007

PROFESSIONAL DISTINCTIONS

Designated by Karlsbad Chairman to represent him to:
- Welcome the Queen of England and Queen of Denmark on royal visits to Italy and Argentina (2017, 2013)
- Receive on his behalf the "Lifetime Achievement Award" from the World Tourism Organization (Paris, 2017) and "Hotelier of the Year Award" from the International Hotel Association (New York, 2012)

Member, Chaîne de Rôtisseurs and Skål International

Board of Directors, Hoteliers International (Australia); Association National des Hôtels (France), Cinque Terre Hotel Association (Italy)

Guest Speaker at international forums, universities, and private institutions

RESUME 84: by Vivian VanLier, CPRW, JCTC, CEIP, CCMC, CPBS • www.CareerEmpowermentCoach.com

DENISE CHAN

San Francisco, CA 94132
San Francisco, CA 94132 • 415-555-3344

TRAVEL & TOURISM INDUSTRY EXECUTIVE

Extensive Knowledge of Tour and Cruise Industry
Innovator in Packaging Cruise Programs and Tours

- Well-respected Industry Executive with 20+ years of professional and managerial experience leading tour companies from start-up through fast-track growth and market expansion.
- Consistently successful in identifying and capitalizing on market opportunities to drive revenue growth and expand market penetration.
- Pioneer in strategic alliances and business partnerships to grow business.
- Strong leadership and team-building skills with a participatory management style.

Sales & Marketing / Key Account Management / P&L Management / Information Technology
Team Building / Public Relations & Promotions / Strategic Business Partnerships

PROFESSIONAL EXPERIENCE

President • 2012 to Present
INTERNATIONAL SPECIALTY TOURS, LTD., San Francisco, CA

Recruited by Chairman to spearhead growth of mass-market tour company with programs to Europe, Britain, and the Mediterranean. Charged with full responsibility for US operations, including P&L accountability, business and market planning, sales training and management, IT, and administrative affairs. Negotiate and manage strategic partnerships with travel agencies, airlines, and cruise lines.

> *Delivered consistent increases in sales performance, building revenues from **$12 million to $32 million** within 2 years. During the same period, reduced expenses by **15%** and improved bottom line by more than **$1 million**.*

- Evaluated market trends and implemented strategies to reposition company as a niche operator.
- Developed key strategic partnership with leading international cruise line.
- Secured sole representation for major airline vacation packages.
- Introduced new technologies, including online connection to Apollo Leisure Shopper.
- Improved brand recognition through focus on improved product and service.
- Awarded "Office of the Year" in 2015 and "Executive of the Year" in 2017.

Sr. Vice President Sales & Marketing • 2010–2012
WORLDTRAVELER TOURS, Tampa, FL

Charged with all sales and marketing functions for $150 million Caribbean tour operator. Hired, trained, and managed sales team. Developed and implemented marketing budget. Created sales/marketing strategies, materials, and seminar presentations.

> *Increased revenues by **30%** within 1 year.*

- Repositioned regional company as a national competitor.
- Brought a "Sales and Reservations" approach to focus on top producers, which increased revenues and reduced selling cost.

Strategy: Accent key points in bold and italics to promote this candidate's expertise, strengths, and record of innovation. Throughout the resume, highlight the bottom-line results she contributed throughout her career.

DENISE CHAN   Resume (Page 2)

PROFESSIONAL EXPERIENCE, continued

Vice President Sales and Marketing • 2005–2010
BARKELEY TOURS, INC., New York, NY

Recruited for newly formed company to package and market tours of Europe and Eastern Mediterranean. Defined marketing strategy, established initial marketing infrastructure, and developed long-term strategic and short-term tactical marketing plans.

> *Drove revenues from start-up to $120 million, positioning company as the mass-market leader to Europe.*

- Obtained exclusive contracts with airlines, including vacation tour program to Europe with major airline.
- Created innovative, distinctive, and successful direct-mail, advertising, promotion, and business-development campaigns.
- Built national sales and marketing network, negotiating strategic partnerships and alliances.
- Awarded "Salesperson of the Year," 4 straight years.

EDUCATION

OXFORD POLYTECHNIC, Sheffield, UK
Degree in Hotel Management and Tourism

Management Training: Suisse Hotels and Restaurants, Switzerland; Hotel Genève, Geneva, Switzerland.

Continuing Education / Professional Development: Stephen Covey seminar: *7 Habits of Highly Effective People;* Tom Peters *WOW Seminars;* Harvard Business School training.

Certified Travel Counselor Course, 2005

FOREIGN LANGUAGE SKILLS

Fluent in French; working knowledge of Spanish

PROFESSIONAL AFFILIATIONS

Member—USTOA (United States Tour Operators Association)
Member—ASTA (American Society of Travel Agents)
Member—New York Athletic Club
Member—SKAL

ADDITIONAL SKILLS

Accomplished and articulate public speaker, frequently selected to deliver presentations to industry gatherings of 250 to 1,500 people.

—Available for Domestic and International Travel and/or Relocation—

RESUME 85: *by Louise Kursmark, MRW, CPRW, JCTC, CEIP, CCM • www.louisekursmark.com*

CELIA BRADLEY

New York Metro | 212-789-5432 | celiabradley@gmail.com | LinkedIn profile

SENIOR CREATIVE EXECUTIVE: MULTIMEDIA PLATFORMS

Brand-Aligned Creative Strategy & Detailed Execution | Creative Team Leadership | Viewership & Revenue Gains

Multiple award-winning creative director with 20+ years of MaxTV, CineVu, and independent producer experience. Driving force behind multi-platform storytelling that attracts target audiences, engages viewers, and expresses brand personality.

Leadership Strengths

→ Melding big vision with detailed execution
→ Conceiving new ideas in a changing media landscape
→ Getting things done in volatile, high-pressure environments

→ Maximizing both financial and human resources
→ Inspiring and leading creative teams
→ Driving the business forward

PROFESSIONAL EXPERIENCE

MaxTV – New York, NY
2013–2020
Cable television network with 90 million subscribers in the US; owned by the Turner Broadcasting System division of Time Warner.

SVP CREATIVE SERVICES, 2018–2020 | **VP CREATIVE SERVICES,** 2013–2018

Member of executive team that defined and promoted the network's direction, philosophy, and brand identity to consumers, advertisers, and the trade.

- Held full executive responsibility for the conception, creation, development, and implementation of creative content for the brand across all platforms.
- Created the network's on-air architecture and promotional programming to fully utilize all assets ($85M in inventory).
- Built and cultivated a talented team of 30+ creative professionals, instilling a culture where individuals were willing to take risks and achieve unexpected results.
- Repeatedly retained as lead creative following corporate leadership changes—thrived through 4 executive transitions.

Key Challenges and Results

- **BRAND TRANSITION:** Delivered one of the most successful rebrands in cable history (Docu Channel to MaxTV) and 3 additional brand transitions as the network repeatedly transformed itself in response to changing entertainment trends and shifts in audience expectations.

  → **1M+ new viewers in first year following rebranding.**
  → **9 quarters of ratings growth.**
  → **35% increase in prime demographic viewership in 5 years.**
  → **Top-10 network ranking, up from mid 30s.**

- **UPFRONT:** Spearheaded creation of high-budget, high-profile, high-pressure annual upfront events, designed to attract advertisers and build media buzz. Forged exceptional team spirit through intensive multi-month development process.

  → **Rave reviews for first event—and the best sales results in the network's history.**
  → **Consistent year-over-year growth in upfront advertising dollars.**

- **MULTI-PLATFORM EXPANSION:** Pivoted and expanded creative services to develop programming for new media. Worked closely with Marketing to ensure strategic content that promoted the brand holistically across all platforms.

  → **Short-form stories that quickly engage audience.**
  → **Long-form digital content for website and YouTube.**
  → **Documentaries that attract new demographics.**

- **BUSINESS LEADERSHIP:** Stepped into leadership void after 2017 departure of network president. Rallied leadership team, established processes, improved communications, and instilled purpose and passion for getting the job done.

  → **Well-oiled machine that advanced toward goals and transitioned smoothly to new president.**
  → **Culture of collaboration, open flow of information, and teamwork enhanced through regular meetings and consistent communication processes.**

Strategy: Distinguish diverse activities from the resulting achievements by offsetting strong results in bold type in a shaded box that makes those results the focal point of the resume.

CELIA BRADLEY   212-789-5432 | celiabradley@gmail.com

CineVu – New York, NY   2003–2013
CREATIVE DIRECTOR | SENIOR PRODUCER | PRODUCER

Advanced quickly to creative leadership role with responsibility for developing all on-air promotion for CineVu movies, CineVu original pictures, and 4 MovieVu networks.

Performance Highlights

- **BRAND EXPANSION:** Conceived idea for 4 channel expansions to extend the CineVu network. Led creative team in developing new brand names, packaging, promotions, and launches.
- **BRAND RELAUNCH:** Re-introduced CineVu with a major launch event.

PRIOR EXPERIENCE

- **BUSINESS LEADERSHIP:** Owned and operated a production company producing on-air campaigns, sales tapes, and industrial videos for high-profile clients.
- **VIDEO PRODUCTION:** Produced and directed more than 150 music video programs for the XYZ Network.
- **ENTERTAINMENT EVENTS:** Began career in the music business producing live events for a 3,000-seat arena.

EDUCATION

Columbia University – Film and Media Studies   New York, NY
University of Connecticut – Mathematics   Storrs, CT

PROFESSIONAL AWARDS AND AFFILIATIONS

- Honored with more than 50 industry awards, including Promax, BDA, CLIO, and New York Festivals.
- Member of PromaxBDA – International Association for Entertainment Marketing Professionals.

RESUME 86: by Myriam-Rose Kohn, CCM, CJSS, CCMC, UJCTC, CEIP, CPRW • www.jedaenterprises.com

JEREMIAH GEND

jeremiahgend@gmail.com

(555) 999-3456

www.linkedin.com/in/jeremiahgend

VICE PRESIDENT, DIGITAL CONTENT

Influential Media Executive — Driving cross-platform content and programming strategy — delivering remarkable outcomes.

- Originated groundbreaking program to convince 10 schools to form a new men's soccer-driven Big East conference. Resulted in a 12-year, 9-figure rights agreement for over 400 hours of premium programming for Sly Sports.

- Pioneered short-form content strategy for distribution during live, linear broadcasts and wide consumption across social platforms: YouTube, Instagram, Twitter, soccerchannel.com.

- Conceived new strategies for identifying opportunities to compete with traditional and disruptor media organizations.

Performance & Process Improvement | Strategic Alliances | Negotiations | Strategic Brand Management

PROFESSIONAL EXPERIENCE & ACCOMPLISHMENTS

VICE PRESIDENT, HEAD OF PROGRAMMING　　　　　　　　　　　　　　　　　　　　　　2016–2020
Soccer Channel · San Raphael, CA

Soccer Channel (www.soccerchannel.com) is the only 24-hour multimedia destination dedicated to both the professional sport and soccer lifestyle—a hybrid of sports, health, fitness, pop culture, entertainment, lifestyle and travel programming

- Executed network's cross-platform content and programming strategy, oversight of $25M+ annual department budget, telecast rights negotiations, acquisitions, and scheduling for nearly 7500 live domestic and international events plus original programming via best-in-class, digital OTT subscription service, *Soccer Channel Plus*.

- Worked closely with Production, Integrated Sales, and Marketing to maximize endemic sponsor engagement, media buying up-fronts, and partnership activation within linear and digital content to generate revenue growth.

- Fostered collaborative culture and provided vision and leadership to department of 9 full-time employees.

- Attended and networked at worldwide events with telecast rights: World Cup, Premier League finals, US Soccer finals, NCAA championships, and more.

  Key Performance Goals Achieved:
  - **Raised annual revenue and year-over-year ratings +20% in first year.**
  - **Elevated digital subscription revenue to 36 months ahead of plan by end of year 2.**
  - **Achieved highest EBITA in company history.**
  - **Acquired multiple domestic and international tournament rights, ousting incumbent broadcaster ESPN.**

VICE PRESIDENT, COLLEGIATE SPORTS AND RIGHTS ACQUISITIONS　　　　　2012–2016
EXECUTIVE DIRECTOR, COLLEGIATE SPORTS　　　　　　　　　　　　　　　　　2010–2012
Sly Sports Media Group · Los Angeles, CA
Sly Sports is the nationwide leader in sports programming.

- Oversaw the implementation of comprehensive programming and acquisition strategy for over 500 live events annually across 30 cross-platform distribution networks. Managed 4 direct reports.

- Built strong relationships throughout the college sports industry as the primary contact for Commissioners, Conference staff, Athletic Directors, coaches, Olympic Sports coaches, and marketing and PR directors.

- Administered scheduling, network designation, game selection, TV timeout formats, supplier inventory delivery, program flow, and contingency programming.

- Redesigned company scheduling software to comply with evolving media landscape for 7 distinct television networks.

  Key Performance Goals Achieved:
  - **Inked more than $6 billion in television rights agreements over 2-year period, negotiating deal terms for all college sports acquisitions and sublicensing agreements.**
  - **Launched new department to manage emerging networks, such as Big Ten Network (BTN) and FX Sports.**

Strategy: Highlight "Key Performance Goals Achieved" for each position to make impressive achievements stand out for this sports/digital media executive.

JEREMIAH GEND

jeremiahgend@gmail.com

(555) 999-3456

www.linkedin.com/in/jeremiahgend

Page 2

(ACTING) ASSOCIATE COMMISSIONER, BIG EAST CONFERENCE
Los Angeles, CA

2009–2010

- Tapped to fill interim position on short notice, rapidly took the reins and created a 160-game basketball schedule in time for looming conference playoffs.

- Interacted daily with athletic directors and basketball coaches at St. John's University, Villanova, Georgetown, Marquette, Xavier, Butler, Creighton, Providence, Seton Hall, and DePaul.

- Coordinated directly with facilities such as Madison Square Garden, Verizon Center, Wells Fargo Center, and others.

DIRECTOR OF NATIONAL PROGRAMMING AND COLLEGIATE SPORTS	2006–2009
MANAGER OF SCHEDULING	2003–2006
SENIOR NATIONAL SCHEDULING COORDINATOR	2001–2003
REGIONAL SCHEDULING COORDINATOR	2000–2001

Sly Sports Net · Los Angeles, CA

EDUCATION

Bachelor of Arts, Broadcasting, Radio and Television, San Francisco State University, San Francisco, CA — 1998

PROFESSIONAL AND COMMUNITY ACTIVITIES

The California State University Entertainment Advisory Council

Youth Soccer and Basketball Coach – AYSO (17 years), YMCA (4 years)
Invited Speaker – San Francisco State University, University of Oregon, USC

RESUME 87: by Louise Kursmark, MRW, CPRW, JCTC, CEIP, CCM • www.louisekursmark.com

CHARLIE DOCKER

213-445-5543   Los Angeles, CA   charliedocker@youmail.com

MULTI-PLATFORM ENTERTAINMENT EXECUTIVE

Strategist … Storyteller … Branding & Marketing Innovator … Ratings, Revenue, Community Builder

Marketing Executive & Brand Strategist instrumental in building some of TV's most recognizable brands.

Strategic leader, passionate about entertainment on any screen/device, known for collaboration, inspired creative oversight, and innovative thinking. Big idea generator who derives maximum value from available resources through bold concepts and buzz-worthy initiatives. Team player, team leader, talent developer.

PROFESSIONAL EXPERIENCE

StreamTV, Glendale, CA   2016–2020

Chief Marketing Officer | Chief Creative Officer

Scope: *Cross-Channel Consumer Marketing Campaigns; Brand Strategy, Maintenance, and Evolution; Media Planning and Analysis; Creative Services; Social/Digital Media; Ad Sales and Content Distribution Support. Eleven high-performing direct reports, $15M annual marketing budget, oversight of deep vendor bench and freelance production talent.*

Snapshot: Led all multi-platform consumer marketing activities that helped transform a fledgling network into a more formidable and competitive brand positioned for growth, innovation, and ever-expanding viewership and ratings.

- **Performance Highlights:**

  Q1 and Q2 2020 ....2 strongest quarters in network history
  Primetime Ratings ....+26% in 2020, topping 3.5 years of primetime rating growth
  Primetime Viewership .....+32% and +27% key demographics, Q2 2020
  Ratings Drive Revenue ....Q1 2020 biggest revenue quarter in the network's history
  Social/Digital Media ....Triple-digit YOY growth: +264% Facebook fans, +135% Twitter followers, +727% Instagram and streamtv.com page views

- **Brand Management:** Drove the brand experience within and beyond network walls through oversight of the design and architecture of a cohesive network voice and narrative.

- **Content Elevation:** Directed strategic marketing campaigns that drove ratings growth as StreamTV shifted from acquired to more brand-defining original programming. Generated record-breaking results for individual programs, programming blocks, social/digital media, and overall viewership, supporting climb to "Top 10 Cable Network" status.

- **Social/Digital Media:** Drove the creation of sticky, shareable, engaging content born of low-cost, high impact ideas and partnerships with like-minded brands and influential social and digital stars. Clever content and data-driven paid and organic targeting garnered record-breaking premiere-night social activity for high-profile, high-premium originals. Supplied Ad Sales team with series-based digital content successfully monetized through advertiser sponsorship.

- **Ad Sales Support:** Orchestrated multiple effective Upfront events that drew wide participation among key decision makers, increased awareness of StreamTV's USP, garnered high scores post-event (50% "very likely" or "likely" to increase advertising investment), and contributed to year-after-year increases in new advertisers and incremental spending by existing clients.

- **Strong Leadership:** Built and managed a high-performance, award-winning team by fostering a culture that placed a premium on ideas and creativity and encouraged risk-taking, collaboration, and audience experience.

Strategy: Lead the experience section with "Performance Highlights" and segue to detailed descriptions of how those results were attained. Maintain readability with ample white space throughout.

213-445-5543   **CHARLIE DOCKER**   charliedocker@youmail.com

---

NuTV (formerly Law & Justice TV), Los Angeles, CA   2000–2016

VP, Brand Strategy & Development (2015–2016) ▪ **VP, Marketing** (2009–2015)

Scope: *Branding, Marketing, Advertising, Promotions, Ad Sales Support, Creative Services (Print) & Outside Creative Agencies*

Snapshot: Integral member of marketing leadership team that drove the industry's most successful rebrand, transforming Law & Justice TV from a narrowly focused, mid-tier performer to NuTV, a diversified cable network with a top-10 ranking. Network rebrand exceeded all expectations, delivering performance gains in multiple areas of measurement.

- **Performance Highlights:**

  Viewership .... Most watched year in network history, 2016
  Demographic .... Median viewer age dropped 8 years since 2014
  Key Demos .... Double-digit growth quarter after quarter

- **Upfront:** Co-orchestrated 2015 Upfront, NuTV's first solo event after years of co-presentation with sister networks. Executed entire event from concept to completion in 6 weeks, driving home message of surge in critical 18–49 viewership. Captured 40 new advertisers—best Upfront results in network history.

- **Brand Strategy & Transformation:** Guided affiliates through multi-step rebranding process, from programming innovations through name change to NuTV. In first full year after rebranding, network captured record viewership and—2 years later—continued to set new records.

- **Partnerships & Cross-Functional Initiatives:** Cultivated relationships with cross-functional groups, collaborated with research team, and engaged internal and external media buying agencies to maximize cross-promotion opportunities on sister networks. Network achieved Top 10 ranking and continued to break records in all major categories.

Director, Marketing (2000–2009)

Scope: *In-house Print Design Group; Creative Staff & Outside Agencies; Ad Sales Support; Trade Show Marketing, PR & Promotions*

Snapshot: Brand watchdog and marketing strategist instrumental in growing subscriber base from +15M to +80M homes, quadrupling asset value, and helping establish the network as a viable business that delivered value to distribution partners, viewers, and advertisers alike.

- **Program Innovation:** Spearheaded concepts through detailed execution of local market campaigns, affiliate promotions, and award-winning public service initiatives that extended the network's brand, generated revenue for distribution partners, and supported sales team in ultimately driving the network to full distribution.

Early Career

- **True Crime Television**—Promotion Director ▪ Manager On-Air Promotion ▪ Senior Writer/Producer
- **Children's Television Workshop**—Researcher, "Sesame Street"
- **Teen TV Network**—Associate Director Post-Production, "Growing Up"
- **California Public Television**—Crew Chief/Studio Tech

EDUCATION

M.A., University of California   Berkeley, CA
B.A., Southern California State University   Los Angeles, CA

CHAPTER 12

Military, Government, and Nonprofit

- Director Office on Disability
- Supervisor, US Department of Veterans Affairs
- City Planning Director
- Municipality Value Economist Manager
- Association Executive Director
- Vice President of Foundation
- Development Director
- Foundation CEO

RESUME 88: *by Diane Hudson, CCMC, CPCC, CLTMC, CPRW, FJSTC • www.cpcc-careercoach.com*

JOE SMITH

Philadelphia, PA, 19119 • 555.714.4570 • jsmith@gmail.com

PUBLIC POLICY EXECUTIVE

Business Forte: **Idea-maker** • **Disability Advocate** • **Public Disability Policy Change Agent** • **Political Prodigy**
High-volume Producer • **Problem-solver** • **Corporate Turnaround Expert** • **Senior Executive and Board Member**

RESULTS SNAPSHOT

Defying the Odds	**Legally blind** since a young age and one of the very few elected officials to serve as a person with a disability. Elected as Republican in heavily Democrat district.
M&L Transit Systems	**Reversed critical downward spiral** of company's cash flow and credibility; recreated forecasting and resolved cash-flow hemorrhaging. Guided turnaround and strong re-growth.
City of Philadelphia	**Negotiated** the most successful Surrounding Community agreements in Pennsylvania. Led effective effort to keep taxes, fees, and regulations in check.

LEADERSHIP VALUE DRIVERS

- **Business Model and Process Change:** Affect positive change and improve the common good, providing strong leadership to improve the human condition. Skilled with applying technology as a force multiplier.

- **Hands-on, Forthright Leadership:** Clarify, confront and resolve the most complicated challenges. Fluidly navigate parallel projects crossing organizational boundaries with tight deadlines and clashing priorities.

- **Personal Credibility:** Anchored by the fundamental principles of integrity, objectivity, and professional competence. Politically and socially sensitive; communicate well with different people.

- **Forensic Communications / First-class Speech Writer & Inspiring Presenter:** Write and deliver speeches to large audiences without tele-prompters. Comfortable on camera and with the media.

LEADERSHIP PROGRESSION

Director • **Office on Disability** • **Philadelphia, PA** • **2013–Present**
Leadership Impact: Gubernatorial Appointee • Direct a staff of 12 • Report to the Secretary of Administration & Finance • Administer $2M budget • Communicate with state HHS for disability programs; policy development, and implementation • Highest ranking Disability Official in the state • Member of Interagency Council • Grant Writer

- Spearheaded Memorandum of Understanding (MOU) with Department of Communities and Housing Development (DCHD) on the American Disabilities Act (ADA), creating a policy and first-of-its-kind program to ensure funds earmarked for the disabled were properly spent on facilities creating access to everyone.

- Designed MOU policy to include architectural access to all new construction and renovations.

- Navigated shift to new ADA standards, designing a novel municipal program allowing cities and towns to access grant money for ADA accessibility improvements. Convinced top-level stakeholders to include funds in the capital budget.

- Championed "Work Matters" framework, a collaborative initiative by the Council on State Governments (CSG) and the National Conference of State Legislatures (NCSL) to create disability program "best practices guide" for all 50 States.

- Member, Council of State Governments (CSG) and National Conference of State Legislatures (NCSL) National Task Force on Workforce Development for Persons with Disabilities.

- Co-chair of the Transportation, Technology, and Other Employment Supports Subcommittee.

City Councilor At Large • **Elected 2011** • **City of PA** • **Philadelphia, PA** • **2012–Present**

Leadership Impact: Elected to City Council 3 times • Set policy; adopt ordinances, orders, and resolutions • Review and approve the City's annual budget of greater than $173M • Approve/confirm appropriations and appointments

- Create new political and public policy proposals. Chief Negotiator for the PA Casino "Surrounding Communities Agreement," positioning the city to receive $20M in future revenue.

Strategy: Focus on upward progression in the public policy and advocacy field for this high-level government official and then showcase Board and community work in an addendum.

Joe Smith | jsmith@gmail.com   Page | 2

PAGOP Nominee ▪ Candidate for Secretary of State ▪ Statewide ▪ 2014
Leadership Impact: Won Nomination for Secretary of State ▪ First statewide person with a disability to reach a statewide general election ballot in PA.

- Broadened and enhanced the perception of the PAGOP slate by putting forth a candidate with a disability, which may be a first and/or be a rarity.
- Delivered highly inspirational speeches by memory and encouraged audiences by taking 'selfies.'
- Focused the Secretary of State Campaign to energize and identify voters.
- Received more endorsements from PA newspapers than any other candidate, except the Governor.

Founder & Managing Director ▪ Arc Communications ▪ Philadelphia, PA ▪ 2008–2014
Leadership Impact: Stood up a select-consultancy Public Relations and communications company specializing in issue advocacy and online promotion

- Created and implemented PR plans and direct mail campaigns for clients. Obtained major market media coverage, achieving top ranking in both Google and Yahoo searches for websites created and maintained by Arc.

Regional Development Manager ▪ CSI Support & Development Services ▪ Philadelphia, PA ▪ 2007–2008
Leadership Impact: Identified multimillion-dollar parcels of land for disabled and senior housing for the nation's largest non-profit rental co-op comprising 53 buildings and 6,200 apartment units across 4 states.

- Identified and approached C-suite executives, Mayors, Councilors, and other community officials and built proposals to procure major development sites for as little as $1.
- Catalyst for establishing policies and procedures to locate developable sites.

Chief Communication Officer ▪ M&L Transit Systems, Inc. ▪ Philadelphia, PA ▪ 2004–2007
Leadership Impact: Developed organizational communication systems ▪ Optimized websites

- Identified severe lack of funds. Designed a corporate budget and turnaround plan and turned $40K monthly losses into $10K monthly gains. Streamlined company spending.
- Revised $2M company budget to maximize revenue and trim costs without cutting jobs.
- Drafted proposals using complex costing methods. Responded to RFPs. Negotiated multimillion-dollar contracts.
- Wrote successful grant applications that yielded $235,000 from the federal government. Implemented programs funded by the U.S. Department of Homeland Security.

Program Coordinator ▪ PA Department of Education ▪ Philadelphia, PA ▪ 1999–2003

- Devised new data collection system for the $50M PA Comprehensive Assessment System (PCAS), Support & Remediation Program, eliminating a 6-month backlog of grant proposals.
- Reduced 18-month backlog within four months by interacting with over 250 school districts.

Communication Coordinator & Municipal Liaison for Senator Jan Ochs ▪ PA State Senate ▪ 1995–1999

- Coordinated, developed, and implemented the Senator's press releases, press strategy and media contacts at the local and state levels. Served as the Senator's spokesperson.
- Landed and placed news stories, analyzed and oversaw legislation, and offered line items and earmarks for the $25B state budget. Drafted and helped maneuver bills through the legislative process.

EDUCATION & CERTIFICATIONS

- Bachelor of Science in Communication & Journalism | Temple University, Philadelphia, PA
  Dean's List | Competed in Lincoln-Douglas Debate competitions | Member, National Forensics Association
- SEO Certification, SEOCertification.org, 2017

Joe Smith | jsmith@gmail.com   Page | 3

Addendum

BOARDS & COMMISSIONS

- **PA Commission for the Blind Rehabilitation Council**   2005–2014
  - **Appointed by Rendell and reappointed by Corbett. Intellectual driving force behind Blind Commission.**
  - Spearheaded development of new reports on vocational rehabilitation for the blind, from the ground up, for the Commission for the Office of Special Education and Rehabilitation Services Administration (RSA).

- **City of PA, Elections Division** | Election Officer, Warden, Clerk & Inspector   2007–2014
  - **Expert in elections:** Filled multiple roles during several election cycles, including the Presidential Election.

- **Tailored for Success, PA** | Board of Directors for 501c3   2009–2013
  - Prepared people in delicate situations (battered women, incarcerated, others) to reenter the workforce. Provided interview and work attire plus interview preparation, resume development, and job coaching skills.

- **The ARC of East,** Philadelphia, PA | Board of Directors for 501c3   2008–2011
  - Provided support to persons with developmental disabilities. Consultant to leadership during executive director position change-over. Managed all PR for 3 months.

- **Resource Partnership,** Statewide | Board of Directors for 501c3   2006–2008
  - Focused on helping people with disabilities enter the labor force.

- **Braille Literacy Advisory Council** (Appointed by the Commissioner of Education)   1999
  - Department of Education Subcommittee; Statutory Advisory Council to the PA Department of Education.
  - Provided recommendations on topics such as Braille instruction, literacy assessment for students with visual impairments, teacher certification and recertification, PCAS testing, and availability of instructional materials and Braille production activities. Partnered with the PA Commission for the Blind.

PROFESSIONAL MEMBERSHIPS, AWARDS & OTHER ACCOMPLISHMENTS

- **Member, Public Relations Society of America,** 2008–2014
- **Member, Publicity Club of Mid Atlantic,** 2008–2014
- **Chairman,** PA Republican City Committee, 2010–2014 & 2004–2008
- **PA Rotary Club** (2012 President); recipient of Paul Harris Fellowship award bestowed by Rotary International for "Service Above Self"
- **PA Chamber of Commerce,** Philadelphia Business Association; former member, PA Planning Board, 2010
- **Chairman,** PA Ward 5 Republican Committee, 2001–present
- **Temple University, Armand Stettler Award winner** as Outstanding Communications and Journalism Alumni
- **5-time elected delegate** to the PA Republican State Convention
- **Perfect 3–0 record as Campaign Manager:** Publicized, planned, coordinated, and executed strategies for successful campaigns. Integrated technology into campaigns, built websites, and leveraged social media.

Walter E. Cook, Jr.

Knoxville, TN 37075 — waltcook@comcast.net — (865) 736-8300

SENIOR-LEVEL MANAGER / ADMINISTRATOR

Veterans Affairs / Disability Claims / VA Health-Care Eligibility / VA Law

- More than 20 years of successful performance in the diverse and complex arena of Veterans Affairs, including 15 years of management experience as a National Service Officer for Disabled American Veterans.
- Sound leadership and business-management abilities complemented by professional, hands-on, administrative style that inspires a goal-oriented work environment and ultimately enhances the quality of care for veterans.
- Consistently achieve budget- and grant-funding goals. Ten-year history of successfully preparing annual grant proposals for DAV Colorado Trust and DAV Charitable Trust.
- Solid business insight, with the ability to ascertain and analyze needs, forecast goals, streamline operations, and implement new program concepts. Proven skill at turning around nonproductive, inefficient operations.
- Strong strategic vision coupled with overall business sense and attention to detail.
- Extensive knowledge of anatomy, medical terminology, and physiology; VA claims processing (from initial application, to rating decision, through appellate process); VA Nursing Program; Aid to States for Care of Veterans in State Homes; and VA Benefit Delivery Network (BDN).
- Accredited to practice before US Department of Veterans Affairs. Have testified before US Congress and state legislatures of Maryland and Montana.

Professional Experience

DISABLED AMERICAN VETERANS — US Department of Veterans Affairs — 1997–Present

Supervisor, National Service Officer, 2007–Present, Knoxville, TN & Fort Hamilton, MT
Associate National Service Officer, 1997–2007, Washington, DC

Operations Management

- Oversee and direct all daily operations, functions, and decisions of state nonprofit veterans' organization that represents veterans in dealing with VA health-care eligibility and processing disability claims.
- Ensure effective representation of DAV clients through application of laws and regulations administered by US Department of Veterans Affairs.

Budget Development / Grant Writing

- Develop budgets and write grant proposals to ensure sufficient funding for Field Service Office program. Secure funding from DAV Colorado Trust and DAV Charitable Trust.
- Create budgets for six field offices, including salary, training, travel, and supplies.

Human Resources Management

- Supervise four National Service Officers, six Field Service Officers, and two secretaries, as well as volunteer support staff throughout the state.
- Created state program to define and develop job descriptions, employment policies, and employee manuals for state field offices.
- Have trained and supervised professional, accredited Service Officers to practice before US Department of Veterans Affairs.

Strategy: Emphasize depth of experience in veterans affairs, along with extensive administrative experience, for this federal government administrator seeking to transition into a management role for the VA at the state level.

Walter E. Cook, Jr.

Professional Experience (continued)

Persuasive Communication

- Develop and nurture effective dialogue and cooperation between DAV state office and directors of each VA Medical Center and Regional Office Center in Tennessee.
- Extensive interaction with elected officials at federal, state, and local levels; nonprofit veterans' organizations; volunteer agencies; and oversight committees.

Educational Background

MANAGEMENT AND LEADERSHIP PROGRAM — 2015 — University of Colorado at Denver

DAV STRUCTURED AND CONTINUING TRAINING PROGRAM, PHASES I, II, & III

BACHELOR OF SCIENCE — University of Baltimore

Military Service / Veteran Status

US Army Military Police, 1993–1997

Presentations / Public Speaking

- **Instructor, DAV Training Academy,** University of Colorado at Denver, October 2019

  Led two-week course on proper application of Parts III and IV of 38 Code of Federal Regulations. Developed detailed lesson plan and created practical models to clearly demonstrate specific rating concepts. Also developed comprehensive final examination to fully evaluate each trainee's knowledge and understanding of principles of rating disabilities.

- **Keynote speaker** before delegates of state DAV conventions; federal, state, and local conferences; and panels with leading veterans' organizations regarding veteran-related issues. Spoke to Johns Hopkins School of Law to argue legal defense of post-traumatic stress.

- **Conducted seminars** on readjustment problems of returning war veterans. **Made numerous presentations** to mental health professionals and medical schools, up to 2,000 audience members.

- **Testified** before Maryland State Assembly, Montana State Assembly, and Veterans Affairs Subcommittee in Washington, DC. **Submitted written briefs** before US Department of Veterans Affairs supporting specific arguments.

Professional Affiliations

Disabled American Veterans' Guild of Attorneys-in-Fact
Life Member, Knoxville Chapter, Disabled American Veterans

RESUME 90: by Birgitta Möller, MRW, ACRW • www.cvhjalpen.nu

LENNART ANDERSSON

📞 0708-94 94 70
✉ lennart.andersson@gmail.com
in linkedin.com/in/lennart-andersson

CIVIL DIRECTOR

- Business-oriented leader skilled at navigating politically governed organizations and architecting/streamlining structures, functions, concepts, processes, and teams of 25–450 staff.
- Directed large change and vision processes for top-5 Swedish cities Västerås and Uppsala.

CAREER

CITY PLANNING DIRECTOR, Uppsala Municipality   2014–Present

Recruited to run large-scale community building projects: new neighborhoods, new infrastructure, and Expo Uppsala 2016. Oversee ≈240 staff and 8 subordinate managers (24 managers total in administration).

- ☑ Fulfilled political demand for increased housing construction in third fastest growing city in Sweden.
- ☑ Designed and implemented long-term strategic and action-oriented development model for land and water use.
- ☑ Introduced policy documents to support and control development according to established strategies.
- ☑ Implemented process management model throughout entire organization.
- ☑ Planned/executed 255K m² housing expo. Member of jury appointing winning proposal.

DEPUTY CITY PLANNING DIRECTOR, Västerås City   2007–2013

Promoted to contribute to extensive change work and maneuver complex steering and management needs in political systems. ≈250 staff and 20 managers.

- ☑ Created new administrative organization and departments.
- ☑ Built streamlined administrative processes. Recruited key personnel and new competencies.
- ☑ Participated in vision for process transforming port area into central districts. Work nominated for and won Swedish Architecture's "Planning Prize" in 2013.

DIRECTOR, Västerås City   2001–2006

Headhunted to lead unit overseeing housing, business, infrastructure, and metropolitan development; 25 staff, 3 subordinate managers.

- ☑ Supported Municipal Chief Executive in critical strategic matters decided by Executive Board and City Council.
- ☑ Developed guidelines for government ownership and management in relation to municipal companies.
- ☑ Outlined local development agreements for vulnerable neighborhoods.

BUSINESS DEVELOPMENT MANAGER, AB Bostäder, Västerås   1999–2001

Brought on board to develop business-driven operations/processes by focusing on analysis of surrounding world, competitors, and customers. ≈250 staff, 9 subordinate managers, 25 heads of administration.

- ☑ Architected new structure for group-wide business planning.
- ☑ Created joint structures for how company's 4–5 subsidiaries worked with new analysis.
- ☑ Contributed to development of business opportunities (products and services).

Previous Managerial Experience: Spearheaded large rebuilding project (1,500 apartments) and developed 50 employees in subject matter expertise and planning, structure, and delivery skills.

BOARD ASSIGNMENTS

Board Member, National Academy of Housing and Sustainable Communities (NAHSC)   2017–Present
Board Member, GIS Advisory Board   2015–Present

EDUCATION

Executive Program in Sustainable Urban Systems, Chalmers   Top Managers Program, Vision
Bachelor in Social Science, Lund University

Strategy: Create a clear, concise, 1-page format that emphasizes context around each position (why he was hired) along with skills and accomplishments.

Carmalina Giovese, PMP

--- Toronto's *next* Strategy and Business Operations Leader ---

DRIVING OPERATIONS, INNOVATION, AND HIGH GROWTH

705-222-1111 | carmalina@icloud.com

10+ years of impactful, diverse leadership and stakeholder engagement experience

"I leverage the City of Toronto's story to deliver overarching benefits to Torontonians."

> A determined and curious intrapreneur with a passion for solving complex business problems as an analytical visionary and project management innovator.
> Transparent and respected leader who employs unconventional strategies grounded in real-world analytics to deliver exponential profit and growth.

▶ Career milestones include outpacing competitors in down markets, guiding corporations through business turbulence, and launching innovative technology solutions with market-disruptive impact.

▶ Brand ambassador who promotes organizational goals, builds vast networks, and inspires internal and external stakeholders to collaboratively visualize the strategic direction.

LEADERSHIP STRENGTHS

Networking | Company Vision & Growth Planning | Business Strategy | Consensus Building |
Business Communications | Team Leadership | Project Management | Process Improvement |
Business-Technology Alignment | Stakeholder Relations | Partnership Building

PROFESSIONAL EXPERIENCE

The City of Toronto – Real Estate and Development Services (RE&DS)   June 2014–Current

VALUE ECONOMIST MANAGER

Reporting to the Executive, review developments for triple-bottom-line (social, economic, and environmental) benefits by researching land development, sale, and acquisition opportunities. Deliver market analysis and feasibility reports.

Select Accomplishments:

▶ Nominated for and completed the Emerging Leaders Program in March 2017.
▶ Spearheaded a new line of service and standard templates for Market Analysis and Feasibility; enabled portfolio approach to ensure department "does the right work at the right time."
▶ Orchestrated and hosted the Living Life initiative, generating over $50K in ad value on a lean $1K event budget. Positioned City as innovative and open for business.
▶ Referred $45M to management for project approvals and delivered $10M in value analysis cost-savings realized over 2.5 years.

Page 1 of 2...

Strategy: Identify this candidate as the "next" Strategy and Operations Leader, right at the top of the resume, to position her for advancement with the City of Toronto. Provide ample evidence of her relevant skills, strengths, and value throughout the resume.

Carmalina Giovese | Page 2 | 705-222-1111

Financial Industries Toronto   October 2013–June 2014

CLIENT SERVICES MANAGER

Prior to landing stellar position with the City of Toronto, managed a book of clients and coordinated various stock option and award plan market transactions with ShelfWorks software.

Select Accomplishment:

▸ Partnered with Delta Corporation client. Facilitated the training and administration of the ShelfWorks platform for smart and sustainable solutions.

Sheldon International Inc.   February 2002–September 2013

MANAGER, STRATEGIC INITIATIVES (2010–2013)
MANAGER, CLIENT SERVICES (2006–2010)
MANAGER OF RESEARCH, LAND ACQUISITIONS (2005–2006)
CLIENT SERVICES REPRESENTATIVE (2002–2005)

Track record of accomplishment led to promotion to strategic initiatives department, reporting directly to COO. Wielded deep expertise in launching continuous improvement initiatives to identify, review, and improve business operations. Managed up to 12 direct reports and project budgets of up to $7M.

Select Accomplishments:

▸ Identified, negotiated, and transferred $700K in investor savings as lead project manager.
▸ Led automation and outsourcing of post-sale communications project initiative that delivered $150K in annual savings and allowed organization to operate in compliance with newly introduced NI 11–111 regulations.
▸ Collaborated with IT to develop standard reports, improve functionality, and increase data integrity. Reduced CRM investment database error rate to less than 6% from 30%.
▸ Played key role in increasing sales by $30M for lead account manager through strategic partnership building and event networking.
▸ Coordinated large-scale roadshows and new product launches. Resulted in successful syndication of full Prospectus offerings over $35.8M.

EDUCATION & PROFESSIONAL DEVELOPMENT

Executive MBA Candidate, Toronto Institute | Expected August 2020

Project Management Professional (PMP) Certification | 2011

B.A. in Business Administration, Management, University of Canada | 2005

ADDITIONAL TRAINING:

Collaborating for Results; Crucial Conversations; Presentation Skills for Supervisors; Smarter Meetings; Increasing Self-Awareness; Effective Decision Making; Canadian Securities Course (CSC); Fearless Presentations Training Leader's Institute; Active Listening & Performance Management Training; Negotiation Skills, level 1; Interpersonal Conflict Resolution

RESUME 92: *by Carol Altomare, ACRW, MRW, CCMC, CBBSC, CJSS • www.worldclassresumes.com*

JON ROSENBERG

Yonkers, NY 10710 ◆ 914-963-8228 ◆ jrosenberg@gmail.com ◆ www.LinkedIn.com/in/jonrosenberg

ASSOCIATION EXECUTIVE

Team Leadership / Strategic Planning / Program Development / Performance Maximization / Staff Development
Strategic Communications / Relationship Building / Program Outreach / Public Relations

High-energy leader who leverages an inquisitive, "out-of-the box" nature to identify solutions …
and a passion for excellence to drive success.

Forward-thinking leader with a record of success in developing and executing strategic plans to drive organization goals while cultivating an environment of excellence. Performance-driven executive focused on maximizing program effectiveness to increase engagement of members. Respected, influential leader; a persuasive communicator who is effective in engaging others to gain support and funding for programs. A consummate relationship-builder with an extensive network of well-placed connections and a polished public presence. Critical thinker who asks the tough questions to consistently deliver results that exceed expectations.

Core Competencies:

- **Providing vision and leadership to organizations;** developing and executing plans to advance strategic goals.
- **Building teams,** attracting strong talent, and providing tools and support to deliver "best-in-class" performance.
- **Serving as public ambassador,** leveraging stellar relationship-building and presentation skills to raise organizational profile.
- **Promoting strategic initiatives,** capably demonstrating value to gain buy-in and support of key stakeholders.
- **Revitalizing organizations and programs,** capitalizing on entrepreneurial spirit to drive growth and improvement.

PROFESSIONAL EXPERIENCE

AMERICAN INSTITUTE OF CHEMICAL ENGINEERS, New York, NY   2015 to present
Executive Director
Oversee day-to-day operations of 40,000-member professional organization, leading 32 staff and managing $3 million budget. Direct program initiatives and oversee marketing, communications, finance, and technology teams. Set strategic direction of organization. Cultivate and maintain relationships across all departments.

Leveraged keen entrepreneurial mindset to refine operations …
implemented organizational and program initiatives to maximize return on investment.

Leadership & Performance Excellence

- Recruited to bring entrepreneurial approach to association and its programs. Launched staff reorganization to gain synergy, unifying programs under a single senior program manager to improve department communications and achieve more efficient utilization of resources.

- Secured 3 new full-time staff positions to help advance goals, highlighting strategic plan, association priorities, and potential return on investment in well-received presentation that was successful in gaining approval and funding.

- Launched comprehensive review of all 74 existing programs, engaging staff to define and implement appropriate performance criteria. As a result, shed underperforming programs, making way for more effective, better-targeted programs. Identified good programs that could be better and implemented changes to improve benefit to members.

- Developed relationships with industry and academia representatives to provide greater collaboration on programs.

(Continued)

Strategy: Emphasize relevant association leadership on page 1 and appropriately feature impressive business success on page 2. Communicate both hard facts and soft skills throughout the resume.

Jon Rosenberg

AMERICAN INSTITUTE OF CHEMICAL ENGINEERS

Program Successes

- Led overhaul of cumbersome, difficult-to-use online application for members, delivering user-friendly engagement website that featured expanded, role-based directory and complete suite of online management tools. Led cross-department team in gap analysis, benchmarking, and product design activities to build top-notch tool.
  - ▷ Generated 35,000+ unique visitors and nearly 2,000 new program registrations in first 6 weeks after site launch.

- Gained funding for and launched new website to meet impending member career needs.
  - ▷ Generated 19,479 unique visits (42,400 total) with 275,000 page views in 16 months.
  - ▷ Attracted 18,000 members to private LinkedIn group and 1400 registrations with free career search tool.
  - ▷ Sparked creation and delivery of a series of career resource seminars across the country.

- Launched new AICHE-branded credit card that, in only 3 months, earned ranking among the top 5 association affinity cards in the nation. Program is projected to be the association's largest revenue generator within 1 year.

CRESTLINE, Lewiston, ME   2000 to 2015
CEO
Oversaw operations of newly purchased promotional products company, growing to $15 million before selling the firm in 2015.

> Rapidly turned around performance of floundering company, driving dramatic sales improvement.
> Once righted, re-invented company to meet ongoing market challenges.

- Taking over struggling business, reversed losing performance, achieving 30% to 40% growth in each of the first 6 years. Totally retooled company, rebuilding it to a market-driven, customer-centric organization. Refreshed product line based on customer preferences to dramatically increase sales and satisfaction.

- After stabilization, launched major rebranding effort and reengineered company to thrive in tough market. Averaged 82% increase in sales in each of the last 5 years of operation, despite having more than 100 competitors.

- Built and managed high-performance sales team, recruiting and attracting seasoned, talented reps from across the industry by persuasively communicating vision and opportunity.

- Garnered industry's most prestigious "Supplier Star Award" and recognition as "Supplier Entrepreneur of the Year."

- Gained acquisition attention from world-class company based on standout growth, products, quality, service, and reputation. Participated in negotiations and successful sale of company to well-known suitor.

EDUCATION

UNIVERSITY OF CONNECTICUT, Storrs, CT
Bachelor of Arts Degree, History

RESUME 93: *by Louise Kursmark, MRW, CPRW, JCTC, CEIP, CCM* • *www.louisekursmark.com*

Stuart Campbell

Houston, TX ▪ 281-555-0001 ▪ stuartcampbell@ymail.com

Senior Philanthropy Executive

VP Foundation ▪ VP Philanthropy ▪ Chief Development Officer

Accomplished executive with 15 years of success driving strategy, influencing culture, and generating record results.

- **Built top-performing philanthropy programs at Houston Regional Hospital and TexasHealth.** Possess full range of executive leadership skills from program vision and strategy to staff recruitment and management, program development and execution, and operational oversight.

- **Pioneered new programs, built powerful relationships, and approached fund-raising challenge with entrepreneurial drive** and deep belief in the mission of the institution and the value of philanthropy.

- **Created a culture of philanthropy that produced "transformative" gifts.**

Professional Experience

VICE PRESIDENT OF FOUNDATION ▪ HOUSTON REGIONAL HOSPITAL, Houston, TX   2016–Present

Chief Development Officer for 400-bed community hospital with 2700+ employees, 700 physicians, and annual operating budget of $400M. Direct report to CEO and member of Senior Management Team for organization rated a "Best Place to Work" by Houston Chronicle, Texas Business Journal, and Fortune Magazine.

➢ **Built comprehensive philanthropy program, creating new programs and partnerships to support giving across all donor constituencies.**
- More than doubled donor base, from 1,500 to 3,252.
- Strengthened ties to the business community, recruiting a high-profile chair of the Business Partners program and sponsoring new events to build awareness and drive donations.
- Founded 15-member Advisory Council of legal/financial professionals to promote planned giving.
- Introduced leadership annual giving with the formation of the Giving Circles.

➢ **Led the most successful capital campaign in hospital history – the *Heart of Houston Campaign.*
- Raised $10M+ in 2 years.
- Secured the organization's first $1M and $2M campaign gifts.
- Achieved 100% participation from hospital leadership (Hospital and Foundation Boards, Medical Executive Committee, and Directors) for the first time in organization's history.
- Established 6 planning committees and engaged more than 120 volunteers.

➢ **Instilled a culture of philanthropy where none had existed.**
- Inspired Medical Staff to raise $3.2M through 63% participation in capital campaign.
- Rallied employees to raise $340K with 53% participation in their first employee capital campaign.
- Instituted first Grateful Patient program to engage medical staff in cultivating potential donors.

➢ **Generated record fundraising results.**
- Achieved highest fundraising revenue in institutional history: $7.1M, 92% more than prior leadership.
- In 2018, increased Annual Giving 45% over previous year through diverse programs that garnered wide support from the Board, Corporators, Medical Staff, past Donors, Patients/Families, and the general public.
- Consistently increased annual special events revenue in a challenging economy: 14% increase in 2019.

VICE PRESIDENT OF PHILANTHROPY ▪ TEXASHEALTH, Dallas, TX   2010–2016

Chief Development Officer for the state's 4th-largest healthcare system – 3500 employees, $360M operating budget. Direct report to President/CEO and member of Senior Management Team.

Strategy: Create bold introductions to numerous achievements, providing both big-picture and detail views that can be quickly skimmed and then easily read.

Stuart Campbell ▪ Page 2 ▪ 281-555-0001 ▪ stuartcampbell@ymail.com

TEXASHEALTH, continued

➤ **Built the hospital's philanthropy program from the ground up.**

- Grew overall giving from $1M in 2010 to $6.2M in 2016.
- Increased overall donors 123%, from 2,450 to 5,460.
- Led the largest capital campaign in the history of hospital and entire region. Exceeded goal of $10M by 62%.

➤ **Identified, pursued, cultivated relationship, and captured first donation from major donor whose generosity transformed the institution.**

- Secured initial $7M gift that launched the James Beeman Pediatric Center.
- Built relationship with the Beeman Foundation that led to second major gift of $35M to build a new hospital.

DEVELOPMENT OFFICER ▪ HILL COUNTRY HEALTH SYSTEM FOUNDATION, San Antonio, TX   2007–2010

Spearheaded annual fund, planned giving, community relations, volunteers, and alumni relations, reporting directly to Executive Director of the Foundation.

➤ **Improved fundraising results through programs engaging employees, volunteers, business sponsors, and the community.**

- Tripled event revenue, doubled employee giving, and increased in-kind gifts 40%.
- Engaged 100 new corporate and business sponsors.
- Founded, recruited, and led 50-member Volunteer Council and its extended committees.

EXECUTIVE DIRECTOR ▪ WE CARE, INC., San Antonio, TX   2004–2007

Directed all aspects of nonprofit with mission to prevent childhood maltreatment through community awareness, education, and advocacy. Managed 5-member staff; reported to Board of Directors.

➤ **Transformed organization by rebuilding relationships, creating new programs and partnerships, and restoring fiscal soundness.**

- Tripled operating budget to more than $500K.
- Turned around poor image and reestablished agency as major player in a number of important collaborations.

Education and Professional Designations

Master's Degree in Philanthropic Studies – University of Houston

AHP Fellow, 2016 • Association for Healthcare Philanthropy

Certified Fund Raising Executive, 2012 ▪ Association of Fund Raising Professionals

Bachelor of Arts in Biology, 2000 ▪ University of Texas, Austin, TX

Board and Professional Affiliations

Board Member, Ex Officio ▪ Houston Regional Hospital	2016–Present
Member, AHP (Association for Healthcare Philanthropy)	2012–Present
Board Member, TAHP (Texas Association for Healthcare Philanthropy)	2007–Present

- Presenter, TAHP Conference, 2015, 2019

RESUME 94: by Stephanie Clark, MRW, MCRS • www.newleafresumes.ca

PHOEBE
HALLMAN |MBA | CFRE

416.555.1111 | phoebe@charitablenotes.com

linkedin.com/in/phoebeh

EXECUTIVE LEADERSHIP | NOT-FOR-PROFIT FUNDRAISING & OPERATIONAL EXPERTISE

Astute strategies build operational effectiveness. | Award-winning appeals drive charitable sector donations.

Executive Summary: Seasoned Thought Leadership, Trendsetting Fundraising

Tenacious, respected, and connected charity executive who has earned a reputation for credibility and trust sustained throughout 20 years of award-winning fundraising and operational leadership.

Driven by passion for community health and genuine desire to build people – in my team, my organization, and my community. Strong chairperson, avid mentor, altruistic volunteer, and decisive and ethical leader.

- Blend traditional not-for-profit methodologies with business-focused tactics, introducing tremendous operational savings and leveraging data to identify funding opportunities.
- Evaluated as *natural born leader* according to Myers-Briggs assessment as "Commander." As an ENTJ who behaves as an ENFJ, balance natural authority with inspiring and guiding others to improve community.
- Inspired by the motto "Great is the work that remains to be accomplished!" (Sylvia Pankhurst), which motivates my own involvement as active sector mentor and community volunteer. "I walk the talk."

"Phoebe is a passionate leader … seasoned fundraising professional with a focus on results … boldy takes on causes others might consider too challenging or awkward … removes barriers … generously shares knowledge."

Professional Experience: $100M+ in Donations; $1.3M in Savings

CHARITEE CENTRAL, MONTREAL, QUEBEC, CANADA

DEVELOPMENT DIRECTOR | Report to Executive Director   2015—Present

Mandate: To reinvigorate fundraising program with a goal of growing fundraising by a minimum of 15% each year – with $200K as a 1st year goal – leading staff in Fundraising Advisory and Golf Tournament Committees.

- Established fundraising program. Developed policies, procedures, donor prospect list, volunteers, programs, communications, and budgets, leveraging capabilities of relationship management system.
- Sourced community to tap into best practices for fundraising in this sector; attended annual conference to build relationships and acquire, as well as share, knowledge.
- Re-energized fundraising priority project, stalled for 4 years, with only $15K raised. Within first year, achieved $225K toward goal of $300K.
- **Results**:
  - Closed >$1.8M in gifts in 13 months, including $1M and 3x 6-figure gifts.
  - Supported colleague's goal to turn around declining education program enrollment by facilitating $425K in new gifts to underwrite a substantially improved program.
  - Developed and executed successful donor stewardship program; reduced operational expenses.

⊃

Strategy: Provide a multi-layered view of this nonprofit executive by including endorsements and references to her LinkedIn profile, where more recommendations can be found.

THE COMMUNITY FOUNDATION

Foundation supports vital services and strengthens its work in social innovation, enhancing self-sufficiency, promoting well-being, and reducing poverty through health services, housing, child care, and more.

EXECUTIVE DIRECTOR   2010–2015

Mandate: To strengthen strategic direction of the program, meet elevated fundraising goals, and improve interactions and relationships with Board of Directors, local community services, and housing boards.

- Led team to achieve "Excellence in Fundraising" award (Association of Fundraising Professionals) in recognition of operational savings and tripling of cash revenue to $2.7M.
- Restructured Board – now noted as among the top-performing Boards in Montreal, with 100% giving and outperforming Boards of larger, more prominent charities.
- Partnered closely with TDBank, identifying and linking its business goals to Community's work and fundraising goals. Successfully introduced women's philanthropy as a market opportunity.
- Increased brand awareness through an award-winning media campaign (DDB Canada), negotiating a pro-bono campaign that earned 8M media impressions and developed a major gift donor.

CANADIAN NATIONAL ORGANIZATION

NATIONAL DIRECTOR, Major Gifts   2007–2010
INTERIM DIRECTOR, Ontario, INTERIM NATIONAL DIRECTOR, Corporate Giving   2006–2007
NATIONAL DIRECTOR, Personal Giving   2004–2006

Managed team of 50 in 11 geographic locations and supervised $400K in annual government and foundation grants, leading a variety of giving portfolios during a time of tremendous leadership and organizational change.

- Promoted through series of increasingly responsible roles, earning recognition as largest individual fundraiser (more than $100M) and building programs that ensured short- and long-term financial stability.
- Slashed expense budget by 50% without loss of revenue.
- Structured unprecedented, multi-stakeholder partnership leading to a $multi-million government funding initiative that attained Health Canada approval.

"Phoebe is a creative, strategic and innovative thinker ... top of the class ... positive, curious, humble, vibrant and dynamic ... fantastic strategist, best combination of strategic and detail oriented."

Education and Executive Development

Schulich School of Business, York University | MBA Diversity Fellow: Non-Profit Management Specialization (2009)
Toronto University | BPhil: Magna cum Laude, Phi Beta Kappa, Community Service Award (2006)
Institute for Corporate Directors | Not for Profit Directors Program (2012)
Certified Fund Raising Executive (1996–Present)

For details on awards, volunteering, and as thought leader, visit my LinkedIn page at linkedin.com/in/phoebeh

Professional Awards: Continued Excellence in Fundraising, Planned Giving, and Events

Recent Professional Volunteer Experience: Deeply rooted in philanthropy

Speaker, Lecturer, Panelist, Author: Sector thought-leader and disruptor of status-quo

RESUME 95: by Emily Wong, ACRW, CPRW • www.wordsofdistinction.net

Theodore Woods

301.555.5555 ▪ twoods22@gmail.com ▪ www.linkedin.com/in/twoods22

Community Advocate ▪ Award-Winning Nonprofit Executive ▪ Board Leader

DONOR OUTREACH…ORGANIZATIONAL TRANSFORMATION…COMMUNITY ENGAGEMENT

➢ **Nationally recognized Community Advocate** who champions change through collaboration and research-backed public policy initiatives that drive improvements in early child development, holistic family health, and general human services.

➢ **Transformational Leader** who excels at steering cross-cultural organizations through complex transitions to improve organizational effectiveness and community engagement.

➢ **Influential Fundraiser** who leverages extensive donor network to mobilize support and achieve ambitious financial goals that help educate and lift entire local communities out of poverty.

Strategic Planning

P&L & Budgeting

Fund Development

Organizational Change

Innovative Solutions

Governance

AWARDS & RECOGNITION

Mellon Lifetime Achievement Award in HIV Services and Advocacy—2018

Honorary Doctor of Public Service, Rutgers University—2014

Frederick County Impact Change Award, Tech Innovators—2014

Pioneer in Community Building (PCB)—2009

Martin Eldridge Performance Award from the American Leadership Forum Forum—2004

CAREER HIGHLIGHTS

CEO | THE HEALTH TRUST | Frederick, MD   2007–Present

Led the strategic direction of a $250M foundation focusing on prevention and wellness programs that address oral health, nutrition, HIV, health insurance, homelessness, and aging, with $4M in annual grantmaking funds. Direct Reports: COO, CFO, HR, Communications, VP Fund Development, and Executive Director of Destinations.

▪ Championed sweeping cultural and organizational changes—including the establishment and scaling of a corporate wellness program that included benefits, work environment upgrades, and on-site services.

▪ Recognized by Tech Innovators as the 2014 Frederick County Impact Challenge winner for the Good Health: Good Life campaign—an urban agriculture initiative designed to improve nutrition through availability of affordable produce.

▪ Earned national recognition for leading a campaign that raised $22M and built a coalition to bring fluoride to the drinking water of 300K residents in the City of Frederick, the largest city in the state previously without water fluoridation.

▪ Worked in partnership with a coalition of stakeholders as the initial funder to pass Measure A, a $950M housing bond of which $750M was dedicated to housing for chronically homeless residents.

▪ Partnered with Yale business professor to introduce grant funding for local nonprofit and government sectors. Grants included Success and Beyond, a $12M social impact funding model for chronic drug abusers.

PRESIDENT | PRINCIPAL CONSULTANT | KEYNOTE SPEAKER | HEALTH CHANNELS | Frederick, MD   2000–Present

Founded national consulting firm that specializes in delivering strategic solutions and project guidance to nonprofits and government agencies. Provide expertise and advocacy for health, family support, and early childhood education.

▪ Designed and facilitated stakeholders in a 9-month process for a Universal Access to Early Care, Education, and Health Pilot Project in 2 low-income school districts with $3.2M in county government funding.

▪ Developed a plan and the contacts to re-open a $15M Laboratory Early Childhood Center at a local community college and position them to become a Center of Excellence in professional development.

Strategy: Structure the resume to draw attention to many different areas of distinction—awards and recognition, strong career achievements, board and community leadership, publications—that amply demonstrate that this executive walks the talk as a community advocate.

NATIONAL TRAINER | ADULT SERVICES PROJECT | Baltimore, MD — 2005–2007

Developed and implemented Adult Leadership Institute (ALI) for the Janice Wright-Smithson Foundation in Baltimore and surrounding counties. Strengthened leadership capacity through family-focused support principles.

EXECUTIVE DIRECTOR | DOMINION FAMILY SERVICES | Baltimore, MD — 2000–2005

Directed nonprofit agency ($1.5M budget/30 staff). Transformed organization from a childcare center serving 85 children to a comprehensive child development and family services program that served 2K children by approaching families holistically to assess challenges and provide solutions. Raised $2M to send 750 children to camp annually.

BOARD LEADERSHIP & COMMUNITY OUTREACH

University of Maryland College of Arts and Science: Leadership Advisory Board	2016–Present
University of Maryland, Filbert Center for Education: Advisory Board Member	2005–2016
Frederick County Blue Ribbon Commission for Diversity and Inclusion: Chair	2016
Donald Fields Endowment: Education Fellow	2015–Present
Legacy & Enterprise Enrichment Council: Board Member	2015–Present
Children's Arts Museum: Advisory: Board Member	2016–Present
Frederick County Public Schools: National Board Chair	2007–Present
Baltimore City Commissioner	2001–2007

TEACHING EXPERIENCE

DEAN'S EXECUTIVE PROFESSOR OF PUBLIC HEALTH & ADJUNCT LECTURER | UNIVERSITY OF BALTIMORE — 2000–Present

Design and facilitate year-long seminar and internship in Public Health Leadership.

ADJUNCT INSTRUCTOR, CHILD DEVELOPMENT AND EDUCATION DEPARTMENT | MORGAN STATE UNIVERSITY — 2000–Present

Provide instruction in child development, health, adolescent psychology, educational leadership, and family engagement.

PUBLICATIONS

Homelessness Inspires Fear, Discomfort—But it Can Inspire Solutions, Baltimore News Op-ed. August 2018.

Food as Relief: Curating Culinary Experience for Nonprofit Leadership
A Case Study of Food Pantries at Children's Art Museum of Baltimore, cited as thought leader. March 2017.

The Power of Actionable Leadership, Nonprofit Leaders in Health. December 2015.

Health Care and Racial Inequality, Baltimore News Op-ed. April 2011.

EDUCATION

Master of Science, Counseling Psychology, UNIVERSITY OF MARYLAND

Bachelor of Science, Developmental Psychology, UNIVERSITY OF BALTIMORE

Strategic Perspectives in Nonprofit Management, HARVARD BUSINESS SCHOOL

Effective Measurement of Nonprofit Organizations, HARVARD KENNEDY SCHOOL OF GOVERNMENT

Executive Residency Program for Nonprofit Leadership, PENN STATE UNIVERSITY

Theodore Woods   301.555.5555 ▪ twoods22@gmail.com ▪ www.linkedin.com/in/twoods22

Part III

LinkedIn Profile Strategies and Formats

Writing Your LinkedIn Profile

A recruiter once mentioned:

"If you're not on LinkedIn, you don't exist."

Those are very wise words for every manager and executive, whether actively engaged in a job search or working to build a professional profile for future opportunities.

At its very foundation, LinkedIn is a social network for professionals. It is the business-suited version of Facebook, Instagram, and other sites that promote interaction, sharing, and self-expression.

When it comes to job search and career management, your LinkedIn profile is as important as your resume. That's because millions of people use LinkedIn, it is the go-to resource for executive recruiters, and your LinkedIn profile will almost always be the first thing that people find when they search for you online.

Equally important, LinkedIn itself is a vast and powerful network. It offers tools and resources that make it easy for you to find and connect with people, broaden your existing web of contacts, and penetrate your target employers.

What's more, LinkedIn is often the first site that people access to find out about *you*—either before or after they've seen your resume or met you in person. It is an opportunity for you to share *more* and *more insightful* information about yourself, your value, and your executive brand.

As recruiters, employers, and job seekers have discovered its value, LinkedIn has grown exponentially, from 37 million members in 2009 to 610 million members as we write this book in 2019. Today a LinkedIn profile is not just "nice" to have; it's a necessity for professionals who are serious about their careers and—of particular relevance to you—in the market for new professional challenges.

Why Not Copy and Paste Your Resume?

We get it. You've spent a lot of time and effort creating a great executive resume that sells your expertise and your value. Why can't you simply copy it into the relevant sections of your profile?

Certainly that's an option, but we don't recommend it. Here's why:

- As mentioned, many readers will view your profile after seeing your resume. If your profile simply reiterates what they already know, they've wasted their time and you've wasted the opportunity to share even more compelling and relevant information.

- LinkedIn is a different medium than a resume, with its traditional structure, fairly formal language, and page limitations. As you'll read later in this chapter, we recommend a different writing style than your resume and the inclusion of different information to help your readers go beyond your resume, learn more about your career, and feel a connection to you.

- The structure of LinkedIn makes it easy for readers to get a quick bird's-eye view of you and your career and then click to "see more" in any section. You have a prime opportunity to share more information because, when they click through, they are already interested.

Now that you understand the value of a powerful LinkedIn profile, let's explore how to write it. And don't worry—all of the material that you uncovered and wrote about in your resume will come into play. You're simply telling your story in a different way, with different details, and in a different tone and writing style.

Four Keys to a Winning LinkedIn Profile

As you begin to write your profile, focus on the following 4 elements. Each is important to create a profile that will attract, interest, and engage your readers.

KEY #1: KEYWORDS

On LinkedIn, perhaps even more so than in your resume, keywords are king. Recruiter and employer searches are keyword-driven, so to be found for appropriate positions, you must include all of the relevant terms throughout your profile.

As we've discussed with regard to your resume, keywords are really nothing more than the language of your profession. They describe your knowledge and expertise. They establish that you have worked in particular functions and industries, held specific responsibilities, have a certain education level, and so much more.

There is no magic, one-size-fits-all approach to keyword optimization on LinkedIn. Use your judgment in integrating keywords into the various sections of your profile. When you've finished writing it, you'll find that keywords naturally fall in everywhere.

As well, consider adding a keyword list at the bottom of your Summary/About section and at the end of each position description in the Experience section. You'll increase your keyword density and reinforce the *right* terms for each job you've held.

Review Chapter 1 for a deeper discussion on keywords, how to find them, and how to use them in your career marketing materials.

KEY #2: PERSONALITY AND INSIGHT

Your LinkedIn profile is not your resume. It can be more personal and less formal. You can share details that don't obviously relate to your professional qualifications but that can help readers understand your leadership style, how you communicate, how you build camaraderie, what excites you or keeps you up at night, what makes you laugh, and other insights into who you are, what you do, and why you do it. It's the *extra* information that will often attract people to you.

Not sure where to start or how to do that? Ask yourself a few questions to spark ideas beyond typical resume thinking, and use what you uncover to inject your personality into the content that you create for LinkedIn.

- How are you different from other candidates for the same positions?
- How do you approach challenges?
- What gives you the most professional and personal satisfaction?
- What do you enjoy doing—on or off the job?
- How do others (your staff, your bosses, your family and friends) describe you?
- How do you bring your personality to work?
- How can you reveal your character?
- How can you help readers understand who you are?
- Who or what has influenced you in your life?
- What motivates you and why?

KEY #3: STORYTELLING

Humans are hard-wired to respond to stories. Stories stir emotions. They activate multiple areas of our brains. And perhaps most importantly, stories are what people remember (over facts and figures).

When you include stories in your career marketing messages—your resume and cover letter, your interviews, and your LinkedIn profile—you instantly make yourself more memorable and more distinctive.

As well, you may create positive perceptions of who you are that cannot be ascertained from a resume or straightforward career facts. You can seem more likeable, funnier, wittier, more sympathetic, more human.

To spark your thinking around stories you might include in your LinkedIn profile, ask yourself questions like these:

- How did you get where you are today?
- How did you choose your line of work?
- How has your past led to your present (and future)?
- What is the accomplishment that you're most proud of?

Then, think about what each story illustrates about you, what themes from your background might connect, and how to help readers see you in your desired future roles. Use the stories that support your current objectives and align with your personal brand.

There are many ways to incorporate stories into your profile. Some stories are brief excerpts that help frame an experience or achievement. Others are complete "origin stories" that take up the entire Summary/About section. Still others provide context for your career choices.

As with all of your career messages, use good judgment in what you share and how you tell your stories. LinkedIn is a *professional* networking site, and everything in your profile, including your stories, should bolster your professional image. But don't be afraid to reveal a bit more about yourself than perhaps you are used to sharing. Authenticity is an important element of your profile, and stories are a great way to exude your genuine self.

KEY #4: STRUCTURE

Just as in your resume, how you structure your profile can affect how easily and how often it is read. Keep these guidelines in mind as you are writing, editing, and polishing your profile.

- **Write in first person and use the word "I."** While it's not a hard-and-fast rule that your profile must be in first person, we strongly recommend it. It creates a friendlier and more social tone than writing about yourself in the third person (using "he" or "she" instead of "I").

- **Use natural language—not "resume speak."** When we write resumes, we deliberately use a succinct writing style to get quickly to the point. In addition to the word "I," we often omit modifiers such as a, an, the, and our. That's fine for a resume—in fact, it's expected. On LinkedIn a more relaxed, conversational style is appropriate. However, relaxed doesn't mean sloppy! Never forget the rules of grammar, spelling, and punctuation.

- **Write in short bursts of information.** Just as in your resume, keep in mind how people actually read: They skim, they seek to pick up information quickly, and they move on if their attention isn't quickly captured. When writing your profile, break up big chunks of text into multiple short paragraphs. Allow ample white space so that readers can quickly absorb one bite of information and then move on to the next.

- **Feel free to use all of the available space.** LinkedIn has strict character allowances for each section of the profile. (They are discussed later in this chapter when we delve into writing specifics.) Some of these allowances are quite expansive. But, as mentioned, readers will see only the first 3 lines of content and then must click to "see more." You can give it to them!

- **Capture attention in the first 3 lines.** What can you say to entice readers to want to "see more"? If you don't engage their interest quickly, they may never take the time to learn more about you.

- **Add emphasis the old-fashioned (typewriter) way.** On LinkedIn you can't use the font enhancements and design elements that you likely employed in your resume. You can use ALL CAPS, and you can use various symbols to create borders and bullets. We recommend that you do so. They really help to add distinction and readability to your profile.

- **Build your visibility through active engagement.** Once your profile is complete, you can multiply its effectiveness by increasing your activity on LinkedIn. Share updates, publish articles, comment on posts from your network, join groups, follow industry leaders, and otherwise maintain an active presence. Investing just a few minutes a day will build your online image quickly and professionally.

Tips for Writing Major Sections of Your Profile

The best way to demonstrate what makes for a winning LinkedIn profile is to show you a few samples—and in the next chapter, we do just that. But it makes sense to briefly touch on best practices for each of the main sections (Headline, Summary/About, and Experience) as well as guidelines for the remainder of your profile.

Headline (120-character limit, including spaces)

Your Headline appears immediately under your name and photo at the top of your profile. The default content is your current or most recent job title ... but you can change that.

We recommend a headline that still quickly tells readers "who you are" but goes beyond simply your job title. You might edit your headline to include:

- Areas of interest or influence
- Distinguishing credentials, qualifications, or awards
- A career achievement highlight
- Your "personal brand"—what you're known for
- Your key areas of expertise

And, by the way, we do recommend that your profile include a photo—a professional-looking headshot. It's a red flag if you don't include a photo, so don't eliminate yourself from consideration instantly.

Summary/About (2000-character limit, including spaces)

The default for this section is blank. Yet it may be the most important section of your profile. It is certainly the most read. Why not give your readers something interesting and informative?

There is no single formula for writing the Summary/About section, as you'll see in the samples that follow. Here are a few guidelines and content ideas.

- Incorporate keywords in your content and possibly in a separate listing at the end of the section.
- Tell a story or stories to give readers insight into who you are, why you've been successful, what motivates and excites you, and the value you bring to your next role.
- Mention a few of your most notable career achievements—be specific.
- Consider touching on intangibles such as leadership skills (how you get teams and people to align behind your vision), communication and persuasion skills, public speaking talents, creativity, work ethic, or any others that help readers understand how you work and why you've been successful.
- Connect the dots from your past experiences to your current goals/future career. This is extremely helpful, particularly if you are changing careers or industries. What caused that choice? Tell the story so readers understand the connection.
- If you are still employed, paint the picture of someone who is a top performer in your current role. Certainly don't say anything about looking for your next job.

- If you are not employed, we still don't recommend that you announce that you are "open to opportunities." Of course you are—who isn't? Instead, focus on your story and your value.

- When listing your employer name, use the drop-down list to populate the exact company name whenever possible. Your profile will then feature the company logo, and that can be a strong and instant identifier.

- Be strategic—be certain that your story line, the achievements you've highlighted, and the insights you've shared are all congruent with your current career objectives.

Experience (2000-character limit, including spaces, for each position)

The challenge in writing your experience is presenting essentially the same information as in your resume but in a different way.

An added complication is that, because LinkedIn is a public profile, you may not want to share financial and other details that are featured prominently in your resume. You do want to give concrete examples of your effectiveness and success, however.

As you rethink how to present your career story, these prompts may help you come up with a framework that feels fresh and differentiated from your resume.

- Share context around each position. Why did you take the job? What was the challenge or opportunity? What did you do about it?

- Highlight major projects, challenges, assignments—perhaps similarly to your resume, but in a more relaxed, storytelling style.

- Share specific results whenever possible, because specifics are impressive and memorable.

- Connect to or continue themes that you wrote about in your Summary/About section. For example, if you talked about being energized by tough challenges, frame each position in the context of a steep challenge, how you conquered it, and what the results were.

- Consider closing out each position with a list of relevant keywords.

Additional Profile Sections

Most of the remainder of your profile is self-explanatory, but here are a few tips:

- In the **Education** section, use the drop-down box to select your college or university and, if appropriate, the specific school at which you studied. When you do that, your profile will include the school logo—a nice visual enhancement and a way for fellow alumni to instantly feel a connection to you.

- Don't hesitate to add stories and details to your **Education** section if you believe they will help you. Let's say you studied at a university for 3 years but never finished your degree. A brief story can overcome a potential objection. For example, "I left school after 3 years when my startup reached $1M in sales and I needed to devote 100% of my time to running, building, and ultimately selling the company."

- Re-order your **Skills and Endorsements** if need be so that the top 3 shown are indeed your most valuable and relevant skills. This is particularly important if you are changing careers, changing industries, or looking for a big step up in responsibility. Many of your contacts may know you and endorse you for "Project Finance," for example, but you would prefer that "Corporate Strategy" be the first skill listed. You can put it there.

- Do your best to secure several **Recommendations.** These must be written by others—you can't populate that section yourself. You might need to reach out to a few past and/or current colleagues and ask them to write a testimonial for you.

- Write **Recommendations** for others. These recommendations also populate your profile, and writing endorsements for others may prompt them to write one for you. And it's a nice way to initiate some networking outreach.

- In the **Interests** section, choose companies, colleges/universities, and thought leaders to follow. These listings will help populate your daily feed, provide a regular source of business and industry news, and expand your networking opportunities.

LinkedIn Profile Samples

In the following chapter, you will find 8 LinkedIn profiles, each one preceded by its companion resume. You can see the wide variety of styles in which the profiles are written and structured to attract attention, provide insight, express personal brand, and showcase career successes.

Then, look at the resume that accompanies each profile. Note what's similar and what's different, how the 2 documents complement each other, and how they showcase different facets of the same person. Your own resume and LinkedIn profile should also work together to tell your story, convey your value, and advance your career.

Once complete, you'll be all set to launch your job search with resume and LinkedIn profile in hand!

CHAPTER 14

Portfolio of LinkedIn Profiles

- Emergency Preparedness Director
- Biotechnology Consultant
- Global Merchandising Director
- General Counsel
- Software Engineering Executive
- Global Sales Executive
- National Marketing Manager
- CEO and President

TRAVIS T. WAGNER

312-345-6789 | travis.wagner@comcast.net
Lincoln, IL | LinkedIn Profile

▪ *Environmental Health* ▪ *Public Health* ▪ *Emergency Preparedness* ▪ *Food Safety*

Targeted Role: **Director of Quality Management**

**Forecasting long-range needs while managing short-range objectives and shifting resources.
Making timely decisions, initiating plans to solve problems,
and guiding others towards shared objectives.**

**COMPETENCIES: Efficiency Improvement | Stakeholder Relations | Education/Training | Risk Management
Safety | Culture Change | Staff Development | Performance Improvement | Negotiation
Fiscal Planning/Budgeting | Public Speaking | Written/Verbal Communication**

Emergency Planning & Resource Management	**Developed a volunteer 40+-member Medical Reserve Corp and joined a regional preparedness and emergency response coalition.**
Leadership	**Reinvigorated the team's culture by resolving morale issues, retraining employees, and setting clear expectations.**
Crisis Communications	**Department of Public Health Public Information Officer – Logan County, with prior experience as PIO for two local health departments.**

PROFESSIONAL EXPERIENCE

LOGAN COUNTY HEALTH DEPARTMENT | *Lincoln, IL*   3/2013–Present
EMERGENCY PREPAREDNESS DIRECTOR
Manage all Environmental Health Division operations—development, planning, implementation, reporting, and evaluation. Coordinate, execute, and track $900K annually in Local Health Protection and Public Health Emergency Preparedness grant deliverables.

- Lowered foodborne illness risks by implementing the Federal Food Code across 700+ restaurants. Extensive undertaking took nine months and involved retraining inspectors and upgrading hardware/software.
- Procured $340K in grants for power generators and mobile evacuation trailers to proactively ensure essential operations would continue in emergencies.
- Conserved resources during two-year budget impasse. Prioritized resources, reduced staff hours, and cut all non-essential expenses to accomplish grant deliverables.

Recruited to serve as **Midwest Region Public Information Officer**. Tasked with disseminating critical information to entire 25-county region.

LOGAN COUNTY HEALTH DEPARTMENT | *Lincoln, IL*   9/2011–3/2013
REGIONAL MANAGER / PUBLIC INFORMATION OFFICER
Oversaw the rollout of a new Affordable Care Act healthcare program. Led the region in education, coordination, and technical support (15 health departments serving a 25-county area). Monitored outreach and community education progress as well as fiscal performance of each In-Person Counselor (IPC) agency.

- Increased health insurance enrollees by 38%, bringing 8000+ individuals from uninsured to insured.
- Educated and supported the public on their health insurance options by training 25 in-person counselors.
- Collaborated with internal and external stakeholders, including the Illinois Department of Health, the CDC, and other Health Department Administrators and Environmental Health Directors.

Strategy: Create an engaging career summary with multple textual and visual components. Use call-out boxes and graphics to emphasize this candidate's most significant achievements.

TRAVIS T. WAGNER | 312-345-6789 | travis.wagner@comcast.net

BASCOM INSURANCE CENTER | *Lincoln, IL*   4/2007–9/2011
PRESIDENT
Sold automobile, fire, life, property, medical, and dental insurance policies to businesses and individuals. Managed day-to-day tactical and long-term strategies. Customized insurance programs and ensured policy requirements were filled. Coached and mentored seven staff members on individual performances.

- Brought company from start-up to nearly $3M in premiums in less than 10 years.
- Monitored insurance claims to ensure they were settled equitably for both the client and the insurer.
- Increased clients and developed a local pipeline by networking within the community.

EDUCATION

DEPAUL UNIVERSITY | *Chicago, IL*
Master of Business Administration (MBA) – Operations Management

UNIVERSITY OF ILLINOIS | *Champaign, IL*
Bachelor of Science (BS) – Education

PUBLIC SERVICE EXPERIENCE

LOGAN COUNTY BOARD | *Lincoln, IL*   2014–2018
BOARD MEMBER
Budgeted, appropriated, and oversaw the management of funds. Reviewed and approved tax levies and managed county properties. Provided executive oversight of county agencies and construction/maintenance of public buildings.

- Member of the Logan County Board of Health and the Emergency Management Agency.
- Helped pass county safety tax referendum raising $700K yearly to support public safety capital projects.

LINCOLN BOARD OF EDUCATION | *Lincoln, IL*   2010–2015
VICE PRESIDENT   2013–2015
Oversaw long-range strategic planning to promote student achievement. Approved budgets, secured financial support, and reviewed financial statements. Sanctioned and negotiated collective bargaining agreements and other contracts.

- Helped direct a 10,000-square-foot addition to the middle school.
- Member of search committee that hired several key staff members, including Superintendent and two Principals.

EMERGENCY MANAGEMENT EDUCATION AND CERTIFICATION

2019:	CDC–Crisis and Emergency Risk Communication
2018:	An Introduction to Exercises	Mass Fatalities Planning and Response for Rural Communities	National Weather Service SKYWARN Spotter	Homeland Security Exercise and Evaluation Program (HSEEP)	CDC Inventory Management and Tracking System (IMATS)
2017:	National Incident Management System (NIMS) Introduction	Introduction to Incident Command System	ICS for Single Resources and Initial Action Incident	National Response Framework Introduction	Intermediate ICS – Illinois Emergency Management Association	Advanced ICS – Illinois Emergency Management Association	Emergency Support Function (ESF) – Public Health and Medical Services	NIMS Multi-Agency Coordination System (MACS)	National Incident Management System (NIMS) Public Information Systems	NIMS Resource Management	Emergency Support Function – External Affairs: A New Approach to Emergency Communication and Information Distribution

Travis Wagner LinkedIn Portfolio

Headline:
Emergency Preparedness Director: Environmental Health Administration | Public Health Management | Disaster Response

About
I manage Environmental Health and Emergency Preparedness divisional operations, focusing on efficiency improvements and staff development. I am responsible for the timely implementation of the Public Health Emergency Preparedness Grant deliverables. Strengths of mine include the ability to see the big picture and forecast long-range needs while adapting to short-range objectives and managing shifting resources.

▶ DIVERSE BACKGROUND: I have owned a successful insurance and financial services agency. Starting a business from scratch was tough. It taught me to think on my feet and perform well under pressure. In ten years, I built a successful agency and later sold it for a profit. This insurance experience helped me gain entry into the field of public health. As Regional Manager/Public Information Officer, I oversaw a group of insurance counselors executing the Affordable Care Act rollout.

▶ LOCAL GOVERNMENT: Through my experience serving on county and school boards, I have gained knowledge of how local governments work, allowing me to more effectively form partnerships with them.

▶ SERVANT LEADERSHIP: I try to focus primarily on the growth and well-being of those I lead, putting their needs first and helping them develop and perform as highly as possible. My staff appreciates my easy-going nature and willingness to tell it like it is.

▶ CRITICAL THINKING DURING STRESSFUL SITUATIONS: Some folks run from a fire and some run into it. I enjoy running into it and being prepared to handle the consequences. I pride myself on being a problem solver in high-pressure situations.

▶ CUSTOMER SERVICE: Taking good care of the public we serve and developing trustful relationships is critical. I'm passionate about making a difference in people's lives. Being involved with public health and especially emergency management/preparedness is very rewarding.

My wife and I are relocating to Chicago this fall. I would love to connect via LinkedIn or at travis.wagner@comcast.net.

Experience
LOGAN COUNTY HEALTH DEPARTMENT | *Lincoln, NE* | 3/2013-Present
ENVIRONMENTAL HEALTH / EMERGENCY PREPAREDNESS DIRECTOR
I manage Environmental Health Division operations including development, planning, implementation, reporting, and evaluation. I coordinate, execute, and track grant deliverables ($900K) and assist in budget development/monitoring. A central part of my job is directing the agency's response to public health emergencies.

For the past year, I have served as the Northeast Region Public Information Officer. My primary responsibility is to release information from the Illinois Department of Public Health to the Logan Region local health departments.

Strategy: Add keywords to the headline to brand this candidate for positions he is targeting—and improve his searchability by hiring managers and recruiters. In the summary, quickly engage readers with his professional story. Highlight his diverse experience and success performing under pressure.

ACHIEVEMENTS:

• In Illinois, the most significant change in Environmental Health has been the adoption of the Federal Food Code. Our division implemented the new code across 360 restaurants. This extensive undertaking took nine months and involved retraining inspectors and upgrading hardware/software.

• Developed an Emergency Response Healthcare Coalition to ensure all entities involved in emergency management work together.

• Conserved resources during the two-year budget impasse. Prioritized resources, reduced staff hours, and cut all non-essential expenses to accomplish grant deliverables.

• Increased productivity and saved money by centralizing Environmental Health operations.

• Collaborated with internal and external stakeholders, including the Tennessee Department of Health, the CDC, and other Health Department Administrators and Environmental Health Directors.

I'm known for making timely decisions and preventing emergencies by proactively preparing for them. Former managers have commended my ability to perform well under pressure and communicate well with stakeholders inside and outside of our agency. My relationships at the Illinois Department of Public Health and the Logan Preparedness and Response Coalition have helped our department procure grants for backup power generators and a mobile evacuation and sheltering trailer.

LOGAN COUNTY HEALTH DEPARTMENT | *Lincoln, IL* | 9/2011-3/2013
REGIONAL MANAGER / PUBLIC INFORMATION OFFICER
As Regional Manager I oversaw the rollout of the Affordable Care Act healthcare program. Our team led the region in education, coordination, and technical support (15 health departments serving a 25-county area). I was responsible for monitoring outreach and community education progress as well as the fiscal performance of each In-Person Counselor (IPC) agency.

ACHIEVEMENTS:

• Trained 25 in-person counselors (many with limited experience) to assist with new insurance regulations and make product recommendations.

• Increased health insurance enrollees by 38%, bringing 8000+ individuals from uninsured to insured.

BASCOM INSURANCE CENTER | *Lincoln, IL* | 4/2007-09/2011
PRESIDENT
I owned and ran a successful insurance agency, selling automobile, fire, life, property, medical, and dental insurance policies. I customized insurance programs for clients and ensured policy requirements were filled.

ACHIEVEMENTS:

• Brought company from start-up to nearly $1M in premiums in less than 10 years.

• Increased clients and developed a local pipeline by networking within the community and building lists of prospective clients.

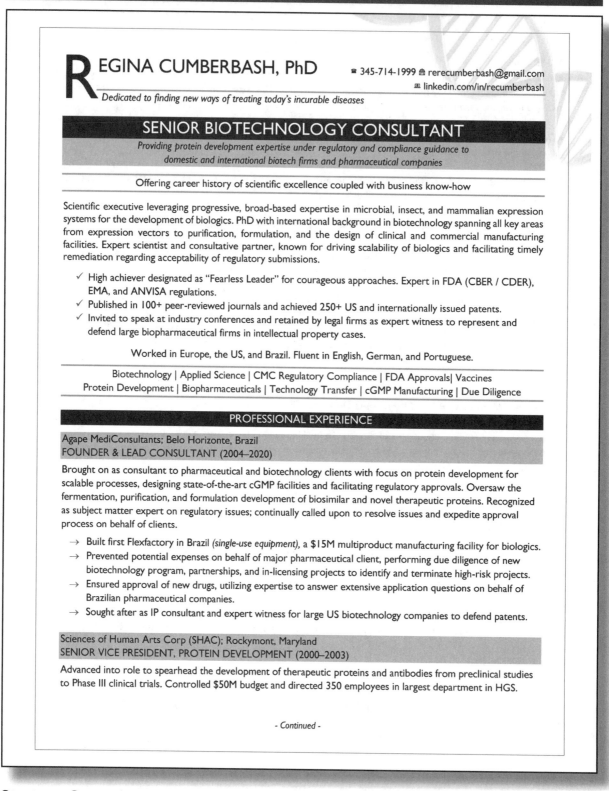

REGINA CUMBERBASH, PhD

☎ 345-714-1999 ⌨ rerecumberbash@gmail.com
🖳 linkedin.com/in/recumberbash

Dedicated to finding new ways of treating today's incurable diseases

SENIOR BIOTECHNOLOGY CONSULTANT

Providing protein development expertise under regulatory and compliance guidance to domestic and international biotech firms and pharmaceutical companies

Offering career history of scientific excellence coupled with business know-how

Scientific executive leveraging progressive, broad-based expertise in microbial, insect, and mammalian expression systems for the development of biologics. PhD with international background in biotechnology spanning all key areas from expression vectors to purification, formulation, and the design of clinical and commercial manufacturing facilities. Expert scientist and consultative partner, known for driving scalability of biologics and facilitating timely remediation regarding acceptability of regulatory submissions.

✓ High achiever designated as "Fearless Leader" for courageous approaches. Expert in FDA (CBER / CDER), EMA, and ANVISA regulations.
✓ Published in 100+ peer-reviewed journals and achieved 250+ US and internationally issued patents.
✓ Invited to speak at industry conferences and retained by legal firms as expert witness to represent and defend large biopharmaceutical firms in intellectual property cases.

Worked in Europe, the US, and Brazil. Fluent in English, German, and Portuguese.

Biotechnology | Applied Science | CMC Regulatory Compliance | FDA Approvals| Vaccines
Protein Development | Biopharmaceuticals | Technology Transfer | cGMP Manufacturing | Due Diligence

PROFESSIONAL EXPERIENCE

Agape MediConsultants; Belo Horizonte, Brazil
FOUNDER & LEAD CONSULTANT (2004–2020)

Brought on as consultant to pharmaceutical and biotechnology clients with focus on protein development for scalable processes, designing state-of-the-art cGMP facilities and facilitating regulatory approvals. Oversaw the fermentation, purification, and formulation development of biosimilar and novel therapeutic proteins. Recognized as subject matter expert on regulatory issues; continually called upon to resolve issues and expedite approval process on behalf of clients.

→ Built first Flexfactory in Brazil *(single-use equipment)*, a $15M multiproduct manufacturing facility for biologics.
→ Prevented potential expenses on behalf of major pharmaceutical client, performing due diligence of new biotechnology program, partnerships, and in-licensing projects to identify and terminate high-risk projects.
→ Ensured approval of new drugs, utilizing expertise to answer extensive application questions on behalf of Brazilian pharmaceutical companies.
→ Sought after as IP consultant and expert witness for large US biotechnology companies to defend patents.

Sciences of Human Arts Corp (SHAC); Rockymont, Maryland
SENIOR VICE PRESIDENT, PROTEIN DEVELOPMENT (2000–2003)

Advanced into role to spearhead the development of therapeutic proteins and antibodies from preclinical studies to Phase III clinical trials. Controlled $50M budget and directed 350 employees in largest department in HGS.

- Continued -

Strategy: Convey the unique selling point of this biotech executive: the ability to overcome regulatory red tape to gain approval for newly developed drugs through her perfect mix of scientific excellence and business know-how.

REGINA CUMBERBASH, PhD ☎ 345-714-1999 ✉ rerecumberbash@gmail.com | Page 2 of 2

Sciences of Human Arts Corp (Cont'd)
- → Initiated the development of Anthrax antibody, expressed and purified bacterial toxin, and selected binding site for mAb.
  - ○ Gained approval by FDA. Drug purchased by US government under Project BioShield, generating $300M+ in revenues for SHAC.
- → Oversaw design and construction of commercial manufacturing facility for monoclonal antibodies.
- → Purified novel B-cell growth factor protein determined as disease factor in systemic lupus erythematosus.
  - ○ Led to development of Benlysta, first FDA approved drug for the treatment of lupus in 30+ years.
  - ○ Generated over $550M in 2018, projected to exceed $1B in 2 years.
- → Identified novel cytokines and cell surface receptors, ultimately patenting ~150 genes.
- → Key contributor in raising $2B+ in equity capital, presenting to investor groups, biotech firms, and pharmaceutical companies.
  - ○ Pitched to Bayer, GlaxoSmithKline, Pfizer, Bristol Myers Squibb, Hoffman La Roche, Schering Plough, Synthelabo, Merck, and J&J.

VICE PRESIDENT, PROTEIN DEVELOPMENT (1998–2000)
Drove bioprocess development and scale-up activities in expression systems, including bioreactor, refolding, chromatographic purification processes, and formulation of IND candidates.

- → Expressed and purified 150+ novel proteins within 5 years, setting industry record.
- → Oversaw design and construction of $43M clinical manufacturing plant / launch facility; delivered project on time and under budget.
  - ○ Gained publicity from several media outlets.

DIRECTOR, PROTEIN EXPRESSION AND PURIFICATION (1996–1998)
Selected to establish 5 new departments (Cell Culture, Fermentation, Analytical Development, Purification, Formulation, and Stability).

- → Advanced 2 therapeutic proteins into clinical trials 18 months ahead of schedule and achieved Nasdaq listing within 2 years of company's founding
- → Advocated building clinical manufacturing suites at early stage, resulting in production facilities being ready by time first candidates obtained.
- → Sourced and hired all team members.

EDUCATION

University of Heidelberg; Heidelberg, Germany
DOCTOR OF PHILOSOPHY, MOLECULAR BIOLOGY
MASTER OF SCIENCE, BIOLOGY

PUBLICATIONS, PATENTS & PRESENTATIONS

- → Published in 100+ peer-reviewed journals including Science, PNAS, JBC, Cell, EMBO Journal, and FASEB.
- → Earned 250+ US and internationally issued patents.
- → Invited scientist and lecturer at Federal University of Minas Gerais (Brazil).
- → Keynote Presenter at Chinese Biopharmaceutical Association USA.

Regina Cumberbash LinkedIn Profile

Headline

Senior Consultant | Chief Scientific Officer » Dedicated to finding new ways of treating today's incurable diseases

Summary

With expertise in protein development, I'm a Senior Scientific Consultant to international and domestic biotech and pharmaceutical companies for commercial biologics candidates.

Working in Europe, the US, and Brazil has enabled me to gain international expertise that encompasses conducting research on therapeutic proteins / antibodies, designing state-of-the-art biologic production facilities, and ensuring the approval of drugs from governing bodies like FDA / CBER / CDER / ANVISA.

Throughout my career, I have become known as the "Fearless Leader" for my courageous approaches. In essence, biopharmaceutical firms come to me to expedite the drug approval process, defend their patents as an expert witness, and drive the scalability of newly developed biologics.

Some of my notable achievements include:

✔ Playing a vital role in the development of Benlysta® (belimumab), the very first drug approved by the FDA for treatment of lupus in 30+ years.

✔ Earning more than 250 patents in the US and abroad and being published in 100+ peer-reviewed journals, including Science, PNAS, JBC, Cell, and FASEB.

✔ Building the first Flexfactory in Brazil, $15M multiproduct facility for biologics and spearheading the design of a $43M clinical manufacturing plant in the US.

✔ Submitting 6 successful Investigational Drug Filings (INDs) and inventing 6-histidine tag.

✔ Gaining recognition as a successful consultant and expert witness in IP litigations.

Being able to help discover new breakthroughs in curing disease has been a rewarding journey.
Let's connect!

» Key Skills:
✔ Biopharmaceuticals
✔ FDA Approvals
✔ CMC Regulatory Compliance
✔ Molecular Microbiology
✔ Protein Development
✔ cGMP Manufacturing
✔ Biologics development
✔ Purification
✔ Drug Development
✔ Expression Vectors
✔ Monoclonal Antibodies

Strategy: Transform a lackluster profile into one that clearly conveys this executive's diverse talents, many accomplishments, status as an industry leader, and enthusiasm for her work.

Experience

Agape MediConsultants (2004–2020)
Founder / Lead Consultant » Biopharmaceuticals | cGMP Manufacturing| Regulatory Approvals

I was brought in to advise pharmaceutical and biotechnology clients on driving scalability, designing state-of-the-art clinical laboratories, and facilitating regulatory approvals. I also oversaw the fermentation, purification, and formulation development of biosimilar and novel therapeutic proteins. Many of my clients recognized me as a subject matter expert on regulatory issues, and I was continually called upon to resolve issues and expedite approval processes on behalf of these corporations.

✔ Built first Flexfactory in Brazil (single-use equipment), a $15M multiproduct facility for biologics.

✔ Prevented potential expenses on behalf of major pharmaceutical client, performing due diligence of new biotechnology program, to identify and terminate projects with poor outlook.

✔ Performed due diligence of in-licensing candidates and proposed international partnerships for multiple companies.

✔ Ensured approval of biosimilar, utilizing expertise to answer extensive application questions on behalf of Brazilian pharmaceutical company.

✔ Sought after as successful IP consultant and expert witness to defend patents of Pharmaceutical and Biotechnology companies.

Sciences of Human Art Corp (2000–2003)
Senior Vice President, Protein Development » Team Leadership | Protein Development

I was promoted to SVP role to spearhead the development of therapeutic proteins and antibodies from preclinical studies to Phase III clinical trials. Here, I also controlled a $50M budget and directed 350 employees in the company's largest department.

✔ Initiated the development of Anthrax antibody, expressed and purified bacterial toxin, and selected binding site for mAb.
- Gained approval by FDA. Drug purchased by US government under Project BioShield, generating $300M+ in revenues for HGS.

✔ Expressed and purified novel B-cell growth factor protein determined as disease factor in systemic lupus erythematosus.
- Led to development of Benlysta, first FDA approved drug for the treatment of lupus in 30+ years.
- Generated $ 550M in 2018, projected to hit $1B in 2 years.

✔ Created search motifs to identify novel cytokines and cell surface receptors, ultimately discovering and patenting ~150 genes.

✔ Key contributor in raising $2B+ in equity capital, presenting to investor groups, biotech firms, and pharmaceutical companies.

- Pitched to Bayer, GlaxoSmithKline, Pfizer, Bristol Myers Squibb, Hoffman La Roche, Schering Plough, Synthelabo, Merck, and J&J.

✔ Oversaw design and construction of commercial manufacturing facility for monoclonal antibodies.

(1998–2000)
Vice President, Protein Development » Purification | Project Management

During this time, I established 5 new departments (Cell Culture, Fermentation, Analytical Development, Purification, Formulation, and Stability) and hired team members as we grew from 10 to 350 employees.

✔ Expressed and purified 150+ novel proteins within 5 years, setting industry record.

✔ Oversaw design and construction of $43M clinical manufacturing plant / launch facility; delivered project on time and under budget. Gained publicity from several media outlets.

(1994–1998)
Director, Protein Expression and Purification » Bioprocess Development | Protein Isolation | cGMP

Earlier in my tenure with HGS, I drove bioprocess development and scale-up activities in various expression systems, including bioreactor development, protein isolation, refolding, chromatographic purification processes, and formulation of IND candidates.

✔ Advanced therapeutic proteins into clinical trials ahead of schedule.

✔ Facilitated Nasdaq listing within 2 years of company's founding.

Hoffman La Chair CG
Group Leader/Scientific Specialist » Protein Development

While working in Switzerland, I produced and purified therapeutic proteins and vaccines in prokaryotic and eukaryotic cells. Some of my projects included:

✔ Expression of soluble TNF receptors, interferon γ and its receptor, renin, PDGF β, Human Immunodeficiency Virus (HIV-I) and malaria antigens, endothelin receptors.

✔ Development of eukaryotic expression systems.

RESUME 98: by Norine Dagliano, NCRW, NCOPE • www.ekminspirations.com

Robert A. Nichols

Sai Ying Pun, Hong Kong SAR | +846 9628 7365
robert.nichols@gmail.com | www.linkedin.com/in/robertnichols

Global Merchandising/Buying Executive

Senior Director... Vice President... Divisional/General Merchandising Manager

Value Proposition: Bringing expertise, passion, and sophistication to international retailers of fashion and luxury brands.

HIGHLIGHTS OF EXPERIENCE

Leadership Oversight Includes:
- Consumer Focus
- Merchandising Strategies
- Open-to-Buy Management
- Assortment Planning & Allocation
- Competitive Landscape & Behaviors
- Digital Strategies & eCommerce
- Brand Planning & Launch
- Fiscal & Seasonal Budgets
- Forecasting & Goal Setting
- Product Lifecycle
- Pricing Optimization
- Growth Plans & KPIs
- Qualitative & Quantitative Feedback

- **REGIONAL & COUNTRY MANAGEMENT:** Demonstrate strong command of Asia-Pacific markets, specializing in Greater China region with a deep knowledge of local business practices and customs across multiple channels.

- **CROSS-FUNCTIONAL GLOBAL COLLABORATION:** Consistently achieve goals and objectives by partnering with corporate and Asia-Pacific senior management, corporate merchandising and design, global brand planning, merchandise planners, allocation, brand presentation, marketing and PR, supply chain, regional and country retail operations and management, and local talent.

- **CULTURAL SENSITIVITY & TEAMBUILDING:** Build and retain best-in-class merchandising, planning, and allocation teams, learning cultural nuances and overcoming language barriers while leveraging synergies among local talent.

- **CHANGE MANAGEMENT:** Maintain laser focus on achieving corporate sales and margin targets in midst of leadership changes, shifts in corporate direction and distribution, brand realignment, and rapid adoption of new buy processes.

Professional Experience

GYPSY LA RUE ASIA PACIFIC, Hong Kong SAR | 2014 to Present

OVERVIEW: Selected to join newly established Asia-Pacific HQ, created to reenergize Asia-Pacific market and rapidly penetrate China's growing luxury goods industry. Collaborated with local teams across Asia-Pacific and NY partners to bridge Gypsy La Rue's vision and brand with local markets and drive luxury initiatives, strategies, and sales. Rapidly advanced through 4 positions encompassing multiple categories and brands while developing expertise on consumer behavior and in-country trends.

SENIOR DIRECTOR, Regional Merchandising for Greater China & Southeast Asia | Dec. 2018 to Present

- Handpicked for newly created position, partnering with APAC buying, visual merchandising, and creative services to define and manage assortment needs and key categories customized to multiple markets (China, Taiwan, Hong Kong, Singapore, Malaysia) and consumer profiles to ensure sustainable and profitable growth.

- Established diverse, globally minded team of nine strong performers with deep understanding of local markets. Manage geographically dispersed team comprised of regional merchandising managers and assistants.

- Designed infrastructure, processes, merchandising strategies, and road map for achieving sales targets and maintaining sustainable, profitable growth trajectory in company's fastest developing market.

  ↗ Opened 40 new stores across Greater China, on track to open 52 points of sale (POS) by year end with additional 38 stores targeted for FY21.

  ↗ Led team in quickly reading and reacting to product performance and business analytics, creating foundation for reaching FY24 goal of 150+ new stores and $500 million annual revenue.

FY20 RTL SLS Target: $222.7M

FY20 Performance through Q2

Revenue: +48%

Gross Profit: +36%

Comp Performance: +3.4%

Strategy: Convey this candidate's command of the Asia-Pacific luxury market, broad functional expertise, and rapid career advancement with a globally recognized brand. Distinguish his resume from the competition through graphics that illustrate performance metrics.

Robert A. Nichols | +846 9628 7365 | robert.nichols@gmail.com | Page 2

SENIOR DIRECTOR – *achievements*

↗ Developed digital strategy for China, including launching e-commerce platforms on China's two largest B2C online retailers, relaunching premiere digital flagship store in China, and creating concept for WeChat mini-program e-shop through China's largest social media network.

Digital FY2020 Projections

Annual SLS: $5.8M → Comp SLS: $4.3M → Tmall 11.11: $1.03M

PRIOR POSITIONS AND ACHIEVEMENTS

DIRECTOR OF MERCHANDISING, Men's and Women's Luxury Apparel and Accessories | Jun. 2016 to Dec. 2018
DIRECTOR OF MERCHANDISING, Women's Luxury and Amberina Brands | Jan. 2016 to Jun. 2016
MERCHANDISING MANAGER, Women's Luxury Brands | May 2015 to Jan. 2016

↗ Managed $100 million men's and women's luxury apparel and accessories retail and wholesale business in Greater China, Japan, Korea, Singapore, Vietnam, Thailand, Malaysia, Australia, and The Philippines.

↗ Co-created new buy process in partnership with key internal and external partners, improving average end-of-season (EOS) sell-through by 30–50 percent and decreasing inventory liability.

↗ Drove launch of Amberina brand in Asia Pacific, converting 144 points of sale across Japan and Korea from Blue Label brand to Amberina within aggressive timeline and establishing $90-million line of business.

↗ Managed luxury apparel brands, a $30-million business across 35 doors, primarily in Japan, Korea, China, and Hong Kong and opened APAC's first dual-gender luxury flagship store.

↗ Spearheaded VIC client engagement activities across APAC network, building brand equity, capturing preorders, and selling OTR products to improve regular price selling, resulting in $0.3M reserved (SP15) and $1.0M reserved (FA15).

↗ Led 2015 Chinese New Year capsule initiative and structured line list of SKUs on behalf of APAC merchandising. Grew brand awareness with Chinese consumer and generated $690,000 RTL SLS (80% driven by APAC +400bps to prior LY).

↗ Created and promoted a 5-star experience for women's luxury apparel, awarding Very Important Customers (VIC) with annual spend threshold >$100,000 USD first-class trips to NY Fashion Week and other exclusive activities.

GYPSY LA RUE AMERICAS, New York, NY | 2009 to 2015

OVERVIEW: Began rapid career progression from intern to merchandising assistant, assistant buyer, and associate buyer. Acquired broad knowledge of fundamentals of retail buying through close executive mentorship and exposure to wide array of business environments.

ASSOCIATE BUYER *(promoted from Assistant Buyer)* | June 2014 to May 2015
■ Made transition to Vintage & Antiques Global as Assistant Buyer in July 2011, assuming sole ownership of *Carefully Curated Collection* and boosting retail sales 533.5% within 2 years. Promoted to handle end-to-end management of V&A retail business, including open-to-buy, inventory, sales plan, and key product strategies/initiatives, ultimately driving sales and growth +6.0% above total retail sales plan. Supervised and developed 4 direct reports.

↗ Tagged by division director and finance team to create an end-to-end inventory management process that rectified pattern of inventory losses and established framework to account for every dollar spent by creative team.

↗ Collaborated cross-functionally with asset protection, inventory control, supply chain, and finance (including CFO) to develop, deliver, and implement efficient open-to-buy strategy.

Education

BACHELOR SCIENCE, Business Administration | 2010
GEORGETOWN UNIVERSITY, Washington, DC

Robert Nichols LinkedIn Profile

Headline
Global Merchandising Executive ★ Bringing expertise, passion, and savoir-faire to the international fashion market

About
Within the global apparel and fashion industry, Gypsy La Rue has redefined a style of luxury that is recognized around the world. As a senior director of merchandising, I take a great deal of pride in collaborating with our talented team of professionals to help drive luxury brand initiatives, strategies, and sales across the Asia-Pacific market.

I launched my career with Gypsy La Rue as an intern in NYC, and over the last decade rapidly advanced through various roles, seizing every opportunity to learn and grow with the company. Having worked and lived in New York and Hong Kong, supporting three major markets (US, APAC, and EMEA), I'm equally globally minded and regionally attuned to product trends and consumer preferences.

MY TRADEMARKS:
I work hard. I take calculated risks and approach challenges as opportunities, with an open mind and creative flair. And I deliver – increased revenues, higher gross profits, multiple store openings, explosive ecommerce sales, and creative experiences that allow customers to dream.

HOW I ACCOMPLISH GOALS:
Building relationships at every level of the organization… collaborating with colleagues… establishing clear objectives and milestones… and solving problems. I value people and as a result can work effectively with various types of people, bring them together, and achieve goals. I've developed best-in-class merchandising teams— training, mentoring, and empowering individuals to embrace change and attain greater productivity and performance. And I do so while making sure that the people working alongside me are having fun.

Consumer demographics and behaviors are changing rapidly; consequently, the retail market is constantly changing and evolving. It is imperative that we in the industry have a strong understanding of our buyers and how they consume goods and commodities. I'm passionate in my desire to continue being part of this evolution and welcome opportunities to connect and collaborate with like-minded professionals.

Experience
Senior Director, Regional Merchandising for Greater China ✓ $222M+ RTL SLS ✓ Stores & eCommerce
Gypsy La Rue Asia Pacific – Hong Kong
Dec. 2018 to Present
Following measurable success in prior merchandising director/manager roles, I was handpicked for this newly created position to plan and drive strategies aimed at gaining a stronghold on the luxury fashion market across China, Taiwan, Hong Kong, Singapore, and Malaysia and ensuring sustainable and profitable growth.

PARTNERS: APAC buying, visual merchandising, and creative services teams. We define and manage assortment needs and key categories that are customized to each market.

DIRECT REPORTS: Geographically dispersed, globally minded team of 9 strong performers with deep understanding of their local markets.

Strategy: Go beyond work performance and communicate "trademarks" and other insightful information about how he does his work and accomplishes his goals. In the experience section, expand job titles with keywords that quickly communicate details about each job.

INITIATIVES:

✓ Lead team in quickly reading and reacting to product performance and business analytics; create foundation for reaching FY24 goal of 150+ new stores and $500 million annual revenue.

✓ Developed digital strategy for China, including launching e-commerce platforms on China's two largest B2C online retailers, relaunching premiere digital flagship store in China, and creating concept for WeChat mini-program e-shop through China's largest social media network.

Impact:

★ 40 stores opened across the region and on track to open 52 POS by year end

★ +48% revenue

★ +36 % gross profit

★ +3.4% comp performance

★ $5.8M projected for annual digital SLS (FY2020)

Director of Merchandising ✓ Multiple Categories & Channels ✓ Luxury Apparel & Accessories
Gypsy La Rue Asia Pacific – Hong Kong
May 2015 to Dec. 2018
Secured international transfer from NY corporate office to the newly established Asia Pacific headquarters in Hong Kong. Joined forces assembled to reenergize the Asia Pacific market with a focus on penetrating the rapidly growing luxury goods industry across mainland China.

Helped shape collaboration between local cross-functional teams from various cultural/geographic backgrounds and NY partners to effectively bridge Gypsy La Rue's vision and brand with local market and drive luxury initiatives, strategies, and sales.

ALL ROLES:

☛ Director of Merchandising, Men's and Women's Luxury Apparel and Accessories (Jun. 2016 to Dec. 2018) ✓ $100M retail and wholesale business ✓ Greater China, Japan, Korea, Singapore, Vietnam, Thailand, Malaysia, Australia, and The Philippines
Director of Merchandising, Women's Luxury and Amberina Brands (Jan. 2016 to Jun. 2016) ✓ Retained women's luxury and added $90M Amberina brands business
☛ Merchandising Manager, Women's Luxury Brands (May 2015 to Jan. 2016) ✓ $30-million business across 35 doors ✓ Japan, Korea, China, and Hong Kong

INITIATIVES AND IMPACTS:

✓Co-created new buy process ★ Boosted average end-of-season (EOS) sell-through by 30%–50% and decreased inventory liability.

✓ Drove launch of women's Amberina brand in Asia Pacific ★ Converted 144 points of sale across Japan and Korea from Blue Label brand to Amberina.

✓ Spearheaded VIC client engagement activities around runway across APAC network ★ Built brand equity, captured pre-orders, and sold OTR products to improve regular-price selling ★ $0.3M reserved (SP15) and $1.0M reserved (FA15).

✓ Led 2016 Chinese New Year capsule initiative and structured line list of SKUs on behalf of APAC merchandising ★ Increased brand awareness with Chinese consumer ★ Generated $690,000 RTL SLS (80% driven by APAC +400bps to prior LY).

✓ Created and promoted a 5-star experience for women's luxury apparel Very Important Customers (VIC) with annual spend threshold >$100,000 USD.

✓ Opened APAC's first dual-gender luxury flagship store.

Associate Buyer ✓ Retail Buying ✓ Multiple Promotions ✓ Home Décor ✓ Vintage & Antiques
Gypsy La Rue – New York City
Mar. 2009 to May 2015
I launched my career as an intern in men's made-to-measure and quickly moved through progressively responsible positions while acquiring broad knowledge of the fundamentals of retail buying.

In July 2012, I transitioned from home décor to vintage and antiques, first as an Assistant Buyer and then Associate Buyer. I handled end-to-end management of the V&A retail business, including open-to-buy, inventory, sales plan, and key product strategies/initiatives. Direct reports: 4

INITIATIVES AND IMPACTS:
★ Drove sales and growth +6.0% above total retail sales plan.
★ Created an end-to-end inventory management process (tasked by division director and finance team).
★ Developed, delivered, and implemented efficient open-to-buy strategy (collaborated with asset protection, inventory control, supply chain, finance, and CFO of Gypsy La Rue Americas).

JI-MIN BAHK

jiminbahk@gmail.com • linkedin.com/in/jiminbahk • 917.976.0150 • New York, NY 10021

GENERAL COUNSEL

15+ Years of Executive Experience Fueling Innovation and Revenue Growth at Fortune 500 Companies

Business lawyer who negotiates revenue-generating transactions on the world stage and counsels innovative businesses on cross-border strategies. Background in entertainment, new media, and technology.

❖ **Business Value:** Provided strategic leadership to monetize and grow three pioneering startup divisions.

❖ **Pioneering:** Described as *"the most entrepreneurial person at Showz"* with passion to bring new ideas to life.

❖ **Leadership:** Energized teams and built capabilities for crafting multimillion-dollar deals.

CAREER HISTORY

SHOWZ, INC.   New York, NY • 2008-Present

Senior Vice President, Legal Affairs, 2015–Present
Vice President, Legal Affairs, 2010–2015
Senior Counsel, 2008–2010

Licensing • Domestic & International Distribution Agreements • Program Acquisition Agreements • Intellectual Property • Data Privacy Issues • Compliance • Trademark • Copyrights

Facilitate growth of Showz World, the company's syndication business and second-largest revenue source. Lead a legal team to structure and negotiate transactions for domestic and international distribution. Provide business direction for program acquisition, production, and marketing.

- Met the fast-paced challenge of a startup group to maximize intellectual property value of original programming; leveraged strong licensing skills to establish a framework for structuring deal parameters for theatrical, broadcast, cable, and home video viewing of films, television programs, and sporting events.

- Achieved a complex balance of protecting the Showz brand and digital download revenues while enabling the business to seize opportunities in ecommerce, video games, satellite radio, digital video recording, video-on-demand, and other growing technologies.

- Shaped practical strategies to drive tremendous growth, leading to profitable licensing transactions with third-party payers in 130 countries.

- Completed the company's first exclusive deals with Verizon and Vodaphone, working with business units enterprise-wide to define exclusive distribution for wireless platforms.

- Served as Executive Sponsor of the company's business resource group for Asian-Americans; also served on Diversity & Inclusion Council.

AMERICAN GAMING & VIDEO ENTERPRISES   New York, NY • 2003-2008

Vice President, Legal Affairs

Licensing Agreements • Purchasing Agreements • Intellectual Property • Corporate Law • Regulatory & Compliance Issues • Litigation • Data Privacy • Rights Management • Copyrights • Trademarks • Human Resources

Guided a start-up division to innovate and compete in a changing media environment. Acted as general counsel on the senior management team for a mobile game service using pioneering technology. Supervised a legal team and outside legal counsel. Protected intellectual property by directing patent clearance and prosecution efforts.

- Provided business leadership for building and commercializing a greenfield technology; drove fast and calculated planning and execution of product, operational, marketing, and licensing strategies.

- Overcame revenue challenges by shaping a business model that balanced technology with consumer acceptability objectives, an imperative for an entertainment company.

Strategy: Focus on themes of innovation and growth to elevate this candidate above typical general-counsel territory and establish her as a true business leader.

JI-MIN BAHK

WORLD BUSINESS NEWS, INC.	New York, NY • 2000-2003

Associate Counsel

Licensing • Domestic & International Distribution Agreements • Program Acquisition Agreements • Intellectual Property

Provided legal and analytical expertise for the company's new media and information technology groups. Partnered with business leaders on business planning and financial transactions.

- Broke new ground for business opportunities in the emerging arena of Internet publishing; drafted and negotiated agreements for content and software licenses, online distribution, and joint marketing.
- Limited risk for online versions of all magazine brands by conceptualizing approaches for an evolving framework of data privacy and regulatory compliance issues.
- Catalyzed the launch of the company's *New Media* magazine; moved quickly to prioritize a master growth plan and enable execution for a trailblazing publication.
- Authored a regular column on new media issues, becoming a thought leader in an evolving business space.

BAKER & MEADOWS LLP	New York, NY • 1995–1999

Associate

Licensing • Distribution Agreements • Services Transactions • Trademarks • Copyrights • Intellectual Property

Advocated on behalf of clients at the country's first technology law firm. Managed legal strategies in industries that included media, financial services, technology, telecom, and consulting. Drafted licensing, distribution, and services transactions and achieved positive outcomes in intellectual property and commercial litigation cases.

EDUCATION

Juris Doctorate (JD), NEW YORK UNIVERSITY School of Law – New York, NY   1995
Bachelor of Arts, Communications, UNIVERSITY OF CALIFORNIA – Santa Barbara, CA   1993

BAR MEMBERSHIP

New York State • Southern & Eastern Districts of New York

PROFESSIONAL DEVELOPMENT & VOLUNTEER ACTIVITIES

Graduate, BETSY MAGNESS LEADERSHIP INSTITUTE (Women in Cable Telecommunications' leadership program)
Board Member and Programming Chair, WOMEN IN CABLE TELECOMMUNICATIONS – NY Chapter
Volunteer Mentor, WOMEN IN CABLE TELECOMMUNICATIONS – NY Chapter

AWARDS, PUBLICATIONS, & SPEAKING ENGAGEMENTS

Distinguished Alumna of the Year, ASIAN AMERICAN LAW STUDENTS ASSOCIATION
Published Author, New York Law Journal • Brooklyn Journal of International Law

Ji-Min Bahk LinkedIn Profile

Headline

SVP, Legal Affairs – Showz | Sr. Counsel / Attorney for Corporate Transactions, Intellectual Property, Content Licensing

About

Across 15+ years as corporate counsel for the startup divisions of Fortune 500 companies, I have provided legal and business expertise as well as the entrepreneurial leadership to achieve growth against the uncertainties of emerging market opportunities.

In my current role as head of the global legal function for Showz World, I guide my team to partner with businesses on new growth areas. A catalyst for innovation, I helped grow the business in international markets, shaping decisions on global strategy, deal-making, intellectual property, governance, and operations. From our early days, the company now distributes original programming in 130 countries.

Previously, I served as a key strategic, business, and legal advisor and decision-maker at American Gaming & Video Enterprises and World Business News' new media group. At these technology-driven companies, I gained substantial experience in content distribution, technology transactions, digital marketing, and intellectual property.

Throughout my career, I have been a strong champion for diversity and inclusion, supporting employee resource groups and inclusivity initiatives where everyone is welcome and valued. I thrive in environments where talented employees are encouraged and inspired to drive company and customer success.

Experience

Showz, Inc.
Senior Vice President, Legal Affairs
2008–Present

Promoted several times to current role providing strategic, business, and legal direction for Showz World, the company's syndication business. Oversee a global legal team engaged in negotiating and structuring profitable distribution agreements and handling other business and legal matters.

Joined the business in its startup phase and played a key role in its growth to the company's second-largest business by revenue by delivering third-party licensing agreements in 130 countries. Focused on maximizing the intellectual property value of original programming (films, television programs, and sporting events) through deals for theatrical, broadcast, cable, and home video viewing.

Managed legal risks while enabling business expansion to a proliferation of distribution platforms such ecommerce, wireless devices, satellite radio, digital video recording, and video-on-demand. Negotiated exclusive distribution deals with major telecom companies' wireless divisions.

Supported the company's cultural values as the executive sponsor of the employee resource group for Asian-Americans and as a member of the Diversity and Inclusion Council.

Strategy: Create a fairly formal presentation of this attorney's career, focusing on business leadership and notable "firsts." Summarize experience in concise, well-written paragraphs that convey depth and breadth of her expertise.

American Gaming & Video Enterprises
Vice President, Legal Affairs
2003–2008

Handled business and legal affairs as the startup division's chief legal officer, providing strategic and operational guidance for success in the new media environment. Served as a member of the senior management team and supervised outside counsel.

Took a lead role in developing and executing a thriving business model and commercialization strategy for a pioneering mobile game service. Protected intellectual property with patent and prosecution efforts, enabling the technology's ongoing growth.

World Business News, Inc.
Associate Counsel
2000–2003

Managed all legal needs for the company's new media and information technology groups. Participated in setting business strategy and implementing strategic goals.

Negotiated and drafted complex commercial agreements for digital publishing that spanned content and software licenses, online distribution parameters, and joint marketing. Mitigated risks by assessing and managing privacy and compliance considerations. Assisted with problem solving when legal issues arose.

Became a new media industry specialist, authoring a regular column and mobilizing the launch of the company's New Media magazine.

Baker & Meadows LLP
Associate
1995–1999

As a business lawyer for the country's first technology law firm, represented clients in the media, financial services, technology, telecom, and consulting sectors. Acquired broad experience in intellectual property, copyrights, trademarks, and commercial litigation cases, and drafted agreements for licensing, distribution, and services transactions.

SENIOR TECHNOLOGY ARCHITECT

OSCAR HERNANDEZ

North Pasadena CA 86753 | (397) 309-8675
oscarhernandez@gmail.com | https://www.linkedin.com/in/oscarhernandez

Software Engineering | IT Client Solutions | Project Management
Expertise: cash payment systems flows, processing systems design and development

Technology change agent, enhancing user experience, reducing operating expenses, and optimizing operational efficiencies through technology solutions innovation, design, and management.

Certified Agile Scrum Master and system technology owner for Jim Jones Financial's institutional cash and securities settlements system that processes trillions in monthly securities and cash transactions.

Influential project manager, passionate about driving transformational change and creating value through strategic roadmap development, business stakeholder engagement, and focused execution and delivery.

Authentic relationship builder with entrepreneurial spirit, engaging stakeholders and gaining buy-in on strategic initiatives while taking full ownership of project direction and accountability for success.

Charismatic leader of 6 VPs and global organization up to 25 spanning Budapest, Mumbai, and North America.

Agile Scrum Master
Project Management
System Architecture
Stakeholder Management
Enterprise Solutions
Database Administration
Systems Integration
Process Improvement
Technology Operations
Business Infrastructure

Self-taught technologist and architect, highly proficient in Java, Sybase, and DB2 database development; specialist in building low-latency data replication and DB2 / Sybase database persistence solutions and message-based data streaming architectures (JSON, XML).

PROFESSIONAL EXPERIENCE

Project Delivery Manager (Executive Director) | Jim Jones Financial (2014 – 2020)
Advanced into role with focus on executing portfolio of enterprise-wide software projects with $3M–$5M budgets designed to optimize systems that support institutional trade and cash payments settlements. Led 6 VPs in the US and India. Handled database and data streaming, technical architecture and design, budget management and planning, and audit engagement facilitation with internal, external, and regulatory audits.

- **Avoided $1.8M in annual mainframe costs** by redirecting expensive mainframe queries sent from institutional settlements system's GUI, servicing 2,000+ users globally, to new real-time distributed DB2 database replica.

- **Replaced $20M legacy system** with the deployment of renovated global cash and securities settlements system pilot as first go-live for Canadian Fixed Income securities.

- **Served as agile scrum master** delivering java-based SOAP middleware plant, highly scaled DB2 HADR database backend, and web-based Angular GUI interface to support the platform.

- **Spearheaded rollout of highly visible regulatory project** to ensure compliance with Office of the Comptroller of the Currency (OCC) and enforce sanctions-screening program for all incoming cash across 88 markets.
    - **Controlled $4M over aggressive 6-month window** through extensive engagements with key stakeholders spanning operations, financial controllers, legal and compliance, global financial crimes, and technology.
    - **Directly supervised team of 20** and oversaw technology team leaders while working closely with business units to deliver new settlement system on time and within budget.

- **Improved control framework** around payment functions subsequent to OCC regulatory program.

Strategy: For this software project manager, focus on major IT projects he had led and use a modern design that conveys freshness and energy. Highlight his career moving through the ranks at a major financial institution and briefly showcase achievements from his early career.

OSCAR HERNANDEZ

North Pasadena CA 86753 | (397) 309-8675
oscarhernandez@gmail.com | https://www.linkedin.com/in/oscarhernandez

Project Delivery Manager (VP) | Jim Jones Financial (2005 – 2014)
Appointed to ensure the delivery of 70 – 100 business-critical projects annually to transfer trade settlement data supporting 20 million daily transactions from institutional settlements system to 50 internal applications spanning front, middle, and back office functions. Assembled and groomed high-performing distributed development teams of highly skilled Java, C#, Web, and Database development professionals in New York, Mumbai, and Budapest.

- **Conceptualized state-of-the-art exception-based workflow** to eliminate redundant data analysis and steered the integration of internal cash and check payment system for US, Canadian, and Latin American currencies.
  - **Led 12 resources globally** in decommissioning legacy system and deploying solution to 1,500 users.
  - **Established interfaces with 30+ internal systems** supporting trillions of dollars in yearly cash payments.

- **Enabled firm to repurpose mainframe subject matter experts** to build a new strategic web-based GUI for US, Canadian, and Latin American currencies within 6 months of delivering innovative development paradigm and supporting infrastructure.

- **Recruited new distributed systems production support team** located in India and Mexico through strategic vendor partner Tata Consultancy Services.

- **Facilitated migration of support for all 10 legacy distributed applications** to newly established distributed production support team.

EARLY CAREER

Started career as Account Analyst at National Freedom Bank, managing monthly corporate trust account distributions and accounting for several large banking clients and their corporate and municipal bond affiliates.

Joined Jim Jones Financial organization as Operational Risk Reporting Analyst and progressed throughout organization, leveraging self-taught technology skills and consistently outstanding talents in producing value-added results. Previous roles include Developer and Data Services Manager.

EDUCATION

BS, Economics & Finance *(Summa Cum Laude)* | University of Miami (1995)

Certified Agile Scrum Master | Agile Project Management (2020)

Oscar Hernandez LinkedIn Profile

Headline
Senior Technology Architect / Project Manager » innovating, designing & managing business-critical technology solutions

About
I'm a senior technology executive with expertise in driving the innovation, delivery, and maintenance of enterprise-wide systems within a global financial services organization.

I have a knack for driving transformational change that ultimately enhances engagement and user experience, reduces operating expenses, and optimizes operational efficiencies.

Specializing in steering the execution of cash payment, trade settlement, and data-driven projects, I'm a Certified Agile Scrum Master with expert knowledge in high-performance database, data streaming, and message-based systems architecture as well as processing systems design and development.

Known as an outside-the-box thinker and innovator, I'm passionate about implementing high-value technology solutions that solve the most pressing and impactful business problems in new inventive ways.

While leveraging partnerships and nurturing relationships with stakeholders, colleagues, and executive teams, I take full ownership and accountability for delivering results.

During my long-standing tenure at Jim Jones Financial, I worked my way up from a reporting analyst to a technology executive as a result of repeatedly taking the initiative to improve day-to-day functions. As Project Delivery Manager, I was accountable for managing a portfolio of up to 100 projects with total annual development budgets in the $3M – $5M range.

I've successfully led teams of up to 25 both locally and remotely across the North America, India, and Europe. My team members consider me not only a boss, but a confidant who is invested in their professional success.

Let's connect!

► Key Skills ◄

✔ Enterprise Architecture Planning
✔ Enterprise Solution Design
✔ Project Portfolio Management
✔ Strategic Technology Initiatives
✔ Project Delivery
✔ IT Strategy
✔ Agile Project Management
✔ Change Management
✔ Enterprise IT Strategy
✔ Software Project Management
✔ Business Transformation

Strategy: Use a conversational tone to convey leadership skills, highlight strong results throughout his career, and tell the story of how he successfully transitioned from finance to technology.

Experience

Jim Jones Financial (2014–2020)

Project Delivery Manager (Executive Director) » Project Portfolio Management | Agile Project Management

I was promoted into this role to oversee a portfolio of enterprise-wide software projects with $3M–$5M budgets. These initiatives were designed to optimize systems that support institutional trade and global cash payments settlements. I led 6 VPs in the US and India handling data warehousing and provisioning systems supplying key settlement data to 50 internal systems. I also handled database and data streaming, technical architecture and design, budget management and planning, and audit engagement facilitation.

✓ Avoided $1.8M in annual mainframe costs by redirecting expensive queries sent from institutional settlements system's GUI, servicing 2,000+ users globally, to new fault-tolerant DB2 database replica.

✓ Eliminated $20M legacy system and deployed renovated global cash and securities settlements system pilot as first go-live for Canadian Fixed Income securities.

✓ Took the lead on highly visible regulatory project to ensure compliance with Office of the Comptroller of the Currency (OCC), implementing a sanctions-screening program for all incoming cash across 88 markets.
– Controlled $4M budget throughout aggressive 6-month timeline, engaging with key stakeholders spanning operations, financial controllers, legal and compliance, global financial crimes, and technology.
– Supervised team of 20 direct reports and matrix-managed leads from technology teams while working closely with business units to deliver new settlement system on time and within budget.

✓ Led initiatives focused on improving control framework around payment functions subsequent to OCC regulatory program integration.

Jim Jones Financial (2005–2014)

Project Delivery Manager (VP) » Enterprise IT Strategy | Strategic Technology Initiatives

I was selected as project delivery manager to ensure the execution of 70–100 business-critical technology projects annually. These processes supported 20 million daily transactions across 50 internal applications spanning front, middle, and back-office functions. I assembled and groomed top-performing teams of highly skilled Java, C#, web, and database development professionals across New York, Mumbai, and Budapest.

✓ Directed 12 global resources in decommissioning legacy system and deploying state-of-the-art exception-based cash and check payment system to 1,500 users over 2-year period.

✓ Established interfaces with 30+ internal systems supporting trillions of dollars in yearly free-cash payments.

✓ Enabled firm to repurpose mainframe subject matter experts to build a new strategic web-based GUI for US, Canadian, and Latin American currencies. In 6 months delivered innovative development paradigm and supporting infrastructure.

✓ Hired new distributed systems production support team located in India and Mexico through strategic vendor partner Tata Consultancy Services.

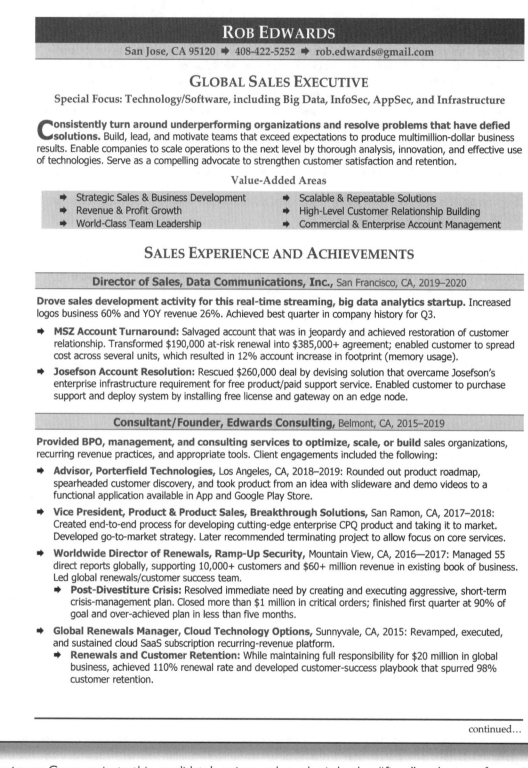

ROB EDWARDS

San Jose, CA 95120 ➡ 408-422-5252 ➡ rob.edwards@gmail.com

GLOBAL SALES EXECUTIVE

Special Focus: Technology/Software, including Big Data, InfoSec, AppSec, and Infrastructure

Consistently turn around underperforming organizations and resolve problems that have defied solutions. Build, lead, and motivate teams that exceed expectations to produce multimillion-dollar business results. Enable companies to scale operations to the next level by thorough analysis, innovation, and effective use of technologies. Serve as a compelling advocate to strengthen customer satisfaction and retention.

Value-Added Areas

- ➡ Strategic Sales & Business Development
- ➡ Revenue & Profit Growth
- ➡ World-Class Team Leadership
- ➡ Scalable & Repeatable Solutions
- ➡ High-Level Customer Relationship Building
- ➡ Commercial & Enterprise Account Management

SALES EXPERIENCE AND ACHIEVEMENTS

Director of Sales, Data Communications, Inc., San Francisco, CA, 2019–2020

Drove sales development activity for this real-time streaming, big data analytics startup. Increased logos business 60% and YOY revenue 26%. Achieved best quarter in company history for Q3.

- ➡ **MSZ Account Turnaround:** Salvaged account that was in jeopardy and achieved restoration of customer relationship. Transformed $190,000 at-risk renewal into $385,000+ agreement; enabled customer to spread cost across several units, which resulted in 12% account increase in footprint (memory usage).

- ➡ **Josefson Account Resolution:** Rescued $260,000 deal by devising solution that overcame Josefson's enterprise infrastructure requirement for free product/paid support service. Enabled customer to purchase support and deploy system by installing free license and gateway on an edge node.

Consultant/Founder, Edwards Consulting, Belmont, CA, 2015–2019

Provided BPO, management, and consulting services to optimize, scale, or build sales organizations, recurring revenue practices, and appropriate tools. Client engagements included the following:

- ➡ **Advisor, Porterfield Technologies,** Los Angeles, CA, 2018–2019: Rounded out product roadmap, spearheaded customer discovery, and took product from an idea with slideware and demo videos to a functional application available in App and Google Play Store.

- ➡ **Vice President, Product & Product Sales, Breakthrough Solutions,** San Ramon, CA, 2017–2018: Created end-to-end process for developing cutting-edge enterprise CPQ product and taking it to market. Developed go-to-market strategy. Later recommended terminating project to allow focus on core services.

- ➡ **Worldwide Director of Renewals, Ramp-Up Security,** Mountain View, CA, 2016—2017: Managed 55 direct reports globally, supporting 10,000+ customers and $60+ million revenue in existing book of business. Led global renewals/customer success team.
  - ➡ **Post-Divestiture Crisis:** Resolved immediate need by creating and executing aggressive, short-term crisis-management plan. Closed more than $1 million in critical orders; finished first quarter at 90% of goal and over-achieved plan in less than five months.

- ➡ **Global Renewals Manager, Cloud Technology Options,** Sunnyvale, CA, 2015: Revamped, executed, and sustained cloud SaaS subscription recurring-revenue platform.
  - ➡ **Renewals and Customer Retention:** While maintaining full responsibility for $20 million in global business, achieved 110% renewal rate and developed customer-success playbook that spurred 98% customer retention.

continued...

Strategy: Communicate this candidate's unique value—he is both a "fixer" and a transformation driver—and clearly convey his sales successes in both text and graphics.

ROB EDWARDS

408-422-5252 ➡ rob.edwards@gmail.com ➡ Page 2

Manager-Americas Renewals, Forsman/TopApp Company, Menlo Park, CA, 2009–2015

Held hybrid sales/sales management role. Focused on service contract renewals, account management, and pursuit of growth opportunities for incremental revenue with existing customer base. Maintained end-to-end responsibility for $20 million in renewals. Led 4-person global team and managed APAC territory accounts. Executed actions to maintain stability and protect book of recurring business during Forsman acquisition.

➡ **Renewals/Recurring Revenue Program:** Created and implemented comprehensive Renewals Process and Customer Success program from scratch.

➡ **Major Account Expansion:** Partnered with customer's senior VP of worldwide operations to prevent continued erosion of revenue potential. Created MSSP true-up program that turned $480,000 contract into 3-year, $2.5 million agreement—the largest in company history.

➡ **Business Increase:** As APAC territory account manager, closed more than $590,000 of new business on top of renewals responsibility in 2012.

➡ Increased maintenance revenues 10%, YOY, 2009—2012.
➡ Over-achieved quota between 108% and 121%, 2009—2014.
➡ Earned President's Club membership three years, 2009—2011.
➡ Ranked as "top performer" in 2014.

Additional value-added contributions:
➡ Managed macro-level strategy, analysis, channel direction, and conflict resolution.
➡ Improved efficiency of information flow organizationally.
➡ Enhanced CRM functionality and utilization.

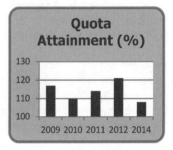

EARLIER EXPERIENCE

Regional Sales Director, Transition Relocation Systems, Sunnyvale, CA, 2008–2009

Directed sales of commercial moving services in Northern California. Implemented and managed sales process for new team. Generated additional business in 20 target accounts in Silicon Valley "Top 100" within a year.

Territory Account Manager, Hitachi Data Systems, Santa Clara, CA, 2007–2008

Sold storage infrastructure solutions, storage management software, and professional services in SMB space. Collaborated with value-added partners and end-users to close and fulfill new business. Achieved 102% of quota.

Sr. Service Sales Representative, Sun Microsystems, San Francisco, CA, 2005–2007

As inside sales rep, serviced $10 million territory. Exceeded targets for 5 consecutive quarters, with results between 161% and 954%. Singlehandedly captured $10+ million in revenue on HDS branded storage arrays. Established and maintained proprietary "best practices" knowledge repository/intranet. Led sales training at both company and account level; included importance of understanding customers' needs and presenting solutions.

EDUCATION

Master of Business Administration (MBA), in-progress, San Jose State University
Bachelor of Science (BS), Computer Science, San Jose State University, 2002

Rob Edwards LinkedIn Profile

Headline
SALES EXECUTIVE: World-Class Team Leader Revenue/Profit Growth; Customer Relations; Scale Operations to the Next Level

About
PROBLEMS I FIX

I thrive on challenges. For example, I build and lead world-class sales teams, increase revenues and profits 10% or more, position organizations to scale up cost-effectively, and turn around underperforming organizations.

I love to fix what's broken, improve what isn't, and over-achieve goals.

MY VALUE STATEMENT

Key elements I bring to the table in every position include the following:
♦ Turn around underperforming organizations by resolving problems that have defied solutions.
♦ Build, lead, and motivate teams that exceed expectations to produce high-value business results.
♦ Enable companies to scale operations to the next level by thorough analysis, innovation, and effective use of technologies.
♦ Serve as a compelling advocate to strengthen customer satisfaction and retention.

WHAT DRIVES ME

I'm largely self-driven. Yes, I've had help from people along the way, but here's the crux of my story: Coming from the inner city of San Diego in a single-parent household and being the first in my family to go to college, I didn't exactly have a blueprint to follow. Both my personal life and my professional career have centered on being smarter, grittier, and hungrier than the next person—and on a relentless commitment to figuring it all out!

MY SPECIALTIES
♦ Technology/Software: Big Data, InfoSec, AppSec, Infrastructure
♦ Strategic Sales & Business Development
♦ Commercial & Enterprise Account Management

HOW I GIVE BACK

It's not all about winning or being better than someone else. I love soccer—have enjoyed coaching it in the past and plan to do so again in the future.

Also, in my early career I spent 7 years working with emotionally disturbed children in group homes and with a family services organization. That fulfilling work indirectly led me to a career in sales.

HOW YOU CAN CONTACT ME

I'm open to having conversations and exchanging ideas regarding sales-related topics. You can connect with me on LinkedIn or contact me at rob.edwards@gmail.com.

Experience
Data Communications, Inc., San Francisco, CA
2019–2020
DIRECTOR OF SALES – Start-up, Business Development

Strategy: Echo and build on the themes established in the resume: that this individual is a top sales performer, a fixer, a turnaround expert, and someone who solves problems that have been considered unsolvable. Weave his personal story into the summary and show what drives and motivates him.

I drove sales development activity for this real-time streaming, big data analytics startup. My team increased the logo business 60% and YOY revenue 26%. While there, I also achieved the best quarter in company history for Q3.

Actions and Results:

♦ Salvaged an account that was in jeopardy. Transformed an at-risk renewal into an agreement that nearly doubled revenue and enabled the customer to spread cost across several units. This resulted in a 15% account increase in footprint (memory usage).

♦ Rescued a 6-figure deal by devising a solution that overcame the customer's enterprise infrastructure requirement for a free product/paid support service. The solution enabled the customer to purchase support and deploy its system.

Edwards Consulting, Belmont, CA
2015–2019
CONSULTANT/FOUNDER – Product Development, Go-to-Market Strategy, Global Business Operations

I provided diverse clients with BPO, management, and consulting services to optimize, scale, or build sales organizations and maximize recurring revenue.

Client engagements, actions, and results:
♦ Advisor, Porterfield Technologies, Los Angeles, CA, 2018—2019: Rounded out the product roadmap, spearheaded customer discovery, and took the product from an idea with slideware and demo videos to a functional application available in App and Google Play Store.
♦ Vice President, Product & Product Sales, Breakthrough Solutions, San Ramon, CA, 2016—2018: Created an end-to-end process for developing a cutting-edge enterprise CPQ product and taking it to market, including the go-to-market strategy.
♦ Worldwide Director of Renewals, Ramp-Up Security, Mountain View, CA, 2015—2016: Managed 60 direct reports globally, supporting more than 10,000 customers and a multimillion-dollar existing book-of-business. Led the global renewals/customer success team.
– – Created and executed an aggressive, short-term crisis-management plan that resolved an immediate crisis. Finished the first quarter at 90% of goal and over-achieved plan in less than 5 months.
♦ Global Renewals Manager, Cloud Technology Options, Sunnyvale, CA, 2015: Revamped, executed, and sustained the cloud SaaS subscription recurring-revenue platform.
– – While maintaining full responsibility for $20 million in global business, achieved an 111% renewal rate and developed a customer-success playbook that spurred 98% customer retention.

Forsman/TopApp Company, Menlo Park, CA
2009–2015
MANAGER-AMERICAS RENEWALS – Contract Renewals, Account Management & Expansion, Incremental Revenue Growth

While holding a hybrid sales/sales management role. I maintained end-to-end responsibility for $20 million in renewals, led a 4-person global team, and served as APAC territory account manager. I also executed actions to maintain stability and protect TopApp's book of recurring business during the acquisition by Forsman.

Actions and Results:

♦ Created and implemented a comprehensive Renewals Process and Customer Success program from scratch.

♦ Partnered with a customer's senior VP of worldwide operations to prevent continued erosion of revenue potential. Created a program that turned a $500,000 contract into a 3-year, multimillion-dollar agreement—the largest in company history.

♦ As APAC territory account manager, closed $600,000 of new business on top of my renewals responsibility in 2012.

Sales Highlights:

♦ Increased maintenance revenues 10%, YOY, 2009—2012.

♦ Over-achieved quota between 108% and 121%, 2009—2014.

♦ Earned President's Club membership three years, 2009—2011.

♦ Ranked as "top performer" in 2014.

Transition Relocation Services, Sunnyvale, CA, 2008—2009
REGIONAL SALES DIRECTOR

I directed the sales of commercial moving services in Northern California, which included implementation and management of the sales process for a new team. My team and I generated additional business in 21 target accounts in the Silicon Valley "Top 100" within a year.

Hitachi Data Systems, Santa Clara, CA, 2007—2008
TERRITORY ACCOUNT MANAGER

I sold storage infrastructure solutions, storage management software, and storage-related professional services in the SMB space. I collaborated with value-added partners and end-users to close and fulfill new business. Results included achieving 102% of quota.

Sun Microsystems, San Francisco, CA, 2005—2007
SENIOR SERVICE SALES REP

As inside sales rep, I serviced a $10-million territory. In this position, I exceeded targets for five consecutive quarters, with results between 161% and 954%. I singlehandedly captured $11 million in revenue on HDS branded storage arrays. I also established and maintained a proprietary "best practices" knowledge repository/intranet. In addition, I led sales training at both the company and the account level.

RESUME 102: *by Carolyn Whitfield, CERM, CEIC, CMRW, COJSRM, CARW • www.totalresumes.com.au*

JOEL BARLOW, MEIT, MIS

Montmorency, VIC ■ 0425 862 021 ■ joelbarlow@gmail.com ■ LinkedIn Profile

NATIONAL MARKETING MANAGER | PRODUCT MANAGER | BUSINESS OPERATIONS MANAGER

Mid to Large Multinational Corporations (MNCs) → Consumer Electronics, IT Hardware, and HVAC Companies

Skyrocketing Revenues by Optimising Brand Visibility, Launching New Products, and Building Multi-Channel Alliances

PIONEERING BUSINESS OPERATIONS LEADER with 18+ years of verifiable background in leading strategic business operations, marketing, and product management for globally recognised brands Totaline and Emax. Expert in boosting multimillion-dollar sales by unifying brand identity, increasing product visibility, and negotiating win-win channel partnerships and alliances.

INNOVATIVE MARKET STRATEGIST with demonstrated success in developing and implementing well-researched go-to-market (GTM) strategies and plans that identified untapped business opportunities, invigorated product potentials, discovered new channel partnerships, and outpaced heavy industry competitors.

GROWTH-CENTRIC B2B / B2C PARTNER and expert in devising and executing sustainable marketing and advertising programs to establish market presence in the Australian, Indian, and GCC (Saudi Arabia, Kuwait, United Arab Emirates, Qatar, Bahrain, and Oman) regions. Credited for launching world-class product commercials, campaigns, and tradeshows.

MARKETING & LEADERSHIP STRENGTHS

- Business Operations Management
- Product Development & Management
- Strategic Marketing Communications
- Brand Strategy & Image Building
- Multi-Channel Partnerships & Alliances

- New Product Introduction & Launch
- Stakeholder Relationship Building
- KPI Setting & Profitability Analysis
- Revenue & Margin Maximisation
- Budget / Cost Control & Forecasting

- Territory / Area Management
- Sales / Demand Generation
- Regulatory Compliance
- Team Leadership & Development
- Project & Program Management

CAREER IMPACTS

Achieved revenue growth of $50M+ over 3 years after designing and executing Totaline's Australian-specific business plan.

Boosted top-line revenue to 20%+ by launching 6 new products for Totaline.

Grew Emax Electronics' overall sales through e-commerce channel to 140% (4% of total company revenue) by pioneering introduction and implementation of integrated e-commerce marketing platform.

Achieved $120M gross revenue for AV segment in GCC for over 2 years at Emax Electronics.

CAREER NARRATIVE

TOTALINE ■ Melbourne, Australia ■ 2010–Present
Fully owned subsidiary of Air-Conditioning & Heating International (AHI) with $550M+ and 250+ employees.

NATIONAL PRODUCT & MARKETING MANAGER – AUSTRALIAN MARKET

Managed: 7+ reports | P&L: $48M | EBIT: 7% | Reported to: Business Unit Manager

Promoted to provide strategic product management and marketing oversight across 4 business segments. Drove launch of new products and improved existing product portfolios by assessing market needs, developing unique value propositions, crafting go-to-market strategies, boosting brand awareness, and architecting coherent product roadmap tied to revenue targets.

> Helped drive year-on-year growth since 2010 by launching new products to targeted market and revamping go-to-market plan in quick reaction to shifts in trends, demand, and global economy.

- **Achieved revenue growth of $50M+ over 3 years** after designing and implementing Australian-specific business plan.
- **Increased top line revenue to 30%+ with additional $4.4M gross margin** by facilitating in-depth market review that addressed product gaps, then launching 11 new products that boosted company's product line-up.
- **Topped revenue expectation by 11%+** through spearheading full 360-degree overhaul of company's go-to-market preseason strategy focusing on marketing and promotional activities tied with existing products.

Strategy: Pack this resume with robust metrics showcasing the candidate's strong achievements in marketing, specifically with mid to large multinational corporations in consumer electronics, IT hardware, and HVAC.

JOEL BARLOW, MEIT, MIS | 0425 862 021| joelbarlow@gmail.com

- **Generated 25% revenue and 5% gross margin improvement** by successfully restructuring single pricing strategy into multi-layered pricing model, delivering added value to customers and manufacturing unit partners.

- **Boosted company sales 160%+ in Australia** by spearheading highly competitive marketing campaigns via "Above the Line (ATL)" and "Below the Line (BTL)" communication tools. Adopted inclusive product GTM strategy.

- **Achieved new product target and profitability within first 4 weeks** by strengthening internal and external marketing communication strategies (launch plan, sales training, campaign, promotion) to multiple channel partners and customers.

- **Strengthened overall brand performance** after convincing reluctant top management to allocate $1M add-on investment focused on brand building. Created and launched all-inclusive marketing plan that generated positive results from 150+ dealers and 200+ network partners.

EMAX ELECTRONICS ■ Dubai, UAE ■ 2000–2010
Leading global manufacturer of consumer electronics with $174B+ (2016) revenue and 489K+ employees worldwide

HEAD OF MARKETING DEPARTMENT – AV, IT, MOBILE, AND WHITE GOODS
Managed: 11+ reports | Budget: $22M | Reported to: Managing Director

Promoted as Head of Department from Marketing Manager role. Led all aspects of consumer marketing, branding, visual merchandising, and promotional campaigns (ATL and BTL approach) across multiple platforms. Built strategic multi-channel partnerships to improve product visibility, control budgets/costs, enhance consumer brand awareness, and build sales.

> Boosted product showcasing performance by 33%+, media coverage by 24%, and target rating point (TRP) by 15% to 18% —by converging marketing focus across all 4 business verticals at Emax Electronics.

- **Created unique, synergised marketing tagline** that leveraged overall brand value and was adopted to all advertising campaigns across GCC nations. *Key results:*
  — Achieved $120M gross revenue for AV segment in GCC for over 2 years.
  — Increased brand visibility by 33%, generating $70M sales across product categories.
  — Improved channel visibility across 8 countries and 150+ outlets.
  — Received "Best Ad Campaign Award" across GCC for LCD technology print advertisement.

- **Grew territory sales more than 15%** after taking corporate showcasing platform to below-the-line (BTL) advertising across 150+ stores. Enhanced visibility and attracted thousands of consumers. *This was achieved on the backdrop of a long-term deal with premium channel partners on investment-sharing basis.*

- **Earned praise from business partners and competitors** after securing $300K additional budget (from Emax HQ Design team) to create a truly world-class corporate showcasing platform during annual electronics exhibition attracting 300K+ visitors.

- **Boosted company sales by 55%+ in Middle East** by spearheading highly competitive marketing campaigns.

- **Bolstered channel sales to 4% of total company revenue** after pioneering introduction and implementation of e-commerce marketing platform—later adopted enterprise-wide by Emax in 2006.

- **Attained cost advantage of 25% to 30% and sales increase of 20%+** by leveraging promotional advertising that utilised resources better and gained premium positions in leading print media partners.

PRIOR SUCCESS

- **Commercial Officer, Emax Group, Dubai:** Charged with complex commercial and administrative functions relating to project scoping, investment planning, and business pitches, leading to revenue growth via repeat business from multiple clients.

- **Business Development** roles at Intertec Software in Bangalore, India, and Grundig Gulf Fze in Dubai, UAE.

CREDENTIALS

Certificate in Advanced Management (Strategy and Scenario Planning) – National University of Singapore – Singapore, 2007
Master's Degree in Information Systems (Database Management) – Bond University – Gold Coast, QLD, Australia, 2002
Master's Degree in Economics (International Trade) – MODUL University – Dubai, 1999

Joel Barlow LinkedIn Profile

Headline
National Manager → Product Development. Marketing. Operations → Consumer Electronics and HVAC Companies

Summary
Leveraging my hands-on operational background in leading all aspects of business operations, marketing, and product management, I have helped globally known consumer brands (Totaline and Emax) achieve multimillion-dollar sales, strong global market presence, and solid brand identity — loved by global consumers! I do this by:

✔ Building scalable go-to-market strategies…
✔ Launching world-class marketing and advertising campaigns…
✔ Establishing win-win multi-channel partnerships.

I have gained significant international experience across the Australian, GCC, and MEA regions — supporting aggressive business growth and consolidation, strengthening product stewardship, and driving brand awareness to peak levels.

Here are a few examples of how I've delivered results:

GROWTH AND PROFITABILITY
✔ Achieved revenue growth of $50M+ after implementing Totaline's Australian-market specific business plan.
✔ Attained $120M gross revenue for Emax Electronics' AV segment in GCC for more than 2 years.

MARKETSHARE OPTIMISATION
✔ Boosted Totaline's market share by 120%+ in Middle East and 70%+ in Australia by spearheading highly competitive marketing campaigns via Above the Line (ATL) and Below the Line (BTL) communication tools.

BRAND VISIBILITY
✔ Increased Emax Electronics' brand visibility to 35%, covering 8 countries and 150+ outlets.

Are you looking for a results-driven Product and Marketing Leader? I am willing to challenge the status quo and produce tangible results within organisations. I'd love to sit down and chat about how your needs align with my experience.

--> Joel Barlow, MEIT, MIS
0425 862 021 | joelbarlow@gmail.com

Experience
National Product & Marketing Manager – Australian Market ▶ Business Operations ▶ Marketing Strategy
Totaline
2010 – Present | Melbourne, Australia

Promoted to provide strategic product management and marketing oversight across 4 business segments — during period of evolving market changes.

Strategy: Build an easy-to-skim profile, with symbols and borders that accentuate important information while improving readability. In the About section, highlight important achievements in 3 distinct areas that align with all of his potential job targets.

Launch new revenue-generating products and improve existing product portfolios by assessing market needs, developing unique value propositions, crafting go-to-market strategies, boosting brand integrity and awareness (campaigns and promotions), maintaining regulatory compliance, and architecting coherent product roadmap (structure) tied to overall revenue targets.

--- ---

REVENUE GROWTH AND PROFITABILITY

✔ Achieved overall revenue growth of $50M+ over 3 years after designing and implementing Australian-market specific business plan.

✔ Increased top line revenue to 20%+ with additional $2.4M gross margin by launching 4 new products that boosted company's product line-up (long-term).

✔ Generated 25% revenue and 7% gross margin improvement by successfully restructuring single pricing strategy into multi-layered pricing model, delivering added value to customers and manufacturing unit partners.

MARKETSHARE IMPROVEMENT

✔ Boosted market share by 120%+ in Middle East and 70%+ in Australia by spearheading highly competitive marketing campaigns.

COST REDUCTION

✔ Cut inventory holding cost by $1.2M annually, contributing 1% directly to annual EBIT, by analysing 3-year sales history, introducing product segmentation and categorisation, and optimising stock holding per warehouse.

Marketing Head – Av, It, Mobile, And White Goods ▶ Marketing ▶ Branding ▶ Multi-Channel Alliances
Emax Electronics
Dubai, UAE | 2000–2010

Promoted as Head of Department from Marketing Manager role to lead all aspects of consumer marketing, branding, and promotional campaigns (ATL and BTL approach) across TV, print, media, tradeshows, etc.

Built strategic multi-channel partnerships to improve product visibility, control budgets/costs, enhance consumer brand awareness, and overall generate sales/revenues.

--- ----- ----- ---

MULTIMILLION-DOLLAR SALES GROWTH

✔ Achieved $120M gross revenue for AV segment in GCC for more than 2 years.

BRANDING VISIBILITY

✔ Increased brand visibility to 35% covering across 8 countries and 150+ outlets.

E-COMMERCE MARKETING OPTIMISATION

✔ Bolstered overall sales to 40% (3% of total company revenue) after pioneering introduction and implementation of e-commerce marketing platform — later adopted enterprise-wide by Samsung in 2006.

Commercial Officer ▶ Investment Planning ▶ Client Management ▶ Project Scoping And Delivery
Samsung Group
Abu Dhabi, UAE | 1995–2000

Charged with complex commercial and administrative functions relating to project scoping, investment planning, and business pitches, leading to revenue growth via repeat business from multiple clients.

RESUME 103: *by Louise Kursmark, MRW, CPRW, JCTC, CEIP, CCM • www.louisekursmark.com*

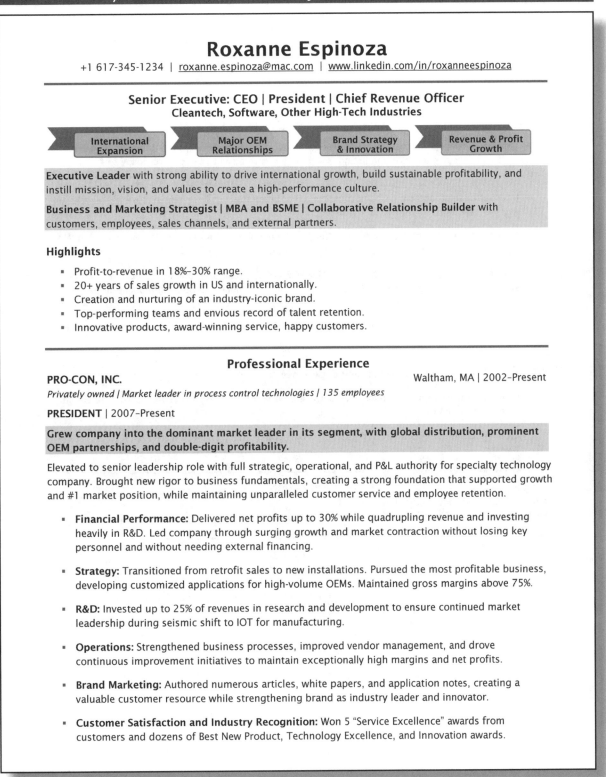

Roxanne Espinoza

+1 617-345-1234 | roxanne.espinoza@mac.com | www.linkedin.com/in/roxanneespinoza

Senior Executive: CEO | President | Chief Revenue Officer
Cleantech, Software, Other High-Tech Industries

| International Expansion | Major OEM Relationships | Brand Strategy & Innovation | Revenue & Profit Growth |

Executive Leader with strong ability to drive international growth, build sustainable profitability, and instill mission, vision, and values to create a high-performance culture.

Business and Marketing Strategist | MBA and BSME | Collaborative Relationship Builder with customers, employees, sales channels, and external partners.

Highlights

- Profit-to-revenue in 18%–30% range.
- 20+ years of sales growth in US and internationally.
- Creation and nurturing of an industry-iconic brand.
- Top-performing teams and envious record of talent retention.
- Innovative products, award-winning service, happy customers.

Professional Experience

PRO-CON, INC.   Waltham, MA | 2002–Present
Privately owned | Market leader in process control technologies | 135 employees

PRESIDENT | 2007–Present

Grew company into the dominant market leader in its segment, with global distribution, prominent OEM partnerships, and double-digit profitability.

Elevated to senior leadership role with full strategic, operational, and P&L authority for specialty technology company. Brought new rigor to business fundamentals, creating a strong foundation that supported growth and #1 market position, while maintaining unparalleled customer service and employee retention.

- **Financial Performance:** Delivered net profits up to 30% while quadrupling revenue and investing heavily in R&D. Led company through surging growth and market contraction without losing key personnel and without needing external financing.

- **Strategy:** Transitioned from retrofit sales to new installations. Pursued the most profitable business, developing customized applications for high-volume OEMs. Maintained gross margins above 75%.

- **R&D:** Invested up to 25% of revenues in research and development to ensure continued market leadership during seismic shift to IOT for manufacturing.

- **Operations:** Strengthened business processes, improved vendor management, and drove continuous improvement initiatives to maintain exceptionally high margins and net profits.

- **Brand Marketing:** Authored numerous articles, white papers, and application notes, creating a valuable customer resource while strengthening brand as industry leader and innovator.

- **Customer Satisfaction and Industry Recognition:** Won 5 "Service Excellence" awards from customers and dozens of Best New Product, Technology Excellence, and Innovation awards.

Strategy: Create a visually distinctive resume that succinctly presents 18 years of leadership experience and notable achievements with one company.

Roxanne Espinoza | Page 2 | +1 617-345-1234 | roxanne.espinoza@mac.com

PRO-CON, continued

VP SALES AND MARKETING | 2002–2007

Tripled sales in 5 years and made the PRO-CON brand a household name in the industry.

Hired to expand sales for innovative technology company with narrow focus in the domestic US market. Developed and executed all sales, marketing, and branding strategies to catapult company to #1 worldwide in its niche.

- **International Expansion:** Built the company's first international sales channel, covering all relevant worldwide markets within the first year.

- **Growth Strategy:** Conceived and led strategy to drive high-volume sales growth by cementing OEM agreements with numerous leading machine vendors.

- **Brand Marketing:** Developed the famous "PRO-CON PRO" branding—tagline, iconic image, and vendor incentives that elevated PRO-CON into a visible, credible, essential component in the electronics assembly process.

- **Sales Performance:** Exploded brand awareness and quickly jumped from distant #3 to solid #1 in global sales.

Prior Sales & International Development Experience

- **Standard Technologies:** Launched company into target markets in Europe. Recruited, trained, and motivated key VAR partners.

- **Inter-Tech:** Developed European operations from scratch and grew sales from $750K to $7.5M in 2 years.

Education

MBA, Marketing Major | Boston University | 2006
BE MECHANICAL ENGINEERING | Polytechnic University of Catalonia, Barcelona, Spain | 1996

Additional

Languages Fluent Spanish and English | Conversational French

CEO Memberships Invited member of 2 Boston-based CEO Councils—peer advisory and mentoring groups of CEOs for mid-sized and larger companies.

Roxanne Espinoza LinkedIn Profile

Headline
President/CEO for Profitable, High-Growth Technology Companies: Vision + Strategy + Execution

About
Growing a business in international markets is the kind of challenge I enjoy most. Currently President and previously VP Sales and Marketing for high-tech company PRO-CON, I created the strategy and led the execution that made us #1 in worldwide sales in our niche.

Previously, I launched Standard Technologies into new markets in Europe and, for Inter-Tech, built the entire European operation from the ground up to $7.5M revenue in 2 years.

"Going global" has been a natural fit for me, as I am multicultural (born in Spain, worked across Europe, have lived in US for 20+ years) and multilingual (fluent Spanish and English, plus a bit of conversational French from my on-the-ground efforts there for several years). My education, too, has taken 2 paths—first a bachelor's degree in Mechanical Engineering, then an MBA—that provide business and technical acumen, plus logical problem-solving skills, to break complex situations into simple components with achievable solutions.

Together, these diverse experiences and perspectives fuel the vision, strategy, tactics, and problem-solving approach needed to crack new markets and identify new paths to profitability.

Of course, nothing is accomplished alone. I'm proud to have a talented team of employees who throw their heart and soul into making the company successful and making our customers and partners happy.

At PRO-CON, we've won dozens of awards from industry media, and OEM partners. The recognition is nice, but even more valuable is the knowledge that we are innovating (numerous Best New Product and Technology Excellence awards) and exceeding our customers' expectations (5 Service Excellence awards).

Currently we're investing millions in R&D to support the growing shift to IOT for manufacturing. We are projecting exponential growth … and we'll keep the same customer-first, employee teamwork approach that has helped us dominate our market niche.

Experience
President, 2007–Present
PRO-CON

COMPANY: Market leader in process control technologies — privately owned.

SCOPE: Strategy, Operations, Sales & Marketing, International Expansion, Vendor Management, P&L

STRATEGY — LEADERSHIP — RESULTS:
► #1 in worldwide sales for 15+ years.
► Robust OEM partnerships and support — major electronics manufacturers of all sizes in all global markets.
► Highly profitable.
► Award-winning products.
► Strong brand recognition.
► Award-winning customer service.
► Exceptional employee morale and retention.

Use a narrative, storytelling approach in the About section to reveal interesting personal details as well as leadership style. In the Experience section, provide a very concise and easy-to-skim presentation of career experience, company and job scope information, and notable successes.

VP Sales and Marketing, 2002–2007
PRO-CON

SCOPE: Sales, Marketing, Branding, International Expansion

LEADERSHIP — EXECUTION — RESULTS:
► Company's first international sales channel.
► OEM partnerships for high-volume growth.
► Iconic "PRO-CON-PRO" branding and global positioning.
► 3X sales growth in 5 years.
► Surge from #3 to #1 in worldwide sales.

Director International Sales, 1998–2002
Standard Technologies

COMPANY: Innovator in security software with industry-leading "Open Sesame" that let automatic IT software back up files even if open and active.

SCOPE: Sales, VAR partners, International Expansion

LEADERSHIP — EXECUTION — RESULTS:
► Launch and leadership of entire sales operation in key European markets.
► Recruitment, training, and motivation of key VAR partners.

Director European Sales, 1996–1998
Inter-Tech

COMPANY: Printers and accessories for semiconductor back-end applications.

SCOPE: Startup European Operations, Sales, Marketing, Distributor Relationships, Team Recruitment & Leadership

LEADERSHIP — EXECUTION — RESULTS:
► Relocation to France for operational startup.
► Close collaboration with European distributors to educate/motivate them to sell MPM products.
► 10-fold sales growth to $7.5M.
► High margins, exceptional profitability.

APPENDIX A

Resume and LinkedIn Profile Preparation Worksheet

A resume is only as good as the information that it showcases.

To write a great resume, you must take the time to document your complete career history, whether 2 years or 22 years. This "raw data" is the foundation for everything that you will write. The more raw data the better, so be as comprehensive as possible when collecting and documenting all of your experience. You won't necessarily include it in all of your final documents, but you want to have it all initially to best determine what to include and how.

Keeping a running log of your career successes (for example, project highlights, revenue and profit results, productivity and efficiency gains, customer satisfaction scores) and then updating your resume every 6 months or so is a smart way to be prepared at a moment's notice when a great career opportunity presents itself.

Use the following worksheet as a guide when assembling all of your career information as the foundation for a powerful and well-positioned resume.

RESUME AND LINKEDIN PROFILE PREPARATION WORKSHEET

Contact Information

Name:		
Address:		
City:	State:	Zip:
Primary Phone:	Email:	
LinkedIn URL:	Personal website:	
Willing to relocate? YES NO	Willing to travel? YES NO	
Current Salary:	Expected Salary:	

Career Objectives

Answer the following questions as completely and accurately as possible. Not all questions will apply to you—simply mark those N/A. Use additional sheets if necessary.

Position/Career Objective: List top 3 job title choices in order of preference:

1.

2.

3.

Is this a career change for you?   Yes ( )   No ( )

Long-Range Career Goals:

What are some terms (or keywords) that are specific to your industry and profession?

What skills do you possess that you want to highlight?

Work Experience

As you consider each position, ask yourself: *"How is this organization better off now than when it hired me?"* Here are some questions to get your thoughts flowing.

- Did you increase profits? If so, by what percentage or amount?
- Did you increase sales? If so, by what percentage or amount?
- Did you generate new business, bring in new clients, or forge affiliations?
- Did you save your company money? If so, how much and how?
- Did you design and/or institute any new system or process? If so, what were the results?
- Did you meet an impossible deadline through extra effort? What difference did this make to your company?
- Did you bring a major project in under budget? How did you make this happen? How were the dollars you saved used?
- Did you suggest and/or help launch a new product or program? If so, did you take the lead or provide support? How successful was the effort?

- Did you take on new responsibilities that weren't part of your routine responsibilities? If so, did you ask for the new projects or were they assigned to you, and why you?
- Did you introduce any new or more effective techniques for increasing productivity?
- Did you improve communication? If so, with whom and what was the outcome?
- How did your company benefit from your performance?

Begin with your present employer. If you're not currently working, you *might* want to start with your volunteer experience—treating it just like a paid position—if it relates to your current career objective. List different positions at the same company as separate jobs (at least at this point in the information-collection process).

Company:

City/State: Dates of employment:

Your title or position:

Who do you report to (title)?   Number of people you supervise:

Their titles or functions:

What does the organization do, make, or sell?

Where does it rank in its industry in terms of competitors?

Briefly describe your duties, responsibilities, and level of authority. Use numbers (size) and percentages, quantify budgets, state with whom you interacted, and so on.

Why were you hired (or promoted or selected)? What was going on at the company? Was there a particular challenge or problem you were brought on to solve? Did you have specific performance measurements? (If so, please describe them as specifically as possible.) Where was your company headed? Why did they need you?

Describe 4 to 6 accomplishments, successes, project highlights, contributions, or other achievements in this position. Give lots of details, facts, and figures.

_____

_____

_____

_____

_____

_____

_____

_____

_____

_____

_____

Previous Employment

You will likely need to make multiple copies of this page and the next so that you have one copy for each position.

Company:

City/State:

Dates of employment:

Your title or position:

Who do you report to (title)?   Number of people you supervised:

Their titles or functions:

What does the organization do, make, or sell?

Where does it rank in its industry in terms of competitors?

Briefly describe your duties, responsibilities, and level of authority. Use numbers (size) and percentages, quantify budgets, state with whom you interacted, and so on.

Why were you hired (or promoted or selected)? What was going on at the company? Was there a particular challenge or problem you were brought on to solve? Did you have specific performance measurements? (If so, please describe them as specifically as possible.) Where was your company headed? Why did they need you?

Describe 4 to 6 accomplishments, successes, project highlights, contributions, or other achievements in this position. Give lots of details, facts, and figures.

Education

List all degrees, certificates, and diplomas you've received; dates you received them; and the school or college, with location. Begin with the most recent and work backwards.

College/University:		City/State:	
Major:	Degree:	Year	GPA:
Honors:			

College/University:		City/State:	
Major:	Degree:	Year	GPA:
Honors:			

Relevant Courses/Seminars/Workshops

Certifications and Licenses

Certifications:

Licenses:

Military

Include branch of service, locations, positions, rank achieved, years of service, honorable discharge, key accomplishments, special recognition, awards, and so on.

Professional Organizations/Affiliations

Include offices held.

Publications / Presentations

Include titles, names of publications, locations of speaking engagements, and dates.

Computer Skills

Include hardware, software, operating systems, networks, programming languages, and so on.

Foreign Languages

Indicate level of fluency—verbal/written.

Hobbies

Note that you will only want to include hobbies that are out of the ordinary and might make a great conversation topic.

Community Activities

List names of organizations, years involved, and positions held.

APPENDIX B

Resume Verbs: Write with Power & Clarity

Here are 400+ of our favorite verbs for writing resumes, cover letters, thank-you letters, LinkedIn profiles, career biographies, achievement profiles, and a host of other online and offline career marketing communications. Use these verbs wisely, and remember the following tips:

- Write with verbs and stay away from phrases such as "Responsible for" and "Duties included." Verbs communicate action and results, and that's precisely what you want to accomplish when writing your career communications.

- Each verb conveys a different message. For example, "manage," "coordinate," and "facilitate" seem to say the same thing, but upon closer examination, that's not the case. Each verb has a unique meaning, and very few verbs are interchangeable.

- Don't use verbs that overstate your level of responsibility for a particular company, organization, project, product, etc. If you have to defend what you wrote, then you've lost the opportunity.

- Not all verbs will be appropriate for you, your industry, your profession. Don't use a verb just because you like it. Rather, use a verb that communicates precisely the right message.

NOTE: In descriptions for your current job and in your resume summary, you will use verbs in the present tense, as shown here. For previous jobs, and for accomplishments that you've completed, convert the verbs to past tense.

Accelerate	Achieve	Adjudicate	Advocate
Accentuate	Acquire	Administer	Align
Accommodate	Adapt	Advance	Alter
Accomplish	Address	Advise	Analyze

Anchor	Close	Create	Drive
Apply	Coach	Critique	Earn
Appoint	Cobble	Crystallize	Edit
Appreciate	Collaborate	Curtail	Educate
Arbitrate	Collect	Cut	Effect
Architect	Command	Decipher	Effectuate
Arrange	Commercialize	Decrease	Elect
Articulate	Commoditize	Define	Elevate
Ascertain	Communicate	Delegate	Eliminate
Assemble	Compare	Deliver	Emphasize
Assess	Compel	Demonstrate	Empower
Assist	Compile	Deploy	Enact
Attain	Complete	Derive	Encourage
Augment	Comply	Design	Endeavor
Authenticate	Compute	Detail	Endorse
Author	Conceive	Detect	Endure
Authorize	Conceptualize	Determine	Energize
Balance	Conclude	Develop	Enforce
Believe	Conduct	Devise	Engineer
Bestow	Configure	Differentiate	Enhance
Brainstorm	Conserve	Diminish	Enlist
Brief	Consolidate	Direct	Enliven
Budget	Construct	Discard	Ensure
Build	Consult	Discern	Entrench
Calculate	Contemporize	Discover	Equalize
Capitalize	Continue	Dispense	Eradicate
Capture	Contract	Display	Espouse
Catalog	Control	Distinguish	Establish
Catapult	Convert	Distribute	Estimate
Centralize	Convey	Diversify	Evaluate
Champion	Coordinate	Divert	Examine
Change	Correct	Document	Exceed
Chart	Corroborate	Dominate	Excel
Clarify	Counsel	Double	Execute
Classify	Craft	Draft	Exhibit

Exhort	Honor	License	Officiate
Expand	Hypothesize	Listen	Operate
Expedite	Identify	Locate	Optimize
Experiment	Illustrate	Lower	Orchestrate
Explode	Imagine	Maintain	Order
Exploit	Implement	Manage	Organize
Explore	Import	Manipulate	Orient
Export	Improve	Manufacture	Originate
Extract	Improvise	Map	Outpace
Extricate	Increase	Market	Outperform
Facilitate	Influence	Marshall	Outsource
Finalize	Inform	Master	Overcome
Finance	Initiate	Mastermind	Overhaul
Focus	Innovate	Maximize	Oversee
Follow up	Inspect	Measure	Participate
Forecast	Inspire	Mediate	Partner
Forge	Install	Mentor	Perceive
Form	Institute	Merge	Perfect
Formalize	Instruct	Minimize	Perform
Formulate	Integrate	Model	Persuade
Foster	Intensify	Moderate	Pilot
Found	Interpret	Modify	Pinpoint
Freshen	Interview	Monetize	Pioneer
Fulfill	Introduce	Monitor	Plan
Gain	Invent	Motivate	Position
Garner	Inventory	Navigate	Predict
Generate	Investigate	Negotiate	Prepare
Govern	Judge	Network	Prescribe
Graduate	Justify	Nominate	Present
Guide	Land	Normalize	Preside
Halt	Launch	Obfuscate	Prevent
Handle	Lead	Obliterate	Process
Head	Lecture	Observe	Procure
Helmed	Leverage	Obtain	Produce
Hire	Liaise	Offer	Program

Progress	Reinforce	Service	Systematize
Project	Rejuvenate	Set up	Tabulate
Project manage	Relate	Shepherd	Tailor
Proliferate	Remedy	Simplify	Target
Promote	Render	Slash	Teach
Propel	Renegotiate	Sold	Terminate
Qualify	Renew	Solidify	Test
Quantify	Renovate	Solve	Thwart
Query	Reorganize	Spark	Train
Question	Report	Speak	Transcribe
Raise	Reposition	Spearhead	Transfer
Rate	Represent	Specialize	Transform
Ratify	Research	Specify	Transition
Realign	Resolve	Standardize	Translate
Rebuild	Respond	Steer	Trim
Recapture	Restore	Stimulate	Troubleshoot
Receive	Restructure	Strategize	Uncover
Recognize	Retain	Streamline	Unify
Recommend	Retrieve	Strengthen	Unite
Reconcile	Reuse	Structure	Update
Record	Review	Study	Upgrade
Recruit	Revise	Substantiate	Use
Rectify	Revitalize	Succeed	Utilize
Recycle	Salvage	Suggest	Validate
Redefine	Sanctify	Summarize	Verbalize
Redesign	Satisfy	Supervise	Verify
Reduce	Save	Supplement	Win
Reengineer	Schedule	Supply	Work
Regain	Secure	Support	Write
Regulate	Select	Surpass	Zero in
Rehabilitate	Separate	Synergize	
Reimagine	Serve	Synthesize	

EMERALD
CAREER PUBLISHING

Other Career Books from Emerald Career Publishing

CURRENTLY AVAILABLE

Modernize Your Resume (2nd Edition)
GET NOTICED ... GET HIRED
By Wendy Enelow and Louise Kursmark

Modernize Your Job Search Letters
GET NOTICED ... GET HIRED
By Wendy Enelow and Louise Kursmark

COMING FALL 2020

Modernize Your Executive Job Search
GET NOTICED ... GET HIRED
By Louise Kursmark and Jan Melnik

www.emeraldcareerpublishing.com